The Life of the Parties

The Life of the Parties

A History of American Political Parties

A. JAMES REICHLEY

ROWMAN & LITTLEFIELD PUBLISHERS, INC.
Lanham • Boulder • New York • Oxford

301536

ROWMAN & LITTLEFIELD PUBLISHERS, INC.

Published in the United States of America
by Rowman & Littlefield Publishers, Inc.
4720 Boston Way, Lanham, Maryland 20706
http://www.rowmanlittlefield.com

12 Hid's Copse Road
Cumnor Hill, Oxford OX2 9JJ, England

British Library Cataloguing in Publication Information Available

Library of Congress Cataloging-in-Publication Data

Reichley, James.
   The life of the parties : a history of American political parties / A. James
      Reichley.
     p. cm.
   Originally published : New York : Free Press, 1992.
   Includes bibliographical references and index.
   ISBN 0-7425-0888-9 (alk. paper)
     1. Political parties—United States—History. I. Title.

JK2261 .R33 2000
324.273'09—dc21   00-031102

Printed in the United States of America

♾ TM The paper used in this publication meets the minimum requirements of American
National Standard for Information Sciences—Permanence of Paper for Printed Library
Materials, ANSI/NISO Z39.48-1992.

For BILL and MARY SCRANTON

CONTENTS

CONTEMPORARY PARTIES

1

INTRODUCTION:

The American Two-Party System

THE CENTRAL PROBLEM of democracy is to combine effective administration of government with accountability to the public and constitutional protection of personal liberties. If government cannot efficiently perform its primary domestic and international duties, admirably set forth in the Preamble to the United States Constitution, the nation will suffer and probably eventually perish. But if the political system provides no means for citizens to determine the course of government, or for safeguarding the rights of individuals and minority groups, there is of course no true democracy.

The American political system, broadly understood, maintains a number of institutional means for combining governmental effectiveness with accountability and protection of rights, including the courts, the election process, and the balance between the executive and legislative branches within the federal government. One of the most valuable of these means, perhaps essential, has been the institution of the political party.

Parties have provided voters with instruments for choosing between alternative policy directions in the conduct of government and have enabled minority interests to participate in coalitions that taken together form majorities. On the side of effectiveness, they have given political leaders bases on which to build support among both the general public and elected officeholders, and have supplied channels for two-way communication between leaders and the electorate. Parties have helped maintain continuity in government policies over time and have brokered compromises among social groups pursuing different goals within a common party coalition. At their most effective, they have mobilized voter participation in politics and elections, stimulated the interest of citizens in public issues, and acted as watchdogs against authoritarian tendencies in government.

To some extent in recent years some of these roles have been taken over by other institutions, such as interest groups and the mass communications media. But these alternative institutions do not perform some major civic functions as well as parties. The steep fall-off in national voter turnout since 1960 can plausibly be related to the weakening of grassroots party organizations and the decline in pub-

1

lic support for parties that were taking place at the same time. And the federal government's trouble in recent years in developing a coherent approach to entitlement programs in part reflects the growing power of interest groups at the expense of parties.

Since the American Political Science Association in 1950 issued a manifesto-like report calling for a "more responsible two-party system," by which was meant more programmatic parties like those in Europe, American political scientists have argued over whether the United States would be better served by more centralized and pro grammatic parties, or whether so large and diverse a nation is best governed through a system of relatively decentralized and pragmatic parties of the kind that until recently characterized American politics. Both sides of this debate, however, have agreed on the need for effective parties. James Sundquist, from the programmatic party side; writes that parties are "crucially necessary to formulate governmental programs, to enact and execute those programs, and to account for them to the electorate afterward." Larry Sabato, who favors more pragmatic parties, regards them as "vital, umbrella like, consensus-forming institutions that help counteract the powerful centrifugal forces in a country teeming with hundreds of racial, economic, religious, and political groups."[1]

Parties have brought with them some liabilities. They develop institutional interests of their own that sometimes undermine both governmental efficiency and democratic values. Party machines have often fostered political corruption. When contending groups are arrayed in opposing parties, party competition sometimes makes social conflict more heated. During periods of divided party control of the executive and legislative branches of the federal government, as has existed during 32 of the 46 years between 1954 and 2000, party rivalry intensifies the natural tendency of the two branches to pull against each other, making action on serious governmental problems more difficult.

On the whole, however, most political practitioners and commentators agree, parties have helped American democracy balance governmental efficiency with accountability and freedom. E. E. Schattschneider, the American political scientist who probably did most to advance the study of parties, wrote: "Political parties created democracy . . . and modern democracy is unthinkable save in terms of parties." Maurice Duverger, the leading European scholar of parties, concurred: "Liberty and the party system coincide."[2]

A DURABLE SYSTEM

Some political scientists, journalists, and practicing politicians in recent years have regularly buried, or at least downgraded, parties as decisive actors in American politics. Considerable evidence supports this view. About one-third of voters now tell pollsters they regard themselves as political independents—up from 15 percent in 1942. The old patronage-based state and local party machines that used to play a dominant role in politics, at least in the Northeast and Midwest, are almost everywhere in ruins. The startling 19 percent of the popular vote won by Ross Perot in 1992 was rightly interpreted as a sign of the declining appeal of the two traditional major parties.

Yet parties have endured. Party identification is still by far the best predictor of how voters will cast their ballots in most elections. Parties continue to supply most of the workers who do such political chores as stuffing envelopes, organizing rallies, distributing yard signs, serving as poll watchers, and driving voters to the polls on election day. Since Ronald Reagan was elected president in 1980, party unity on roll-call votes in Congress has steadily risen (partly as a result of reduction in the ranks of conservative southern Democrats and progressive northeastern Republicans). Parties have become more ideologically consistent, and voters are better able to identify parties with distinct ideologies. In contrast to the old one-party South, most states now maintain genuinely competitive party systems. National party organizations, including congressional campaign committees, have hugely increased their fund-raising and spending for party candidates.

We clearly are not going back to the condition of the late nineteenth century when the major parties were like great popular armies, almost churches, which fought in well-drilled and enthusiastic ranks in each campaign. There is no reason for complacency among those who believe that strong parties make an essential contribution to democracy. But parties of some kind will continue to play important roles in national and state politics.

Will the United States, however, continue to operate under a predominantly two-party system? Most democratic polities, even in relatively homogeneous countries such as Sweden and the Netherlands, have tended to divide into three or more major parties. Maurice Duverger pointed out years ago (in his formulation known as Duverger's law) that polities that maintain single-member, first-past-the-post systems of election, principally the United States and Britain and its dominions, tend to foster the development of two major parties. Systems including two rounds of election or using some form of proportional representation tend to produce a multiplicity of parties.

Even polities such as Britain, Canada, and Australia, however, which, like the United States, use the first-past-the-post system, have generally had at least one significant minor party represented in parliament alongside the two major ones. Why have enduring minor parties with significant impact been so rare in the United States?

I have argued that American politics has usually been formed, at least loosely, around two great ideological traditions, which I have called the republican tradition and the liberal tradition. These are, roughly, the tradition descended from Alexander Hamilton and represented since the Civil War by the Republican Party on one side, and the competing tradition descended from Thomas Jefferson and represented since the time of Andrew Jackson by the Democratic Party on the other.

Both traditions cherish individual freedom as a fundamental human value—differing in this respect from both old-fashioned Tory monarchists and collectivist socialists. But the republican tradition has particularly advocated freedoms that are least likely to conflict with public order, specifically economic freedoms; and the liberal tradition has specifically championed freedoms that are most likely to be compatible with equality, notably freedoms of personal behavior and expression. The traditions agree that government in a democratic society has a responsibility to "promote the general welfare," but the liberal tradition particularly in the twentieth century has tended to identify such promotion with direct government intervention and support, while the republican tradition has emphasized government's role in securing economic and social conditions favorable to individual, family, and community achievement. Republicans accept substantial inequality as a necessary source of investment and motivation for economic growth, while liberals are prepared to take risks with disorder and pay some price in economic inefficiency in return for almost unlimited right to socially unrestrained expression and behavior not physically harmful to others. I will define both traditions more fully in the chapters that follow.[3]

The point here is that a two-party system representing these two traditions is in this sense natural to our politics.

I do not doubt, however, that without the shaping influence of electoral institutions, the political system of a nation so large and so economically and culturally diverse as the United States would long since have produced a substantial number of competing parties. First-past-the-post elections push us toward a two-party system. But the thing that really has kept this system locked in place has been the institution of the electoral college for selecting presidents.

Quite contrary to the Founders' intention, the electoral college, as long as most states retain the at-large system for choosing electors (not required by the Constitution), effectively limits the presidential candidates with a real chance of winning to the nominees of the two major parties (or at least has done so since 1860). Ross Perot's 19 percent of the popular vote did not earn him a single vote in the electoral college. This system even makes it improbable that a minor party could hold the balance of power between the two major parties, as has sometimes occurred in Britain and Canada. Constitutional change to eliminate the electoral college would entail a political effort that is unlikely to be forthcoming—at least until the winner in the popular vote loses in the electoral college, as occurred several times in the nineteenth century and almost happened in 1976.

The high visibility of the presidential election shapes our entire political system. As long as the electoral college confines the real presidential competition to the candidates of the two major parties, the United States will probably continue to have a two-party system in most congressional and state elections.

This does not, however, necessarily mean that the two major parties will continue to be the Republicans and the Democrats. Even in countries with institutionally fortified two-party systems, new parties have at times displaced one of the major existing parties, as the Republicans did the Whigs in the United States in the 1850s and Labour Party did the Liberals in Britain in the 1920s.

It has seemed anomalous to many observers that the United States has never had a true left-Wing party in the European sense, and some have predicted that the Democrats will eventually break up and give way to a socialist successor. The world-wide decline of socialism in recent years has perhaps made this less likely, but there is still the possibility that intraparty revolt against an unpopular centrist Democratic president might produce a serious break-away party on the left. On the other side, at low ebbs of the Republican Party, such as 1964 and 1976, some conservatives have proposed abandonment of the Republican label and creation of a new national conservative party. And there is recurring sentiment among the electorate that what we really need is a new centrist party, divorced from the extremes of the Republicans and Democrats, which Perot to some extent tapped in 1992 and 1996.

The difficulties of forming a new major party, nevertheless, are formidable. Perot, running as the candidate of his largely self-created third party in 1996 received 8.5 percent of the popular vote—still impressive, but less than half of his showing as an independent in 1992. It is no accident that no enduring new major party has emerged in American politics for more than 130 years. The existing major parties have proven adept at picking up issues attracting support to new parties, as the Democrats did with the Populists in the 1890s, the Republicans and the Democrats with the Progressives in the 1910s, the Democrats with various labor and socialist minor parties, and the Republicans with various states' rights parties.

The representatives of the two major parties have taken pains to enact election laws that strongly favor major party candidates. Public financing of presidential election campaigns heavily advantages the Republican and Democratic nominees. At the state level, barriers against third-party candidates are even more severe. In Pennsylvania, for example, major party candidates for the state senate need only two thousand signatures on petitions to get their names on the ballot, whereas minor party candidates require twenty-nine thousand (reduced from fifty-six thousand by court order).

A major national disaster or conflict might lead to the creation of a new major party, as the struggle over slavery gave birth to the Republicans in the 1850s. Barring such a catastrophe, it is probable not only that we will continue to have a two-party system but also that the Republicans and Democrats will be the main competitors. After all, even the Great Depression of the 1930s failed to put enduring cracks in the existing two-party system, though for a time it spawned some successful third parties at the state level, such as the Farmer-Labor Party in Minnesota and the Progressives in Wisconsin.

THROWING THE RASCALS OUT

Let us, then, concentrate on the two-party system as we know it and consider what appear to be its operational characteristics, particularly those that may give some clue to our likely political future. We still really do not have very extensive spans of experience for studying the long-range behavior of democratic party systems (two-party or otherwise): about two centuries in the United States and Britain; somewhat less in France, some countries of northwestern Europe, and the British dominions; only since World War II in Germany, Italy, Japan, and most of the other democracies; and only nine or ten years in Eastern Europe and the countries of the former Soviet Union.

Nevertheless, some characteristics of the electoral effects of party competition seem discernible. First, there seems to be a tendency for voters to grow disenchanted with a party in power, even if no major disasters occur, after eight to ten years. The normal result is for the incumbent party to be voted out, often by a large majority, and the former opposition installed. This tendency may be countered or outweighed by special circumstances, as when the fear of including Communist parties in government in France and Italy kept conservative parties in power for extended periods; or when voters' distrust of the opposition or lack of a fully developed party system produced long-lasting dominance by one party, such as the Socialists in Sweden from the 1930s to the 1970s, Labor in Israel from independence to the early 1970s, the Congress Party in India from the 1940s to the 1970s, the Liberal-Democrats in Japan from the 1950s to the 1990s, and the Party of Institutional Revolution (PRI) in Mexico during most of the twentieth century. Even in these instances, however, accumulation of voter discontent and stagnation or corruption within the incumbent party eventually led to change, or at least interruption, of party control.

The operation of the ten-year cycle appears particularly pronounced in countries with two-party systems, probably because this system inhibits formation of new coalitions through which incumbent parties sometimes are able to hold onto power under multiparty systems. In the United States, the normal incumbency span translates into two or three presidential terms. From the 1950s to the 1990s, the Republicans and Democrats regularly alternated in control of the White House, with three two-term spans, one three-term (the Reagan-Bush years), and one that was confined to a single term (Carter).

Going back somewhat further, since the present party system was formed in the 1850s, the average duration of party control of the White House has been eleven years. The only markedly longer periods of party domination were the twenty-four-year tenure of the Republicans during and after the Civil War, and the twenty-year period of Democratic supremacy during and after the Great Depression.

Similar cycles appear to operate for the governorship in states with competitive two-party systems. In the seven most populous states with truly competitive systems, the average period of party control of the governorship from 1950 to 1996 was 8.7 years. In Pennsylvania, Ohio, and New Jersey, the two parties alternated in control of the governor's office with almost rhythmic regularity. In New York, Illinois, and Michigan, parties tended to hold gubernatorial dominance for somewhat longer periods, but alternation nevertheless occurred. In California, the two parties exchanged control of the governorship every eight years until Governor

Pete Wilson in the 1990s stretched Republican supremacy to sixteen years. Cyclical party turnover now seems to be developing in some of the southern states where the Democrats used to enjoy one-party dominance, such as Texas, Virginia, and North Carolina.

The impulse of voters to "throw the rascals out" by changing party control at regular intervals is both understandable and rational. After two or three terms of party control of a nation or state, enough things are likely to have gone wrong to give voters a taste for change. This tendency may sometimes be unjust to the party in power, but it at least keeps incumbent parties on their toes, seeking to come up with policies and solutions that will cause voters to relent and give them "four more years." Moreover, under conditions of modern government, a party team that has held office for two terms or more is likely to be run-down, reduced to petty bickering, and bereft of new ideas. Henry Kissinger used to say that an administration begins to use up its intellectual capital from the day it takes office.

From 1954 to 1994, regular shifts in party control did not occur in Congress. Between the Civil War and the Eisenhower administration, control of Congress normally accompanied, or slightly preceded, the presidential cycle. In only four two-year periods did the president's party not control at least one house of Congress (under Hayes, 1879–1880; Cleveland, 1895–1896; Wilson, 1919–1920; and Truman, 1947–1948). From 1954 to 1994, however, the Democrats controlled the House of Representatives without interruption and the Senate for all but six years. As a result, Republican presidents during this forty-year span regularly confronted Congresses controlled by their partisan opposition, producing the famous deadlock that disrupted the policy-making process. After the 1994 election, the shoe was on the other foot, with a Democratic president facing a Republican Congress—creating even more spectacular instances of deadlock.

The failure of cyclical turnover in Congress from 1954 to 1994 had damaging effects on the entire political system. Even apart from the policy results of deadlock, the long dominance of Congress by the Democrats produced an impression among many voters that the system was impervious to electoral change, contributing to voter cynicism and disaffection. It was probably bad for the congressional Democrats themselves (as a party, though not of course in terms of individual careers). The results of long duration in power by one party that special circumstances have produced in the politics of, for example, Japan, Italy, and Mexico had become all too evident in Congress: arrogance, preoccupation with "perks," outright corruption, and stagnation of ideas. Whether the 1994 turnover will lead to more normal alternation in party control remains to be seen.

CYCLICAL THEORIES

Beyond the normal two- to three-term alternation in party control of the presidency, the existence of party cycles (or ideological cycles) in national politics becomes speculative. However, such cycles, if they exist, are important and must be included in any overall consideration of parties. Probably the best known of the theories of long-term political cycles is that of the historian Arthur Schlesinger, Jr., carrying on work begun by his father. Schlesinger's theory is more closely related to ideology than to parties, but it also has party manifestations.[4]

According to Schlesinger, throughout American history regular alternations between spans of liberalism and conservatism have occurred, each lasting about sixteen years or four presidential terms. The most recent spans have been the liberal one, launched by John Kennedy in 1960, and its conservative successor that began in the late 1970s. Right on time, Schlesinger claimed after the 1992 election, a new liberal span was initiated by Bill Clinton's victory.

This theory—like almost all cyclical theories—requires some nimble tucking. The Civil War Republicans, "liberal" under Lincoln, somehow become "conservative" under Grant, though in many cases they were the same people, and hang on long beyond their allotted span; Theodore Roosevelt, William Howard Taft, and Woodrow Wilson are lumped together in a liberal span, despite the fierce inter- and intraparty battles of the time; Richard Nixon and Gerald Ford become part of a liberal span that began in 1960; and Jimmy Carter is designated a harbinger of the return of conservatism. The 1994 Republican landslide seemed to bring a premature end to the new liberal span that had begun only two years before—though perhaps Clinton's reelection in 1996 could be interpreted as having got it back on track. Still the theory has enough resonance in history to suggest the presence of a real phenomenon. What Schlesinger is on to, I think, is the succession of phases in a much longer cycle, which I will describe below.

The most widely discussed cyclical theory developed in political science was introduced by V. O. Key. It links cycles to "realigning" or "critical" elections, which, its advocates claim, have periodically purged American politics and government of accumulated detritus and opened the way to new growth.[5] Key's work has been carried on by, among others, Walter Dean Burnham, James Sundquist, Gerald Pomper, and Paul Allen Beck. In most versions of this theory, realigning elections, ending the dominance of one political party and ushering in normal majority control by another, have occurred every twenty-eight to thirty-six years. The root of these cycles appears to be policy upheaval, coupled with generational change.

There is some dispute over which were the actual realigning elections, but general agreement places realignments at or just before the elections of Thomas Jefferson in 1800, Andrew Jackson in 1828, Abraham Lincoln in 1860, William McKinley in 1896, and Franklin Roosevelt in 1932. (Some scholars drop the elections of Jefferson and Jackson, on the ground that the party system did not achieve mature development until the 1830s.)

A puzzle for believers in the theory of realigning elections is the apparent failure of one to occur on schedule in the 1960s. Burnham deals with this problem by arguing that a realignment *did* occur with the election of Richard Nixon as president in 1968 and the creation of a new Republican majority in presidential politics. Certainly the shift of the South away from the Democrats at the presidential level after 1968 was a major change in national politics. But if this was a realignment, why did it not produce a change in control of Congress or of most of the major states, as previous realignments had done?

The elections usually identified as critical to realignments—1800, 1828, 1860, 1896, and 1932—were clearly times when something important happened in American politics. But were all of these major realignments in the sense of changing one major party for another? The victories of the (Jeffersonian) Republicans in 1800, the Republicans in 1860, and the Democrats in 1932 certainly were. But what of the 1828 and 1896 elections, which are needed to maintain the thirty-six year cycle?

Jackson won in 1828 after a period of about ten years in which national politics had been in flux and the old hegemony of Jefferson's party appeared shaken. But Jackson was clearly in the line of the Jeffersonians, and was so recognized at the time. Martin Van Buren, one of Jackson's principal lieutenants and his successor as president, wrote, "The two great parties of this country, with occasional changes in their names only, have, for principal part of a century, occupied antagonistic positions upon all important political questions. They have maintained an unbroken succession. Jackson carried every state Jefferson carried in 1800 and lost every state Jefferson lost. Jefferson's narrow victory over John Adams in 1800 was converted into Jackson's landslide triumph over John Quincy Adams in 1828 by the addition of new western states in which the Democrats were strong. So the 1828 election *restored* the dominance of the Democrats (under their new name) instead of bringing in a new majority party.

Similarly, McKinley's victory in 1896 followed a period during which Republicans and Democrats had taken turns controlling the federal government, or dividing control, and in which there had been no clear majority party. The 1896 election represented a rallying of the forces, temporarily in eclipse, that had made the Republicans the clear majority party from 1860 to 1876. McKinley won through renewal of the coalition of northeastern and midwestern states on which the Republican Party had been founded. William Jennings Bryan, his Democratic opponent, swept the South, the Democrats' principal stronghold since the end of Reconstruction. Bryan also tapped the farmers' revolt and the silver issue in the West to win some of the normally Republican western states that had been admitted to the Union since the Civil War. But within a few years most of these were back in the Republican column where they normally remained until the Great Depression of the 1930s. The 1896 election, therefore, did not displace the former majority party but renewed and strengthened the party that became dominant after the last major realignment.

What, then, do we have? Not five or six major realigning elections but three: 1800, 1860, and 1932. Each of these began a cycle in which one party was generally dominant, lasting not thirty-six years but *sixty to seventy years*. The climactic elections won by Jackson and McKinley, which I identify as 1832 (rather than 1828) and 1896, were in this scheme elections in which the dominant force of the cycle that had begun about thirty years before met and decisively defeated a force trying to turn back the clock to the prevailing ideological orientation of the preceding cycle (the conservative opposition directed by Nicholas Biddle in 1832 and the populist crusade championed by Bryan in 1896).

The mystery of why no true realignment occurred in the 1960s is thus explained: it was not due. What actually happened in the 1960s was the climax of the cycle dominated by liberalism and the Democratic Party that had begun in the 1930s. In 1964, Lyndon Johnson decisively defeated Barry Goldwater, representing a radical version of the laissez-faire economic doctrine that had prevailed during the preceding cycle. The movement of the South away from the Democrats at the end of the 1960s was an early sign of the breakup of the New Deal cycle—similar to the move of the Northeast away from the Democrats in the 1840s and the swing of major northern cities away from the Republicans in the era of Woodrow Wilson.

As shown schematically in Figure 1–1, each of the sixty- to seventy-year-long cycles moved through roughly similar phases: (1) a breakthrough election in which the new majority gained power under a charismatic leader (Jefferson, Lincoln, F. D. Roosevelt), followed by an extended period during which the new majority party changed the direction of government and enacted much of its program; (2) a period

Figure 1–1   American Political Cycles

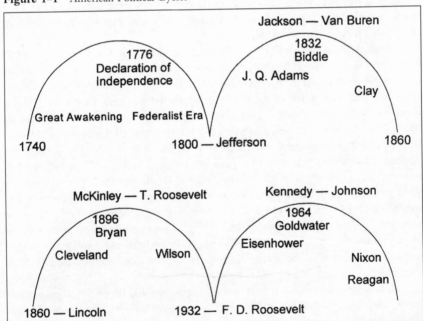

of pause in which the new majority lost some of its dynamism and forces that dominated the preceding cycle staged a minor comeback (J. Q. Adams, Cleveland, Eisenhower); (3) a climactic victory by the majority party over a more radical expression of the ideology of the preceding cycle (Jackson over Biddle, McKinley over Bryan, Johnson over Goldwater), followed by enactment of remaining items in the majority party's program; and, finally, (4) the gradual decline and ultimate collapse of the majority party, opening the way for a new realignment and a new majority. Only three such fully developed cycles have occurred in our national history, though, as Figure 1–1 shows, the outline of an earlier cycle can be seen in the nation-building process that reached its climax with the American Revolution and went through its declining, though still institutionally fruitful, phase during the Federalist era.

The phases of the sixty- to seventy-year-long cycles correspond roughly to some of Schlesinger's sixteen-year spans. The long-cycle theory, however, explains why the Jeffersonians after 1800, the Republicans after 1860, and the Democrats after 1932 held onto power for longer than Schlesinger's theory would predict. These were all periods covered by the initial phase of the long cycle, during which the new majority is fresh and holds the support of the public through an extended series of elections. The separate cycles posited in the twenty-eight- to thirty-six-year theory correspond neatly to the rise and decline segments of the long cycle.

The possibility of a sixty- to seventy-year cycle has occasionally been glimpsed by political scientists and historians. It was first discussed, to my knowledge, by the political scientist Quincy Wright in 1942. In recent years, William Riker and Jerome Mileur have suggested the possibility of a sixty- to seventy-year cycle. Political scientists have generally been reluctant to consider the possibility of sixty- to seventy-year party dominances largely, I think, because the limited time over which democracies have so far extended gives us little material against which to test such a hypothesis. Such skepticism is understandable and even reasonable. But the long-cycle theory fits the evidence better than any of the other cyclical schemes. There is also some indication that long cycles have been at work in Britain and France, although this matter requires further study.

If such long cycles exist, what causes them? Perhaps to some extent they reflect cycles in the underlying economic system, such as the "long-wave" cycles suggested in the 1920s by the Russian economist Nikolai Kondratieff, and discussed often since by futurist economists. Kondratieff and his followers have claimed to detect cycles lasting about fifty years in which market economies swing between booms and major depressions caused by "overbuilding of the capital sector." Kondratieff long waves correspond roughly to the long party dominance cycles in American history. The economic expansion that started in the 1790s petered out through the 1840s and 1850s, and the expansion that began in the 1860s, though interrupted by several pauses, did not truly collapse until the depression of the 1930s. According to Kondratieff theorists, we are now in the downswing of the expansion that began in the 1940s. Many of them have been predicting for some time that a new economic collapse is just around the corner.[6]

Political cycles are also probably rooted to some extent in generational change. Schlesinger argues that his sixteen-year spans reflect the succession of political generations. Members of the political generation of John Kennedy, for example, were putting into effect values and attitudes acquired during their youth in the liberal environment of the 1930s. The Reaganites of the 1980s were applying views they had developed during the relatively conservative 1950s (though many of the Reaganites regarded themselves as revolting *against* Eisenhower moderate Republicanism). Members of the generation of the 1990s, in this theory, should have been eager to reintroduce the liberal values with which Kennedy inspired them during their college years in the 1960s.

Schlesinger's analysis, like his larger cyclical theory, captures part of the truth. Genuinely major changes in political direction, however, seem to occur only after persons whose political values and party loyalties were formed by the realignment, including many who were in childhood at the time, have largely passed from the political scene. So long as generations whose party ties were shaped by the Civil War remained politically active, even voting in substantial numbers, the normal Republican majority in national elections was hard to shake. Similarly, party loyalties formed by the Great Depression and the New Deal have been exceptionally durable. In the 1990s, the generations whose attitudes were most deeply marked by the Great Depression and the New Deal, roughly those born from 1905 to 1930, included a sharply declining share of the total electorate—already in 1996 less than 15 percent. This, I think, is a major reason for the presence of an increasing segment of voters who feel no particular loyalty to either major party.

The last two major realignments, in the 1860s and 1930s, came at times of massive traumas within the larger social system—namely, the Civil War and the Great Depression. The first realignment, in the 1800s, coincided with huge territorial growth and migration of population. Probably a major realignment requires *both* extraordinary social upheaval *and* an electorate in which ties to the existing party system have grown weak. We certainly now have the latter. If the Kondratieff theorists are right, we may soon encounter severe economic turmoil. But the causes of social upheaval need not be primarily economic—those of the 1800s and 1860s were not. Possibly an ecological crisis could trigger the next political realignment. Or continuation of current trends toward moral and social disorder and decay could bring it on. The point is that the political system is now open, as it was not in the 1960s when the hold of the New Deal alignment remained strong, for transformation by a major economic or social shock.

THE LIFE OF PARTIES

The history of the origin and development of parties provides many lessons that will be of direct benefit to policy-makers and would-be policy-makers, as well as to citizens seeking means to improve the practice of American politics. It is also worth studying for its own sake, as a record of remarkable human endeavors, intrigues, rivalries, conflicts, and civic achievements—indeed, one of the great political stories in human experience, fully comparable in drama to those reported in the *Iliad* and the chronicle plays of Shakespeare, and far richer in historical significance.

This book will argue that the work and creed of American democracy have been carried forward by two great contending but not incompatible ideological traditions, the republican and the liberal; that these traditions have been conveyed for the most part by parties that have competed within the two-party system; that the two-party system was not intended or foreseen by the Founders, but rather developed gradually, largely through the efforts and ingenuity of some extraordinary master politicians; that parties are now endangered by a number of cultural, technological, social, political, and legal changes in American life; and that concerned supporters of a free society should therefore seek means for renewing the vitality of parties and the dynamism of the party system.

This argument will be presented through a series of historical chapters describing and analyzing crucial episodes in the evolution of American parties, followed by a series of chapters reporting and commenting on recent developments in the life of parties at the national, state, and local levels. The final chapter will examine developments during the 1990s, and conclude with recommendations on how parties can be made to serve better the needs and ideals of American democracy.

FROM THE FOUNDING
TO THE CIVIL WAR

2

INTENTION OF THE FOUNDERS

A Polity Without Parties

IN GOVERNMENT OF A MONARCHICAL CAST," George Washington observed, "Patriotism may look with indulgence, if not with favor, upon the spirit of the party. But in those of popular character, in Governments purely elective, it is a spirit not to be encouraged . . . A fire not to be quenched; it demands a uniform vigilance to prevent its bursting into a flame, lest instead of warming it should consume."[1]

The other principal Founders fully shared Washington's distrust of parties—at least until they began running parties themselves. Thomas Jefferson declared in 1789 that if he "could not go to heaven but with a party," he "would not go there at all." Alexander Hamilton associated parties with "ambition, avarice, personal animosity." James Madison wrote in *Federalist* Number Ten of the "mischiefs of faction." John Adams expressed "dread" toward "division of the republic into two great parties, each arranged under its leader, and concerting measures in opposition to each other."[2]

The Founders' low regard for parties was in part derived from prejudices formed by their studies of classical writers and British and European political theorists. But they also had before them what they considered the baneful effects of parties in the colonial and state governments: the tendency of parties to sharpen class antagonisms; the emergence of parties, with their attendant functionaries, as interests in themselves; the openness of parties to corruption, and the ease with which they could be mastered by demagogues.

Beyond these acquired biases and empirical observations, the Founders' rejection of parties grew out of their conviction that such political divisions are inherently subversive of republican ideals. The Founders, almost to a man, were Old Whigs, in the British as well as the American sense. They realized that any political system will be shaped in part by clashing interests and personal ambitions. But they believed that republican government must finally be rooted in the ideal of a disinterested citizenry coming together, either directly or through elected representatives, to legislate for the common good. They were Lockeans, but Lockeans of the original school, holding, like Locke himself that the social contract once con-

17

cluded exerts moral authority of its own, rather than merely providing a playing field for unremitting struggle among private interests.

They were convinced, as James Madison wrote, that while "there is a degree of depravity in mankind which requires a certain degree of circumspection and distrust," there are also "other qualities in human nature which justify a certain portion of esteem and confidence." The natural inclination of mankind toward corruption requires the checks and balances and other safeguards built into the Constitution. But if man is totally driven by self-interest, then Thomas Hobbes, who argued that the egoistic drives in human nature are so strong that without authoritarian government life will be "nasty, brutish, and short," not Locke, was right, and republican government is impossible. Only authoritarian government with unchallengeable power is sufficient to curb total egoism this side of anarchy. If on the other hand there are indeed qualities of generosity and forbearance in human nature that make some measure of disinterested judgment achievable, then good citizens can be trusted, on genuinely public issues, to reason together on what is good for the nation as a whole, rather than to insist on the last pound of gain for particular interests, personal appetites, or individual greed. Republican government then is possible. The American experiment may succeed.[3]

Parties, by framing every issue in terms of winners and losers, the Founders believed, undermine this indispensable willingness to seek at some level the common good rather than the satisfaction of special interests. Parties, therefore, are socially destructive and must be considered, as Madison wrote, a potentially "mortal disease"; as Hamilton claimed, an "avenue to tyranny"; and as Washington insisted, a source of "frightful despotism."[4]

PARTIES AND DEMOCRACY

Parties, defined (minimally) as organized social groups formed to exercise or influence governmental authority through elective means, have usually been associated with democratic polities. In societies run politically by a single ruler or a dominant class, as most societies in history have been, the dominant establishment naturally feels threatened by organized opposition and acts to suppress it. Even in the oligarchic republic that governed medieval Venice, parties were legally prohibited for fear they would split the dominant aristocracy and give the lesser orders political leverage.

Parties of a kind existed in classical Athens of the Periclean age and in republican Rome. In Athens, the two main parties, known as oligarchs and democrats, differed over how much democracy was good for the state. In Rome, in the period just before Julius Caesar replaced republican institutions with authoritarian dictatorship, the parties, known as *optimates* and *populares,* clashed over the division of social benefits between the upper classes and the common people. In both cases, political conflict between parties was held by later historians to have played a part in the downfall of democracy—contributing to the unpopularity of parties with the American Founders, many of whom closely studied antiquity.[5]

Parties began to develop in late seventeenth-century Britain, at first during the controversy in 1679 over whether James, Duke of York, a Catholic and therefore held suspect by the nation's Protestant majority, should be permitted to succeed to the throne upon the death of his brother, Charles II, who had no legitimate off-spring. Those defending James's right to succeed became known as Tories (originally an Irish term for highwayman), and those insisting on a Protestant heir were known as Whigs (a Scottish term for horse thief). The Tories won the first round, and James did in fact become king when Charles II died in 1685. As James II, however, the new monarch proceeded to rule in an authoritarian manner and appointed Catholics to high office, outraging not only Whigs but Tories, most of whom were Anglican Protestants. In 1688 a coalition of upper-class Whigs and Tories ousted James and installed in his place the Dutch William of Orange, the Protestant hero of Europe at the time, and William's wife Mary (James's daughter).

The difference between Whigs and Tories as contending groups in Parliament, and as contenders for the favor of succeeding monarchs, continued into the eighteenth century. Historians have argued over how much significance should be attached to party divisions in Britain during most of the eighteenth century. The parties had no formal organizations and even in the House of Commons were not much more than loose coalitions of politicians, held together largely, Harold Perkin has observed, "by the hope and expectation of 'place.' " But even Louis Namier, the great historian of eighteenth-century British politics, who attached relatively little importance to parties, acknowledged that Whigs and Tories represented differences in "temperament and outlook, in social types, in old connections and traditions." In general, Tories stood for the older view of a hierarchically organized feudal society and an established church, while Whigs gave more rein to the social and political individualism that was associated with growing economic enterprise and the philosophy of John Locke. Both parties, however, remained distinctly aristocratic in their outlook.[6]

During most of the eighteenth century the parties existed mainly in Parliament and developed no campaign structures among the general population. In the late 1780s, however, the Whigs established party clubs in London and other cities and towns "specifically designed to increase the party's strength among the electorate." The Tories responded by forming a council of party leaders that before the 1790 election "regularly dined together to plan the campaign."[7]

Eighteenth-century party divisions in Britain sent political tremors through the British colonies in North America. Bernard Bailyn has traced the major ideas that contributed to the outbreak of the American Revolution to the writings of British libertarian Whigs of the 1720s, such as John Trenchard and Thomas Gordon. "These coffeehouse radicals," Bailyn writes, "more than any other single group of writers . . . shaped the mind of the American Revolutionary generation." When clashes developed in the 1760s and early 1770s between the British government and colonial interests seeking more freedom, Americans who took the side of the British crown called themselves Tories and those who placed themselves in opposition were generally known as Whigs.[8]

When independence came, former Tory leaders such as James DeLancey in New York and Thomas Hutchinson in Massachusetts fled or were expelled, along with most of their followers. The victorious Whigs, however, soon experienced new party divisions within their ranks.

CLASH OF FACTIONS

In the early years of the American Revolution, political disputes among the revolutionaries were mainly over the conduct of war. But by the late 1770s ideological divisions had begun to develop in most of the states. The two loose groupings that formed in most state governments may be called *conservatives* and *populists* (though neither term was used at the time). Both sides were committed to the Revolution. Both supported republican government and were intensely individualist in their social values and economic attitudes. But they began to split over the question of how far the principle of equality being advanced by some patriot politicians and publicists should be carried.[9]

In the state legislatures of the early 1780s studied by Jackson Turner Main, conservatives generally supported and populists opposed payment of the public debt and giving more authority to state governors. Populists favored and conservatives opposed legislation to issue paper money and to permit delay in payment of private debts. Conservatives voted to stop the confiscation of property owned by former loyalists, while populists supported continuation of such seizures. In most legislatures neither bloc normally achieved majority control. Independents, who switched back and forth between the two blocs depending on the issue, usually held the balance of power.[10]

Conservatives were concentrated in and around the coastal cities of Boston, Salem, New York, Philadelphia, Baltimore, Annapolis, and Charleston, and in the tidewater regions of Virginia and the Carolinas. Populists came from the inland valleys of New England, New York, Pennsylvania, Maryland, and Virginia, and the highlands of Pennsylvania, northern New Jersey, Virginia, and the Carolinas—though the conservatives controlled a few back-country constituencies like the Berkshire mountain region of western Massachusetts and the wilderness area of Virginia that became the state of Kentucky. Most Episcopalians and Quakers were conservatives, while most Baptists were populists. Congregationalists and Presbyterians divided on the basis of residence, dwellers in the coastal areas tending to be conservatives and inlanders tending to be populists.[11]

In most states, political organization was usually so slight that true parties cannot be said to have existed. The major exception was Pennsylvania. The Pennsylvania state constitution of 1776, "the principal official American embodiment of revolutionary radicalism," so divided the supporters of independence that well-defined parties quickly organized, one to maintain the radical state constitution and the other to replace it with a more moderate charter. The pro-constitution party, whose political and demographic characteristics were similar to those displayed in other states by the populists, took the name Constitutionalists. Their opponents, who paralleled the conservatives, called themselves Republicans (a name chosen to make clear their distinction from the state's substantial body of Tories).[12]

The Republicans dominated Philadelphia and also attracted support from conservative German (Pennsylvania Dutch) farmers in Lancaster and York counties along the Maryland border. The Constitutionalists held sway in the rural Susquehannah Valley around Harrisburg (which they made the state capital) and among the Scotch-Irish in the western highlands. The two groups established party organizations to conduct election campaigns and formed caucuses in the legislature. Battle lines were tightly drawn and the percentage of independents was much smaller than in any other state. The difference separating the two parties, a Constitutionalist leader wrote, was between "the few and the many. . . aristocraticks and the democraticks." A Republican, in contrast, described the more conservative party as composed of "Whigs of a more moderate and deliberate cast, of more property and more respectable capacities. . . ."[13]

The Republicans faced an uphill fight, as the Constitutionalists for some time successfully identified the 1776 state constitution with the Revolution itself. Attempts to change the constitution, they claimed, showed disloyalty to the new nation. Both sides at times resorted to violence. In 1779 a Philadelphia mob attacked the home of James Wilson, a signer of the Declaration of Independence and leader of the Republican party. The assault was met with gunfire, Setting off a riot in which six persons were killed and 20 wounded. Gradually, however, the more moderate elements in the rural counties swung to the Republicans. In 1790—after the new federal Constitution had been ratified—the state constitution of 1776 was scuttled and a more conservative basic law was put in its place.[14]

In New York the populist faction was organized around Governor George Clinton, a talented demagogue who used government patronage to assemble the first state party machine in American history. At the peak of its power, the Clinton organization dispensed 15,000 state jobs as political plums. Before the Revolution, New York politics had revolved around a struggle between the DeLancey family, wealthy New York City merchants, and the Livingston family, based in the Hudson Valley. The DeLanceys had remained loyal to the crown and had fled to England after independence. The more conservative and moderate forces in state politics in the 1780s gathered behind the Schuylers, another family of Hudson Valley aristocrats, led by General Philip Schuyler and his brilliant and ambitious son-in-law, Alexander Hamilton. The Livingstons, leaders of the Whig party under the colonial government and therefore on the winning side in the Revolution, decided that for the time at least they feared Clinton even more than they disliked the Schuylers and Hamilton and joined a common "Anti-Clintonian" party that became a formidable competitor in state politics.[15]

In Virginia, the largest and most populous of the States, party lines were loose, but two discernible blocs took shape. One, relatively conservative, was based on the "Northern Neck," the peninsula between the Potomac and Rappahannock Rivers that in early colonial times had been owned by the Fairfax family, who sold it off in vast tracts, including George Washington's huge plantation beside the Potomac. The other bloc, inclined to populism, took root in the "Southside," the region south of the James River, where farms were smaller and society more democratic. More than a quarter of the members of the state house of delegates, particularly those from the Shenandoah Valley and the central piedmont, including young James Madison, avoided regular identification with either faction. In most districts, John Randolph observed, members were elected on the basis of "personal and local, rather than political, considerations."[16]

In Massachusetts there was little party organization before 1787, but political divisions there were as bitter and rancorous as those in Pennsylvania. Conservatives, concentrated in Boston and Salem but attracting support from fishing villages on Cape Cod and Martha's Vineyard and from hamlets in the Berkshires, charged that the more radical faction in state government favored "an agrarian law [to equalize property] and a revolution." Their populist opponents, scattered across the Connecticut Valley and the Narragansett Basin, complained that the "overgrown rich" in the coastal seaports were seeking to put down the "smaller sort of folks."[17]

Populists usually held the upper hand in the Massachusetts legislature, while the governorship passed back and forth between the conservative James Bowdoin and the populist John Hancock. When economic depression struck in 1786, conservatives in the legislature succeeded in blocking passage of a "stay law" to postpone the collection of debt. State courts ordered numerous foreclosures on small farms. Finding the state government unresponsive to their demands, a body of armed Connecticut Valley farmers led by Daniel Shays, a hero of the Revolution (who had been driven by poverty to sell a ceremonial sword presented to him by Lafayette), marched on Springfield to prevent the state court sitting in that city from carrying out further foreclosures. The rebels achieved some initial successes, and panic for a time took hold in Boston. Winter fell, however, and Shays and his men, rather than pressing on to the state capital, decided to hole up in Worcester. Bowdoin, who was governor at the time, called up the state militia, which soon routed the rebels without much difficulty. Shays fled to Vermont.

In the spring of 1787 a move by populists in the Massachusetts legislature to pardon leaders of the rebellion failed by a vote of only 100 to 108. "The natural effects of a pure democracy are already fully produced among us," wrote Theodore Sedgwick, a Berkshire lawyer active in politics on the conservative side. "A very large party in both branches of the legislature filled with a spirit of republican frenzy are now attempting the same objects by legislation, which their more manly brethren last winter would have procured by arms. In both instances it is a war against virtue, talent and property carried on by the dregs and scum of mankind."[18]

In most states during the mid-1780s, conservative Whigs, for whom one revolution was enough, generally held their own in gubernatorial and legislative elections. Conservative leaders, however, were increasingly fearful that equalitarian radicals would soon impose their will on exposed fragments of the decentralized nation. "People once respected their governors, their senators, their judges, and their clergy . . . ," lamented John Dickinson of Pennsylvania, but now "men of sense and property have lost much of their influence by the popular spirit of the war." Henry Knox, who had served on Washington's staff during the Revolution, wrote to his old chief in 1786 that the "creed" of many small farmers was "that the property of the United States has been protected from the confiscation of Britain by the joint exertions of all, and therefore ought to be the common property of all." Alexander Hamilton, Washington's other former principal subaltern, warned that government was being invaded by people "of the *levelling sort.*" James Madison, following events from his seat in the Virginia house of delegates in Richmond, observed, more cautiously, that Shays' rebellion had been an "alarming symptom."[19]

TRIUMPH OF THE CONSERVATIVES

The delegates who gathered in Philadelphia in the spring of 1787 to consider amendments to the Articles of Confederation, on which such national government as existed was based, were concerned over the growing acrimony among the states. Even more, they were determined to erect constitutional safeguards for social order and established rights, including property rights.

With Washington in the chair, and Hamilton, Madison, James Wilson, and the octogenarian Benjamin Franklin among the delegates, the Philadelphia convention went far beyond its legal mandate and produced a Constitution that embodied the spirit of the Revolution in a moderately conservative structure of national government. A major purpose of the Constitution, Charles Beard wrote, was to place "the fundamental private rights of property . . . beyond the reach of popular majorities." With the stipulation that the framers regarded this goal as a necessary condition for their larger purpose of creating a viable republic, Beard was right. While preserving a federal system, the Constitution specifically prohibited the states from issuing paper money or legislating to impair contracts to relieve debtors—both favorite projects among populists at the state level.[20]

Hamilton, Madison, and John Jay, in their classic defense of the Constitution, *The Federalist,* made no bones about the conservative nature of their objectives. The proposed new structure of government, Hamilton maintained in *Federalist* Number Nine, would be "a barrier against domestic faction and insurrection." A strong national government, insulated against parochial pressures, Jay argued in *Federalist* Number Three, would override the tendency of "the governing party in one or two States to swerve from good faith and justice. . . ."[21]

Madison, more than his two colleagues, spelled out the underlying moral, political, and psychological assumptions on which the Constitution is based. The "great object" of the Constitution, Madison wrote in the familiar *Federalist* Number Ten, was to "secure the public good and private rights against the danger of . . . faction, and at the same time to preserve the spirit and the form of popular government. . . ." The causes of faction, "actuated by some common impulse or passion, or of interest, adverse to the rights of other citizens, or to the permanent and aggregate interests of the community," are "sown in the nature of man." Differences over religion and forms of government contribute to the development of faction. "But the most common and most durable source of faction has been the various and unequal distribution of property."[22]

Economic inequality results from "diversity in the faculties of men. . . ." Proponents of pure democracy "have erroneously supposed that by reducing mankind to a perfect equality in their political rights, they would, at the same time, be perfectly equalized and assimilated in their possessions, their opinions, and their passions." Democracies taking this approach "have ever been spectacles of turbulence and confusion; have ever been found incompatible with personal security or the rights of property; and have in general been as short in their lives as they have been violent in their deaths."[23]

Faction growing out of differences in economic interest, though a constant threat to republican government, cannot be avoided without suppressing freedom. "Liberty is to faction what air is to fire. . . ." Since faction in a republic cannot be avoided, its effects must be mitigated through constitutional design. A faction consisting of "less than a majority . . . may clog the administration, . . . may convulse the society," but in the end it must give way to the will of the majority, so long as republican forms are maintained. But "when a majority is included in a faction, the form of popular government . . . enables it to sacrifice to its ruling passion or interest both the public good and the rights of other citizens." It is then that popular government becomes vulnerable to such pernicious schemes as "a rage for paper money, for an abolition of debts, for equal division of property. . . ."[24]

The surest way to avoid this danger, Madison contends, is to make it unlikely that such a majority will form. In relatively small constituencies, like the individual states, the majority of have-lesses will tend to combine politically against the minority of have-mores. But in a nation as large as the federal union to be formed by the new Constitution, economic interests will divide into "a landed interest, a manufacturing interest, a mercantile interest, a moneyed interest, [and] many lesser interests. . . ." Politics, then, will focus on functional and regional differences rather than on class rivalries—a politics, that is, of many minorities, rather than of majority against minority.[25]

Sheer size, moreover, will make it difficult for radical agitators, like the populist leaders coming to power in some of the states, to mobilize the discontented into an effective national majority. "The influence of factious leaders may kindle a flame within their particular states, but will be unable to spread a general conflagration through the other states."[26]

In *Federalist* Number Fifty-one, Madison returned to the need under republican government "to guard one part of the society against the injustice of the other part." Madison takes note of the Rousseauian view that this end can be achieved "by creating a will in the community independent of the majority—that is, of the society itself." This may work under dictatorships administered by "hereditary or self-appointed authority." But in a republic, given Madison's Puritan and Lockean understanding of human nature, it is impossible.[27]

In a republic, the avaricious will of a transitory majority may be countered in part by a system of governmental checks and balances: first dividing "the power surrendered by the people" between the states and the national government; then within the national government balancing the executive against the legislature; and finally by dividing the legislative branch into different houses, rendering "them by different modes of election and different principles of action, as little connected with each other as the nature of their common functions and their common dependence on the society will admit." The surest protection for minorities, however, is extension of governmental authority over a territory so vast and a population so varied that government will have to achieve consensus rather than a simple majority in order to act. Society "will be broken into so many parts, interests, and classes of citizens, that the rights of individuals, or of the minority, will be in little danger from interested combinations of the majority."[28]

Resort to such devices, Madison concedes, may be a reflection on human nature. "But what is government itself, but the greatest of all reflections on human nature? If men were angels, no government would be necessary."[29]

The populist leaders in the states, who had been little represented at the Philadelphia convention, did not have to read *The Federalist* to recognize what the framers of the Constitution were up to. Populist strategists and spokesmen like Samuel Adams in Massachusetts, George Clinton in New York, and Patrick Henry in Virginia fought ratification in their respective states. Among state legislators whose position on the Constitution is known, more than four-fifths of the populists opposed ratification while an even larger share of conservatives were pro-Constitution.[30]

The Antifederalists, as opponents of the Constitution were called, could not match the Federalists' national organization, directed by much of the former high command of the Revolution. The inability of the Antifederalists to mount an effective national campaign provided a demonstration that seemed to bear out Madison's thesis. Populist appeals might work state by state, but when the issue was framed in national terms—in this case, the survival of a united republic—the moderates and conservatives appeared to have the advantage.

The Antifederalists issued propaganda blasts but deployed no intellectual artillery approaching the force of *The Federalist*. Tom Paine, the Revolution's most articulate publicist of equalitarian ideology, had earlier attacked the principles of social balance and mixed government on which the Constitution was based. But in 1787 Paine was otherwise engaged, working on various political and business projects in England, soon to depart for France to participate in the Revolution of 1789. Thomas Jefferson, absent in France as American ambassador but in touch with political associates at home, wrote to friends that he hoped the Constitution would not be ratified—an interesting first effort, he told Madison, but needing another try. Jefferson did not, however, publicly align himself with the Antifederalists. Looking back after the fight for ratification had been won, he maintained that he had been "neither federalist nor antifederalist; . . . of neither party, nor yet a trimmer between parties."[31]

In some states, notably Massachusetts, New Hampshire, New York, and Virginia, the vote on ratification was close. But by March 4, 1789, 11 states had ratified and the Constitution was declared adopted. Eight months later, North Carolina added its vote for ratification. In May 1790, Rhode Island, by a majority at the state convention of only 34 to 32, became the last of the original 13 states to join the federal union. By that time, George Washington had been President for more than a year.

WERE THE FOUNDERS WRONG?

When James Madison argued in *The Federalist* that factions will inevitably develop in a free society, he did not imply approval of political parties nor did he suggest that parties as institutions would necessarily play a major role in the political life of the United States. Like all the other principal Founders, Madison regarded parties as a political evil and believed that a wisely framed constitution would minimize their influence.

The Founders recognized that competition among different economic and social interests was bound to find outlet through politics. But they believed that the varying kinds of representation provided by the states and the federal government, and by the executive and bicameral legislative branches at the federal level, would themselves offer sufficient advocacy for contending interest groups and would make extensive recourse to formally organized parties unnecessary.

The low opinions of parties voiced by the major Founders, including Washington, Jefferson, Hamilton, Madison, and John Adams, are well known. Political leaders and theorists just below the first level were even more outspoken. James Monroe argued that "the existence of parties is not necessary to free governments" and urged supporters of republican government to "exterminate all party divisions in our country." Patrick Henry warned that to "split into factions . . . must destroy that union upon which our existence hangs." Tom Paine wrote disparagingly of "dupes of faction" and "the cloven foot of faction." John Taylor of Caroline, the most systematic thinker among the Virginia libertarians, commented: "The situation of the public good, in the hands of two parties nearly poised as to numbers, must be extremely perilous. Truth is a thing, not of divisibility into parts, but of unity." John Jay, staunch Federalist of New York, cautioned, "If faction should long bear down law and government, tyranny may raise its head. . . ." Abigail Adams, after observing the effects of party division during her husband's single term as President, concluded: "Party spirit is blind, malevolent, uncandid, ungenerous, unjust and unforgiving. It is equally so under federal and under democratic banners."[32]

Yet, as I will show in the next chapter, recognizable parties had begun to take shape in Congress within three years of Washington's first inauguration as President. By the time John Adams stood for reelection in 1800, well-defined parties were competing for state and local as well as national offices. Since that time, except for a brief lapse in the 1820s, parties have been a major structuring force in American politics.

Were the Founders, who were right about so many things, simply wrong then when they turned their attention to parties? Did prejudice or lack of experience with how republican government actually works lead them to overlook the valuable role that most political scientists now claim parties play in free societies? Or is it possible that they were in fact right: that the nation would have been better off if the development of institutionalized parties had somehow been avoided; and that parties not only are not necessary to democracy, but also, as many ordinary Americans have always believed, dangerously undermine the efficiency and integrity of republican government?

The Founders were certainly wrong in underestimating the value of parties in coordinating action between the legislative and executive branches, and, to a lesser extent, between the federal and state governments. As many commentators in the nineteenth and twentieth centuries have pointed out, parties have supplied "the tie that binds, the glue that fastens" between government agencies that are constitutionally divided.[33] The current weakness of the parties has helped remind us how useful they can be.

Parties, moreover, by providing an institutional opposition to the regime in power have served as a check on the tendencies in human nature and society that justify "a certain degree of circumspection and distrust." Attempts at one-party democracy, as in Mexico and some African countries, or for that matter in many American cities today, have demonstrated that lack of organized political opposition can open the way to disastrous levels of corruption and governmental inefficiency.

But the Founders were not wrong in maintaining that democracy will fail if there is no sense of a common national interest that at some point transcends particular interests, or in identifying party and party spirit as potential impediments to the development of such awareness. Parties have all too often in American history been instruments of corruption, preservers of prejudice, burdens on effective government, and disrupters of social harmony. If party interest can help bridge the natural tension between legislative and executive branches, it can also aggravate that tension when the branches are wholly or partially controlled by different parties—as has recently occurred more often than not.

Democracy over the long run cannot be successful, particularly in the conduct of foreign policy, but also in settling great internal issues such as the shape of the national budget, if party leaders are not prepared at some point to put aside party identification and operate as trustees for a common nationality—or even as sharers of responsibility for the direction of a functionally connected world community.

The Founders erred in not appreciating the essential contribution that parties make to republican government. But their warnings against the potentially harmful effects of party and excessive party spirit had a good deal of validity and deserve to be heeded today.

In any case, the Founders' statecraft was completely at odds with their objective of establishing a polity without parties. The constitutional structure they put in place practically guaranteed the development not only of parties but of a particular kind of party system: two-party democracy.

3

THE FIRST PARTIES

Federalists and Republicans

THE FUTURE DEVELOPMENT of a two-party system was not foreseen, even dimly, when the first electoral college gathered in February 1789. George Washington of Virginia was elected President, and John Adams of Massachusetts, Vice President. Washington received the votes of all 69 participating electors. Adams, in second place, was strongly backed by New England, Pennsylvania, and Virginia for 34 votes. The remaining votes were scattered among ten others.

The United States appeared headed toward being a one-party democracy. At least 18 of the 24 members of the first Senate and 37 of the 65 members of the House of Representatives identified with the Federalist party that had won ratification of the Constitution.[1]

The Antifederalists were in disarray. The strongest potential leader of a political opposition, Thomas Jefferson, had been persuaded by President Washington to join the administration as secretary of state. Under the circumstances, the Federalist party could fairly claim to be essentially identical with the political nation—as the Founders had intended. That is, the Federalists in 1789 were not a party in the Founders' pejorative sense but a kind of committee or club formed to manage the national polity.

Before the First Congress had concluded its business in March 1791, tensions and cleavages had developed within the political community. At first these reflected "rival claims for pre-eminence" among the four largest states, Virginia, Pennsylvania, Massachusetts, and New York. Soon, however, an ideological divide began to form in response to the ambitious economic program proposed by Alexander Hamilton, secretary of the treasury and dominant intellectual force within the administration. This division was caused in part by personal rivalries. Long after, John Quincy Adams traced the beginning of parties to the fact that, unlike his father John Adams, Hamilton and Jefferson were "spurred to the rowels by rival and antagonist ambition."[2]

But important substantive differences, rooted in the competition between what were to become the republican and liberal ideological traditions, also separated the two groups.

HAMILTON V. JEFFERSON

Hamilton's economic program included formation of a national bank, assumption of prior national and state debts by the federal government (bringing huge profits to speculators who had invested in these securities when their market value was low), and enactment of a tax on whiskey (shifting some of the tax burden from northeastern business to western farmers). The program was immediately attacked by those who feared collaboration between a relatively strong national government and aggressive business interests. Critics accused the dynamic young secretary of the treasury—Hamilton was only 34 when the administration took office—of being a secret monarchist and an aspiring Julius Caesar.[3]

Hamilton argued that government support for commerce and manufacturing served the long-term interest of the entire nation. "Everything tending . . . to increase the total mass of industry and opulence," he wrote, "is ultimately beneficial to every part of it." Though a political Whig (he had, after all, been a military hero of the Revolution, as well as Washington's favorite aide), Hamilton was of the school of Whiggery that attached little value to social equality. Rising from humble origins (the "bastard brat of a Scotch pedlar," John Adams, his reluctant sometime political collaborator, sarcastically described him), he had, through marriage to the daughter of General Philip Schuyler and his own gifts of personality and intellect, positioned himself at the apex of the conservative New York society that had taken the place of the DeLancey connection after the Revolution.[4]

Hamilton's view of the rich was not particularly flattering, but he had no doubt that enlisting the interest of wealthy investors and enterprises was vital to the success of the new nation. He minced no words. "Look through the rich and the poor of the community; the learned and the ignorant," he told the New York convention considering ratification of the Constitution in 1788. "The difference indeed consists, not in the quality but kind of vices . . . ; and here the advantage of character belongs to the wealthy. Their vices are probably more favorable to the prosperity of the state, than those of the indigent; and partake less of moral depravity."[5]

The core of Hamilton's political philosophy from the moment he entered public life was his commitment to a strong national government. "In every civil society," he wrote, "there must be a supreme power, to which all members of that society are subject; for, otherwise, there could be no supremacy, or subordination, that is no government at all." Like all Whigs, he acknowledged the danger of giving too much power to the state. But "powers must be granted, or civil society cannot exist; the possibility of abuse is no argument against the *thing*." His efforts in the Washington administration were concentrated on building a robust national economy, but his ultimate goals were always political. The national bank, he wrote, "is not a mere matter of private property, but a political machine of the greatest importance to the state."[6]

Thomas Jefferson, member by birth of Virginia's higher gentry, at first gave gingerly support to part of Hamilton's program. In return for locating the new national capital in a federal district on the banks of the Potomac River between Virginia and Maryland, Jefferson helped get the administration's proposal for federal assumption of state debts through Congress. By February 1791, however, Jefferson was writing privately to Robert Livingston in New York: "Are the people in your quarter as well contented with the proceedings of our government as their representatives say they are? There is a mass of discontent gathered in the South, and how and when it will break God knows." At the same time he queried his old political ally in Virginia, George Mason: "What is said in our country on the fiscal arrangements now going on? . . . . The only corrective of what is corrupt in our present form of government will be the augmentation of the numbers in the lower house, so as to get a more agricultural representation, which may put that interest above that of the stock-jobbers."[7]

In May 1791, Jefferson set out with his friend, James Madison, on a trip to Lake Champlain, the Connecticut Valley, and Long Island, "to observe the vegetation and the wild life of the region." Madison, a member of the House of Representatives from Virginia (having been blocked from election to the Senate by Patrick Henry), had begun to speak out against some items in Hamilton's program, including the national bank and federal assumption of state debts. The trip involved a stopover of several days in New York City. While there, Jefferson and Madison seem to have met with Robert Livingston and George Clinton, who were trying to settle their differences and make common cause against the Schuylers and Hamilton. They also visited newly elected Senator Aaron Burr, an audacious schemer who was building his own political machine among the urban masses (including the Tammany Society, founded to promote equalitarian ideals). "There was every appearance," one of Hamilton's lieutenants reported to him, "of a passionate courtship between the Chancellor [Livingston], Burr, Jefferson, and Madison when the two latter were in town. . . . Delendo est Carthago I suppose is the maxim adopted with respect to you."[8] Noble Cunningham, historian of the Jeffersonian Republicans, has expressed doubt that much real political business was transacted, pointing out that Jefferson made no political references to the trip in his correspondence while leaving an abundance of notes on the types of trees, flowers, and other plant life . . . , on the size of lakes, and on the type of soil." Even so, the meetings among the New York and Virginia leaders, however informal, were among the most fateful in American political history. The first links were forged in an alliance that was to last, in one form or another, for almost 150 years and that was to be a major shaping force in national politics from the administration of Jefferson to that of Franklin Roosevelt.[9]

MADISON IN OPPOSITION

The national bank, the centerpiece of Hamilton's program, had been approved a few days before the First Congress wound up its business in March. But the midterm congressional elections produced some of the "augmentation" that Jefferson had hoped for.

Madison became de facto leader of the opposition in the House during the Second Congress. Analysis of roll-call votes shows that of the 65 members of the House, 17 usually voted with Madison, 15 consistently voted against him, and the rest shifted back and forth depending on the issue. "We have," wrote Fisher Ames, Federalist member of the House from Massachusetts, "nearly twenty *Antis,* dragons watching the tree of liberty, and who consider every strong measure and almost every ordinary one as an attempt to rob the tree of its fair fruit." Most members from Virginia, North Carolina, and Georgia, and a few from Pennsylvania and New York, usually followed Madison's lead. Only the delegations from New England were solidly against him. "It was not till the last session," Hamilton wrote in May 1792, "that I became unequivocally convinced of the following truth: that Mr. Madison, cooperating with Mr. Jefferson, is at the head of a faction decidedly hostile to me and my administration; and actuated by views, in my judgment, subversive to the principles of good government and dangerous to the union, peace, and happiness of the country."[10]

At about this time the two emerging groups acquired auxiliaries among the press—beginning the long and intimate relationship that was to exist between the press and party politics in the United States. John Fenno's *Gazette of the United States,* published in Philadelphia, and richly favored with government advertising from Hamilton's Treasury Department, became a spirited advocate of the administration's program. It was, Jefferson complained privately, "a paper of pure Toryism, disseminating the doctrines of monarchy, aristocracy, and the exclusion of the influence of the people." Seeking to offset the influence of Fenno's paper, Jefferson invited Madison's Princeton classmate, Philip Freneau, "the poet of the Revolution," to come down from New York to Philadelphia to start a rival sheet. To make the venture financially feasible for Freneau, Jefferson put him on the State Department payroll as a "translator clerk." In the spring of 1792, the new paper, called the *National Gazette,* began attacking not only Hamilton and the national bank but "stockholders and speculators [occupying] seats in the Congress."[11]

Madison contributed to the *National Gazette* an article calling for laws to prevent "an immoderate, and especially unmerited, accumulation of riches" and "to reduce extreme wealth toward a state of mediocrity, and raise extreme indigence toward a state of comfort." Such laws, he said, would head off the development of parties. But in a second article he identified two "natural" parties that he claimed exist in "most political societies" and are "likely to be of some duration in ours. On one side were persons more partial to the opulent than to the other classes of societies," who, "having debauched themselves into a persuasion that mankind are incapable of governing themselves," relied politically on "the pageantry of rank, the influence of money and emolument, and the terror of military force." Against these were arrayed the "friends to republican government," who represented the interest of "the mass of the people in every part of the union." The anti-republicans, "by reviving exploded parties" and through their access to wealth, might temporarily hold political power. But since the republicans' "superiority of numbers is so great, their sentiments . . . so decided, . . . no temperate observer of human affairs will be surprised if the issue in present instance should be reversed, and the government be administered in the spirit and form approved by the great body of the people."[12]

What had become of the earnest young conservative of *The Federalist,* who had been so eager to protect the rights of the affluent minority against the "passion or interest in a majority"? In the first place, Madison even in 1787 had not been as conservative as the well-known *Federalist* Ten and Fifty-one make him sound. Having assured the well-off minority that their interests would be protected under the proposed Constitution, he shifted in later letters to identify with the sentiments of the less well-off majority. In *Federalist* Fifty-two, he argued that the House of Representatives because of frequent elections would "have an immediate dependence on, and an intimate sympathy with, the people." In *Federalist* Fifty-seven he pointed out that the voters electing members of the House would be "not the rich, more than the poor; not the learned, more than the ignorant; not the haughty heirs of distinguished names, more than the humble sons of obscurity and unpropitious fortune."[13] Once the Constitution was approved and the new government launched, Madison drafted and took the lead in enacting the Bill of Rights.

Nevertheless, the difference in ideological point of view between the Madison of 1787 and the Madison of 1792 seems inescapable. Some personal factors may have been involved: In the early 1790s Madison was losing out to Hamilton as Washington's most trusted adviser, and Jefferson, who had been in Paris in 1787, was on the scene, no doubt exerting strong influence on his younger associate. (Jefferson was 47 in 1790; Madison, 39.) Or deeper thought and experience may have led Madison to feel greater sympathy for the poor. Madison's own explanation, given near the end of his life, was that his apparent change was only a response to the radical direction in which Hamilton was leading the government: "I abandoned Colonel Hamilton—or Colonel Hamilton abandoned me—in a word, we *parted*— upon its plainly becoming his purpose to administer the government into a thing totally different from that which he and I both knew perfectly well had been understood and intended by the Convention which framed it, and by the people in adopting it."[14]

Beyond all these factors, Madison may by 1792 have developed a different understanding of the power relationships in the Republic than he had held when he contributed to *The Federalist.* In 1787 he had identified, at least partly, with the interest of the planter class of Virginia, which might be threatened by a local version of Shays' Rebellion. After serving for several years in the House of Representatives, first in New York and then in Philadelphia, he may have concluded that the Virginia way of life was challenged less by economic have-nots, or have-lesses, than by the growing force of New York and New England mercantile capitalism. If libertarian republicanism of the kind cherished by the Virginians—which

Madison probably valued at least as much on moral as on economic grounds—was to be maintained, it would need allies against the aggressive financiers and industrialists of the North for whom Hamilton spoke. Where better to find these than among the have-nots and have-lesses, particularly among the small farmers in the inland valleys, but also among the masses whom Burr and others had begun to organize, who were the capitalists' natural antagonists within their own bailiwicks? If the Clintons and the Burrs, along with the upper-class northern libertarians like the Livingstons, could be aligned with the South, the "superiority of numbers" that Madison claimed for "republicanism" might well be preserved.

The ticking time bomb in this prospect, of course, was slavery. How could southern libertarians claim with a straight face to champion the interest of economic have-nots when they consented to, indeed lived off, a system based on the ruthless exploitation of more than half a million enslaved blacks? The more thoughtful among the upper-class southerners recognized this paradox but looked to time for its solution. Jefferson's words are well known: "I tremble for my country when I reflect that God is just; that his justice can not sleep for ever. . . ." Madison's less so: "We have seen the mere distinction of colour made in the most enlightened period of time, a ground of the most oppressive dominion ever exercised of man over man." But: "Great as the evil is, dismemberment of the union would be worse."[15]

"THE CAUSE OF MAN"

In the second presidential election, in 1792, the opposition to Federalist domination was considerably better organized than it had been four years before. Aaron Burr indicated some interest in opposing Adams for Vice President. But a caucus in Philadelphia of leaders of "the republican interest," or party, as opponents of the administration were coming to be known, determined "to exert every endeavor for Mr. Clinton, and to drop all thoughts of Mr. Burr." Washington again was supported by all 132 participating electors, and Adams was safely reelected as Vice President with 77 votes. But George Clinton obtained all the votes of New York, Virginia, North Carolina, and Georgia, and one from Pennsylvania, for a total of 50. The opposition coalition that had taken shape in Congress was entering presidential politics.[16]

Party divisions were deepened and made more passionate in response to revolutionary France's declaration of war on Britain in 1793. Many Americans had regarded the French Revolution of 1789 as a continuation of the struggle that had begun in America in 1776. Tom Paine's participation in the new rebellion seemed to signify the extension of liberal ideals. Even when the French revolutionaries attacked not only monarchy but traditional Christianity, many enthusiasts for democracy in the United States, John Trumbull of Connecticut critically observed, "threw up their caps, and cried, 'glorious, glorious, sister republic.' "[17]

From the start, some American conservatives and moderates expressed reservations about the direction of the French Revolution. "I know not," John Adams wrote in 1790, "what to make of a republic of thirty million atheists." As the murderous details of the Terror of 1793 became known, such reservations increased and spread.[18]

Among political equalitarians, and among much of the public, however, support for the Revolution remained strong. Early in 1793, Jefferson justified the Terror:

> In the struggle which was necessary, many guilty persons fell without the forms of trial, and with them some innocent. These I deplore as much as any body. . . . But I deplore them as I should have done had they fallen in battle. It was necessary to use the arm of the people, a machine not quite so blind as balls and bombs, but blind to a certain degree. The liberty of the whole earth was depending on the outcome of the contest, and was ever such a prize won with so little innocent blood? My own affections have been deeply wounded by some of the martyrs to this cause, but rather than it should have failed, I would have seen half the earth desolated.[19]

When war came between France and Britain a few months later, many thought the United States should pitch in on the French side. Washington, however, on the grounds of prudence as well as moral judgment, swiftly declared American neutrality. Jefferson, still secretary of state, supported the decision. Many among his followers were not so temperate. "The cause of France is the cause of man," declared a republican journal in western Pennsylvania, "and neutrality is desertion."[20]

The arrival of "Citizen" Genet, the new French ambassador, in Charleston on the day Washington declared neutrality set off tumultuous demonstrations in support of France. Traveling triumphantly up the east coast to Philadelphia, Genet openly commissioned privateers to prey on British shipping and urged Americans to join French forces in Louisiana for an attack on New Orleans, then owned by Spain. At a banquet held to honor the ambassador in Philadelphia, Freneau read his translation of a French revolutionary ode, "while the red cap was passed from head to head." At another banquet, "guests marched round and round an obelisk, Singing the 'Marseillaise,' and staggering a little from the effects of revolutionary toasts." John Adams, perhaps overexcited, was sure that only the scourge of yellow fever prevented an actual rebellion. He later wrote:

> You certainly never felt the Terrorism, excited by Genet, in 1793, when ten thousand People in the streets of Philadelphia, day after day, threatened to drag Washington out of his House, and effect a Revolution in the Government, or compel it to declare war in favour of the French Revolution and against England. The coolest and the firmest Minds, even among the Quakers in Philadelphia,

have given their Opinions to me, that nothing but the Yellow Fever . . . could have saved the United States from a total Revolution of Government.[21]

Supporters of the French cause in Philadelphia formed a political club which they called the "Democratic Society." Philadelphia soon had two Democratic societies, one English-speaking and the other German-speaking. Similar clubs, taking the names Democratic or Republican, sprang up all over the country, numbering 35 by the end of 1794. These clubs were active in several congressional campaigns in 1794, always on behalf of Republican candidates. In New York the emerging parties were for a time identified as "Gallician" or "Anti-Gallician." In Charleston the local Democratic club petitioned to be adopted by the Jacobean club in Paris. Hot-blooded South Carolina Democrats toasted the guillotine as the proper fate for "all tyrants plundering, and funding speculators." Genet's subsequent marriage to George Clinton's daughter Cornelia (after the fall of the Jacobins in France had made it imprudent for him to return home) neatly symbolized the union of equalitarian spirit in the two countries. The war between France and England "kindled and brought forward the two parties," Jefferson wrote to James Monroe in 1793, "with an ardor which our own interests merely, could never excite."[22]

THE REPUBLICAN INTEREST

The Whiskey Insurrection in western Pennsylvania in 1794 (set off by farmers furious over the federal levy on whiskey, their principal means for converting grain into a marketable commodity), and controversy over the commercial treaty negotiated by John Jay with Britain in 1795, further hardened party lines. Madison and other Republican strategists (not yet including Jefferson) saw that the key to defeating the Federalists was to combine the old Antifederalist base with former Federalists who had grown dissatisfied with some, or all, policies of the Washington administration.

Some modern scholars have doubted that there was much connection between the Antifederalists and the Republicans of the 1790s, pointing out that a few leading Antifederalists crossed over to the Federalist side and that Madison and some others who argued for ratification became Republicans. Except in New England, however, the great majority of Antifederalists seem to have moved smoothly into Republican ranks, including such future party leaders as James Monroe of Virginia and Albert Gallatin of Pennsylvania. In New York the old Clintonian party became "the center of the Republican interest." (Jefferson, however, warned Madison that "the cause of republicanism will suffer and its votaries be thrown into schism by embarking it in support of this man," and Monroe told Jefferson that he found Clinton's character "highly exceptionable.") The Livingstons, following Chancellor Livingston's dictum to "yield to the torrent if they hoped to direct its course," joined the Clintonians and Burr in the new alignment. In Pennsylvania, remaining supporters of the radical state constitution of 1776, including Scotch-Irish Presbyterians in the west, joined forces with the newly organized Democratic clubs. In Virginia, enough Antifederalists lined up with Madison and his followers to make the Republicans the majority party in 1795 (though the Federalists retained pockets of strength in the tidewater and the Shenandoah Valley). In Massachusetts, John Adams claimed, his cousin Sam Adams and John Hancock were conspiring with other "Detesters of the present national Government" to oust the Federalists at both the national and state levels so that "the Stone House Faction [Hancock's mansion on Beacon Hill was built of granite] will be sure of all the Loaves and Fishes, in the national Government and the State Government as they hope."[23]

In the fall of 1793, Jefferson, complaining that Hamilton was gaining control over foreign as well as domestic policy, resigned as secretary of state. In 1794 Hamilton, too, left the administration, but he kept close ties with Washington and saw to it that the cabinet was packed with reliable Federalists. "General Washington," Jefferson observed, "after the retirement of his first cabinet and the composition of his second, entirely Federal, . . . had no opportunity of hearing both sides of any question. His measures consequently took more the hue of the party in whose hands he was."[24]

Washington continued to regard himself as above parties and to deplore the development of party spirit in the nation. In 1794 he lashed out at the Democratic clubs, which he characterized as "self-created societies," formed to undermine the government. He identified the clubs with the recently suppressed Whiskey Insurrection, which he said had been "fomented by combinations of men who, regardless of consequences and disregarding the unerring truth that those who rouse cannot always appease a civil convulsion, have disseminated, from an ignorance or perversion of facts, suspicions, jealousies, and accusations of the whole Government."[25]

Madison reacted angrily that the administration's "game" was "to connect the democratic societies with the odium of the insurrection, to connect the Republicans in Congress with these societies, [and] to put the President ostensibly at the head of the other party in opposition to both." Theodore Sedgwick of Massachusetts, now Federalist whip in the Senate, remarked with satisfaction: "Poor Madison is indeed very much chagrined and mortified, but not disheartened. He has been calling out for several days past the *Sans Cullotes* of the House one after another. This has been invariably the prelude to some effort to do mischief."[26]

Jefferson increasingly shared Madison's view that the administration, and indeed Washington himself, had deserted true republican principles. "In place of that noble love of liberty and republican Government which carried us triumphantly through the war," he wrote privately in the spring of 1796, "an Anglican, Monarchical and Aristocratical party has sprung up, whose avowed subject is to draw over us the substance as they have already done the forms of the British government." On the side of the Federalists Jefferson included "all the officers of the government, all who want to be officers, all timid men who prefer the calm of despotism to the boisterous sea of liberty, British merchants, and Americans trading on British capital, speculators, and holders in the banks and public funds. . . ." To these he added "apostates who have gone over to these heresies; men who were Samsons in the field, and Solomons in the council, but who have had their heads shorn by the harlot England"—apparently with Washington specifically in mind. But Jefferson did not despair. "The main body of our citizens . . . remain true to their republican principles. The whole landed interest is republican, and so is a great mass of talent."[27]

Albert Gallatin of western Pennsylvania, a rising star among the Republicans who had already called Hamilton "the Judas Iscariot of our country," asked if Washington might "become the tyrant instead of the saviour of his country." Paine, writing from France, where things were going badly for him, joined the attack. From the time of the Revolution, he maintained, Washington had been a "hypocrite" who would "desert a man or a cause with constitutional indifference."[28]

Perhaps saddened by these reproaches and suffering the effects of advancing age, Washington decided not to allow his name to go forward for a third term. He used the occasion of his retirement from public life to deliver his final advice to the American people. The Farewell Address (never actually given as a speech, but published in newspapers) was based on a draft written by Madison in 1792 and substantially revised by Hamilton in 1796. The sentiments and the final language were Washington's own.

After warning against "foreign alliances, attachments, and intrigues" and recommending avoidance of "overgrown military establishments," Washington turned his attention to political parties. In their efforts to "direct, control, counteract, or awe the regular deliberations and actions of the constituted authorities," he said, parties "serve to organize faction, to give it an artificial and extraordinary force, to put in the place of the delegated will of the Nation the will of a party, often a small but artful and enterprising minority of the community. . . ." Parties "may now and then answer popular ends," but "they are likely, in the course of time and things, to become potent engines by which cunning, ambitious, and unprincipled men will be enabled to subvert the power of the people and to usurp for themselves the reins of government. . . ." The spirit of party, "unfortunately, is inseparable from our nature, having its roots in the strongest passions of the human mind." But "the common and continual mischiefs" of this spirit "are sufficient to make it the interest and duty of a wise people to discourage and restrain it."[29]

THE SEDITION ACT

Although Washington did not announce his intention to step down until a few weeks before the election, both parties proceeded throughout 1796 on the assumption that he would not seek a third term. "It is now generally understood," Madison wrote to Monroe in May, "that the President will retire. Jefferson is the object on one side, Adams apparently on the other." Federalist members of Congress agreed at an informal meeting in Philadelphia that their party's electors would cast ballots for Adams and Thomas Pinckney of South Carolina, with the understanding that Adams was to become President. The Republicans seem to have had no doubt that Jefferson would be their candidate for President, but congressional Republicans met in Philadelphia to try to reach agreement on a running mate. Chancellor Livingston had substantial support but was blocked by Burr from receiving unified backing from New York. Burr, in turn, was regarded by some of the southerners as "unsettled in his politics." The meeting adjourned without reaching agreement.[30]

In the campaign that followed, a few candidates for elector refused to announce their choice in advance—like the candidate in Maryland who promised only that he would "vote for that man, who to my judgment, after all I can obtain, shall appear best qualified, and likely to support the honor, and to preserve and promote the freedom, the tranquility, and the prosperity of our common country." But most identified openly with one party or the other—like the Massachusetts candidate who placed a newspaper announcement that his vote would be for "uniform Federalism," or the Maryland aspirant who assured a Baltimore paper that he was "decidedly in favor of Jefferson."[31]

Neither Adams nor Jefferson conducted an active campaign. Jefferson, who had tried to dissuade his friends from putting up his name, wrote to Madison from Monticello: "There is nothing I so anxiously hope, as that my name may come out either second or third. These would be indifferent to me; as the last would leave me at home the whole year, and the other two-thirds of it." The Federalists seem to have relied on the influence of local notables to carry their ticket to victory. The Republican organizations in several states, in contrast, campaigned vigorously to turn out votes for Jefferson. Gallatin reported that he had been "tolerably industrious" in western Pennsylvania. Burr barnstormed through Connecticut, Rhode Island, Massachusetts, and Vermont.[32]

When the electoral college met, Adams, carrying all of New England, New York, New Jersey, and Delaware, and picking up a few votes in Pennsylvania, Maryland, Virginia, and North Carolina, achieved a narrow majority of 71. Apparently aiming to guard against defections from Adams by southern Federalists, 11 Federalist electors from New Hampshire, Massachusetts, and Rhode Island cast their votes not for Pinckney but for Oliver Ellsworth of Connecticut, Chief Justice of the Supreme Court. As a result, Jefferson, with 68 votes, was elected Vice President—carrying out in a way the intention of the framers but placing rival leaders of opposed parties in the two highest offices. Pinckney received 59 votes, and Burr with 30 votes was in fourth place.

With Washington gone from the scene, party warfare blazed through national politics without restraint. Republicans charged that the Federalists not only were bound to the "money power" but were actually plotting to establish a monarchy. "Changes in the principles of our government are to be pushed," Jefferson warned, "till they accomplish a monarchy peaceably or force a resistance which, with the aid of an army, may end in monarchy." John Taylor of Caroline went so far as to suggest that Virginia and North Carolina should consider secession to escape the "saddle" being imposed on the Union by Massachusetts and Connecticut.[33]

The Federalists responded by accusing the Republicans of contemplating treason. Senator George Cabot of Massachusetts gloomily predicted, "Our country is destined to act over the same follies, to practice the same vices, and of consequence to suffer the same miseries which compose the history of revolutionary France." Senator Robert Goodloe Harper of South Carolina declared that the Republicans were "a conspiracy, a faction leagued with a foreign power to effect a revolution or subjugation of this country, by the arms of that foreign power." George Washington, observing events from retirement at Mount Vernon, wrote to Lafayette that the Republicans were attempting "to Subvert the Constitution."[34]

When corrupt politicians claiming to control the French government demanded bribes from and insulted American emissaries in 1798—the so-called "XYZ affair"—public opinion in the United States swung heavily against France. Invasion by French armies of "the two sacred homelands of the Reformation, Switzerland and the Netherlands," produced shock and outrage among American Protestants. Theodore Sedgwick sensed that the shift in public attitudes afforded "a glorious opportunity to destroy faction," unlikely to be repeated. "Improve it," he advised.[35]

With Adams' approval, the Federalist majority in Congress whipped through the Sedition Act, making it a crime to speak, write, or publish anything "with intent to defame" public officials, along with a package of Alien Acts, making it easier for the government to deport political antagonists who were not citizens. Between 1798 and 1800, 14 indictments were brought under the Sedition Act. About ten of these led to convictions. In one case, Justice Samuel Chase instructed the jury that the defendant, a Republican publicist named John Cooper, had attempted "to mislead the ignorant, and inflame their minds against the President, and to influence their votes in the next election." Cooper got six months in federal prison and a fine of $400.[36]

The Republicans responded, at Jefferson's instigation, by persuading the legislatures of Virginia and Kentucky to enact resolutions condemning and defying the Sedition Act. The Virginia Resolution, written by Madison, charged that the act was "levelled against the right of freely examining public characters and measures, and of free communication among the people . . . , which has ever been deemed the only effectual guardian of every right."[37]

Other southern legislatures, however, hung back from following the examples of Virginia and Kentucky. Popular wrath against France continued to rise. Seaboard residents worried that the French fleet might attack American ports. "I fear Congress will close the session without a declaration of War," wrote Federalist Senator James Lloyd of Maryland, "which I look upon as necessary to lay our hands on traitors."[38]

The decisive obstruction to the hope of many Federalist politicians for a patriotic war against France turned out to be President Adams. As Richard Hofstadter pointed out, Adams, "as a scorner of parties and partisan politics, . . . accepted no sense of obligation to the Federalists as a party." Responding to Federalists like Hamilton, who insisted that taking a militant stand against France was a party as well as a national duty, Adams declared: "Arrogance shall be made to feel a curb. If anyone entertaining the idea that, because I am a President of three votes only, I am in the power of a party, they shall find that I am no more than the Constitution forces upon me."[39]

FIRST REALIGNMENT

By the time the climactic presidential campaign of 1800 came around, anti-French feeling had subsided and the Republicans were in the political ascendancy. But this time Jefferson felt he could not afford to be detached. The outcome of the election, he believed, would determine the future direction of the United States. Writing to Madison in the fall of 1799, he urged that the Republicans campaign on a kind of platform: "1. peace even with Great Britain 2. a sincere cultivation of the Union 3. the disbanding of the army on principles of economy and safety 4. protestations against violations of the true principles of our constitution. . . ." Once the campaign was underway, he distrusted the federal mails for political communication. "Postmasters," he wrote to Taylor, "will lend their inquisitorial aid to fish out any new matter of slander that can gratify the powers that be."[40]

Gallatin argued that Burr should be included on the Republican ticket as a means for carrying Pennsylvania and New York. Burr, complaining that he "was certainly ill used by Virginia and North Carolina" in 1796, asked, through an emissary, that "assurances . . . be given that the southern states will act fairly." Republican members of Congress already committed to Jefferson for President met at Marache's boarding house in Philadelphia, the unofficial party headquarters, and voted unanimously to support Burr for Vice President—the first formal endorsement of a national ticket by a body claiming to represent the entire party.[41]

The Federalists decided to team Adams with General Charles Cotesworth Pinckney—another member of that numerous and politically active South Carolina family. "We have had a meeting of the whole federal party, on the subject of the ensuing election," Sedgwick reported, "and have agreed that we will support, *bona fide,* Mr. Adams and General Pinckney." Some historians have speculated that Hamilton secretly intended to have Pinckney elected President. If electors from South Carolina voted for Jefferson and Pinckney while Federalist electors in other states voted for the two Federalist candidates, Pinckney might come in first. In his correspondence, however, Hamilton warned that there must be no defections of the kind that had occurred in 1796. "To support *Adams* and *Pinckney* equally," he wrote, "is the only thing that can save us from the fangs of *Jefferson.* It is therefore, essential that the Federalists should not separate without coming to a distinct and solemn concert to pursue this course *bona fide.*"[42]

Both parties used their strength in state legislatures to alter electoral systems to their advantage. In Virginia the legislature shifted from choosing presidential electors by congressional district to a statewide winner-take-all system, to assure that Jefferson would win the state's entire vote. The *Virginia Argus,* the Republican paper in Richmond, explained: "The same game is playing off in New England, and some other Eastern States: and in plain English, it is necessary to fight an adversary at his own methods." In Massachusetts the choice was shifted from popular vote by congressional district to the legislature, "to guard against *one* antifederal vote" from the Bay State.[43]

In New York, which both sides recognized held the key to the election, the Federalists defeated a move by the Republicans to change from choosing the electors by the legislature to having them elected by district. When the Republicans won control of the legislature, Hamilton wrote to John Jay, the Federalist governor, proposing that a lame-duck legislative session adopt the district system of election in order to salvage some electoral votes for Adams. "In weighing this suggestion," Hamilton argued, "you will doubtless bear in mind that popular governments must certainly be overturned . . . if one party will call to its aid all the resources which vice can give, and if the other (however pressing the emergency) confines itself within all the ordinary forms of delicacy and decorum." Jay, like Adams, was unwilling to sacrifice principle for party. With a note to himself that the stratagem would serve "party purposes, which I think it would not become me to adopt," he did not reply to Hamilton's letter.[44]

As in 1796, the Republicans deployed the stronger party organizations in most of the battleground states. In New York Burr once more led the Republican canvass. The campaign in New York City was coordinated by a committee "composed of deputations from the respective ward committees in favor of the republican interest." During the first two of the three days of balloting, Burr moved from poll to poll, frequently encountering Hamilton, with whom he "debated the issues of the day before the assembled voters." On the last day, Burr "remained at the Poll of the Seventh Ward *ten Hours,* without intermission." The polls closed at sundown. By midnight a dispatch was on its way to Gallatin: "Republicanism Triumphant. To Col. Burr we are indebted for everything." The Republican organization was remarkably successful at obtaining a uniform vote for the party ticket for electors. In the seventh ward, the highest vote received by a candidate on the Republican ticket was 784 and the lowest, 780.[45]

In Pennsylvania the Republican governor, Thomas McKean, elected in 1799, began "the practice . . . of making political removals and appointments for partisan considerations." Political jobholders were expected to work for the party cause. "Every man who is not for the whole Republican Ticket," exhorted the Philadelphia *Aurora,* "Regards the Public Good Less than his Prejudices." The Republican slate included candidates for Congress, the state legislature, and, in Philadelphia, county sheriff.[46]

In Virginia, though there was less party machinery, cooperation between party leaders was "systematized—regular plans are formed and correspondence." Local party workers saw to it that voters were treated to "rum punch or other drinks on election day." (When Madison first ran for the legislature in 1777, he abstained from such inducements on the ground that they were "inconsistent with the purity of moral and republican principles." He lost to a former tavern-keeper and thereafter conformed to local practice.)[47]

The Federalists, too, made more use of campaign organization than they had in 1796. In New York City Hamilton's organization fought toe-to-toe with Burr's. "I have been night and day employed in the business of the election," reported Robert Troup, one of Hamilton's lieutenants. "Never have I witnessed such exertions on either side before. I have not eaten dinner for three days and have been consistently on my legs from 7 in the morning till 7 in the afternoon."[48]

In many states the Federalists used federal government patronage to build up their organizations. Secretary of War James McHenry instructed a subordinate in North Carolina that commissions in the provisional army (formed when war with France seemed imminent) should be awarded only to men "whose attachment to the Government is unquestioned." A Maryland Federalist congressman wrote McHenry asking that one of his "most spirited and best Friends" be commissioned as a captain because he "will be a most valuable Man on the Days of Election." Like the Republicans, the Federalists pressed for a straight party vote. *"Fellow Citizens,"* a Federalist broadside in New Jersey appealed, "let no slight dislikes or preferences induce you to relax your effort, or *break* the ticket; if you are for President Adams, be *wholly* so; by omission of any on the federal nomination, or *taking up* any of the other, we shall defeat our intention, and we may (the supposition is not too distant) ruin our country."[49]

The Federalist campaign in New England received major support from the Congregationalist clergy. In Massachusetts, Connecticut, and New Hampshire, where Congregationalism was still state-established, church members seem to have regarded Federalism as their protector against disestablishment. The Connecticut Valley, where the Shaysites had been strong, became "the most staunch Federalist region in the nation." Timothy Dwight, president of Yale and a grandson of Jonathan Edwards, preacher of the Great Awakening of the 1730s, identified supporters of Jefferson with "profaneness of language, drunkenness, gambling, lewdness. . . ."[50]

Jefferson's reputation as a religious skeptic reinforced the dislike of conservative Calvinists for Republicans in general. Martin Van Buren recalled hearing New York clergymen preach that Jefferson's election would lead to "burning of Bibles, the prostration of religion, and the substitution of some Goddess of Reason." The Federalist press took up the religious issue. "The charge of infidelity against Mr. Jefferson," said the New York *Spectator,* "is legitimate." The *Gazette of the United States* put the question succinctly: "GOD—AND A RELIGIOUS PRESIDENT; OR . . . JEFFERSON—AND NO GOD!!!"[51]

Evangelicals, on the other hand, who traced their origins to the Great Awakening, for the most part rallied to the Jeffersonian cause. Presbyterians were split: rationalist Old Lights backing Adams, and evangelical New Lights supporting Jefferson.

The presence of Burr, another grandson of Jonathan Edwards, on the Republican ticket was thought to offset Timothy Dwight's impassioned Federalism among evangelicals. Baptists and the recently founded Methodists (formed in the United States in 1784), both of whom were winning masses of converts among rural families in the South and on the western frontier, tended to be ardently Republican—attracted by the equalitarian enthusiasm that antagonized conservative Congregationalists and Presbyterians. The Republicans also appealed to the evangelicals' opposition to state-established religion. A New Jersey Republican circular argued that Jefferson was being branded an infidel "because he is not a fanatic, not willing that the *Quaker,* the *Baptist,* the *Methodist,* or any other denominations of Christians, should pay the pastor of other sects; because he does not think a catholic should be banished for believing in transubstantiation, or a Jew, for believing in the God of Abraham, Isaac, and Jacob." Pennsylvania Republicans claimed that "to religious men, Mr. Jefferson has indisputably been the most helpful character since *William Penn.*"[52]

Figure 3–1   Electoral vote by states, 1796

Source: Congressional Quarterly's Guide to U.S. Elections, Congressional Quarterly, Inc., Washington, D.C., 1975

Quakers, concentrated in Pennsylvania and Delaware, were largely Federalist, continuing the conservative political inclination they had developed before the Revolution. Episcopalians were Federalist, except in New England, where their resentment against paying taxes to support established Congregationalism drew some of them to the Republicans. The small number of Catholics, mainly Irish in New York and French Canadians in upper New England, plus a few old families in Maryland and Pennsylvania, were overwhelmingly Republican.

When the electoral vote was counted, the Republican ticket was found to have won a narrow victory. The switch of New York from the Federalists in 1796 to the Republicans in 1800 carried both Jefferson and Burr to national totals of 73 electoral votes. Adams received 65, and Pinckney 64 (one Federalist elector in Pennsylvania voted for John Jay). As Figures 3–1 and 3–2 show, the swing of electoral votes was not massive, but it was enough to produce the first major party realignment in American history. South Carolina cast its votes for Jefferson and

Figure 3–2   Electoral vote by states, 1800

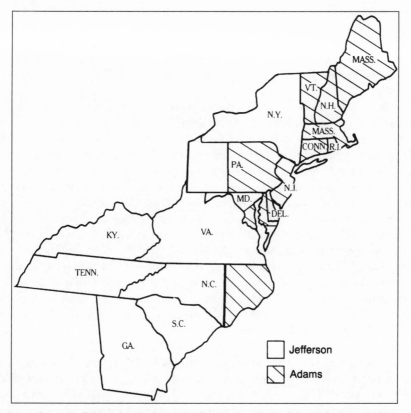

Source: Congressional Quarterly's Guide to U.S. Elections, Congressional Quarterly, Inc., Washington, D.C., 1975

Burr, confounding whatever plot may have existed among Federalist ultras to throw the election to Pinckney. Adams actually did better in Pennsylvania and North Carolina than he did in 1796, but it was not enough to offset New York's switch. The strength of the Republicans in the frontier states of Kentucky and Tennessee, admitted since the formation of the Union, was essential to their victory.

WHY THE FEDERALISTS FAILED

Under the rules set forth in the Constitution, the electoral-vote tie between Jefferson and Burr threw the election into the House of Representatives, where the Federalists controlled enough state delegations to prevent a choice without their approval. But Federalist domination of the executive branch had definitely ended. Divisions among party factions loyal to Adams and Hamilton, and among other factions that did not care much for either man, moreover, were so deep and bitter that it seemed unlikely that the party, deprived of executive branch patronage, would soon achieve a comeback. As matters turned out, the Federalists never again won a national election. The party, though it remained a presence in politics for another quarter-century, became a vessel for New England parochialism and reactionary social attitudes, something like the extreme right-wing parties that lingered on in some western European countries after the Second World War. The Federalist era was over.[53]

Why did the Federalists fail? In terms of their impact on history, the Federalists were, of course, a fantastic success: drafting and securing ratification of the Constitution, launching the new government, establishing the executive authority of the presidency under Washington, enacting Hamilton's economic program. Not the least of the Federalists' contributions to republican government was the law-abiding willingness with which they turned over control to the executive branch after losing the 1800 election. It is hard to find earlier examples in history of such a transition. British governments in the eighteenth century sometimes changed in response to shifting coalitions in the House of Commons, but it was not until 1841 that "the opposition won a general election and the Crown accepted the decision at the polls." The newly established capital city, named after Washington, who had just died, had been designed to withstand a siege. But it seems never to have crossed John Adams' stern Yankee mind not to turn over power to his lawfully elected successor—though only after naming John Marshall as Chief Justice, thereby assuring a Federalist slant to judicial interpretation of the Constitution for the next 34 years.[54]

Despite these achievements, however, the Federalists as a party of government had a remarkably short tenure—particularly considering the political advantages they had seemed to enjoy only 12 years before. The Federalists failed in part because they did not understand the underlying nature of American democracy. The longer they clung to office, the more many of them began to talk and act, not like conservative republicans, but like hierarchical Tories in the British sense.

Fisher Ames of Massachusetts, acclaimed by fellow conservatives as "the American Burke," derided "the dreams of all the philosophers who think the people always mean right, and if the governments do not oppress, the citizens will not resist." Noah Webster of Connecticut, a relatively moderate Federalist, argued that republican government requires "the advantage and superior influence of particular men, derived from their property, their education, their age, their tried virtue and integrity, and their public services." Many Federalists, John Quincy Adams later declared, were "warm admirers of the British Constitution, disposed to confide rather to the inherent strength of the Government than to the self-evident truths of the Declaration of Independence for the preservation of the rights of property and perhaps of persons." The Federalists, observed D. W. Brogan, the British political scientist who perceptively studied American parties, were "of the temper of Coriolanus; even when they wooed the plebs, they did it ungracefully and unconvincingly."[55]

Neither Adams nor Hamilton, the two great Federalist leaders, if Washington is not included (as he wished not to be), was fully committed to democracy as it has come to be understood and practiced in the United States. Adams throughout his career expressed horror of the "tyranny" produced by the doctrine of "all power in the people." There was, he agreed with Jefferson, a "natural aristocracy" of "Talent," but against this must be balanced the aristocracy of "Beauty, Wealth, and Birth." Observing the trend of the times during the Jefferson administration, Adams suggested the period be called "the Age of Folly, Vice, Frenzy, Fury, Brutality, Demons, Bonaparte, Tom Paine, the Age of the Burning Brand and Bottomless Pit; or anything but the Age of Reason."[56]

Hamilton was even more outspoken in his rejection of the equalitarian ethos. Democracy, he wrote, is "our real disease." Democratic politicians, he warned, pursue "the bait of popularity at the expense of the common good." Gouverneur Morris, his friend and political ally, wrote: "General Hamilton detested democratical government because it must end in despotism, and be, in the meantime, destructive to public morality."[57]

The Federalists lived, it is easy to forget, in a world that had no real experience with successful democracy. The examples of antiquity were not encouraging. Even republican government based on rule by an upper-class oligarchy, like that of Venice, seemed to many a frail craft on which to brave the oceans of political turmoil. Even Washington, while prepared to "lose the last drop of blood" to assure that republican government should have "a fair chance for success, at times, according to Jefferson, privately expressed uncertainty about its "duration."[58]

Despite endlessly repeated charges by Jefferson, Taylor, and the Republican publicists, few if any of the Federalists hoped or conspired to restore monarchy. They believed in freedom, in the sense of affirming that individuals have rights derived from God or nature that no government can legitimately trample. They favored some kind of representative government—though, as the institutions of the Senate and the electoral college show, they were far from enshrining the concept of "one man–one vote" (let alone "one person–one vote"). But they were convinced that legitimate rights and genuine representation are best preserved through a system that assures, as Fisher Ames wrote, rule by "the wise, and the good, and the rich."[59]

Looking back now at the Sedition Act, most of us, I think, feel, after disapproval, amazement that the Federalists thought they could get away with it. And yet among the leading Federalists only John Marshall is reported to have expressed any doubts—and he on grounds of expediency, not legality. Washington, living in retirement, viewed it as "simply an effort toward stronger national unity." Most of the Republicans were cautious about following Jefferson's lead in calling for defiance of the act. Even Jefferson, when the shoe was on the other foot, responded to attacks by the Federalist press in 1803 by writing to Governor McKean of Pennsylvania that a "few prosecutions" at the state level "of the most prominent offenders would have a wholesome effect in restoring the integrity of the presses." The First Amendment concepts of freedom of speech and freedom of the press, as we conceive them, had not yet been fully defined in the public mind, or even among judicial experts or political philosophers. In a way, the Federalists, by offending the spirit of these rights, helped the nation arrive at a clearer understanding of what it really believed.[60]

The Federalists tried to govern in part on the basis of principles that turned out to be contrary to American values. As a result, they did not survive as a political force. A kind of conservatism was to play a major, indeed often dominant, role in American society and politics. Hierarchical conservatism was to be an enduring influence in shaping family life, in many forms of religion and education, in structuring communities, in internal governance of both public bureaucracies and private firms. But never again would a significant political party identify itself with rule by "the wise, and the good, and the rich" or openly promote governmental prohibition of public criticism. The Federalists had tried those options. Their political failure, as well as their many governmental achievements, helped establish the terms and conditions for the future practice of democracy.

aristocracy means.

NO ROOM FOR PARTIES

Madison and Jefferson, more than other leaders or theorists of the period, began to sense that a party system might be an inevitable or even beneficial adjunct to republican government. Madison wrote of a "division . . . natural to most political societies" and "likely to be of some duration in ours." Jefferson, in a letter to Taylor in 1798, conceded: "In every free and deliberating society there must, from the nature of man, be opposite parties and violent dissensions and discords; and one of these, for the most part must prevail over the other for a longer or shorter time. Perhaps this party division is necessary to induce each to watch and relate to the people the proceedings of the other." When he came to compose his first inaugural, Jefferson wrote in an early draft: "Wherever there are men there will be parties and where there are free men they will make themselves heard. . . . These are the whigs and tories of nature." Significantly, he did not include this passage in the address as finally presented.[61]

Some of the lesser Federalists—though not, so far as I know, Adams or Hamilton—at times acknowledged that a party system might serve a useful purpose.

In the end, however, each side disliked the other so intensely that neither could countenance the continued existence of a party institution embodying the views of the other. How could an honest Republican admit a legitimate role for monarchists? How could decent Federalists make room for men who would lead the country into "the same miseries which compose the history of revolutionary France"?

When Jefferson declared, in the passage he *did* include in his first inaugural, that "We are all republicans; we are all federalists," he meant really that the party wars were over; that the Republicans had won; and that the Federalists should fit themselves into the new regime as best they could. For a time, it again seemed that the United States might achieve one-party or no-party democracy. But then the "violent dissensions and discords" that Jefferson had predicted did in fact occur, and he proved a more accurate prophet than he would have hoped.

4

ONE-PARTY HEGEMONY

The Jeffersonians

THE ELECTION of Thomas Jefferson as President in 1800 ushered in a period of almost 60 years during which the party representing the liberal tradition was normally dominant. For a time, in the administrations of James Madison and James Monroe that followed Jefferson's two terms, the supremacy of the party of liberalism was so complete that the Founders' ideal of a political system without party divisions seemed within grasp. But at the end of Monroe's second term in 1824, the renewal of competition between parties representing the two great American traditions revealed that both traditions were deeply imbedded in the national political culture and showed that the two-party system was useful, perhaps essential, to American democracy.

"The Revolution of 1800," Jefferson wrote, "was as real a revolution in the principles of our government as that of 1776 was in its forms."[1]

Some scholars, finding continuity as well as change in the administration that took office in 1801, and noting the absence of "violence and bloodshed," have concluded that Jefferson exaggerated. Henry Adams, no doubt with a certain family bias, pointed out in his classic history of the period the extent to which Jefferson maintained Federalist policies and structures he had earlier attacked. Jefferson himself privately admitted in 1802: "It mortifies me to be strengthening principles which I deem radically vicious, but the vice is entailed by the first error." Fresh opportunities as well as inherited constraints caused Jefferson at times to behave differently as President than his earlier utterances would have suggested. His purchase of Louisiana from Napoleon in 1803 showed that he was prepared to go beyond a narrow interpretation of the Constitution when such action was required by his view of the national interest.[2]

Yet the Republican victory of 1800, whether or not revolutionary, did indeed mark a major turning point in American history. The Jeffersonians made good on some of their campaign promises: expenditures for national defense were slashed; the national debt, which had reached $83 million in 1800, was cut to $27.5 million by 1812; the national Bank was allowed to expire when its charter ran out in 1811 (though a new Bank was established, with Madison's reluctant approval, in

1816). More importantly, the Republicans sought and to a great extent achieved substantial shifts in the values and ideological assumptions on which the direction of national government was based.

Even in underlying ideology, the break with the immediate past was far from complete. Jefferson and his colleagues had no intention of returning to the loose confederation of states that had existed before the Constitution. Nor did they show much inclination toward social or economic collectivism. In some ways the Jeffersonians were more radically individualistic than the Federalists had been.

The Jeffersonians, however, took the viability of national government more for granted and concentrated on pursuing equalitarian ideals. The issue that most sharply divided the Jeffersonians from the Federalists was not states rights, nor the national debt, nor the national Bank, all of which both sides regarded as instruments to larger ends, but the question of social equality. The Federalists had gone beyond the American Tories, and beyond British practice at the time, in establishing the equality of individuals before the law (with usually unexamined exceptions for women, slaves, Indians, and others regarded as unsuitable for the full exercise of citizenship). But they did not doubt the need for some kind of hierarchical structure in society, and therefore in government. The Jeffersonians, and Jefferson himself, were not consistent in challenging the inevitability of hierarchy, or even in maintaining the right of all adult human beings to full individuality. But their ideal was a society in which individuals were equal in fact as well as in narrowly prescribed legal rights—a society more open in spirit, more tolerant of human differences, more evenly distributing the products of human toil and the bounty of nature. The idea of equality, never rigorously defined and often violated in practice by even its warmest theoretic advocates, had become a force of enormous consequence in American life and politics.

A CONSTITUTIONAL CRISIS

The Jeffersonian era, even after the Republicans had won the election of 1800, almost failed to get off the ground. The tie in the electoral college between Jefferson and Burr gave the defeated Federalists a chance to play a role in determining which Republican would become President. The Constitution required that the House choose between the two candidates tied for first place, with each state delegation casting one vote. Support from an absolute majority of nine of the sixteen state delegations was needed to declare a winner. The Republicans controlled eight delegations and the Federalists six. Delegations from the remaining two states, Vermont and Maryland, were evenly divided and therefore unable to vote. The Federalists could not by themselves select the President, but, if they held firm, they could prevent the Republicans from achieving a majority.[3]

Many Federalist leaders argued that the party's members in the House should support Burr, in the expectation that the wily New Yorker would be able to pry loose enough Republican members to shift a few state delegations in his favor. The Federalists would then have participated on the winning side and could claim some share of federal patronage and even a role in setting administration policy. The Republican party would be split, perhaps beyond repair. And, most satisfyingly, the hated Jefferson would be kept out of the presidency for at least another four years.

Burr stayed away from Washington and played a cautious game. He apparently did not approach the Federalists, but he also did not do the one thing that would have ended the crisis: announce that under no circumstances would he accept the office of President.

Hamilton, deciding that his distrust for Burr outweighed even his dislike for his old colleague in Washington's cabinet, came down on the side of Jefferson. (Hamilton's preference for Jefferson was based in part on contempt. Jefferson, he wrote, was not "zealot enough to do anything in pursuit of his principles, which will contravene his popularity or his interest." Burr, on the other hand, was America's "embryo Caesar.")

Still the needed Federalist votes in the House were not forthcoming. At last, as the entire system of constitutional government seemed headed for the rocks, the single member of the House from Delaware, James Bayard, a Federalist, yielded to Hamilton's urging and announced he would vote for Jefferson. (Once the outcome was settled, Federalist members from Vermont and Maryland, in order to spare Bayard the pain of actually voting for the party's archenemy, agreed to abstain, thereby allowing their delegations to make the required majority for Jefferson.)[4]

BUILDING PARTY ORGANIZATION

In March 1801, Jefferson led the Republicans into control of the executive branch, with Madison as secretary of state and Gallatin as secretary of the treasury. Almost at once the new administration began cleaning Federalists out of politically sensitive posts in the national civil service (almost 30 years before the presidency of Andrew Jackson, popularly remembered as the launcher of the spoils system at the federal level). In the Internal Revenue Department, 15 of the 16 superintendents were identified as Federalists. Of these, six were fired outright, and the other nine lost their jobs when Gallatin reorganized the department in 1802. Of the 146 customs officers appointed directly by the President, 50 were fired. In New York and Philadelphia, where party warfare was particularly hot, Jefferson replaced all but one of the customs officers. In New Jersey, all five port collectors were turned out. Federalist collectors were removed in Portsmouth, New Hampshire; New Haven, Connecticut; Norfolk, Virginia; and Savannah, Georgia. The Federalists who were fired as customs collectors had under their authority about 270 subordinates, most of whom were dismissed and replaced by Republicans.[5]

Jefferson claimed that only a few of these firings were for political activity, the rest being because of "misconduct" or "delinquency." The port collector of York,

Maine, for instance, was fired not only because he was "a violent *federalist*" but also on the charge that he was "constantly drunk and incapable of business." The town of York immediately convened a town meeting and voted 106 to 0 to clear the former collector of this charge. "In spite of this impressive denial . . . no further investigation was made and a Republican succeeded to the collector's post."[6]

Deprived of federal patronage, nascent Federalist organizations in most parts of the country outside New England withered. Mercantile interests and the Congregational clergy in New England sustained Federalism as a potent force in that part of the country, and the party remained fairly active in New Jersey, Maryland, and Delaware. But in the critical states of New York and Pennsylvania, Federalism went into steep decline. In most of the South and West the Republicans were soon virtually unchallenged.

"Federalism," Jefferson wrote with satisfaction in 1802, was sinking "into an abyss from which there will be no resurrection for it." He had always believed, he confided to a correspondent, that "the body of the people as thought themselves federalists, would find they are in truth republicans, and would come over to us by degrees."[7]

Republicans at the state and local levels continued to run against John Adams, much as Democrats of a later era were to run year after year against Herbert Hoover. "Sir," declared a circular distributed for Republican legislative candidates in Maryland in 1802, "you cannot have forgotten the unjust and oppressive measures of the late administration . . . WHO imposed, unnecessarily, upon the people a debt of upwards of ten millions?—The Federalists . . . WHO laid and continued the tax on your stills?—The Federalists . . . WHO taxed your lands?—The Federalists . . . WHO raised a useless standing army?—The Federalists . . ."[8]

Republican organizations were most developed in states where the Federalists continued to be serious contenders for power. "It was recognized very early," Richard P. McCormick writes, "that if a party did not concentrate its entire vote behind a single candidate for each office it would dissipate its strength and risk defeat." In New England, both parties organized around party caucuses in the state legislatures. "Nominations were made" by the caucus "for statewide elective offices and, in addition, a central committee was appointed to exercise supervision over local party committees." Legislative caucuses also exercised some authority over party organizations in New York, Pennsylvania, and the newly admitted state of Ohio. New Jersey and Delaware experimented with state conventions to nominate state party tickets. In most of the South and West party organizations were weak and elections were candidate-oriented.[9]

The politicians who manned state and local Republican organizations were drawn for the most part from the ranks of "new men." Paul Goodman writes: "The party attracted persons either outside the elite or enjoying a recently acquired and insecure position in local society. They . . . came from rising families that had been excluded from the highest levels of influence and standing. . . . Rising from obscurity or modest circumstances, they identified revolution and republicanism at home

and abroad with opportunity." The Republicans were generally st
rural hinterlands, but they also maintained effective organizati
nineteenth-century boomtowns like New York and Baltimore.[10]

JEFFERSONIAN IDEOLOGY

What was the nature of the ideology the Jeffersonians brought to government? The
best source is Jefferson's own voluminous writings and correspondence.

Before he went to France as ambassador in 1784, Jefferson was a relatively
moderate Whig, influenced mainly by Locke, the Scottish realists, and Mon-
tesquieu. In Paris he imbibed some of the radical intellectual elixir of the Enlightenment that a few years later helped produce the French Revolution. He became,
and remained for the rest of his life, a critic and antagonist of all kinds of establishment—political, social, economic, and religious. He greeted the onset of the
French Revolution in 1789 with enthusiasm, and, though he conceded the revolutionaries made some mistakes, he defended the Terror in 1793, as noted above.
He developed a taste for violent metaphors and anarchistic aphorisms: "The tree of
liberty must be refreshed from time to time with the blood of patriots and tyrants.
It is its natural manure." And (to Madison, on Shays' Rebellion, in 1787): "I hold
it that a little rebellion now and then is a good thing, and as necessary in the political world as storms in the physical." And (again to Madison, in 1789): "Every constitution . . . , and every law, naturally expires at the end of 19 years. If it be enforced
longer, it is an act of force, and not of right." And (to John Adams, when both were
old men): "To attain all this [the triumph of democracy] rivers of blood must yet
flow, and years of desolation pass over."[11]

Jefferson's dislike for cities and his disdain for urban masses are well known.
"The mobs of great cities," he averred, "add just so much to the support of pure
government as sores to the strength of the human body." Democracy, he believed,
is achievable only in an agrarian society in which most people own their own land.
The "degree of freedom" already possessed by the common man in America would
"in the hands of the *Canaille* of the cities of Europe . . . be instantly perverted to
the demolition and destruction of every thing public and private." (He may have
picked up this expression from his reading of Rousseau, who also warned that civil
order was threatened by the "*canaille* of cities.")[12]

Believing that strong, centralized government is the natural enemy of freedom,
Jefferson was convinced that the government that governs least governs best. "I own
I am not a friend to a very energetic government," he wrote to Madison. "It is always
oppressive." But this did not prevent him from favoring intervention by government
to redistribute wealth. On the contrary, "the consequences of . . . enormous inequality producing so much misery to the bulk of mankind, legislators cannot invent too
many devices for subdividing property, only taking care to let their subdivisions go
hand in hand with the natural affections of the human mind."[13]

The great threat to personal freedom and social equality in America is the insidious attempt by the "monocrats"—Hamilton, and the bankers and manufacturers for whom he spoke—to steer the nation toward "licentious commerce and gambling, speculations for a few, with eternal war for the many." This danger is to be averted through maintenance of a primarily agrarian economy, characterized by "restricted commerce, peace, and steady occupations for all."[14]

No American statesman save Lincoln has more profoundly influenced the shape and substance of politics and society in the United States than Thomas Jefferson. During his lifetime—indeed, within his own administration—the principles he advocated were compromised, the political party he helped found was torn by internal dissension, and the agrarian idyll he celebrated began to seem anachronistic. But he raised a standard of equalitarian individualism that has ever since remained one of the great ideological themes around which the main currents of American politics have circulated.

For many Americans, and for many others as well, Jefferson's vision of democracy has seemed definitive. Freedom and equality, the values he most cherished, are still given highest priority by modern theorists of liberalism like John Rawls. One person–one vote, progressive taxation, public education, and the right to privacy are among the concepts that are drawn, directly or indirectly, from the Jeffersonian model.

To some, both in the United States and elsewhere, Jefferson's rejection of rapid economic growth based on commerce and manufacturing has seemed shortsighted and left behind by history; his praise of equality while doing nothing to end slavery has seemed hypocritical; and his belief in the perfectibility of man through social reform has seemed morally flawed and politically naive. Henry Adams's quip that Jefferson's real aim was to turn the whole world into eighteenth-century Virginia carries weight. Yet Jefferson continues to speak persuasively to socially downtrodden city dwellers and urban intellectuals whom he probably would have disliked, as well as to economic and social populists who were always his most reliable constituency.[15]

To what extent was Jefferson's social vision and political philosophy shared by other Republicans—Madison and Gallatin, Clinton and Burr, Monroe and Taylor, the Livingstons and old Sam Adams (taking one last whack at cousin John), and the host of lesser officeholders, politicians, publicists, lawyers, small businessmen, and farmers who gathered behind the Republican banner? Like participants in every successful political coalition in American history, they were a varied lot, representing and driven by a multitude of interests, attitudes, and ambitions, some of which, in the case of Burr at least, appear sinister. In general, they seem more cautious, less altruistic, and less original than their leader. Also, at the leadership level, more practical. Gallatin dissuaded Jefferson from dismantling much of Hamilton's economic system, arguing for its utility. Madison tactfully disputed Jefferson's idea that every constitution and law should automatically expire at the end of 19 years, pointing out that the resulting instability would expose society to assault by "pernicious factions."[16]

Richard Matthews argues that the term Jeffersonian is actually a misnomer—that Jefferson's views were so much more radical than those of his collaborators and followers that they were never given a fair try and remain an untested possibility for American democracy.[17]

The Republican party that Jefferson led into office was, by later European standards it is true, relatively nonideological. But it did represent a distinct point of view, based on ideas that Jefferson developed or at least articulated in both public utterances and private correspondence. This point of view provided Jefferson's party, and its descendant under Andrew Jackson and his successors, with a body of principles through which to give direction to government and to mobilize public support.

EXTENSION OF SUFFRAGE

Probably the most concrete effect of Jeffersonian ideology on American politics and government was the broad extension of suffrage. Qualifications for voting were liberalized in most states, including New York, New Jersey, Connecticut, and Maryland, where property-owning requirements had been particularly high. By 1824, 50 years before the establishment of mass male suffrage in most of western Europe, virtually all adult white males were eligible to vote in all states except South Carolina, Rhode Island, and Louisiana.[18]

Changes also were made in electoral procedures to facilitate voting. In many states, electoral districts were reduced in size so that it was easier for voters, particularly in lightly settled rural areas, to get to the polls. Previously, voting in most districts had been done by the ancient *viva voce* method: voters were required to announce publicly at the voting place their preference among candidates, often a time-consuming process as the list of elected offices lengthened, as well as notoriously open to manipulation and intimidation. During the early years of the nineteenth century, most states converted to the use of printed ballots. Though the ballots were still cast without secrecy and were supplied by the parties or candidates, they encouraged wider voter participation.

Turnout among voters substantially increased, though at first more in gubernatorial than in presidential elections. (Until 1832 all states except New York held state and national elections on different days.) In Massachusetts, turnout in elections for governor rose from 31 percent of the eligible voters in 1800 to 67 percent in 1812—the highest level it was to reach until 1860. In New York, turnout in gubernatorial elections in 1810 and 1813 was more than 90 percent—practically the entire eligible electorate.[19]

In presidential elections national turnout in 1796 was only 20 percent. By 1800 it had risen to 31 percent, and by 1812 to 42 percent. It then declined as national party competition slackened. But the more open election system assured that turnout would sharply increase once presidential elections again became meaningful for voters.[20]

THE RUIN OF FEDERALISM

Surveying the wreckage of the Federalist party in 1802, Alexander Hamilton hit upon a strategy that he hoped would reverse the trend of national politics: alliance between political and religious conservatives. Most Congregational and Episcopal and many Presbyterian clergy were already enthusiastic supporters of Federalism. Hamilton proposed to institutionalize this association through a "Christian Constitutional Society" which would work to elect to public office candidates pledged to uphold the Constitution and apply Christian principles to government. The association would be financed by a five-dollar fee paid by each of its members and would form local branches in as many cities and towns as possible. Besides participating in election campaigns, it would sponsor "charitable and useful" activities, such as assisting immigrants in the rapidly growing cities and operating vocational schools for workers. The plan for increased church involvement in politics, though rich in future potential, was still in the idea stage when Hamilton died.[21]

Determined that there should be no repetition of the electoral crisis of 1801, the Republicans pushed through the Twelfth Amendment, which provided for the separate election of President and Vice President. Otherwise the amendment kept the selection system pretty much unchanged, except that if no candidate had a majority in the electoral college the House was to choose the President from among the top three finishers instead of from among the top five—a provision that was to have fateful consequences in 1824. As an added precaution, Jefferson dropped Burr from the Republican ticket in 1804 and replaced him with George Clinton, who had again been elected governor of New York in 1801.

Never long at a loss, Burr offered himself as candidate for governor in 1804 to the New York Federalists, who were seeking desperately to check their party's decline. Over Hamilton's strong objection, the Federalists accepted Burr's offer. In the election that followed, Burr was easily defeated by the Clintonian Republican candidate. Choosing to blame his defeat on Hamilton, Burr took umbrage at some abusive remarks his old rival had made during the campaign and challenged him to a duel. Hamilton reluctantly accepted.

The two met on an island in the Hudson River, beneath the heights of Wee-hauken. Hamilton fired his pistol into the air. Burr shot to kill, and succeeded. Henry Adams caught the picture: "The death of Hamilton, and the Vice President's flight, with their accessories of summer-morning sunlight on the rocky and wooded heights, tranquil river, and distant city, and behind all, their dark background of moral gloom, double treason, and political despair, still stand as the most dramatic moment in the early politics of the Union."[22]

"This American world," Hamilton had complained in 1802, "is not for me." On the day before his death, he had written to Theodore Sedgwick, who, with other New England Federalists, had become so disheartened with the course of national events as to consider secession. "Democracy," Hamilton agreed, was a national "disease," a "poison." But "dismemberment of our empire will be a clear sacrifice of great positive advantages without any counterbalancing good. . . ." Hamilton deeply imprinted the nation's political and economic life, but he left no stable political party.[23]

The Republican ticket of Jefferson and Clinton easily won the national election of 1804. Four years later, Clinton, by now almost 70, urged on by New Yorkers growing restless over their subordinate role in the Virginia–New York axis, made a pass at the presidential nomination. Madison, however, easily outmaneuvered him and was nominated by the Republican caucus in Congress for President, with Clinton again nominated for Vice President. The ticket won a landslide victory, carrying all but five states.

The Republicans held large majorities in both houses of Congress and controlled most state governments outside New England. In 1807 they even elected the governor of Massachusetts (though the Federalists regained that office in 1812 and held it thereafter until 1823). Even John Quincy Adams, son of the last Federalist President, went over to the Republicans—partly because, like his father, he could not abide the grumpy Sedgwicks and Adamses who dominated Massachusetts Federalism, and partly because, also like his father and later Adamses, he considered himself too large for any party. The remnant of Federalism, despite some continued regional strength and despite considerable public resentment over the economic effects of Jefferson's embargo on trade with Britain in 1807 (to protest raids on American shipping), was unable to challenge the Republicans' national hegemony.[24]

FISSION IN NEW YORK

John Randolph, who had been the Republican floor leader in the House of Representatives, turned against the administration during Jefferson s second term and led a few Virginia libertarians, the so-called Tertium Quids (Third Force), into opposition. But the first real sign of serious fission within the Republican ranks came in the ever-turbulent politics of New York.

Burr's defection in 1804, and its aftermath, had done little real damage to the party. But by 1807 the Clintons and the Livingstons were again feuding. When George Clinton returned to the governorship in 1801, he had placed his nephew DeWitt in charge of dispensing patronage. DeWitt Clinton quickly showed that he was at least his uncle's equal in the techniques of building a state political machine. While allowing some well-connected Federalists, including John Jay's son, to stay in their state jobs, he distributed an ample supply of plums to deserving Republicans and had himself made mayor of New York City, then an appointed office.[25]

The key to state patronage was the Council of Appointment, which consisted of the governor and four state senators. In 1807, the Livingstons got a majority on the council. Having tired of their partnership with the Clintons, they replaced a large number of Clintonians with Livingstonites and fired DeWitt Clinton as mayor of New York.

In 1812 DeWitt Clinton, though out of power at the state level, ran against Madison for President as the candidate of a coalition of national Federalists and New York Republicans who felt their state was not getting its fair share of federal spoils. (George Clinton having died early in 1812, the Republicans nominated in his place as Madison's running mate Elbridge Gerry of Massachusetts, another old Antifederalist. Gerry was the progenitor of the notorious "Gerrymander"—a method of apportioning congressional districts through contorted boundaries to produce maximum party advantage.) In an effort to whip up popular support, DeWitt Clinton organized conventions in eleven states to place his name in nomination. Capitalizing on opposition to the War of 1812, then underway, Clinton carried New York, New Jersey, Delaware, and all of New England except Vermont, for 89 electoral votes, against 128 for Madison. If Clinton had been able to win Pennsylvania's 25 electoral votes, he would have been elected President.

Frustrated in his national ambitions, Clinton used his position on the Erie Canal Commission, to which he had been appointed in 1810, to increase his popularity in western New York, where the Clintonians formerly had been weak. Opposition to the Clintonians in the state Republican party increasingly centered on a young state senator from rural upstate Columbia County, Martin Van Buren. For the sake of state solidarity, Van Buren had supported DeWitt Clinton for President in 1812. But the "Little Magician," as Van Buren came to be called, placed great emphasis on party regularity, in contrast to Clinton's more personal style of politics. Entertaining lavishly in Albany, the state capital to which he moved after being elected state attorney general, Van Buren established close relationships with the remaining Livingstons and with Tammany Hall, already the dominant force in New York City politics. He organized an alliance of ambitious young upstate politicians, later known as the Albany Regency.[26]

When the governorship became vacant in 1817, Clinton demonstrated that Van Buren was not yet quite his match as a master of New York politics. Van Buren's faction, known as the Bucktails (after the tail of a buck that Tammany had used as its official badge since the 1790s), controlled the state party machinery. But Clinton managed to have the nominating authority shifted to a state party convention in which the western part of the state was heavily represented. To Van Buren's surprise, Clinton was nominated and elected governor. The old Clintonian entourage flocked back into state offices.[27]

Van Buren countered by gaining control of the Canal Commission, which was building the Erie Canal, thereby distributing thousands of construction jobs to loyal Bucktails. By 1821, the Bucktails were able to outvote the governor on the Council of Appointment. The *Albany Argus,* which had become allied with the Bucktails when Clinton tried, unsuccessfully, to shift state printing to another newspaper, called for a "cleansing of the Augean stables." State employees, along with county sheriffs, judges, and district attorneys, were swept out "in windrows." Among the newly installed Bucktails, Van Buren's brother became a county judge and his brother-in-law was appointed state printer. The "ingenuity of man," Clinton ruefully observed, could not have devised a system more likely "to produce continued intrigue and commotion in the state."[28]

In 1821 Van Buren moved to Washington as United States senator. But he left the Bucktails so strongly entrenched in Albany that Clinton decided not to seek reelection as governor. Thinking to finish Clinton off, the Bucktails removed him from his seat on the Canal Commission. Though the Bucktails had held a majority on the Commission for several years, Clinton was still identified in the public mind with the Erie Canal, which he had always ardently championed. Van Buren moaned from Washington: "There is such a thing as killing a man too dead." Public support rallied behind Clinton and he was again elected governor in 1824. He remained in that office, at the top of his form, until he dropped dead in 1828— sparing Andrew Jackson the problem of choosing between Clinton, one of his earliest supporters in national politics, and his more recent New York ally, Martin Van Buren.[29]

DeWitt Clinton has been identified by historians as one of the last of a vanishing breed—a practitioner of the old politics of personality and family faction, differing from the new politics of party as practiced by Van Buren. He was in part that. But he was also harbinger of a type in American politics that was not to reach full development until the twentieth century. Clinton may be called a developmental populist. He possessed none of the antagonism toward market capitalism and urban concentration characteristic of Jefferson and other southern agrarians. He had no misgivings about massive government expenditures on public works. The Erie Canal, which he zealously promoted, served the interest of western agriculture, but it also assured that New York would be the economic gateway to the West and advanced Manhattan's bid to replace Philadelphia as the financial capital of the United States. The stockjobbers and money men of Wall Street whom Jefferson feared were Clinton's political allies. But he never took up the standard of the party of capitalist development, as Hamilton had done earlier and Henry Clay did later. Despite his defection in 1812, he continued to align himself with the party that claimed to represent the interest of the common man. A rising tide, Clinton might have said, lifts all boats. His political descendants would be numerous.

POLITICS WITHOUT PARTIES

As President, James Madison had to deal not only with contentious Clintonians in New York but with a new breed of Republicans in Congress. In the House of Representatives elected in 1811, 61 of the 142 members were first-termers. Among their number were Henry Clay of Kentucky, 34, and John C. Calhoun of South Carolina, 29. (Daniel Webster, the third of the congressional Olympians who were to feud and collaborate over the next 40 years, was elected to the House from New Hampshire as a Federalist, at the age of 30, in 1812.) Clay, supported by Calhoun and most other first-termers, was elected Speaker of the House.

Though overwhelmingly Republican, many of the new members expressed a belligerent nationalism that seemed more Hamiltonian than Jeffersonian. Both Clay and Calhoun favored federal government support for "internal improvements," such as roads and canals, to facilitate development of the West. The external target at which they directed their antagonism, however, was the traditional object of Jeffersonian loathing, Great Britain. Thinking to take advantage of Britain's mortal struggle in Europe with Napoleon's France, and angered by the continued instigation by British agents of Indian uprisings and raids on the frontier, they pressed for a conflict they felt sure would produce territorial gains for the United States.

Clay went beyond earlier Speakers in using the powers of his office to build a personal political machine in the House. During Jefferson's administration, a Speaker who leaned toward the Quids had been removed for failing to give total support to the President. Clay made prudent use of the Speaker's authority to appoint all House committees, thereby assuring that most members put loyalty to him above obedience to the administration. He formulated and pushed a legislative program of his own and soon rivaled Madison both as party leader and shaper of national policy.[30]

Madison proved ineffective as President. His tendency to deliberate endlessly over nuances of policy, which had served him well as party-builder and constructor of coalitions in the House, turned out to be a handicap. He tried to conciliate the new members in Congress, an effort they interpreted as a sign of weakness. Spurred on by the "war hawks," as the press dubbed Clay, Calhoun, and their associates, and given ample provocation by further British outrages on the high seas and the frontier, Madison stumbled into the War of 1812.

Though the war was poorly managed, the Republican party came out of it even stronger than it had been before. When the conflict with Britain seemed to be going badly in the fall of 1814, leading New England Federalists convened secretly in Hartford, Connecticut, to formulate demands for increased regional autonomy. Talk of secession was in the air. By the time the convention's negotiating committee got to Washington in January 1815, however, the war was over, settled on terms reasonably favorable to the United States. (The British government, weakened by the cost of defeating Napoleon, had been anxious for a quick peace.) A few spectacular American naval victories, together with Andrew Jackson's triumph at the Battle of New Orleans, fought after the peace treaty had been signed but before the news crossed the Atlantic, enabled patriotic Americans to regard the war as a success. Republican orators and publicists branded the Hartford convention an act of subversion during wartime, ending what was left of Federalism as a national political force.

James Monroe, who succeeded Madison as President in 1817, was determined to make the Republican party supreme as a prelude to abolishing parties altogether. Monroe fully shared Jefferson's and Madison's prejudices against parties, but he lacked the power of reflection that led them at times to concede that a party system might be useful or at least inevitable. "There can be," Monroe wrote to John

Taylor, "but two permanent parties among us, one of which is friendly to free government, the other to monarchy, in which latter I never did include many persons. Every other division should cease with the cause which produced it." When Andrew Jackson suggested that Monroe include a Federalist in his cabinet to encourage national unity, Monroe replied: "To give effect to free government, and secure it from future danger, ought not its decided friends, who stood firm in the day of trial, to be principally relied upon?" Some, he observed, "are of the opinion that the existence of the federal party is necessary to keep union and order in the republican ranks, that is that free government cannot exist without parties. This is not my opinion." His policy toward the Federalist party, he said, was to "annihilate" it.[31]

THE STRUGGLE FOR SUCCESSION

In the election of 1820, Monroe seemed to get his wish. The Federalists failed to put up even a token candidate for President, and Monroe was reelected with the votes of all the electors except one. (An elector from Pennsylvania voted for John Quincy Adams, Monroe's secretary of state, explaining that only George Washington deserved unanimous approval.) The nonpartisan ideal of the Founders seemed within reach.

It was not to be. "The first year of Mr. Monroe's second term had scarcely passed away," Van Buren later recalled, "before the political atmosphere became inflamed to an unprecedented extent. The Republican party, so long in the ascendant, and apparently so omnipotent, was literally shattered into fragments, and we had no fewer than five Republican candidates [for President] in the field."[32]

Three of the candidates came from Monroe's cabinet: Adams, secretary of state; Calhoun, secretary of war; and William H. Crawford of Georgia, secretary of the treasury. The other two were Clay, Speaker of the House; and Andrew Jackson, the hero of New Orleans, now in the Senate from Tennessee.

Monroe seems to have preferred Calhoun, but, perhaps because lack of competition had weakened the Republican party's internal cohesion, he had almost no influence over the choice of his successor. Crawford was the choice of some leaders of state Republican organizations with a states-rights orientation, including Van Buren in New York, Thomas Ritchie in Virginia, and Isaac Hill in New Hampshire. Among the available candidates, they claimed, Crawford came closest to carrying on the true Jeffersonian faith. The Republican congressional caucus, the mechanism by which the party had been selecting its national ticket since 1800, voted to support Crawford. But when the caucus met in Washington in February 1824 to decide on a candidate for President, only 66 of the 231 Republicans in Congress attended.[33]

Calhoun, deciding to seek the more easily obtained office of Vice President, dropped out. But the other three candidates, far from being cowed by the action of the caucus, used its endorsement of Crawford to link him to the old guard—already an unpopular image in American politics. Adams, Clay, and Jackson persuaded their respective state legislatures to pass resolutions placing their names in nomination.

American political parties, it was becoming clear, would not be mere appendages of legislative party caucuses, as parties were in Britain. The effects of the presidential selection process on national politics, as well as the effects of the federal system, were shifting power toward party organizations based on the states.

Adams put together a solid bloc of support in New England (over the opposition of Hill's machine in New Hampshire), including many former Federalists who, like himself, had switched parties. Clay and Jackson competed for support from the new states of the West, which in a close election would hold the balance of power. Clay's flamboyant personality and generous distribution of political favors had won him a devoted, never-to-be-shaken following in his own state of Kentucky; through his power in the House he also attracted support from Ohio and Missouri. Elsewhere in the West, and also in much of the South, Jackson's military reputation made him the more popular figure. This was a substantial political advantage, since by now presidential electors were chosen directly by the people in all but six states.

Jackson's supporters in 1824 included many who would not later be considered Jacksonians. To the extent that his political views were known (he had been a rather inert member of the Senate), he appeared to be a nationalist, well disposed toward a protective tariff and internal improvements—closer to Adams and Clay than to old-line Jeffersonians like Van Buren and Crawford. In Tennessee he had entered politics in the 1790s under the sponsorship of Senator William Blount, another of the frontier grandees who grew rich while playing the role of popular tribune in state politics. With Blount's backing, young Jackson was elected to the House of Representatives and later to the Senate. In 1797 Blount was expelled from the Senate for participating in a bizarre plot to join with the British in inciting an Indian attack on Spanish Florida. Jackson was not implicated. After Blount died in 1800, Jackson was taken up by one of the Republican factions in Tennessee whose leaders believed his military image would be useful. In 1823 he was again elected to the Senate.[34]

Jackson's presidential candidacy in 1824 was promoted in parts of the Northeast and South by former Federalists who seem to have assumed that because he was a military hero he must be a conservative. In New York, he was the candidate of the Clintonians. In New Jersey, several well-known Federalists put together a "People's Ticket" of electors for Jackson and carried the state.[35]

When the electoral college met, Jackson had the most votes but was short of a majority. Adams was second and Crawford third. Clay, only four votes behind Crawford, was in fourth place, and therefore, under the Twelfth Amendment, was excluded from the pool from which the House could select the President. Calhoun was elected Vice President by a large majority.

Clay had calculated that if he was among the finalists considered by the House, he would be able to use his influence as Speaker to win the poll. Since that option was not available, he backed Adams.

On the day of the vote in the House, Adams, with Clay's help, was within one state of achieving a majority. One more vote in the New York delegation would give him the state, and the presidency. The decision rested finally with the aged Stephen Van Rensselaer, representative from New York, who had promised Van Buren he would vote for Crawford. In the Speaker's room of the House, Clay and Webster put heavy pressure on Van Rensselaer, a former Federalist. The old man wavered. Returning to the House chamber, "he dropped his head upon the edge of his desk and made a brief appeal to his Maker for His guidance." When he lifted his head he found "on the floor directly below him a ticket bearing the name of John Quincy Adams." Regarding this "as an answer to his appeal," he placed it in the election box. "In this way," Van Buren wrote long after, "Mr. Adams was made President."[36]

THE JACKSON COALITION

When Adams appointed Clay secretary of state, Jackson's supporters charged that the two men had made a deal before the vote in the House—an accusation which, though never directly proved, was to hang over each for the rest of his political career.

Jackson, who seems to have felt some genuine reluctance about running for President in 1824, had no such reservations about trying again in 1828. Convinced that he had been dealt with unfairly, he girded himself to deprive Adams of a second term. He moved first to solidify his hold on the political situation in Tennessee. Some of his state lieutenants, notably Senator John Eaton, became agents for his national campaign.

A major accession to Jackson's candidacy in 1828 was the backing of the states-rights Jeffersonian state organizations that four years before had supported Crawford. The most important of these was Van Buren's Albany Regency. If Van Buren had been the purely pragmatic politician he is sometimes described as being, he should have been motivated by the tie between Jackson and DeWitt Clinton to seek accommodation with Adams. But he seems sincerely to have regarded such an alliance as ideologically impossible. He therefore decided to take a chance on the largely unknown quantity of Andrew Jackson.[37]

Some of the former Federalists who had supported Jackson in 1824 found themselves content with the policies of the Adams administration and backed the incumbent President for reelection in 1828. But Jackson continued to draw support from a number of young politicians who had begun as Federalists, including Roger Taney of Maryland (later Chief Justice of the Supreme Court, and author of the infamous Dred Scott decision), and James Buchanan of Pennsylvania (later

President of the United States). After he became President, Jackson appointed more former Federalists to executive branch offices than had all former Republican Presidents combined.

Another important addition to the Jackson coalition was a large share of the rapidly growing body of evangelical Protestants, mainly Methodists, Baptists, Campbellite Presbyterians, and Disciples of Christ (a new denomination founded in Ohio in 1827). During the 1820s the Second Great Awakening, which recreated the spiritual excitement of the 1730s was sweeping through the mountain glens of western Pennsylvania, eastern Ohio, western Virginia, Kentucky, and Tennessee. Though evangelical preachers were critical of Jackson's participation in a duel and his harsh treatment of the Indians, they applauded his equalitarian spirit and were pleased to find that he shared their religious orientation. Jackson, though a somewhat irregular churchgoer, described himself as a "rigid Presbyterian," claimed he read the Bible at least three times a day, and filled his correspondence with expressions of Christ-centered spirituality. Evangelicals, who had already been drawn to the Republican party by Jefferson, became for the most part confirmed Jacksonians. "Every convert to Methodism," claimed one circuit-riding preacher, "in those times became a Republican if he was not one before." Peter Cartwright, one of the best known of the frontier revivalists, told a Democratic convention in Illinois (after the party had changed its name): "I have waged an incessant warfare against the world, the flesh, and the devil, and other enemies of the Democratic party."[38]

By the beginning of 1828, it was clear that a formidable coalition was assembling to deny Adams reelection. Adams did little to put together a political organization of his own. Like his father, he rejected on principle the injection of partisan politics into government administration. Clay and Webster complained that he neglected to reward his political supporters. Thurlow Weed, then a young journalist in upstate New York beginning to make his way in politics on the conservative, or at least anti-Regency, side, later recalled: "Mr. Adams, during his administration, failed to cherish, strengthen, or even recognize the party to which he owed his election; nor as far as I am informed, with the great power he possessed did he make a single influential friend."[39]

HOW THE DEMOCRATS GOT THEIR NAME

During the administration of John Quincy Adams, adherents of Adams and Clay began referring to themselves as National Republicans, partly to express their inclination toward a nationalist ideology, but probably even more to suggest that the Jacksonian opposition was made up of state or local deviationists not entitled to be identified with the national party. (The same tactic was employed in the 1960s by liberal Democrats in control of the national party machinery who called themselves "national Democrats.")

Some of the Jacksonians responded by identifying themselves as Democratic–Republicans. Ever since the founding of the Democratic societies in the 1790s to express solidarity with the ideology of the French Revolution, members of the more equalitarian wing of the Republican party had sometimes called themselves Democrats as well as Republicans. Van Buren in 1821, for example, spoke of restoring the "old democratic party." During the 1820s members of the coalition of northern party bosses, southern and western agrarians, and southern slaveowners who for varying reasons opposed a strong national government began referring to themselves collectively as "the Democracy."[40]

In the 1828 campaign, Jackson's party took the title Democratic–Republican. After Jackson's election, members of the party increasingly spoke of themselves, and were identified in the press, simply as Democrats. At the party's 1840 national convention, the name was formally changed to the Democratic party—as we know it today.[41]

5

FORMATION OF MASS PARTIES

Democrats and Whigs

THE FEDERALISTS and the Jeffersonian Republicans developed some of the attributes of modern parties and laid the foundations of the two-party system. Both, however, despite the equalitarian ideology of the Jeffersonians and Hamilton's attempt to build a mass base for Federalism among religious conservatives, were primarily associations of political elites—almost restricted clubs. As such, they were not very well suited to perform the representative function of popular government. Though this did not greatly trouble many of the leading Federalists, their indifference, even resistance, to representing public opinion was a principal cause of the party's ultimate collapse.

With the renewal of party competition in the second half of the 1820s, and the extension of the suffrage instituted by the Jeffersonians, a new kind of politician appeared who produced a new kind of party that was more useful to democracy. Not surprisingly, it was the politicians who sprang from the liberal tradition who took the lead in creating party organizations adept at rousing public enthusiasm, conducting door-to-door canvasses in every city, town, and hamlet, distributing the spoils of office as a means for motivating armies of party workers, and making sure that voters favoring their cause got to the polls on election day. Soon, however, competing politicians from what was to become the republican tradition had mastered the arts of mass politics. In many cases they even outdid their more equalitarian opposition in building efficient party organizations and publicizing themes that appealed to the aspirations, prejudices, apprehensions, and patriotic impulses of a broad slice of the voting public.

JACKSONIANS IN POWER

The election of 1828, which put Andrew Jackson in the White House, is sometimes identified by historians and political scientists as a realigning election. As comparison of Figure 5–1 with Figure 3–2 shows, in geographic terms at least it was no such thing. John Quincy Adams, ousted from the presidency by Jackson after only a single term, carried every state his father had carried in 1800 and lost every state his father had lost. (There were minor shifts in the electoral votes of Pennsylvania and New York, but not enough to change the majority in either state.) Jackson triumphed by a much larger majority in the electoral college in 1828 than Jefferson had in 1800 because of the addition of seven western states, all carried by Jackson. The coalition of New York, Pennsylvania, and the South had expanded to include the entire West, transforming what had been a narrow majority into an overwhelming preponderance.

Although the Republican party was in the process of changing its name to Democratic, and although there had been a period in the early 1820s when parties almost disappeared, most political observers in 1828 and the period that followed had no difficulty recognizing Jackson's Democrats as direct descendants of Jefferson's Republicans. Jefferson himself, before he died in 1826 (on July 4, the same day as John Adams—exactly 50 years after the signing of the Declaration of Independence), endorsed Jackson for President, declaring that the hero of New Orleans

Figure 5–1   Electoral vote by states, 1828

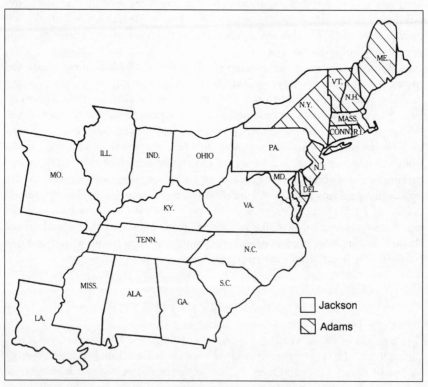

Source: Historical Statistics of the United States, Bureau of the Census, 1961

"has more of the Roman in him than any other man now living." (From Jefferson, high praise.) Jackson maintained that his political philosophy was based on the principles set forth in Jefferson's first inaugural: "A wise and frugal government, which shall restrain men from injuring one another, shall leave them otherwise free to regulate their own pursuits of industry and improvement, and shall not take from the mouth of labor the bread it has earned."[1]

Martin Van Buren, who became Jackson's most trusted lieutenant and was to succeed him as President, traced the Jacksonian Democrats not only to the Jeffersonian Republicans but to the Antifederalists and the earlier populist parties at the state level:

> The two great parties of this country, with occasional changes in their names only, have, for the principal part of a century, occupied antagonistic positions upon all important political questions. They have maintained an unbroken succession, and have, throughout, been composed respectively of men agreeing in their party passion, and preferences, and entertaining, with rare exceptions, similar general views on the subject of government and its administration. Sons have generally followed in the footsteps of their fathers, and families originally differing have in regular succession received, maintained, and transmitted this opposition.[2]

Van Buren, whom Jackson had earlier regarded as too "cunning," rose in the President's esteem as the result of an incident that occurred early in the administration. Jackson had named as secretary of war his old friend and political crony from Tennessee, John Eaton. Shortly before, Eaton had married "a young widow," a former Peggy O'Neale, "of much beauty and considerable smartness, in respect to whose relations with himself before marriage, and whilst she was the wife of another, there had been unfavorable reports." Jackson included among his political allies the newly elected Vice President, John C. Calhoun. But Calhoun's wife, Floride, of the old South Carolina upper class, took it upon herself to snub the new Mrs. Eaton at Jackson's inaugural and to urge cabinet wives to collaborate in the young woman's social ostracism. Jackson, who bitterly remembered snubs directed against his own recently deceased wife, Rachel, urged the Vice President and members of the cabinet to intercede with their wives. Calhoun and most cabinet members declined. Van Buren, however, the new secretary of state, a widower, went calling on the Eatons in their Capitol Hill home (which was still standing in the 1950s when it housed the Capitol Hill Club, a hive of congressional Republicans). Jackson never forgave Calhoun and developed new trust in Van Buren.[3]

A NEW KIND OF PARTY

Jackson's electoral success was accompanied and aided by major changes in the structure and behavior of parties. Van Buren, Amos Kendall of Kentucky, Roger

Taney of Maryland, and other members of Jackson's "kitchen cabinet" built the first extensive national party organization.

Though both the Federalists and Jefferson had used government patronage to reward their political supporters, the Jacksonians were more systematic in distributing federal jobs to loyal party workers. About one-eighth of the local postmasters employed by the federal government were replaced by active Democrats—a relatively small turnover compared to what came later, but enough to lay the foundation for a formidable party machine. The federal bureaucracy, moreover, about doubled during Jackson's two terms, reaching approximately 60,000 civilian employees in 1835. These new jobs provided rich additional stores of patronage.

Jackson defended his policy of "rotation in office" on the ground that "no one man has any more intrinsic right to official station than another." Governor William Marcy of New York, an eminent Jacksonian, stated the principle more bluntly: "To the victor belongs the spoils of the enemy." Marcy elaborated: "When [politicians] are contending for victory, they avow their intention of enjoying the fruits of it. If they are defeated, they expect to retire from office. If they are successful, they claim, as a matter of right, the advantages of success." The expansion of the electorate and the increase in the number and variety of elective offices, Walter Dean Burnham has pointed out, "necessitated the emergence of the plebeian electoral machine staffed by professionals who had to be paid for their services." The public payroll, Democratic politicians like Van Buren and Marcy concluded, was the logical place to find economic sustenance for the growing armies of political workers.[4]

The Jacksonians also went beyond their predecessors in developing a party press to communicate their arguments and point of view to a mass audience. At first, Duff Green's *Telegraph,* published in Washington, was the recognized public voice of the administration. But Jackson soon took angry notice that the *Telegraph* was heaping praise on Green's former patron, Calhoun. At Van Buren's suggestion, Amos Kendall brought his friend Francis Preston Blair (who at the time was in "pecuniary circumstances . . . extremely embarrassing") from Kentucky to Washington to launch and edit a new journal, the *Globe.* Blair, "his face . . . narrow, and of the hatchet kind, according to his meat-ax disposition when writing about his enemies," left nothing to be desired in laying down the national Democratic party line.[5]

Behind the national organization of the Democracy were several strong state machines, notably those of New York, New Hampshire, Virginia, and Tennessee. Each had distinctive qualities but all shared common characteristics. Each was dominated by a single strong party leader, maintained close ties with a widely read newspaper (two of the state bosses also functioned as editor of the party's paper), and espoused agrarian populism.

Foremost of the state Democratic organizations was Van Buren's Regency in New York. "The Regency," writes Donald Cole, "revolutionized American politics, not only by creating a new type of political machine, but also by popularizing a new theory of political parties." The leaders of the Regency, particularly Van Buren, flatly rejected the Founders' anti-party ideology and accepted the party as a political instrument through which individuals could pool their resources for the control of government. Through participation in a party, Van Buren pointed out, persons from humble origins could compete successfully against politicians bearing "great names."[6]

Van Buren not only defended the legitimacy of his own party but acknowledged the political usefulness of an opposition. In comments almost without precedent in the United States, he described the operation of a two-party system and argued for its value to democracy. Competition between parties, he claimed, counters the tendency of persons holding political power to become autocratic or corrupt. The human "disposition to abuse power . . . can by no other means be more effectually checked." Party attachments, moreover, provide "a complete antidote for sectional prejudices by producing counteracting feelings."[7]

For many members of the Regency, the party became a political end in itself—an institutional haven in which individuals could find emotional as well as financial security in a turbulent social environment. The defining characteristic of Regency politicians, wrote a journalist of the time, was that they were "true to their friends." The party became their social home. "Their females kiss each other when they meet—their men shake each other heartily by the hand—they dine, or drink, or pray, or take snuff . . . in each other's company."[8]

Governor Marcy warned against the folly, the absolute iniquity, of placing political principle above the party: "The example of opposing a candidate nominated by political friends is bad not only as to its effect on the pending election but as to others that are to succeed it. An opposition upon the ground of principle will be used to authorize an opposition on the ground of caprice." Regency leaders used military vocabulary to dramatize the need for party solidarity. "Tell them," instructed Silas Wright, another party nabob, "they are safe if they fear the enemy, but that the first man we see *step to the rear,* we *cut down* . . . they *must* not falter, or they perish."[9]

After moving to the national level, Van Buren usually left day-to-day tactics in Albany to a directorate, generally headed by Marcy. Van Buren was careful, like most later successful political bosses, to seek consensus among his associates rather than to issue commands. Writing on a party matter to Jackson in 1832, he reported that he had talked *"in confidence,* with my friends, Marcy, Wright, Flagg, Croswell, and Butler, and they concur fully."[10]

Although the Regency concentrated on winning elections, it would be a mistake to overlook the underlying thread of ideology that helped hold it together. "We must always have party distinctions," Van Buren wrote to Thomas Ritchie, chief of the allied Richmond Junto, "and the old ones are the best of which the nature of the case admits. . . . It would take longer than our lives (even if it were practicable) to create new party feelings to keep these masses together." Though he often worked closely with the New York business community, Van Buren remained an instinctive Jeffersonian agrarian. The "main-stay of the Democratic party," he argued, must always be "the farmers and planters," whose interests led them to resist "the seductive influence of the money power." He regarded "the mechanics not manufacturers, and the working classes" as natural recruits for the Democratic coalition. But Van Buren had no doubt that the continued dominance of the Democrats depended on politically mobilized farmers: "It can only be when agriculturalists abandon the implements and the field of their labor and become, with those who now assist them, shopkeepers, manufacturers, carriers, and traders, that the Republic will be brought in danger of the influence of the money power. But this can never happen."[11]

In New Hampshire, Isaac Hill, editor of the *New-Hampshire Patriot,* built a party machine even more tightly disciplined than the Regency. Loyalty to New England carried the state for Adams in 1828, but thereafter New Hampshire became, until the realignment of the 1860s, the most Democratic state in the nation. Hill, rising from extreme poverty and lamed by a childhood accident, was more radical in policy direction and rhetoric than Van Buren. Issuing fiery populist editorials and directives to the state legislature from his office in Concord, known as the "Dictator's Palace," he mobilized the party around themes of class war and antagonism toward business.[12]

Thomas Ritchie, editor of the *Richmond Enquirer,* in contrast, was personally elegant and belonged to the fox-hunting, classics-quoting elite of Virginia society. The Richmond Junto, which Ritchie led, espoused an equalitarian ideology but retained the Jeffersonian assumption that a society based on small freeholders would preserve a place for a cultivated gentry. Ritchie, who would not have dreamed of playing the part of dictator, conducted the Junto as a kind of gentleman's club established to carry on the political tradition of Jefferson, Madison, and Monroe.[13]

Jackson's own organization in Tennessee, led on the ground by John Overton, a wealthy landowner who had been Jackson's business partner, was the least cohesive and entrenched of the four and in fact lost control of Tennessee politics after Jackson's retirement from the White House.

Jackson had been nominated for the presidency in 1828, as in 1824, through a resolution by the Tennessee legislature. The congressional caucus had been abandoned as a means for selecting national candidates after Crawford, its choice for President in 1824, had finished third in the electoral vote behind Jackson and Adams. But Van Buren, Kendall, and Blair decided that some nominating mechanism with a national base was needed. As the 1832 election approached, this project became linked in their calculations with their determination to replace Calhoun with Van Buren as Jackson's running mate on the Democratic ticket. In the spring of 1831 Kendall visited Isaac Hill in New Hampshire and passed on a letter from another Jackson operative pointing out "the expediency indeed absolute necessity, of advising our friends every where to get up a *national convention* to convene at some convenient point, for the purpose of selecting some suitable and proper person to be placed upon the electoral ticket with General Jackson, as a candidate for the Vice Presidency. . . ."[14]

Hill speedily arranged to have the New Hampshire legislature issue a call for a

Democratic national convention. (Earlier that same year, the Anti-Masonic party, an ephemeral conglomeration of socially conservative populists, of which more below, had held the first national party convention in Baltimore.) The first Democratic convention duly met, also in Baltimore, from May 21 to 23, 1832. Jackson already having been proposed by several legislatures, the convention proceeded to nominate Van Buren for Vice President. In order to placate some of Calhoun's southern friends, who feared the South was being reduced to a minority within the party, a rule was adopted stipulating that to be nominated a candidate must receive "two thirds of the whole number of votes given"—a requirement that was to bedevil many a future Democratic convention until it was finally repealed in 1936.[15]

EMERGING OPPOSITION

When Calhoun broke with the Jackson administration in 1830 on the issue of his version of states rights versus the supremacy of the federal government, he tried to rally the old libertarian wing of the Republican party into a new political alignment based on the South. Outside South Carolina, he had surprisingly little success. Jackson's personality, and even more the ideological consensus represented by the Democratic party, continued to command majority support in most of the South. Following Calhoun's leadership, South Carolina thereafter pursued a somewhat separate course, not only from national politics, but also from the rest of the South.

At the other end of the political spectrum, various small groups of radical equalitarians pressed to go much further than the Democrats in attacking established wealth and emergent capitalism. In New York in 1829, the Workingman's party, originally a dissident faction in Tammany Hall, campaigned for a moratorium on private debt. Eight years later, the New York Equal Rights party—popularly known as Locofocos, after a brand of match that its members lit when the opposition darkened the hall in which they were meeting—proposed the abolition of state charters for corporations and other "artificial" bodies, and the elimination of state licensing requirements for practice of any "profession, business, or trade not hurtful to the community." Van Buren's Democrats, the Locofocos charged, had become a "monopoly aristocratic party."[16]

Neither Calhounites on the right nor Locofocos on the left had much success at mobilizing opposition to Jacksonian hegemony. A more significant effort, sowing seeds for the future, was raised by an odd political construct called the Anti-Masonic party, organized in upstate New York in 1827 and soon active in Pennsylvania and parts of New England. In the late 1820s public wrath was directed against the Masonic Order, in one of those strange bursts of popular frenzy that from time to time sweep through American culture (like later waves of anti-Catholicism and Red scares), when a defector from the Masons disappeared and was believed murdered. Some opponents of the Regency and its counterparts in other states decided to use this uproar to break the Democrats' hold on the socially conservative evangelicals, for whom Masonry must have carried connotations of deism and occult science. "Particularly with rural sectarian audiences who were firm believers in a literal interpretation of the Bible," Leslie Griffen writes, "the Anti-masons had no difficulty in demonstrating that freemasonry was not sanctioned by Holy writ."[17]

Though the Anti-Masons made some headway in upstate New York, their greatest successes were in Vermont and Pennsylvania. In Vermont the party campaigned for the full agenda of evangelical issues, including temperance, Sunday-closing laws, and free public education. In 1831 the Anti-Masons won the governorship (against divided opposition from the National Republicans and the Democrats) and in the following year carried the state for their party's national ticket. In Pennsylvania the Anti-Masons drew most of their support from Germans in a crescent of southeastern rural counties and Scotch-Irish in the southwest around Pittsburgh. Both groups felt they were being discriminated against in the distribution of state benefits. In 1829 the Anti-Masonic candidate for governor of Pennsylvania, Joseph Ritner, won 45 percent of the vote. Six years later, with the Democrats split, Ritner was elected governor.[18]

In New York the principal strategist for the Anti-Masons was young Thurlow Weed, editor of the Albany *Journal,* whom the Regency had already recognized as a dangerous adversary. Business interests had always played a part in American politics, but Weed seems to have been the first to harness business resources to political organization in any systematic way. He saw to it that friendly businessmen received a sympathetic hearing from his allies in the legislature. But he was no mere political fixer. He treated the rising capitalists of New York and Albany as political allies whose aspirations he understood and whose vision of the nation's economic future he shared. As a result, "whenever the bottom of the barrel began to appear" in one of Weed's campaigns, "a trip to New York and consultation with Robert B. Minturn, Moses H. Grinnell, Simeon Draper, Edwin D. Morgan, and other merchants and ship-owners was sure to produce golden results."[19]

Weed was also adept at dealing with the rough-and-tumble of politics. "We are compelled," he privately explained, "to do things that will not bear a blaze of light to elect . . . good men to office." Weed's own ward in Albany had for many years been controlled for the Democrats by Captain James Maher, whose "gang of shoulder-hitters reigned supreme." In 1835, Weed "organized a rival group of toughs, ostensibly for ensuring the personal safety" of non–Democratic voters. "The three-day election of that year saw eyes blackened and heads cracked with merry abandon by the bullies of either side. . . ." The next year, "several of the Democratic heroes, paid off in worthless and even counterfeit banknotes, shook the dust of Democracy off their feet and moved" into Weed's camp. After one more election, Weed's organization controlled the ward.[20]

In 1824 Weed struck up a friendship with a "redheaded, blue-eyed youth named William Henry Seward" whom he had "met by chance in Rochester that summer when Seward's coach broke down." Weed and Seward formed a political partnership that was to be among the most fertile in American history.[21]

At their national convention in Baltimore in 1831, the Anti-Masons nominated William Wirt as their presidential candidate. Wirt, who had been attorney general in the John Quincy Adams administration, had himself once been a Mason and announced that he felt no animus toward Masonry. In the course of the convention, Weed encountered another ambitious young politician who had made the party his vehicle, Thaddeus Stevens of Pennsylvania. Stevens burned with reformist fire against the ponderous Democratic–Republican combination that had dominated his state's politics since the time of Gallatin. As Weed practiced the politics of connections and money, Stevens projected the politics of ideas and passion. Among Pennsylvania Anti-Masons, Stevens led a wing of ideological purists against a more moderate faction. Weed represented the pragmatic side of Anti-Masonry, and Stevens its more ideological side. This distinction continued through the collaboration of the two men in the Whig and Republican parties that followed. It is important to note, however, that, though Weed and Stevens often fought within the parties they shared, they almost always found common ground against the Democracy in the general election.

By the end of the 1832 campaign, Weed had recognized that Anti-Masonry did not provide the basis for a viable national party. The 1831 convention had attracted delegates from 13 states but none from the South. Within New York, the large share of Masons who were eager to vote against the Regency were hardly attracted by a party that called itself Anti-Masonic. Some other issue was needed to pull together an effective coalition. Jackson soon provided that issue with his impassioned war to wreck the second Bank of the United States.

THE BANK WAR

Neither Jackson nor Nicholas Biddle, president of the Bank, had at first sought or anticipated a confrontation between the administration and the nation's central financial institution. Jackson seems to have shared the distrust most westerners felt toward the Bank, but he did not make it a campaign issue in 1824 or 1828. In Tennessee he had not been among those agitating for a state bank to make loans the federal Bank turned down. The Bank, in any case, did not have to be rechartered until 1836. Biddle, for his part, aimed to keep the Bank free of party entanglements. When Daniel Webster in 1828 urged Biddle to extend a loan to a newspaper supporting the reelection of John Quincy Adams as President, Biddle replied: "It would be wrong for us to consider the matter in any other than a pecuniary light or to treat it on any other than business principles. . . . I have striven to keep the Bank straight and neutral in this conflict of parties and I shall endeavor to persevere in that course."[22]

The Bank war began in 1832 when Webster and Clay, believing they could trap Jackson between his western supporters and eastern pro-Bank Democrats, moved to renew the charter before the coming presidential election. Biddle, who had been affronted by some hostile remarks Jackson had made about the Bank, agreed to give "careful and friendly consideration" to requests for loans from newspapers that supported rechartering. Congress passed legislation renewing the Bank's charter at the beginning of July 1832. The President, his back up, issued a scathing veto.[23]

When Van Buren, who had been serving as ambassador to Britain, returned to Washington on the evening of July 7, he found Jackson looking like a "spectre" but still a "hero in spirit." Speaking without "passion or bluster," the President said: "The Bank, Mr. Van Buren, is trying to kill me, *but I will kill it.*" Jackson's veto was sustained by the Senate.[24]

Easily reelected in 1832, Jackson was in a mood to finish off the Bank once and for all. Francis Preston Blair, editor of the *Globe,* who had hated the Bank since he first entered politics in Kentucky, suggested the means: the transfer of federal deposits from the Bank to the struggling state banks. "Biddle," Blair told the President, "is actually using the money of the government for the purpose of breaking down the government. If he had not the money he could not do it."[25]

The proposal to withdraw federal funds from the Bank deeply divided the Democratic party. Members of the financial community who had aligned themselves with the Democracy, particularly in Philadelphia where the Bank was headquartered, were appalled at the idea. An effort by Amos Kendall to line up support among the state banks was only partly successful—many state bank officers feared the economic consequences. Van Buren was of two minds. He bore no affection for the Bank and recognized that eliminating Philadelphia's Chestnut Street as a financial rival to Wall Street would probably serve the long-term economic interest of New York. At the same time he did not wish to be identified as an agent for Wall Street speculators. Most New York financiers with whom he consulted, moreover, thought the economic risks were too high. Van Buren advised delay, but, as usual, promised to follow Jackson s lead.[26]

Receiving the reports of his lieutenants, the President delivered his decision: "Biddle shan't have the public money to break down the public administration. It's settled. My mind's made up." When the secretary of the treasury, a Philadelphian, resisted Jackson's order to remove the federal deposits, Jackson replaced him with Roger Taney, who, though himself a director of the Bank's Baltimore branch, carried out the President's directive with alacrity.[27]

Biddle went down fighting. As federal funds flowed out of the Bank, he began calling loans. The financial panic of 1834 followed—the first of a series of economic disasters in the nineteenth century that much of the public associated with Democratic policies.

WHIGS III

Jackson's war on the Bank helped bring together a new, fairly cohesive national party composed of former National Republicans, Anti-Masons, conservative Democrats, and some state parties that had not previously developed a national connection. Thurlow Weed suggested that the new party be called Republican, as a means of emphasizing its commitment to political and economic liberty. Clay and others rejected this proposal, probably fearing that it would touch off antagonisms left over from the struggles of the 1790s. A few years before there had been two national parties that included Republican in their title. Now there were none. The memory would linger.[28]

The name finally chosen was Whig, first used by a New York journalist and given currency by Clay in a major speech in 1834. The name was intended to recall both the patriot party of the Revolution and the British Whigs of the seventeenth and eighteenth centuries. Jackson, the Whigs claimed, was trying to exercise the powers of a monarch: "King Andrew." Opponents of Jacksonism, therefore, were in the tradition of forebears who had fought Charles I, James II, and George III. Borrowing from British liberal theorists, the Whigs set forth the "Whig theory of government," under which the executive is supposed to act primarily as an administrator carrying out the will of the legislative branch. (Blair complained in the *Globe* that through "metempsychosis . . . ancient TORIES now call themselves WHIGS.")[29]

The Whig enterprise is generally viewed as a failed attempt to establish a second major party. Ultimately it did fail, but during the two decades of the party's existence the Whigs achieved some notable successes. They won the presidency on their second attempt, in 1840, and again in 1848. Unfortunately for the Whigs, both their elected Presidents, William Henry Harrison and Zachary Taylor, died soon after taking office (Harrison within 30 days). Had either survived, and possibly won a second term, the Whigs might have been able to put together a more durable coalition.

By 1840 the Whigs had elected governors of 20 states, including Massachusetts, Ohio, Illinois, Indiana, Kentucky, Tennessee, Georgia, and Louisiana. In 1834 Seward, who had moved with Weed into the Whig party, ran for governor of New York and lost narrowly to Marcy. Four years later, the "political firm of Weed and Seward," as Horace Greeley later called it, finally connected, and Seward became the first Whig governor of the Empire State.

The Whigs were actually the only conservative party in American history before the Republicans in the 1970s to become a truly national party. Unlike the Federalists and National Republicans before them and the Republicans most of the time after, the Whigs were fully competitive in most of the South. Kentucky and Tennessee were Whig bastions in national elections, supporting Whig candidates for President in every election from 1836 through 1852 (even in 1844 against James K. Polk, the Democratic candidate, himself a Tennessean). In Georgia, the states-rights party formed by Governor George Troup, originally anti-tariff and sympathetic to nullification, gravitated into the Whig camp and carried the state for the Whig national ticket in 1840 and 1848. In Louisiana, rivalry between an "American" party (Anglo-Saxon) and a "Creole" party (French) devolved into competition between Whigs and Democrats. Most members of the American party became

Whigs, and most Creoles became Democrats, though both successor parties included some ethnic mix. With the help of large majorities out of Plaquemines Parish, a Creole stronghold already notorious for vote fraud, the Democrats usually held the upper hand, but the Whigs managed to carry the state in 1840 and 1848. Even in Virginia the Whigs, though they never won the state in a presidential election, became ascendant in the old Federalist strongholds of the Northern Neck and the Shenandoah Valley, while the Democrats continued to dominate the more populist Southside. According to an old Virginia saying, "Whigs know each other by the instinct of a gentleman."[30]

In most parts of the country the Whigs attracted support from voters who favored the program of federally nourished economic development that had been initiated by Hamilton and was championed in the 1830s by Clay and Webster. "The Whig party," Daniel Walker Howe writes, "represented those people who, for one reason or another, expected to do well out of economic development and were working to hasten it." The Whigs' economic program was built around Clay's proposals for high tariffs, federal expenditures on internal improvements, and, after the charter of Biddle's Bank expired, establishment of a third Bank of the United States.[31]

The Whigs, however, went beyond their Federalist and National Republican predecessors in adding cultural and moral appeals to economic arguments. Significantly, it was in the 1830s that the word "conservative" came into use as a political term. It had been introduced a little earlier in England by the Tories (who liked it so much they later made it the official name of their party). The National Republican platform of 1832—the first party platform—on which Clay ran for President against Jackson promised to maintain the Senate as "pre-eminently a conservative branch of the federal government." The Whigs used the term to denote association with "law and order," social caution, and moral restraint. "There is a law and order, a slow and sure, a distrustful and cautious party—a conservative, Whig party," proclaimed a Whig journal in 1846, "and there is a radical, innovating, hopeful, boastful, improvident, and go-ahead party—a Democratic, a Loco-Foco party!" Horace Greeley, another young New York journalist, who joined the "political firm of Weed and Seward" as a "junior partner," wrote of Henry Clay: "He was a conservative in the true sense of that much-abused term: satisfied to hold by the present until he could see clearly how to exchange it for the better; but his was no obstinate, bigoted conservatism, but such as became an intelligent and patriotic American."[32]

Many Whigs depicted the contest between their party and the Democrats as a struggle between social virtue and vice. Representative John Bell of Tennessee announced in 1835 that he was joining the Whig party because "We have, in truth, in the last eight or ten years, been in a continual state of moral war." When Clay in 1844 lost the presidency for the third time, a Pittsburgh Whig consoled him: "You had nine-tenths of the virtue, intelligence, and respectability of the nation on our side." Greeley put the same sentiment in more colorful language: "Loafers around the grog-shops of our Manufacturing villages! Subsisting on the earnings of your wives and children in the factories—give an extra glass and an extra yell for Polk and Dallas [the victorious Democratic ticket] and down with Cooney Clay!" According to Greeley, the Whigs' moral and cultural conservatism overrode economic class: "Upon those Working Men who stick to their business, hope to improve their circumstances by honest industry, and go on Sunday to church rather than the grogshop the appeals of Loco-Focoism fell comparatively harmless [Whig publicists liked to identify the entire Democracy with its dissident Loco-Foco faction]; while the opposite class were rallied with unprecedented unanimity against us."[33]

Most Whigs saw no inconsistency, or even tension, between social conservatism and promotion of economic progress. A Whig journal promised that the party would "blend" the "harmonious action" of "conservatism and progress." The link between the two was the reform imperative derived from the Puritan tradition. "The real authors of all benign revolutions," Seward declared, "are those who search out and seek to remove peacefully the roots of social and political evils, and so avert the necessity for sanguinary remedies. . . . The Puritans of England and America have given the highest and most beneficent illustration of that conservative heroism."[34]

The Whigs' support for economic progress did not necessarily attract them to the dreams of "empire" that excited the imaginations of many Americans, particularly in the South and West. Partly because they feared that the acquisition of additional dominions, notably Texas, would increase the political power of the slaveholders, and partly because their innate conservatism led them to favor gradual rather than rapid and destabilizing growth, the Whigs, at least in the North, generally resisted schemes for territorial expansion. Most Whigs opposed the Mexican War of 1846–47, by which the United States confirmed the annexation of Texas and acquired California and a vast territory of mountain and desert later divided into four states. Most of the ardent expansionists were Democrats, including Sam Houston of Texas, Senator Thomas Hart Benton of Missouri (coiner of the phrase "manifest destiny"), President Polk, and Jackson himself.

Participation by the Whigs in campaigns for moral causes like temperance, free public schools, and Sunday-closing laws helped win them the support of many of the evangelicals who had briefly rallied under the Anti-Masonic banner. Weed and Seward brought most of New York's Anti-Masons into the Whig camp. Thaddeus Stevens did the same with the reformist faction from Pennsylvania's Anti-Masons. Vermont, where the Anti-Masons had enjoyed their greatest success, became the most heavily Whig state in the nation. Not all Anti-Masons, however, became Whigs. Benjamin F. Hallett, for instance, who led the Massachusetts delegation to the 1831 Anti-Masonic convention, returned to the Democracy on economic issues and in 1848 became the first chairman of the newly formed Democratic National Committee.

Moral conservatism also helped the Whigs break the hold the Jacksonians had gained on the old Northwest—Ohio, Indiana, Illinois, and Michigan. Many western evangelicals, particularly among the Methodists, continued to support the Democrats, but some of the denominations that had been predominantly Jeffersonian began to shift toward the Whigs. Ronald Formisano has shown that in Michigan most Presbyterians and Baptists favored the Whigs, and William Shade reports a similar trend among the more socially reformist branch of Baptists in Illinois.[35]

There was more than a tinge of anti-Catholicism and nativism to the Whig moral program, as there was to the broader Calvinist and evangelical Protestant involvement in social issues of the time. "The Catholic Church," charged Lyman Beecher, a leading Congregationalist minister and dabbler in Whig politics, "holds now in darkness and bondage nearly half the civilized world. . . . It is the most skilled, powerful, dreadful system of corruption to those who wield it, and of slavery and debasement to those under it." In the 1844 election, the Whigs formed working alliances at the local level in New York with the nativist American Republican party.[36]

Some Whig politicians, including Seward and young Abraham Lincoln in Illinois, saw the danger of turning their party into an agent of Protestant exclusivism. Though Catholics in most parts of the country were even more overwhelmingly Jacksonian Democrat than they had been Jeffersonian Republican, Seward in the early 1840s achieved a cooperative relationship with Bishop John Hughes, Catholic prelate of New York. Hughes, claiming that New York's public schools were Protestant in everything but name, sought state aid for Catholic schools. Seward, stunning many members of the Whigs' Protestant constituency, endorsed Hughes' proposal on the ground that "immigrant children" should be "instructed by teachers speaking the same language with themselves and professing the same faith." When Democrats in the state legislature hedged on the issue, Hughes entered a Catholic slate in several city districts in the 1841 legislative elections, draining off enough normally Democratic votes to enable the Whigs to pick up several seats. Although the legislature still refused to authorize state aid for Catholic schools, it passed a bill, signed by Seward, prohibiting instruction in "any religious sectarian doctrine" in the public schools, thereby effectively depriving Protestantism of its semi-established status.

"MONSTER RALLIES"

During the 1830s, political organizations made increasing use of the new technology of "steamboats, canals, and ultimately railroads" to "hold state and national party conventions, stage 'monster' rallies, . . . and generally manage politics on a grand scale." In 1840 the Whigs pressed these tendencies to new levels of intensity.[37]

Martin Van Buren, who was being held responsible for hard times, was a highly vulnerable incumbent Democratic President. The Whigs, having failed in 1836 with a series of state and regional favorite-son candidates, came together on a ticket composed of General William Henry Harrison of Ohio for President and John Tyler of Virginia, a Calhoun Democrat, for Vice President. The Democrats chose to poke fun at Harrison, whose chief qualification seemed to be that he had defeated an Indian force led by Tecumseh at the battle of Tippecanoe in Indiana 30 years before. "Old Granny" Harrison, they jibed, would be perfectly content to "spend the rest of his days in a log cabin with a barrel of cider." Actually, Harrison, though he had made his military career in the West, was the senior member of one of Virginia's most patrician families. His ancestral home in the tidewater was only a few miles from the estate of John Tyler, another Virginia patrician.

The Whigs, however, shrewdly accepted the Democrats' caricature. In Harrisburg, Pennsylvania, two imaginative party workers set up a reproduction of a log cabin with a cider barrel by the door. The idea caught on and similar displays soon appeared in hundreds of cities and towns. Whig publicists launched an alliterative slogan that continued to resound in American folk memory long after the campaign of 1840 had been forgotten: "Tippecanoe and Tyler too!" Weed and others raised a huge campaign war chest to finance an army of canvassers soliciting votes for "Old Tip." A nationally circulated campaign newspaper, the *Log Cabin,* edited by Greeley, pounded away at the theme, "Van, Van . . . a used up man." During the fall, "monster rallies" featuring a log cabin and a barrel of cider were staged in major cities. Harrison himself followed the recommendation of Nicholas Biddle, who scented victory against his old foes in the Democracy: "Let him say not one single word about principles or creed."[38]

Predictably, John Quincy Adams, now a Whig member of the House of Representatives from Massachusetts, disliked the new kind of campaigning. He deplored the "fearful extent [of] itinerant speechmaking" and wondered where this "revolution in the habits and manners of the people" would end. But the labors of Weed, Greeley, and their associates bore fruit: Harrison carried 19 of the 26 states for an electoral vote majority of 234 to 60. The Whigs for the first, and as it turned out only, time won majorities in both houses of Congress.

After only one month in office, Harrison died as the result of complications from a cold caught at his inaugural. Tyler, a Democrat until the Whigs nominated him for Vice President, succeeded to the White House. The new President kept Harrison's cabinet, including Webster as secretary of state. But when Tyler vetoed a bill to establish a third Bank of the United States that Clay had pushed through Congress, the Whig congressional caucus read him out of the party. All members of the cabinet, mostly followers of Clay, resigned, except Webster, who had little use for the new idea of party. Clay and Webster split. In 1844 the party was in a shambles, and the way was open for the return of the Democrats under Polk.

In 1848 the Whigs tried again with a celebrated military commander—always a device favored by Weed. This time they chose Zachary Taylor, hero of the recently concluded Mexican War. The party was beginning to buckle under the slavery issue, but, assisted by even deeper division among the Democrats, it held together long enough to win the election. (A southern Whig wrote Taylor, who himself was a Louisiana slaveholder but was thought to be under the influence of the anti-slavery wing of the party, demanding: "I have worked hard all my life, and the net product is a plantation with one hundred negroes—slaves. Before I vote, I want to know how you stand on the Slavery question." Taylor replied: "Sir, I too have worked faithfully these many years, and the net product remaining to me is a plantation with *three* hundred negroes." The answer apparently was satisfactory.)[39]

Taylor (who as President in fact quickly broke with the slave-holders) died a little more than a year after taking office, and his running mate, Millard Fillmore of New York, became President. Fillmore belonged to a faction of New York Whigs favoring conciliation of the slaveholders that was hostile to the wing led by Seward and Weed. Once more the party's national structure crumbled.

FOLK POLITICS

The two national parties that developed during the 1830s and 1840s, the Democrats and the Whigs, were political institutions of a kind that had never existed before in history and that existed nowhere else at the time. Unlike the parliamentary parties that had developed in Britain in the eighteenth century, they were broadly organized among the voters and had lives of their own apart from their roles in electing members to Congress or campaigning for the presidency. They were certainly parties of "interest," in that they represented competing economic and social interest groups. But they were also parties of "value," in that they offered distinctive visions of the nation's future. Both were committed to individualism and personal freedom, but one was more equalitarian and the other was more concerned with economic progress and moral order.

In response to the rising party competition, turnout in presidential elections, which had been only 27 percent of the eligible voters as recently as 1824, soared to 57 percent in 1828 and to 80 percent in 1840. The increase was generally greatest in states where the parties were most evenly matched.[40]

The downside of the increased turnout was a sharp rise in vote fraud. Taking advantage of turbulent conditions in rapidly growing cities like New York, Philadelphia, and Baltimore, the party machines recruited armies of voters, particularly among recent immigrants, to act as "repeaters." In New York, Tammany Hall regularly hauled "cart-loads of voters, many of whom had been in the country less than three years," from poll to poll so that they could cast multiple votes for the Democratic ticket.[41]

Whig organizations responded in kind. The Whig machine in Baltimore in 1849 employed among its repeaters a former writer and editor who had fallen on hard times: Edgar Allan Poe. Carted drunk from poll to poll, America's first literary genius finally collapsed in a tavern and five days later died of complications from alcoholism and exposure.

To deal with the new kind of politics, the parties began formalizing and to some extent centralizing their structures. National conventions became the accepted means for choosing party nominees for President and Vice President. After 1840 both major parties usually adopted a platform setting forth the principles and issues on which they sought election. At the Democratic national convention in 1848, the delegates voted to establish a national committee, "composed of one member from each state, to be appointed by the delegations from each state. . . ." Benjamin Hallett of Massachusetts (a former Anti-Mason) became the first national party chairman.[42]

During the Jacksonian era, Richard P. McCormick writes, "campaigns and elections assumed the aspect of folk festivals." Visitors from abroad, McCormick notes, observed that "politics in the United States filled a need that was met in many European nations by the pomp, ceremony, and pageantry of the great established churches." Aroused voters "eagerly assumed the identity of partisans," seeming to find in their parties not only political or economic utility but also a kind of emotional or even spiritual fulfillment.[43]

DISRUPTION OF PARTIES

The social and moral disputes of the 1850s, however, led swiftly to the deterioration of both parties. The Whigs sank into extinction, and the Democrats temporarily fractured.

The slavery issue had already split the major parties in the 1840s. James G. Birney, a former Kentucky slaveholder turned abolitionist, ran for President in 1840 on the Liberty party ticket and picked up a scant 7,000 votes. But the Liberty party, made up of single-issue voters dedicated to the immediate and total abolition of slavery, persevered. In 1842 it elected a few state legislators in Massachusetts and Maine. In 1844 Birney, running again as the Liberty party candidate for President, won 82,000 votes, including more than 8 percent of the total in Massachusetts, New Hampshire, and Vermont. The almost 16,000 votes Birney received in New York were more than three times the margin by which Polk carried the state against Clay. Since Polk would not have won the election without New York's 36 electoral votes, the Liberty party, the great majority of whose members were former Whigs, could fairly be said to have deprived Clay of victory in his third and final run for the presidency.

Four years later the shoe was on the other foot. The Democratic party had been deeply divided by the Wilmot Proviso, an amendment to an appropriations bill introduced in 1846 by Representative David Wilmot, Democrat of Pennsylvania, that would prohibit the extension of slavery in all territories acquired from Mexico. The Wilmot Proviso passed the House, where representatives from states that prohibited slavery were a growing majority, but was bottled up in the Senate, where slave states and free states were still equally represented. Southern Democrats, infuriated by the Wilmot Proviso, looked increasingly to the leadership of the aged Calhoun, who demanded that Congress categorically renounce any authority to prohibit slavery in the territories. Many northern Democrats, too, followed President Polk in favoring conciliation of the southern slaveholders. But a significant segment of the northern Democracy felt that the party must dissociate itself from the extension of slavery.

The division among the Democrats was particularly bitter in New York. One faction, called the Hunkers because "they hankered after spoils," led by former Governor Marcy, resisted any action that would risk losing the South from the Democracy. The other faction, called the Barnburners because they were "radical enough to burn down the barn to get rid of the rats," backed the Wilmot Proviso. The two factions sent rival delegations to the 1848 Democratic national convention. Hostility between the factions ran so high that when the convention voted to give each delegation half of New York's vote, both sides rejected the compromise and New York was unable to participate.[44]

The 1848 Democratic convention nominated as its candidate for President Senator Lewis Cass of Michigan, who held that the voters in each territory should decide for themselves whether they wished their territory to be slave or free—a position that became known as "popular sovereignty." Neither the Calhounites nor the Barnburners were satisfied with Cass's approach. Several southern delegations walked out of the convention, and many Barnburners decided the time had come for independent action.

At this point Martin Van Buren, of all people, agreed to accept the nomination of a new Free Soil party, a broadened and somewhat less radical descendant of the Liberty party. Van Buren may have been motivated in part by frustrated ambition. In 1844, seeking another crack at the presidency, he had received the support of a majority of the delegates to the Democratic national convention on the first ballot. But he was blocked by southern delegations supporting Cass who used the two-thirds rule to prevent his nomination. In the end the convention chose Polk on the ninth ballot—the first "dark-horse" candidate to be nominated for President. This experience, and Cass's role in it, may have weakened Van Buren's normal reluctance to damage the chances of the Democratic ticket in 1848. But Van Buren was able to make the principled argument that the long-term welfare of the Democracy, and the nation, required that the party shed its Calhounite influence, even at the cost of losing an election or two.

That fall Van Buren received support from some northern Whigs, who swallowed hard to forget old antagonisms. In Massachusetts, for example, young Charles Sumner, entering politics for the first time, exhorted: "It is not for the Van Buren of 1838 we are to vote, but for the Van Buren of today. . . ." At least in New York, however, where Van Buren got 45 percent of his 292,000 total national vote, he made his greatest inroad among the Democrats. All but one of the nine New York counties that Van Buren carried, all in the heartland of the "Little Magician's" old Regency machine, had voted Democratic in 1844. Van Buren's 120,000 votes in New York exceeded Zachary Taylor's plurality over Cass in the state. Without

New York's electoral votes, Taylor would have lost the election. Once again an anti-slavery third party in New York had tipped a national election—this time to the Whigs.[45]

In another four years, the slavery issue had fatally split the Whigs as a national party. The Whigs' underlying problem was that their alignment with the moral program of northern Protestantism, a principal source of the political dynamism they briefly enjoyed in the 1840s, brought them into collision with the institution of slavery, thereby antagonizing and alienating their own southern wing.

Most northern Protestants in the early 1850s were not abolitionists. Though morally repelled by slavery, particularly by the open conduct of the slave trade in the national capital, they were for the most part prepared to tolerate continuation of slavery in the areas where it had existed when the Constitution was approved. But the accession of vast new lands in the West following the war with Mexico—a war, ironically, that the South had enthusiastically promoted—put the issue in a different light. For both moral and economic reasons, the majority of northerners were simply not willing to accept the extension of slavery into the developing West.

When the national Whigs hedged on the issue, they cut themselves off from the moral support that had helped make them competitive in New York, Pennsylvania, and the old Northwest. At the same time, the presence in the Whig national leadership of opponents of slavery like Seward and Representative Thaddeus Stevens of Pennsylvania made the party anathema in the South. Burgeoning Whig parties in states like Georgia, Florida, and Alabama collapsed. By 1852 the solid Democratic South, except for Kentucky and Tennessee, was once more a political reality.

NATIVIST EXPLOSION

In the mid-1850s a second deeply divisive issue swept through the nation that for a time seemed to eclipse even the salience of slavery and further weakened the parties. Nativism and anti-Catholicism had long been staples of American politics. Protestants had passed laws discriminating against Catholics in colonial times, and anti-Catholicism had helped spark the Revolution. Protestants in the thirteen colonies were angered by the favorable treatment given by the British crown to Catholicism in Canada after the French and Indian War. George Washington, Benjamin Franklin, and others among the Founders did their best to discourage anti-Catholicism, and the states gradually repealed their laws discriminating on the basis of religion.

With the great influx of Catholics, mainly from Ireland and Germany, in the 1830s and 1840s, anti-Catholic sentiment re-ignited, particularly among working-class Protestants in the big cities. Prejudice against Catholics among middle-class and working-class Protestants was legitimized by the Protestant intelligentsia. Anti-Catholicism became associated with the reform program of Protestant social activists campaigning for the abolition of slavery, free public schools, and the prohibition of liquor. Horace Bushnell, one of the founders of liberal Protestantism in the United States, declared: "Our first danger is barbarism [from immigration], Romanism next."[46]

Riots against Catholics erupted in Boston and Philadelphia, and a pitched battle between Protestants and Catholics in New York was narrowly averted. In the 1840s a secret society was formed to promote legislation against immigration. The members were called Know-Nothings, because they were pledged to tell outsiders they knew nothing about the society's existence.

Since more than 90 percent of Catholics in most cities voted Democratic, many Whig politicians made what capital they could out of nativism. Most Whig leaders, however, resisted having their party turned into a vehicle for Know-Nothingism. Some Whigs, like Seward, Lincoln, and even Greeley, disassociated themselves from nativism. If the Know-Nothings got into power, Lincoln wrote, the doctrine, "all men are created equal," which in practice already meant "all men are created equal, except Negroes," would have to be changed to "all men are created equal, except Negroes and foreigners and Catholics." If it came to that, Lincoln said, he would "prefer emigrating to some country where they make no pretense of loving liberty—to Russia, for instance, where despotism can be taken pure, and without the base alloy of hypocrisy." Greeley conceded in the New York *Tribune,* which he had helped found in 1841, that many immigrants were "deplorably clannish, misguided, and prone to violence." But he denounced the Know-Nothing movement as "essentially anti-Foreign, especially anti-Irish, and anti-Catholic." How, he demanded, "can we regard any movement of this sort as other than hostile to the vital principles of our Republic?"[47]

Disappointed with the Whigs, the Know-Nothings in 1854 formed their own political party, which they called the American party. In its very first election, the American party scored practically a clean sweep in Massachusetts, winning the governorship, every seat in the state senate, and all but two of the 378 seats in the state house of representatives. Know-Nothing state tickets also triumphed in Delaware and, through fusion with the Whigs, in Pennsylvania. In 1855 the American party again won in Massachusetts and added victories in Connecticut, Rhode Island, New Hampshire, Maryland, and Kentucky. American party tickets also ran strong races in Virginia, Tennessee, Georgia, Alabama, Mississippi, and Louisiana and won some minor state offices in Texas.

Nativism seemed on the verge of carrying the country. The New York *Herald* gloomily predicted that in 1856 a Know-Nothing would be elected President. Some American party leaders and sympathizers acknowledged that the party's victory in a national election could produce violence. John Bell of Tennessee, normally a sensible and conservative politician, declared: "It is better that a little blood shall sprinkle the pavements and sidewalks of our cities now, than that their streets should be drenched in blood hereafter" as a result of "deadly conflict, between armed bands—it may be between disciplined legions—Native Americans on one side, and foreigners supported by native factions on the other."[48]

In some states, particularly in the South, the American party was moving into the vacuum created by the demise of the Whigs. But the Know-Nothings were more successful than the Whigs had ever been at reaching across class lines to attract working-class voters. In Baltimore, "the Know-Nothings received great accessions from the Democrats. The most marked change was in the Eighteenth Ward. This ward had been one of the Democratic strongholds, and it became the banner ward of the *Know-Nothings.*" Adjacent to the Baltimore and Ohio Railroad shops, the ward "was inhabited mainly by mechanics and workingmen. . . ." In New Orleans, the American party was controlled by "ward clubs, located in neighborhoods inhabited by workingmen who had moved to [the city] in the last ten or fifteen years. . . . This element did not hesitate to use violence to achieve political success. It was probably they who dressed as Indians, paraded through the streets intimidating Democratic voters, and made the American party the party of thugs."[49]

Perhaps some of the recruits to Know-Nothingism were half-consciously seeking an issue that would transcend the deepening division between North and South over slavery. The 1854 meeting of the American party's national council in Cincinnati adopted a pledge of loyalty to the Union, promising to "discourage and denounce any attempt coming from any quarter . . . to destroy or subvert it or to weaken its bonds."

Whatever the intent of its promoters, nativism failed to inspire a unifying nationalism. Know-Nothingism succumbed in part to ridicule and laughter as newspapers gleefully published its mumbo-jumbo rituals and as jokesters set up "Owe-Nothing," "Say-Nothing," and "Do-Nothing" societies.[50]

Most of all, Know-Nothingism was overwhelmed by the "irrepressible conflict" over slavery that had to be settled before the Republic could proceed. Northern and southern wings of the American party were soon quarreling over slavery, just as the Whigs and Democrats had done. "Thurlow Weed," J. A. Isely writes, "began the decomposition of the American party by compelling its leaders to take notice of the slavery issue." Henry Wilson, leader of the American party in Massachusetts, announced that his purpose from the start had been "to disrupt the Whig and Democratic parties, in the confident hope that, out of the disorganized masses, then would come a great political party antagonistic to the influence of the Slave Power."[51]

In 1856 what remained of the American party persuaded former President Millard Fillmore to run as its presidential candidate. Fillmore, who happened to be visiting Pope Pius IX in Rome at the time of his nomination, disavowed anti-Catholicism. The party was ground between the Democrats and the Republicans. Though Fillmore received 20 percent of the national popular vote, he carried only one state, Maryland. The American party soon after ceased to exist.

THE REPUBLICAN ERA

6

PARTY GOVERNMENT

The Civil War Republicans

D URING THE 1850s the party system that formed around the Democrats and Whigs failed either to resolve or to continue delaying the increasingly bitter national controversy over slavery. In the 1860 election the recently created Republican party, dedicated to checking the further spread of slavery (though not its immediate abolition in states where slavery already existed), won the presidency and achieved majority control in Congress. Within a few months after the election, several southern states seceded from the Union. Abraham Lincoln, the newly elected Republican President, decided to use military force to hold the Union together. The Civil War followed.

Part of the reason neither the Democrats nor the Whigs were able to stand before the divisive force of the slavery issue—as they had failed to contain the challenge of nativism—was that neither had developed a truly cohesive national party in the 1850s Structurally, both major parties were associations of state party organizations, some of which were little more than personal followings of particular politicians. The Democrats, especially in Jackson's time, represented in a general way the liberal tradition; and the Whigs expressed many aspects of what was to become the republican tradition. But neither major party had sufficient ideological coherence to override the competing passions and interests that divided them internally.

The newly formed Republicans, too, were from the start a coalition party. Unlike the Liberty and Free Soil parties of the 1840s, the Republicans were far from being a single-issue party. Besides standing for resistance to slavery, they were committed to an extensive program that included, among other things, federal support for rapid industrial development, distribution of western public lands to small farmers, free public education, and moral reform. Above all, they promised to preserve the Union—one and indivisible.

As a result of their stand against slavery, the Republicans had almost no support in the South or among slave-owners in the Border states. But elsewhere they were more of a national party, with a shared ideology and a centrally coordinated organization, than either the Democrats or the Whigs had been.

In the hands of Lincoln and his associates, this party structure was shaped into a governing institution that not only restored a unified national republic but also over a period of several decades produced a society significantly different—though with problems of its own—from any that had preceded it in history.

A NEW POLITICAL FORCE

As Figure 6–1 shows, the geographic alignment created by the 1860 election did not break completely with the patterns of the past. As in the elections of 1800 and 1828 (Figures 3–2 and 5–1), New England and the South were aligned almost solidly on opposing sides. The crucial shifts came in New York, Pennsylvania, and the states of the old Northwest, all of which had previously been normally Democratic and now swung decisively to the Republicans, producing a new majority coalition.

The election was complicated by the division of the Democracy into two parties, northern and southern, which had split during the summer of 1860 on the issue of slavery. It was made additionally complex by the appearance of a fourth contender, the Constitutional Union party, which sought to rally voters who regarded preserving the Union as more important than either checking or extending slavery, with John Bell of Tennessee as its presidential candidate. Lincoln swept all of the North except New Jersey, winning 180 electoral votes, 28 more than the required majority. John Breckinridge of Kentucky, the candidate of the southern Democracy, carried most of the South and the Border states of Maryland and

Figure 6–1   Electoral vote by states, 1860

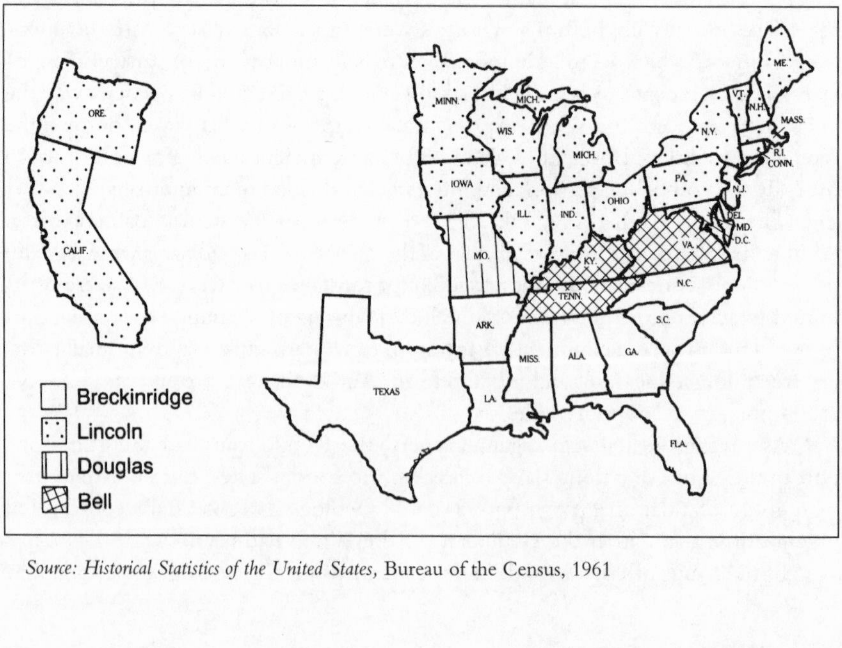

- ☐ Breckinridge
- ⠒ Lincoln
- ⊞ Douglas
- ▨ Bell

Source: Historical Statistics of the United States, Bureau of the Census, 1961

Delaware. Bell carried Virginia (where he defeated Breckinridge by only 156 votes), Kentucky, and Tennessee. And Stephen A. Douglas of Illinois, the candidate of the regular Democratic party that had dominated national politics most of the time for the last 60 years, won only Missouri and three of New Jersey's seven electoral votes. Voter turnout, which had declined in the early 1850s, rose to 82 percent—the second-highest level in American history.

Much has been made of the fact that Lincoln won only about 40 percent of the popular vote. But this was because in the South he received almost no votes at all. Of the 18 states of the North and West, not counting the Border states, Lincoln won solid majorities in all except California and Oregon, where he gained narrow pluralities in three-way contests with Douglas and Breckinridge, and New Jersey, which he lost by 4,000 votes to Douglas. While Lincoln was being elected President, the Republicans were winning (or had won in the last election) the governorships of every northern state and were achieving majorities in both houses of Congress.

Other electoral systems might conceivably have kept the Republicans out of the presidency in 1860. But it is hard to believe that any democratic means would have denied them the apex of national power for long. Like the Jeffersonians and Jacksonians before them, the Republicans in 1860 seemed to embody a social force whose hour had come.

Lincoln won majorities in most counties in the North where the Whigs had been strong and made some important additions. In New York, he swept both the old Clintonian strongholds in the western part of the state and the former bastions of the Regency in the central region, leaving the Democracy in control of only New York City, Brooklyn (then a separate city), western Long Island, and some counties in the Hudson Valley (Figure 6–2). In Pennsylvania, he carried the former Whig counties in the southeast and southwest and added the great swath of northern-tier counties, many of which had been represented in Congress by David Wilmot, who had made the transition from Democrat to Free Soiler to Republican, and the formerly Democratic counties of the northeastern anthracite coal-mining region (Figure 6–3). In Ohio, Lincoln prevailed in the south-central farming counties that had voted reliably for the Whigs and added the six northeastern counties around Cleveland that had voted Free Soil in 1848, plus the rich agricultural counties of the northwest and Hamilton County (containing the city of Cincinnati) in the southwest (Figure 6–4). In his home state of Illinois, Lincoln broke the long Democratic hegemony by carrying the eight northeastern counties around Chicago that had voted Free Soil in 1848 as well as the prosperous northern and central farming counties that had been normally Whig. Southern Illinois, largely settled from the slave state of Kentucky (where Lincoln himself had been born), voted overwhelmingly for Douglas (Figure 6–5).

A new political force, sweeping most of the North and West and totally excluded from the South, had assumed control of the Republic. What manner of coalition was Lincoln leading into national power?

Figure 6–2   New York counties voting for Lincoln, 1860

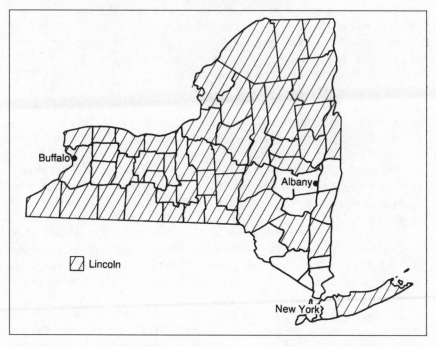

Source: W. Dean Burnham, Presidential Ballots: 1836–1892, Johns Hopkins University Press, Baltimore, 1955

REPUBLICAN ORIGINS

The proximate cause of the formation of the Republican party was indignation in the North over the passage in 1854 of the Kansas–Nebraska bill, which opened the western territories to slavery. "The passage of the Kansas–Nebraska bill by the traitors in the Senate of the United States," Horace Greeley wrote in the New York *Tribune,* "is one further step of Southern chivalry toward effecting the brutal degradation of Mechanical and Laboring men, white and black, in the United States."[1]

Neither the Democrats nor the Whigs, many northern voters concluded, could be trusted to resist the imperial ambition of the southern planter class. Yet the single-issue anti-slavery Free Soil party had turned out to be too narrowly based to win the decisive victory in the North that was needed to produce a majority in the electoral college. What the anti-slavery cause required was a new political combination that would draw on the full range of economic and moral issues that had helped animate the Whigs and that at the same time would attract many of the Democrats who in 1848 had deserted their party to vote for the Free Soil ticket.

During the winter of 1854, while politicians jousted in Washington, a new

Figure 6–3 Pennsylvania counties voting for Lincoln, 1860

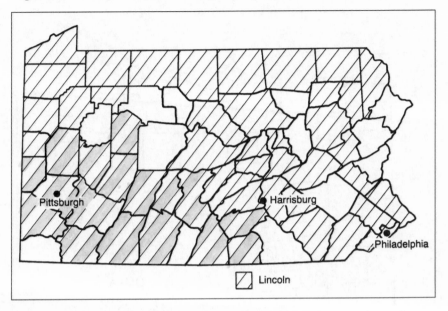

Source: W. Dean Burnham, Presidential Ballots: 1836–1892, Johns Hopkins University Press, Baltimore, 1955

party was coming into being through hundreds of small gatherings in communities throughout the North called to protest passage of the Kansas-Nebraska Act. Several cities of the old Northwest claim to have been the founding site of the Republican party. The claim most generally credited is that of Ripon, Wisconsin, for a meeting held on the night of March 20, 1854. The event was recorded by one of its organizers, Alvin E. Bovay: "We went into the little meeting held in a school-house Whigs, Free-Soilers, and Democrats. We came out of it Republicans."[2]

The name Republican was chosen, Bovay wrote years later, because it recalled Jefferson's party and brought to mind a "common weal," because it could be applied as a noun or an adjective to "a party or to an individual," and because it would be associated by Germans, vital to the new coalition in Wisconsin as in other midwestern states, with *Republicaner,* the name taken by participants in the unsuccessful German revolution of 1848. By June, Horace Greeley was writing in the *Tribune:* "We should not much care whether those (Free–Soilers, Whigs, Abolitionists, etc.) thus united were designated Whigs, Free Democrats, or something else; though we think some simple name like Republican would more fitly designate those who have united to restore the Union to its true mission of champion and promulgator of liberty rather than propagandist of slavery."[3]

Figure 6–4   Ohio counties voting for Lincoln, 1860

Source: W. Dean Burnham, Presidential Ballots: 1836–1892, Johns Hopkins University Press, Baltimore, 1955

In many parts of the North, the Whigs did not make way for the new party without a fight. In Illinois, Abraham Lincoln, who in 1854 had maneuvered himself to the Whig nomination for the Senate, resisted amalgamation with the Republicans, whom he viewed as too radical. In New York, William H. Seward and Thurlow Weed argued that the Whigs were still the best hope for those who aimed to contain slavery without splitting the Union. If a new party "equally right in its principles, and more able and willing to carry them out" should appear, Weed wrote in the Albany *Evening Journal,* "we will urge voters to go for that one."[4]

By the summer of 1855, however, the Whigs had been finished off in many of their former northern strongholds by the Know-Nothings. The only real alternative to the Democrats for politicians who rejected unalloyed nativism was the emerging Republican party, which in the fall of 1854 won victories in state elec-

Figure 6–5   Illinois counties voting for Lincoln, 1860

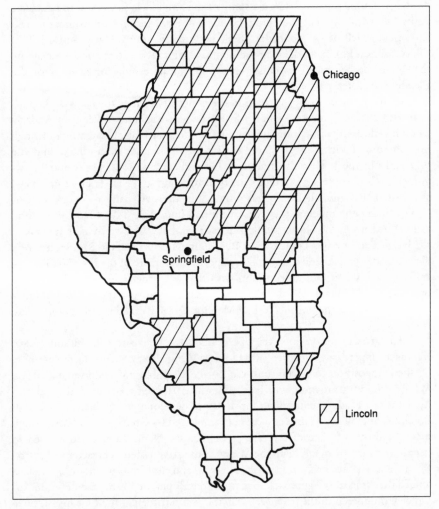

Source: W. Dean Burnham, Presidential Ballots: 1836–1892, Johns Hopkins University Press, Baltimore, 1955

tions in Maine, Vermont, Ohio, Michigan, Wisconsin, and Indiana. Weed, Lincoln, and finally Seward joined the new alignment. In Massachusetts, young Charles Sumner, the embodiment of Boston Brahmanism, elected in 1851 to take Webster's place in the Senate, became a Republican.[5]

Free Soil Democrats, too, gravitated toward the new party. In Indiana, young Oliver P. Morton led a small band of dissenters out of the state Democratic convention "amidst hisses and taunts" after it had endorsed Kansas–Nebraska. "Your heads are getting kinkey," shouted some of the angry delegates. "Go and equalize yourselves with niggers." Reaching the door, one of Morton's companions turned and cried: "Hell dawns upon the Democratic party from this day onward."[6] In Ohio, Salmon P. Chase, denied renomination for a second term in the Senate by the Democrats because of his antislavery views, ran successfully for governor on the Republican ticket.

In the spring of 1855, adherents of the new party formed the national Republican Association. The Association's first president was none other than Andrew Jackson's old journalistic mouthpiece, Francis Preston Blair. Grown rich through his publishing business, Blair aspired to play for a second time the role of midwife to a party in the Jeffersonian tradition. He and his two sons, Frank and Montgomery, who had begun political careers in Missouri and Maryland, respectively, anticipated that enough Democrats would join the new party to overwhelm its Whig contingent, much as the Jacksonians had outweighed the followers of John Quincy Adams in the old Republican party in the 1820s. Two living remnants of the Jacksonian heyday, Thomas Hart Benton in Missouri and old Sam Houston in Texas, made sympathetic sounds. The opposition of many of the Free Soil Democrats to slavery had little in common with that of former conscience Whigs like Sumner. In 1857 Frank Blair led the Free Soilers to victory in the St. Louis municipal elections with the slogan, "White Men for Our City, and Our City for White Men."

The great majority, however, of recruits to the new party—about four out of five, according to one estimate—were former Whigs. They were attracted not only by their opposition to slavery but also by the Republicans' endorsement of the Whigs' economic program, which called for internal improvements and a high tariff. To this was added enthusiasm for the rapid development of the West through homesteading by small farmers, a cause championed by Greeley ("Go West, young man") and others. One of the reasons the Kansas–Nebraska Act had rankled so deeply was that, by opening up the West to "the slave system, characterized . . . by the plantation, the production of staple crops, and non-industrialization," it challenged the "free labor" approach to national development. "Now then Free-men," Greeley thundered in the *Tribune,* "shall the vast territory of the Northwest, once solemnly consecrated to FREEDOM FOREVER, be converted into a new range for the bloodhounds of future monsters?"[7]

Seward, who had been elected to the Senate from New York in 1849, seemed the natural leader of the new party. He was on record as having predicted an "irrepressible uprising" of public opinion against slavery. But he continued to hold out hope that slavery would "give way to the salutary instructions of economy, and to the ripening influences of humanity." He was a strong backer of the Whig economic program, but his opposition to nativism had won him support among Catholic and foreign-born Democrats. Yet he hung back. Perhaps the turning wheel of party change had not yet come to rest. Perhaps the Republicans would prove to be no more stable as a political formation than the discredited American party. Better, Seward decided, to remain another four years in the Senate.[8]

At the first Republican national convention, in Philadelphia in 1856, the former Jacksonians, led by the Blairs, stepped into the breach. Nominated for President at their urging was John C. Frémont, known as "the Pathfinder" for his exploits in the exploration of the West. Frémont's father-in-law was the old Jacksonian leader in Missouri, Thomas Hart Benton. Weed, who probably agreed with Seward that 1856 would be only a trial run for the new party, was content to back yet another military celebrity. The platform invoked the names of only two national heroes: Washington and Jefferson. Its central plank called for exclusion of slavery from the territories—giving rise to another memorable campaign slogan: "Free labor, free speech, free men, free Kansas, and Frémont!"[9]

Weed assumed active management of the campaign. Edwin D. Morgan of New York, who, like his cousin, Junius, father of J. Pierpont, was achieving success in Wall Street, was installed as the first Republican national chairman. Norman Judd of Illinois, a political associate of Abraham Lincoln, became secretary of the Republican National Committee. Greeley, despite tension with Weed (the two had fallen out when Weed had refused to slate the *Tribune* editor as Whig candidate for governor of New York in 1854), was put in charge of propaganda. Frémont's wife (Benton's daughter) Jessie, a formidable personage in her own right, ran the campaign office and answered the mail.[10]

Though the party was not yet fully organized, Frémont's showing in the fall was impressive: victory in all of New England, New York, and every state in the old Northwest except Illinois and Indiana, for 114 electoral votes to 174 for the Democratic candidate, James Buchanan of Pennsylvania. Studying the election results, Weed and other Republican strategists spotted two important gaps in the party's performance: in the crucial state of Pennsylvania, the coalition of former Whigs led by Thaddeus Stevens and Free Soil Democrats led by David Wilmot had not broken the hold of Democratic voting habits that dated from the time of Gallatin; and beer-drinking German–Americans in the Midwest, put off by the Republicans' identification with nativism and prohibition, had for the most part remained loyal to the Democracy.

The first of these problems was dealt with, first, by increasing emphasis on the Republicans' support for a protective tariff popular in both the industrial cities and the coalfields of Pennsylvania, and, second, by putting much of the party's electoral business in the hands of Senator Simon Cameron, a former stalwart of the state's Jacksonian Democratic machine. The German problem was met by playing down some of the moralistic aspects of the old Whig program. By 1858, Democratic orators in the Midwest were reduced to warning German audiences that Republican victory would mean an "end to walks, kisses, and cooked meals on Sunday." In 1860 most German–Americans followed their leader, Carl Schurz, into the Republican ranks.[11]

As the 1860 election approached, Republican prospects seemed distinctly favorable. The controversy over slavery had deepened, and the incumbent Democratic administration was blamed for the financial panic of 1857. The shrewder Republican leaders recognized, however, that the party still needed a broad platform if it was to avoid the fate of the Free Soilers in 1848. "I want to succeed this time," Greeley wrote to a friend. "Yet I know the country is not Anti-Slavery. It will only swallow a little Anti-Slavery in a great deal of sweetening. An Anti-Slavery man *per se* cannot be elected; but a Tariff, River-and-Harbor, Pacific Railroad, Free-Homestead man *may* succeed *although* he is Anti-Slavery. . . . I mean to have as good a candidate as the majority will elect."[12]

In the industrial towns and mining regions of the East, the Republicans emphasized the tariff issue more than opposition to slavery. Andrew Curtin, Republican candidate for governor of Pennsylvania, promised to respond to the "vast heavings of the heart of Pennsylvania whose sons are pining for protectionism."[13]

Seward and Weed decided the time had at last come for Seward to rise to the presidency. Several rivals stood in his way: Chase of Ohio claimed to have a wider appeal among Democrats; Cameron of Pennsylvania put himself forward as his state's favorite son; Greeley and the Blairs busied themselves on behalf of the Speaker of the House, Edward Bates of Missouri. Abraham Lincoln of Illinois, who had gained a national reputation in 1858 through a series of debates with Stephen Douglas, whom he had unsuccessfully challenged for the Senate, indicated his availability. Weed assured Seward, however, that "Lincoln's friends started him only for the second place. . . ."[14]

When party officials met to pick a site for the convention, Seward's people proposed New York City, Chase's people argued for Cleveland or Columbus, and Bates's people insisted on St. Louis. Norman Judd, Lincoln's friend, who was still serving as secretary of the national committee, suggested that since Illinois did not have a serious candidate Chicago was the logical compromise choice. The others went along. Judd also had himself put in charge of seating guests at the convention.[15]

Weed transported several thousand New Yorkers to Chicago to give vocal support for Seward's candidacy. Midwestern Republicans were not impressed. "The New Yorkers," one delegate observed, "are a class unknown to Western Republicans—drunk more whiskey as any crowd of Democrats." When the New Yorkers arrived at the convention hall, the Wigwam, they found that most of their seats were occupied by local Chicagoans who had been issued tickets by the industrious Judd. The placement of Seward's name in nomination for President nevertheless produced a deafening uproar. When Lincoln's name was proposed, Judd's legions responded. An Illinois delegate reported:

> No mortal ever before saw such a scene. The idea of us Hoosiers and Suckers being outscreamed would have been as bad to them as the loss of their man. Five thousand people at once leaped to their seats, women not wanting in the num-

ber, and the wild yell made soft vesper breathings of all that had preceded. No language can describe it. A thousand steam whistles, ten acres of hotel gongs, a tribe of Comanches, headed by a choice vanguard from pandemonium, might have mingled in the scene unnoticed.[16]

The size and enthusiasm of the demonstration, according to some who were there, transformed Lincoln into a serious candidate. On the first ballot, Seward led with 173½ votes, followed by Lincoln with 102, and Cameron, Chase, and Bates, each with about 50. Greeley, whom Weed had denied even a seat in the New York delegation, hurried about the convention floor, assuring any delegates who would listen that "Seward could not even carry New York."

Lincoln, waiting in Springfield, had instructed his managers to make no deals to secure the nomination. In the turmoil of the convention, they did what they believed the situation required. Approaching agents of Simon Cameron, one of the master political spoilsmen of the time, they promised that support now would be rewarded with recognition by a Lincoln administration. (As in fact it was: Lincoln made Cameron secretary of war, a post which he used shamelessly to provide jobs and financial manna for the faithful of the Pennsylvania Republican party.) On the second ballot, Pennsylvania switched to Lincoln, and a rush for the evident victor began. On the third ballot, Lincoln was nominated. Greeley, making his way to the New York delegation, was delighted to find Weed bathed in tears.

Lincoln's managers offered the vice-presidential nomination to Edwin Morgan of New York, who firmly turned it down. The prize was then bestowed on Senator Hannibal Hamlin of Maine. Party leaders worried that the New Yorkers might plan to sit out the election. Their concern was unfounded. Within a week Weed was with Lincoln in Springfield planning the fall campaign.

Faced with a three-way division among their opponents, the Republicans rolled toward victory. Marching clubs known as "Wide Awakes" paraded through northern cities and towns, whipping up enthusiasm for the Republican ticket. A little before midnight on November 6, Simon Cameron wired Lincoln: "Pennsylvania 70,000 for you. New York safe. Glory enough." The Republican era had begun.

REPUBLICAN IDEOLOGY

Lincoln, in one of those aphorisms of his that are more subtle than they at first appear, once said that the two great parties had stolen each other's clothes. And so it seemed: the more equalitarian of the two parties, the Democrats, had become the defenders of slavery; while the Republican party, descended from the relatively conservative Federalists and Whigs, championed human rights and social justice. Underscoring this transformation, the Republicans—and not only those with Democratic origins—emphasized their ties to the individualistic and socially progressive philosophy of Thomas Jefferson. Lincoln said that he had "never had a feeling politically that did not spring from the sentiments embodied" in Jefferson's Declaration of Independence.

Yet the deeper significance of Lincoln's metaphor is sometimes missed: the *clothes* had been changed, but the *bodies* remained the same. The Democrats, despite the incubus of slavery they now carried, and despite the adherence of some prominent businessmen and wealthy individuals, particularly in New York, remained in most parts of the country the party of those, other than blacks, who had not yet made it in American society or who viewed market capitalism with suspicion or dread. The Republicans, while firmly committed to equality before the law and acting as social liberators against slavery, were from the beginning the party more identified with moral puritanism and emerging industrial capitalism.

The Republicans rejected the argument of the philosophers of the Enlightenment and the British utilitarians that self-interest is the only legitimate starting point for moral philosophy. One of the worst aspects of slavery, Lincoln said in 1854, was that it forced "good men into insisting there is no right principle of action but self-interest." For Lincoln, as J. David Greenstone has pointed out, individual freedom was not "natural liberty" to do as one pleased; rather, as it had been for the early Puritans, it was "civil liberty" to do "that only which is good, just, and honest." Freedom, in other words, in the Republican view, was not a self-sufficient political or economic value but a quality that derives its moral authority from the role with which transcendent purpose has vested the human individual. Through both specific reference and rhetorical style, Lincoln invoked the biblical tradition of divine justice and purpose rather than the Enlightenment standard of unconditioned self-fulfillment. The Founders, he said in a speech in Springfield in 1857, "meant to set up a standard maxim for a free society which should be . . . constantly looked to, constantly labored for, and even though never perfectly attained, constantly approximated, and thereby constantly spreading and deepening its influence," to the benefit of "all people of all colors everywhere."[17]

Ordered liberty, the Republicans believed, could best be achieved through political *nationalism* and economic *capitalism*. The Republicans' opposition to slavery, at least to the spread of slavery, was the underlying moral cause of the Civil War and was increasingly invoked by Lincoln as the war continued. But the issue on which the war began, and which chiefly motivated most of the combatants on both sides, was, not slavery, which Lincoln took no step to end until the war was well advanced and then only in areas controlled by the Confederacy, but the question of whether the nation was a pragmatic federation of states, as Democrats such as Stephen Douglas had argued and even many Whigs had believed, or an indissoluble political and social union, as the Republicans insisted.

The secession of seven southern states before Lincoln's inauguration, and of four more when the President resorted to arms to put down the rebellion, directly challenged the Republicans' concept of nationalism. The nation, Lincoln maintained, was anterior to federation and took precedence over even the Constitution.

"Was it possible," he asked, when the constitutionality of some of his wartime measures was challenged, "to lose the nation and yet preserve the Constitution?" The outcome of the war, a Republican journal editorialized in 1865, marked "an epoch by the consolidation of nationality under democratic forms. . . . The territorial, political, and historical oneness of the nation is now ratified by the blood of thousands of her sons. . . . The prime issue of the war was between nationality one and indivisible, and the loose and changeable federation of independent States."[18]

Within the political framework of nationalism, the Republicans claimed, free-enterprise industrial capitalism provided the economic setting most conducive to republican democracy. "In April, 1861," James Garfield told the House of Representatives three years after the war ended, "there began in this country an industrial revolution . . . as far-reaching in its consequences as the political and military revolution through which we have passed." The Republicans saw no conflict between equality under the law and economic competition. Quite the contrary: "Advancement," Lincoln declared, "—improvement in condition—is the order of things in a society of equals." Lincoln's description of a free economy reflected a social ideal that was not far from Jefferson's: "Men, with their families . . . work for themselves, on their farms, in their houses, and in their shops, taking the whole product to themselves, and asking no favors of capital on one hand nor of hired labor or slaves on the other." Yet Lincoln's law practice in Springfield had been largely devoted to representing corporations that already were organizing the economy into larger and larger units. He seems to have had some misgivings about the process but believed that its results would be on the whole beneficial. "I don't believe in a law to prevent a man getting rich," he told striking employees of the New Haven shoe industry in 1859. "It would do more harm than good. So while we do not propose war on capital we do wish to allow the humblest man an equal chance to get rich with everybody else." There was, he said, no "such thing as a free hired laborer being fixed to that condition for life."[19]

Lincoln's view of the social role of property, which was fully shared by the leaders of his party, including such so-called radicals as Thaddeus Stevens and Charles Sumner, was wholly Lockean. "Property," he said in 1863, "is the fruit of labor; property is desirable; is a positive good in the world. That some should be rich shows that others may become rich, and hence is just encouragement to industry and enterprise."[20]

The Republicans were not shy about using the federal government to help achieve their economic and social objectives. While carrying on a war of enormous magnitude accompanied by deep social discord, Lincoln and the Republican majority in Congress pushed through an unprecedented body of domestic legislation: the Homestead Act of 1862, making public land in the West available free to settlers who would promise to develop it; the Agricultural College Act of 1862, sponsored by Representative Justin Morrill of Vermont, offering assistance to the states to establish "agricultural and mechanical colleges" (the origin of most American state universities); creation of the first national paper currency and suppression of the currencies formerly printed by state banks; the National Banking Act of 1863, drafted in consultation with Wall Street financiers like the Morgans, providing capital essential for industrial investment; chartering of the Union Pacific and Central Pacific railroads in 1862, leading to completion of the first transcontinental railroad in 1869; establishment in 1864 of the Immigration Bureau, to help attract labor from abroad; and the Thirteenth Amendment, abolishing slavery, in 1865.

The war itself helped stimulate industrial enterprise. Philip Armour used millions acquired from supplying beef to the Union army to establish a gigantic meatpacking enterprise, making Chicago the center of the industry. Thomas Scott, vice president of the Pennsylvania Railroad and assistant secretary of war, began the rationalization of the railroad industry. John D. Rockefeller plowed back profits from government contracts to underwrite the consolidation of the petroleum industry. Young J. Pierpont Morgan arranged financing for arms manufacturers. In California, Leland Stanford, Mark Hopkins, Collis P. Huntington, and Charles Crocker (the "Big Four") launched a business empire based on subsidies paid by the federal and state governments to help finance construction of the Central Pacific Railroad. Jay Cooke, the Philadelphia financier, directed the marketing of federal government securities, which by the end of the war had produced a national debt of more than $2 billion, largely owned by wealthy individuals and financial institutions. The Hamiltonian strategy of wedding business interests to strong national government once more led to dynamic economic growth—once more at the cost of rampant materialism, increased economic disparity between rich and poor, and widespread governmental corruption.

LINCOLN AS PARTY LEADER

Both to mobilize support for the war effort and to manage social change, Lincoln relied heavily on the political leverage supplied by the Republican party. His first cabinet gave representation to all major party factions: Seward as secretary of state; Chase at the treasury; Cameron (reluctantly appointed) as secretary of war; Edward Bates, Greeley's candidate for President, as attorney general; Montgomery Blair as postmaster general; and Gideon Wells of Connecticut, another former Jacksonian, as secretary of the navy. Seward, with whom the President's relations at first were chilly, soon became his closest ally. Other members of the cabinet tended to band together against Seward, but Lincoln repeatedly invoked the need for party unity to prevent his ouster.

Chase, who thirsted to succeed Lincoln, became the greatest problem. The ambitious treasury secretary believed that his popularity with Radical Republicans in Congress made him invulnerable to removal. Five times Chase submitted his resignation and each time Lincoln refused, in part to limit the Ohioan's freedom to maneuver within the party. When Chase offered his resignation a sixth time in 1864, after Lincoln's renomination for a second term had been assured, the President, to Chase's great astonishment and chagrin, accepted. Lincoln later made Chase Chief Justice of the Supreme Court—after Chase had helped him carry Ohio in 1864.[21]

Chase's departure from the cabinet gave too much weight in the administration to the Blair faction, whose conservative views on race issues were coming under growing fire from Republicans in Congress. Lincoln reluctantly dropped Montgomery Blair, with whom his personal relations were close, as postmaster general. Blair, too, still hoping for future rewards from the Republican party, gave strong support to Lincoln's reelection.

Early in Lincoln's first term a Radical Republican faction developed in Congress, led by Thaddeus Stevens of Pennsylvania in the House and Charles Sumner of Massachusetts in the Senate. The Radicals wanted to move faster and farther on slavery and race issues than Lincoln at first was prepared to go.

Lincoln had attacked slavery as a moral evil throughout his political career. After witnessing as a young man the slave trade in action in New Orleans, he is reputed to have said that if he ever got the chance he would "hit that thing and hit it hard." In 1854 he called for recognition of "the profound central truth that slavery is wrong and ought to be dealt with as a wrong." But Lincoln, at least before he became President, was no believer in social equality between the races. The natural tension between races, he argued, made it impossible for whites and blacks to live together as equals. His preferred solution was the colonization of most blacks to the Caribbean or Central America. "There is an unwillingness on the part of our people," he told a conference of northern black leaders early in his presidency, "harsh as it may be, for you colored people to remain with us."[22]

As the war continued, consuming hundreds of thousands of lives and devastating entire regions, Lincoln's sense of human mutuality and respect for blacks, who after 1863 served in large numbers in the Union army, deepened. By the time of his second inaugural in 1865, he saw the overthrow of slavery, and the war it had required, as a tragic moral drama: ". . . if God wills that it continue until all the wealth piled by the bondsman's 250 years of unrequited toil shall be sunk, and until every drop of blood drawn with the lash shall be paid by another drawn with the sword, as was said 3,000 years ago, so still it must be said, 'The judgments of the Lord are true and righteous altogether.'" But he always gave higher priority to winning the war against the Confederacy than to bringing justice to blacks—believing, no doubt, that the latter depended on the former.

As the end of the war approached, Lincoln took steps to facilitate limited participation by blacks in political life. But he remained sensitive to white resistance. When a free state administration was formed in 1864 in Louisiana, occupied by Union troops, Lincoln wrote the newly installed governor: "I barely suggest for your private consideration, whether some of the colored people not be let in—as for instance, the very intelligent, and especially those who have fought gallantly in our ranks. . . . But this is only a suggestion, not to the public, but to you alone." (The governor, a southern unionist, organized a solidly white administration.)

Lincoln's hope for the postwar South was that the former southern Whigs, the men who had voted for John Bell in 1860, would rally to the Republican party and form state administrations of moderate conservative character.[23]

The Radical Republicans were of quite a different mind. From the start of the war, they pressed for immediate emancipation, enrollment of black troops in the Union army, and confiscation of property owned by supporters of the Confederacy. "We have entered upon a struggle," wrote a Massachusetts abolitionist in 1861, "which ought not to be allowed to end until the Slave Power is completely subjugated, and *emancipation made certain.*" When Lincoln moved slowly on all these matters, the Radicals pressured him relentlessly through their Committee on the Conduct of the War. Yet, as Eric McKitrick has pointed out, the Radicals were tied to Lincoln by shared party interest and basic ideology. Chafe though they might at his relative caution, they never doubted that he was preferable to any Democrat. Some of the Radicals plotted in 1864 to substitute Chase or Frémont as the Republican candidate for President, but when their efforts failed most of them supported Lincoln, both at the convention and in the general election. At "most crucial points" in his administration, Lincoln sought the support of the Radicals, and almost always he got it. The President's relations with Stevens were civil and with Sumner cordial.[24]

The deep division in the North was not between Lincoln and the Radicals, but between virtually all Republicans and those, mostly Democrats, who favored a negotiated settlement of the war and a conciliatory approach to the southern slaveowners. Through skillful use of the Republican party structure, Lincoln was able to hold radicals and moderates together in a coalition that withstood assault from opponents who aimed at a fundamental change in national policy. "The tensions and conflicts of the Lincoln administration . . . were considerable. But without a party apparatus to harness and direct them, they would surely have been unmanageable."[25]

Jefferson Davis, as McKitrick has shown, suffered grievously from lack of a comparable party apparatus in the South. The founders of the Confederacy, in keeping with their claim that they were returning to the constitutional intent of the Founders, abjured political parties. The result was recurring deadlock and ultimate chaos. Unlike Lincoln, who received strong support from the Republican governors who presided over northern statehouses, President Davis could invoke no bond of party loyalty to keep southern governors in line. Lacking a common party interest, some southern governors were soon holding back troops and pursuing their separate courses, at times defying national policies called for by Davis. Alexander Stephens, the Vice President of the Confederacy, a former Whig, disliked Davis, who had been a Democrat, and spent most of the war in a sulk. Hannibal Hamlin, in contrast, gave Lincoln what help he could, and when political expediency in 1864 dictated that he step aside to make room for Andrew Johnson to become Lincoln's running mate, he accepted without a murmur. (He returned a few years later to the Senate, where he served as a loyal Republican until 1881.)[26]

Even the lack of an organized opposition handicapped Davis. There was no structure representing his political opponents with which he could negotiate. And he could not score against a visible antagonistic political force, as Lincoln did against the Democrats in the North.

The Confederacy operated under such dire circumstances, from first to last, that its experience cannot be taken as a fair test of any of its institutions. But it at least showed that the absence of party, far from strengthening administration in time of national crisis, was if anything a source of added political strain.

Lincoln had absorbed well the lessons of party combat in Illinois. As President, he went beyond any of his predecessors in using the resources of the federal government to advance his party at both the national and state levels. In 1862 war weariness in the North produced a reaction against the Republicans, enabling the Democrats to recapture the governorship of New York and control of several state legislatures. Oliver P. Morton, Republican governor of Indiana, faced Democratic majorities in both houses of the legislature, which by refusing to pass an appropriations bill left the state treasury bare. Lincoln for a time dipped into federal funds to keep Morton's administration solvent.[27]

In 1863 prospects appeared bleak for several other Republican governors seeking reelection. Andrew Curtin, Republican governor of Pennsylvania, was challenged by a Democratic opponent who promised to test the constitutionality of the national conscription act, passed earlier that year. Federal government employees from Pennsylvania were assessed 1 percent of their salaries to help pay Curtin's campaign expenses. On election day they were given free railroad passes and sent home to vote. The War Department authorized field commanders to furlough as many Pennsylvania soldiers as could be spared. Workers at the Philadelphia arsenal were marched to the polls "like cattle to the slaughter." Curtin won narrowly by 15,000 votes.

In Connecticut, Republican Governor William Buckingham was opposed by a Democrat who called for an end to the war. Soldiers were sent home to vote, and Connecticut arms manufacturers were advised that future contracts might depend on large turnouts among their workers for the Republican ticket. Buckingham squeaked through with a margin of only 3,000.

The contest the Republicans were most determined to win was in Ohio, where the Democratic candidate for governor was former Representative Clement Vallandigham, the North's most notorious "copperhead," as southern sympathizers were called, who had recently been arrested by military authorities for "seditious utterances" (one of the instances in which Lincoln was accused of violating the Constitution). Federal resources, including furloughed troops, federal employees sent home to vote, and funds assessed from government jobholders, were poured into Ohio. Secretary Chase, joined by Governor Morton from Indiana, stumped the state. Ohio remained under Republican administration by a walloping 100,000-vote majority.[28]

In 1864 Lincoln himself confronted seemingly formidable opposition for reelection from the Democratic candidate for President, General George B. McClelland, who had organized the Union army into a disciplined fighting force after early reverses but never quite succeeded in leading it to decisive victory. Lincoln ran as the candidate of a hastily assembled Unionist party, a coalition of Republicans and Democrats who supported continuation of the war. Former Senator Andrew Johnson of Tennessee, a Democrat who had remained loyal to the Union when his state seceded, was put on the ticket for Vice President to give an appearance of bipartisanship. Republican organizations at the national and state levels, however, retained their identities and carried most of the load in Lincoln's campaign.

Republican operatives swung into action in ways that even the most ruthless or adventurous among today's campaign managers would not dare attempt: "The National Republican Committee," a Washington observer reported, "have taken full possession of all the Capitol buildings, and the committee rooms of the Senate and House of Representatives are filled with clerks, busy in mailing Lincoln documents all over the loyal states. . . . The Post Office Department, of course, is attending to the lion's share of this work. Eighty bags of mail matter, all containing Lincoln documents, are daily sent to Sherman's army." Henry J. Raymond, editor of the *New York Times,* took on the added role of chairman of the Union party. He efficiently assessed campaign contributions from all federal government employees. From Pennsylvania alone, 10,000 soldiers were given furloughs so they could go home to vote.[29]

The capture of Atlanta by General Sherman's army in September probably did more than all the party machinery combined to assure Lincoln's reelection. Nevertheless, the victory was one in which party workers could take justifiable pride: a sweep by the national ticket of every state in the Union except New Jersey, Delaware, and Kentucky; increased "Unionist" majorities in both houses of Congress; and return of Republican control to every northern statehouse.

TRIUMPH OF THE RADICALS

Lincoln's assassination on April 15, 1865, one week after General Lee's surrender to General Grant at Appomattox Court House, removed a vital link that had helped hold the Republican coalition together. Though none of the party factions had been wholly satisfied with Lincoln, his political skill and national popularity had served to keep them all running on the same track.

Andrew Johnson succeeded to the presidency and at first seemed to tilt toward the Radicals. "Treason must be made odious," Johnson had said in 1864, "and traitors must be punished and impoverished." A group of Radical congressmen quickly arranged a meeting with the new President. "Johnson, we have faith in you," said Senator Ben Wade of Ohio, a leading Radical. "By the Gods, there will be no trouble now in running the government." Johnson replied: "I hold this: . . . *treason* is a *crime,* and crime must be punished." Senator Zachariah Chandler of Michigan, another Radical, wrote to his wife: "I believe that the Almighty continued Mr. Lincoln in office as long as he was useful, and then substituted a better man to finish the work."[30]

Johnson had made his political career as an opponent of Tennessee's planter oligarchs, whom he seems genuinely to have hated. What no one at first noticed was that he was also a thoroughgoing racist. "White men alone must manage the South," he confided to a political crony. When his policies were challenged in Congress, he made public his dislike for blacks. In a message to Congress opposing black suffrage, he argued that blacks possessed less "capacity for government than any other race of people. No independent government of any form has ever been successful in their hands. On the contrary, wherever they have been left to their own devices they have shown a constant tendency to relapse into barbarism." This was, probably, as Eric Foner points out, the most blatantly racist statement ever made in an official pronouncement by a President of the United States.[31]

Johnson's fears of the effects of black participation in politics caused him to reassess his former low opinion of the southern planter class. Far from wreaking vengeance on officers and supporters of the Confederacy, he was soon restoring them to power in the southern state administrations established under his authority. The new southern state governments began enacting "Black Codes" that severely limited the political and economic rights of former slaves.

The Radicals had not expected that enactment of federal legislation guaranteeing equal rights for blacks would be easy. Resistance to racial equality, said Thaddeus Stevens, would come from the same groups that formerly had resisted emancipation: "When it was first proposed to free the slaves and arm the blacks, did not half the nation tremble? The prim conservatives, the snobs, and the male waiting maids in Congress, were in hysterics." But with the President's support, they had been confident they would prevail. Finding Johnson leading the opposition, they determined "to draw our swords and throw away the scabbards. . . ." In 1866 the Republican majority in Congress passed the Civil Rights Act, which protected blacks from discriminatory legislation by state governments, over Johnson's veto, and enacted, against his resistance, the Fourteenth Amendment, which established equality before the law.[32]

Breaking with the Radicals, Johnson, who aspired to election to a full term in 1868, looked elsewhere for political support. Leading Democrats, sensing an opportunity to restore their party's fortunes and sharing Johnson's views on southern reconstruction, claimed the President as their own. Horatio Seymour, the Democrat who had been elected governor of New York in the midst of the Civil War, advised Johnson to resist efforts by the Republicans "to keep up hatred towards the South." Seymour, who had close ties to the New York financial community, claimed that the Radicals' plan for reconstruction was a "blind . . . not only to keep the Republicans in power but to keep New England in power." Johnson, however, was shrewd enough to recognize that the Democratic party was still too tainted by the equivocal behavior of many of its leaders during the war to make it a viable base in national politics.[33]

In the Republican party, Johnson at first found his principal allies among the Blairites. When Johnson at his inauguration, apparently under the influence of whiskey he had drunk to ward off an illness, delivered "a rambling and strange harangue," the Blairs hustled him off to the family mansion at Silver Spring, in the Maryland countryside outside Washington, to recuperate. Discovering that Johnson shared their conservative views on race, they took new hope that the Republican party might be made into an instrument of the former Jacksonian consensus, freed of association with slavery, and with the Radicals driven into a separate party of their own. "If we can dispose of the slave question," said Montgomery Blair, "we shall have the miscegenationists [his name for anyone who favored equality for blacks] in a party to themselves and can beat them easily."[34]

The flaw in the Blairs' plan, which Johnson largely approved, was that not only the Radical Republicans, who were indeed a minority within the party, but also the great majority of moderates were appalled by the swift restoration of former supporters of the Confederacy to positions of power in the South. Even Republicans who had qualms about black suffrage were outraged by the Black Codes. "Whoever assented to the President's plan of Reconstruction," observed Representative James G. Blaine of Maine, a rising star among mainstream Republicans, ". . . assented to the full right of the rebellious states to continue legislation of this odious type."[35]

Sturdier support for Johnson came from Seward, who stayed on as secretary of state. Gradually recovering from the effects of an attempt on his life by a participant in the same conspiracy that had killed Lincoln, Seward tried to steer Johnson toward a position that would win the backing of a majority of northern voters. Many in the North, Seward calculated, were not keen on giving the vote to blacks but would not stand for repressive state legislation that would virtually restore slavery in everything but name, as though the Civil War had never happened.

In association with Weed and Henry Raymond, who was still editing the *Times* while serving as a member of the House of Representatives, Seward tried to keep alive the Union party on which Lincoln had run for reelection in 1864, leaving the Republican party to wither into a rump containing a few Radicals. It was a politically fatal misjudgment. The Republican party had become identified in the minds of millions in the North with the cause for which so many had died and practically all had suffered. The period of party fluidity that had preceded the war was over. Party loyalties had hardened. By turning their backs on the Republican party, Seward and Weed seemed to many to be turning against the cause itself.

Events during the campaign leading up to the 1866 midterm election, which Johnson and Seward hoped would increase support for the administration in Congress, ended what small chance there had been for maintaining the Union party as a political force. At a Union party convention in Philadelphia, former copperheads played highly visible roles. In New York the party was drawn into an electoral alliance with Tammany Hall, currently led by the notorious William Marcy Tweed. Early in October, Raymond, who had remained Unionist national chairman, gave up the struggle and scuttled back to the regular Republican ranks. Weed stuck to the end, raising money for the Unionist-Democratic fusion ticket.[36]

Finding themselves cut off from the patronage resources controlled by the administration, Radical Republicans in the House formed their own fundraising campaign committee—direct ancestor of the current National Republican Congressional Committee. Democrats in the House responded by setting up a competing campaign committee—ancestor of the current Democratic Congressional Campaign Committee. (The separate campaign committees now operated by the two parties in the Senate were established after the passage in 1913 of the Seventeenth Amendment calling for the direct election of senators.)

When the returns were counted, the Radical Republicans were found to have strengthened their position in Congress. In New York the regular Republicans, led by Radicals like Greeley and Representative Roscoe Conkling of Utica, won a narrow victory.

Johnson and the congressional Republicans, now dominated by Radicals, moved toward confrontation. "The whole fabric of southern society *must* be changed," Stevens told the House, "and never can it be done if this opportunity is lost." The white-supremacy state governments in the South that Johnson had approved were swept aside, and Republican administrations, elected with the support of blacks enfranchised by congressional edict, took their place.[37]

Johnson did what he could to resist intrusion by Congress into the affairs of the executive branch. On March 13, 1868, the House, with Stevens as chief prosecutor, brought articles of impeachment against the President. After trial in the Senate, presided over by Chief Justice Chase, 35 senators voted for conviction—one short of the required two-thirds majority. Only seven Republican senators voted for acquittal (though more were said to be prepared to support the President if their votes had been needed).

Seeking to pull the party together after the tumultuous divisions of the Johnson administration, the Republicans in 1868 chose as their candidate for President Ulysses S. Grant, who had led the Union army to final victory. The Democrats, after turning aside a bid from the compulsively ambitious Chase (who also had made known his availability to the Republicans), nominated Horatio Seymour, a moderate conservative. Many of the Jacksonians who had defected to the Republicans in the 1850s, foremost among them the Blairs, returned to the Democracy. Awarded the Democratic nomination for Vice President, Frank Blair announced that a Democratic victory would assure the restoration of white-supremacy governments in the South. It proved not to be a popular message. Grant carried every northern state except New York, New Jersey, and Oregon, plus seven southern states in which many former supporters of the Confederacy had been disenfranchised, for a total of 214 electoral votes to 80 for Seymour.[38]

Grant, a military genius who, with his use of advanced technology and logistics against the Confederacy, may fairly be said to have invented modern warfare, had little political interest or skill. Though he had briefly served as secretary of war under Johnson—thereby playing a role in the administrative standoff that had provided the excuse for the House's vote to impeach—he had finally come down on the side of the Radicals, who had approved his nomination. He made no objection to continuation of the patronage machine that Lincoln had installed in the executive branch, but he turned over control of its operation to a quadrumvirate of Radical senators.

The Radicals had won. But it was a somewhat different kind of Radicalism than what had existed during the war and immediate postwar years. Stevens had died in 1868, a few weeks after Johnson's acquittal (to be buried, at his request, in a cemetery for blacks in Lancaster, Pennsylvania, as a symbol of his commitment to racial equality). Sumner remained in the Senate, but he had always been more of an orator and scholar than a political strategist. Active leadership among the Radicals, and therefore as long as Grant was President in the Republican party, passed to the Senate quadrumvirate: Roscoe Conkling of New York, who moved up from the House in 1867; Simon Cameron of Pennsylvania, who returned to the Senate after a tour as ambassador to Russia (where Lincoln had sent him in 1862 when the extent of corruption in the War Department made it prudent to get him out of the cabinet); Oliver Morton of Indiana; and Zachariah Chandler of Michigan.

The Republican party had established itself as more than a wartime or single-issue phenomenon and had made itself, for a time at least, the dominant force in national politics and government. The victorious Republican leaders, while much concerned with the spoils of office, were determined to put into effect the doctrines of nationalism, market capitalism, and traditional Protestant morality that had formed their party's ideological core from the start.

7

MACHINE POLITICS

The Gilded Age

THE PERIOD FROM ULYSSES GRANT'S first election as President in 1868 to the early 1890s is often titled the "Gilded Age"—an era of widespread political corruption and ruthless business conduct, but also a time of astonishing economic growth and intense religious vitality. The period has also been called the "golden age of parties." Party organizations seem to have had more influence on election outcomes than at any time before or since. Parties in government were by American standards unusually united, and parties in the electorate commanded enthusiastic mass followings. Parties, James Bryce wrote in his classic study of *The American Commonwealth,* first published in 1888, had become "to the organs of government almost what the motor nerves are to the muscles, sinews, and bones of the human body."[1]

The Republicans' secure control of the national government ended with the financial panic of 1873 and the withdrawal of Union troops from the conquered South in the mid-1870s. From 1874 to 1894, the Democrats won almost as many presidential contests as the Republicans—three for the Republicans to two for the Democrats. And, though the Republicans controlled the Senate for all but four of those 20 years, the Democrats controlled the House of Representatives for all but four. There were only three two-year congressional terms during which one party simultaneously controlled both the presidency and both houses of Congress (the Republicans in 1881–82 and 1889–90, and the Democrats in 1893–94).

Party competition was close at the national level and in states like New York, Connecticut, New Jersey, Ohio, Indiana, California, and Oregon. Party rivalry was also intense in Pennsylvania, Illinois, Michigan, and Wisconsin, though the Republicans usually prevailed. As a result, the parties developed far more elaborate organizations than had existed before the Civil War. Parties, W. D. Burnham has written, were like "armies drawn up for combat." There was, Arthur M. Schlesinger, Jr., suggests, a "cult of parties." This was the period in which the cartoonist Thomas Nast popularized the symbols of the Republican elephant and the Democratic donkey (as well as the Tammany tiger)—symbols that seemed remarkably apt at the time and have been used ever since.[2]

Elections were marked by torchlight parades, gigantic rallies, and massive pilgrimages to the hometowns of presidential candidates who conducted "front porch campaigns." Voter turnout was consistently higher than during any other period in American history.

In Congress, party unity on roll-call votes fluctuated somewhat from term to term but was generally high, at least by the standards of American politics, reflecting the ability of national party organizations to hold members in line. Party cohesion in the Senate reached a record high in the session that began in 1889: 87 percent for the Republicans and 72 percent for the Democrats. The level of cohesion achieved in the House during the same session was surpassed only in 1903–05.[3]

Political bosses like Matthew Stanley Quay in Pennsylvania and John Kelly in New York introduced major institutional changes into the life of parties. Many of those changes endured at least through the 1960s, and some continue to influence political behavior at the beginning of the twenty-first century.

THE TAMMANY MODEL

New waves of immigration into eastern and midwestern cities, industrial towns, and mining regions produced fresh supplies of voters for a reviving Democracy. In some cities, such as Philadelphia, Pittsburgh, Cincinnati, San Francisco, and even to some extent Chicago, many immigrants were enlisted by local Republican organizations. (In Philadelphia, Republican organizers reminded Italian immigrants that the party of Garibaldi in Italy was called the Republican party and assured them that the American Republicans stood for the same ideals.) But in most cities and industrial towns Catholic immigrants from Ireland, Italy, Poland, and Bohemia generally felt more comfortable in Democratic ranks. (Jews, on the other hand, were heavily Republican.) In many states the Republican party carried more than a tinge of the nativism that had contributed to the party's emergence in the 1850s. The Whig program of moral reform, which the Republicans now championed, included support for causes like prohibition and the outlawing of commercial activity on Sundays—causes that most European immigrants, even German Protestants, found offensive if not threatening. Particularly after the founding of the Prohibition party in 1869, most Republican politicians felt obliged to go on the line for government regulation of morals. As the pace of immigration increased, Republican-controlled legislatures in Illinois and Wisconsin passed laws prohibiting the use of any language except English in the public schools, causing heavy defections among previously loyal foreign-born Republicans, particularly Germans.[4]

Tammany Hall, the principal Democratic organization in New York City, provided a kind of model for what could be done through the mobilization of the new immigrants. "In the weeks prior to the election of 1868," Martin Shefter writes, "the judges allied with the Tweed Ring naturalized several thousand new citizens, and expanded the number of registered voters by more than 30 percent." The immediate result of political control based on an electorate inexperienced in democracy was corruption even more brazen than that practiced by the party bosses in Washington and the state capitals.[5]

Tammany during the Tweed era, Shefter points out, was not only corrupt but politically inefficient and chaotic. Though portrayed in Nast's cartoons and by the popular press as a despotic boss, William Marcy Tweed in fact "was unable to command the obedience of other politicians; instead he was compelled to purchase with cash bribes the support of state legislators, county supervisors, and even his immediate associates." Cash-flow problems drove Tweed and his cronies to dig deeper and deeper into the public till. Between 1867 and 1871, New York's municipal indebtedness tripled, finally arousing concern among members of the city's financial community, who "through purchase of municipal bonds during the period of Ring rule" had permitted their interests to "become intimately intertwined with that of the city government."[6]

After Tweed and his closest associates were packed off to jail in 1871, John Kelly assumed leadership of Tammany and began to build a disciplined machine. Kelly, it was said, "found Tammany a horde and left it a political army." During the Kelly era, which lasted until the middle of the 1880s, Tammany established centralized control over Democratic nominations for all city offices and brought graft down to tolerable levels. The machine shifted from simple vote-buying to providing useful services for the often non-English-speaking residents of the New York slums. "A bucket of coals and basket of food, a rent payment, funeral expenses, clothing and material benefits were made available to those in need, as were interventions with the law such as providing bail, cutting the red tape to receive a license or permit, or getting charges dismissed." Where Tweed had sold political favors to business freebooters like Jim Fiske and Jay Gould, Kelly preferred to deal with "swallowtail" (frock-coated) conservative Democratic attorneys and businessmen like Samuel Tilden, William Grace of W. R. Grace & Co., and Abram Hewitt, an iron manufacturer who became Democratic national chairman in 1876. William Whitney, a leading swallowtail, explained in 1876 that Kelly maintained "efficient control over certain elements of the party," making it unwise to "dispense with his services." By the end of Kelly's reign, and the advent in the late 1880s of the even more businesslike Richard Croker, Tammany was not only supreme in New York City but an important force in state and national politics.[7]

Partly through observation of the Tammany model, and partly through independent recognition of opportunity, Democratic politicians in other eastern and midwestern cities formed similar organizations. In Illinois, Minnesota, Michigan, New Jersey, Massachusetts, and Connecticut, bodies of traditional rural Jacksonian Democrats were joined, and eventually overshadowed, by immigrant-based machines in Chicago, St. Paul, Detroit, Jersey City, Boston, Hartford, and New Haven (all of which, except for St. Paul, had earlier been Whig or Republican strongholds).

THE REPUBLICAN BOSSES

While the Democrats were making headway in eastern and midwestern cities, the Republicans during the early 1870s remained dominant in the national government and most northern states. The Republican Senate leaders, Conkling of New York, Cameron of Pennsylvania, Morton of Indiana, and Chandler of Michigan, joined by John Logan of Illinois after his election to the Senate in 1871, put together a national machine, based largely on federal patronage, that was far more extensive and politically formidable than that of the Jacksonian Democrats in the 1830s.

These senators were, above all, practical politicians: believers in the spoils system, men who pursued politics for material profit and ideological satisfaction, but also for the sheer joy of winning, for delight in the exercise of power for its own sake. Although their personalities varied, most were, as was said of Chandler, "always ready to smoke a cigar, take a drink, play a game of cards, or tell a story." To an extent that not even Van Buren and Weed had been, they were "bosses," a type originated by American democracy—founders and leaders of political organizations based on patronage and governmental favors that dominated entire states for extended periods. They supported black suffrage in the South in part because they believed black voters could turn the South into an impregnable bastion of Republicanism that would guarantee Republican majorities in the electoral college even if the party should lose some of its northern citadels. The Republicans had always been responsive to business interests, but Conkling, pompous and domineering, and Cameron, lean and somber, in particular drew the party close to the business community, raising huge war chests from corporate contributions and establishing interlocking relationships between business and political leaders.[8]

It was no accident that the Radical bosses were senators, not governors. Senators, who until the enactment of the Seventeenth Amendment in 1913 were elected by state legislatures, had special reason to maintain control of state party organizations. Under the Grant administration, they also had access to the means. In the early 1870s the state Republican machines relied for much of their sustenance on federal patronage, which Grant allowed to be doled out by chosen senators.

Following a somewhat different track was James G. Blaine, elected Speaker of the House in 1869. Far more charismatic than the Senate bosses, Blaine ("the Plumed Knight") practiced a form of political leadership that depended more on direct appeal to voters than on command of a patronage-fed organization. He had broader knowledge of the world and seems to have been more interested in policy-making—years later, as secretary of state he was instrumental in founding the Pan-American Union. Yet he was fully as susceptible as the bosses to the lure of financial corruption. Charges of graft, never fully proved, hung over his career. ("Burn this letter," he wrote at the end of a compromising message to a former associate that was read before a congressional committee.)

The bosses distrusted Blaine, in part because they sensed he possessed gifts they lacked, but also because he sometimes violated the rough-and-ready code of their profession. An honest politician, Simon Cameron once said, was one "who, when you buy him, he stays bought." Blaine did not always stay bought. Moreover he had a biting sense of humor that he did not bother to control. His characterization of Conkling's "turkey gobbler strut" fueled an enduring enmity between the two. Although Blaine undoubtedly had more ability and political imagination than most of the Republicans who reached the presidency between the Civil War and the 1890s, he was hindered by moral blinders that prevented him from achieving the first rank of national leaders. He belonged to a class of conservative American politicians, including Alexander Hamilton, Henry Clay, and Richard Nixon, who often have seen further and better than most of their contemporaries but who have ultimately been undermined by their own cynicism.

It is a mistake to think of the leaders of the Republican party in the 1870s as hardhearted conservatives who pushed aside the idealistic founding generation and moved the party in a new direction. Actually it was the moderates, like Carl Schurz of Missouri (elected to the Senate in 1868) and the seven Republican senators who had voted to acquit Johnson, who favored a more conciliatory approach toward the white supremacists in the South and a slower pace on civil rights. The moderates, many of whom became active in the Liberal Republican movement of the 1870s, were also concerned over corruption in the Grant administration. But this was a new issue which, though certainly consistent with the Whig program of moral reform, had not been part of the Republicans' original agenda. Blaine and the Republican bosses in the Senate had at least as good a claim as the moderates to the party's founding principles—perhaps better, since it was they who continued, for whatever reason, to press for racial equality. When the Democratic party in the South, in alliance with the terrorist Ku Klux Klan, set out early in the 1870s to deprive blacks of civil and political rights, congressional Republicans in the Radical tradition enacted a series of Enforcement Acts that for the first time made civil violence and intimidation federal crimes.

THE LIBERAL REPUBLICANS

The Liberal Republicans of the early 1870s were not very liberal in the modern sense of the term. They were reformist in that they attacked the spoils system and promised more honest administration of government, and some of them leaned toward freer international trade in contrast to the Republicans' prevailing protectionism. But they proposed no programs of government help for the economically less fortunate, of the kind that Bismarck and others were introducing in Europe, and showed no inclination to redistribute wealth between the haves and the have-nots. To the contrary, they attacked "the fallacy of attempts to benefit humanity by legislation." Their solution to the southern problem was pretty much the same as Johnson's and the Blairs' had been: turn power over to the former white ruling class.[9]

In 1872 the Liberal Republicans had grown so dissatisfied with the Grant administration that they decided, with the support of several influential newspapers, to run their own national ticket. After considering several plausible reformers, including Charles Francis Adams, son of J. Q. Adams (and father of Henry and Brooks), the Liberal Republican convention, manipulated behind the scenes by Frank Blair, nominated Horace Greeley, who, like Chase, though even less realistically, had never quite given up hope of reaching the White House. For Vice President the Liberal Republicans nominated Governor Gratz Brown of Missouri, an ally of Carl Schurz.[10]

The dispirited Democrats met briefly in Baltimore and allowed their leaders to gavel through endorsements of the Liberal Republican ticket. Though the public was exasperated with the Grant administration, most did not regard Greeley as a feasible alternative. Greeley proved an easy target for the Republican tactic of "waving the bloody shirt"—reminding northern voters that the Republican party had upheld the Union during the Civil War. (Some Republican campaigners literally displayed at rallies a blood-soaked Union army uniform, but the term was used rhetorically as well.) Greeley, in a characteristic burst of generosity and bid for attention, had put up part of the bail that got Jefferson Davis out of prison in 1867. Republican orators, led by Zachariah Chandler, made much of this incident. (Greeley in Chandler's place would probably have done the same.)

Grant was easily reelected, winning 286 out of a possible 366 electoral votes. Greeley died a few weeks after the election, and the electoral votes of the six states he had carried were scattered among five Democrats and independents. A good omen for the Democrats' political future was that three southern states—Georgia, Tennessee, and Texas—in which the federal government had permitted the old order to regain power returned to the Democratic column.

A PARTY MACHINE LIKE A RELIGIOUS ORDER

For the Democrats, the presidential election of 1876 seemed to offer a golden opportunity to win the White House for the first time since the Civil War and perhaps to regain their pre-war status as the national majority party. Many voters blamed Republicans for the hard times that followed the financial panic of 1873, and corruption in the second Grant administration was even more flagrant than it had been in the first. Democratic state parties promising the restoration of white supremacy had regained power in most of the South. The Democrats nominated as their presidential candidate Governor Samuel Tilden of New York, who seemed acceptable to all major elements within the party.

The Republicans, in contrast, were bitterly divided. The Senate bosses, now known as "Stalwarts"—a significant change from "Radicals"—were determined to maintain their hold on federal patronage but could not agree on a single candidate for President. Roscoe Conkling and Oliver P. Morton both sought the nomination, but neither would give way to the other and neither had the support of Pennsylvania's Cameron machine (which backed the state's undistinguished governor as a favorite son). Against them, James G. Blaine, whose followers are known to history as the "Halfbreeds" (though the term seems to have been little used at the time outside New York), presented himself as a candidate who could revitalize both the party and the presidency. Out in the country, many rank-and-file Republicans, including many who had been drawn to Liberal Republicanism in 1872, seem to have felt revulsion toward anyone who had been in any way involved in Washington politics during the Grant administration. The Republican national convention, after six indecisive ballots, turned to former Governor Rutherford B. Hayes of Ohio, whose chief attractions were that he appeared to be a decent man and that, as his nominator put it, he had "no personal enmities."[11]

The election was aggressively contested by both parties. Zachariah Chandler, doing a turn as Republican national chairman, directed the Republican campaign from New York, squeezing hard on the bloody shirt, ruthlessly assessing federal employees, and pouring large sums of money into potential swing states such as New York and Indiana. The Democrats, to the extent that their resources permitted, responded in kind, emphasizing government corruption, economic depression, and the Republicans' alignment with blacks. In the South, local Democratic parties, often aided by the Ku Klux Klan, did their best to intimidate, or "bulldoze," black voters. Voter turnout rose to 83 percent—higher even than in 1860, and still a record for American national elections.[12]

On election night early returns indicated a solid Democratic victory. New York, New Jersey, Connecticut, and Indiana swiftly fell to Tilden, and southern states with Democratic state administrations were producing Tilden landslides. Tilden's national majority in the popular vote seemed certain to exceed 200,000. Across the country, gloom settled over the Republican faithful. In New York, national chairman Chandler concluded that the fight was lost and retired to his hotel bedroom.

As the night wore on, however, Tilden's electoral vote stuck just short of a majority. In the early morning hours, someone at New York State Democratic headquarters sent an inquiry to the *New York Times,* reputed to have the best system in the country for gathering election returns, asking for late results from South Carolina, Florida, and Louisiana—three southern states that still had Republican governors. John Reid, editor of the *Times,* a staunchly Republican paper, calculated that if Hayes lost no more northern states and carried the three southern states of which the Democrats seemed unsure, he would have a one-vote majority in the electoral college.[13]

Hurrying to Republican national headquarters, Reid found William E. Chandler, secretary of the Republican national committee, just returned from voting in New Hampshire, "a small man wearing an immense pair of goggles, his hat drawn down over his ears," mulling over late returns in the almost deserted office. Chandler (no relation to Zachariah), the prototypical staffman, at once grasped the import of Reid's calculation. Together the two men rushed upstairs and roused the national chairman. Zachariah Chandler, "in his nightshirt, rubbing sleep from his eyes," recognized "the possibility of saving the day."[14]

What followed, Matthew Josephson writes, "tells us much of the force of the Republican Party organization as a militant institution, resembling certain church orders . . . rather than a political party." The two Chandlers dispatched telegrams to Republican leaders in the three doubtful states: "Hayes elected if we have carried S.C., Fla., and La. Can you hold your state? Answer immediately." The telegrams were signed simply, "Zach." By late afternoon of the next day, the national chairman was sufficiently reassured to issue a flat claim of victory: "Hayes has 185 [electoral] votes and is elected."[15]

Republican agents recruited from New York, Pennsylvania, Ohio, and Illinois fanned out across the three disputed states. William E. Chandler took personal command of the operation in Florida. General William T. Sherman, on orders from President Grant, directed federal army commanders in the South "to see that proper and legal Boards of Canvassers are unmolested in the performance of their duties." Money was distributed freely by Republican agents to official canvassers.

The national Democratic organization, caught at first off balance, retaliated with its own campaign to produce counts favoring Tilden from the three southern states. Agents for Tilden tried to bribe some of the Republican-controlled counting boards, but the counters, after some vacillation, lived up to Simon Cameron's code: having been bought, they stayed bought.

When Congress met in December to receive the electoral college results, rival returns were delivered from each of the three disputed states. A further complication was added by a Democratic challenge to the vote of one elector from Oregon, who had been a federal postmaster at the time of the election and thus had been constitutionally ineligible to serve. The Democratic governor of Oregon proposed to substitute an elector who would vote for Tilden, thereby giving Tilden a one-vote majority in the electoral college even if all the votes of Florida, Louisiana, and South Carolina were counted for Hayes. But the Republican elector, having resigned his postmastership, insisted that he was now qualified.

The Constitution provided that the President of the Senate "in the presence of the Senate and the House of Representative [shall] open all the certificates and the votes shall be counted." Congress, however, at the time had no rule on how the count should be conducted. The Democratic majority in the House maneuvered to assure the election of Tilden, while the Republican majority in the Senate tried to preserve victory for Hayes.

A few days before the count was to begin, Congress appointed a special commission, consisting of five senators, five representatives, and five Supreme Court justices, to decide all disputes. The congressional members of the commission were divided evenly between the parties, but as there were only two Democrats on the Supreme Court, three of the justices had to be Republicans, giving the Republicans a one-vote majority on the commission. (A political independent on the

Court, David Davis, who had been expected to be the swing vote, resigned at the last minute to accept election to the Senate from Illinois.)[16]

The commission decided all disputes along strict party lines, giving Hayes a one-vote majority in the electoral college. Some northern Democrats in the House threatened a filibuster to prevent completion of the count. But conservative and moderate Democrats, apparently including Tilden himself were prepared to go no further in risking civil discord. "The Democratic business men of the country," James Garfield, who managed the Republican case in the House, wrote to Hayes, "are more anxious for quiet than for Tilden." At a series of confidential dinner meetings in Washington, Republican leaders gave assurances to southern Democratic senators that if Hayes became President he would make no further use of federal authority to prevent the restoration of Democratic administrations in southern states. On March 4, under the watchful eye of federal troops, Hayes was sworn in as President.[17]

THE REPUBLICAN FAITHFUL

The 1876 election ended the postwar era of clear Republican dominance in national politics. But it did not restore the Democrats as the normal national majority party. The Democrats took satisfaction that Tilden had won a majority of more than 250,000 in the popular vote and claimed that a majority in the electoral college had been "stolen" by fraudulent manipulation of returns. (The consensus among modern historians is that an honest count would probably have given Hayes the electoral votes of South Carolina and Louisiana, but that Tilden was entitled to the four votes of Florida, awarding him a seven-vote majority in the electoral college.[18] It can fairly be argued, however, that since Tilden's majorities in many southern states were based on brutal intimidation and violence against black voters, an honest and *open* election would still have brought victory to Hayes.) The Democrats could reasonably look forward to regaining control of the national government in some future election.

The Republicans too, however, came out of the election with renewed confidence. The fact that they had survived the "tight squeeze," that when the chips were down their party organization had proved more highly motivated and more dexterous than the opposition, convinced many of them that they, not the Democrats, were now the authentic party of government.

During the next 20 years, this confidence among the Republicans was at times to be severely challenged. Though the Democrats won control of the Senate only twice, they were usually the majority party in the House.

In 1884 the Democrats finally regained the White House, winning a plurality in the popular vote and a small majority in the electoral college for Governor Grover Cleveland of New York, another pro-business Democrat in the line of Seymour and Tilden.

Going into the final days of the campaign, the Republican candidate, Blaine, had seemed to be ahead. But Cleveland's campaign manager, Senator Arthur Gorman of Maryland, hired a stenographer to follow Blaine in hopes of picking up one of his politically damaging wisecracks. What the stenographer caught was Blaine's failure to disavow an introduction by a Protestant clergyman in New York, who praised him as the opponent of the party of "Rum, Romanism, and Rebellion." Gorman, finding the phrase in the stenographer's notes, realized that it would outrage Irish Catholics, who had been well disposed toward Blaine. At Gorman's direction, handbills reporting the offensive remark were spread through Catholic neighborhoods, tipping New York, and the election, to Cleveland.[19]

Four years later, Cleveland again obtained a narrow plurality in the popular vote but lost in the electoral college. In 1892, Cleveland recaptured the presidency with a solid majority in the electoral college (though again with only a plurality in the popular vote).

Nevertheless, the Democrats were unable to translate these relatively good electoral showings into majority party status. Between 1878 and 1896, the Democrats only once, in 1890, won a majority of the popular votes cast nationally for Congress, and never won a majority for president. From 1880 to 1892, Democratic presidential candidates in 21 northern states that cast a total of 715 electoral votes in four presidential elections received only 45 votes. The Democrats were competitive in national elections only because they had a monopoly of electoral votes in the South.

In most northern states, the Republicans usually maintained control of state governments. From the Civil War to 1890, the Republicans lost the governorship only once in Pennsylvania, Michigan, Wisconsin, Kansas, and Rhode Island, and never in Illinois, Iowa, Minnesota, Nebraska, or Vermont. (Vermont, in fact, did not elect its first Democratic governor until 1962.) Massachusetts also was normally Republican, but in 1874 chose a Democratic governor and in 1882 elected as governor the proto-populist Ben Butler, a former Radical Republican running on a Democratic-Greenbacker fusion ticket. Statewide elections were competitive in New York, Indiana, New Jersey, Ohio, and Connecticut, but in all these states there were many counties that were invariably Republican.

In many rural areas and small towns of the North, Democrats were almost extinct. "The Republican party was not a faction," Brand Whitlock wrote, looking back in 1915 on his boyhood in a small town in Ohio, "was not a group, not a wing, it was an institution like those Emerson speaks of in his essay on politics, rooted like oak trees in the center around which men group themselves as best they can. . . . It was inconceivable that any self-respecting man should be a Democrat. There were, perhaps, Democrats in Lighttown; but then there were rebels in Alabama, and in the Ku Klux Klan, about which we read in the evening in the Cincinnati *Gazette*."[20]

What accounted for this continued Republican hegemony in most of New England, much of New York, Pennsylvania, and the old Northwest, and almost all of the newer states of the Great Plains?

There was, first of all, the enduring legacy of the Civil War. Memories of shared hardships and a common sense of national purpose during the war produced among Union veterans a sense of fraternity, often identified with the Republican party. Many Republican leaders had been Union generals, including Hayes, Garfield, Schurz, Logan, Benjamin Harrison, Ben Butler, and of course Grant. The redoubtable William Tecumseh Sherman, who was commander in chief of the army and served for a time as Grant's secretary of war, maintained ties to the Republican leadership through his brother, Senator John Sherman of Ohio. The equally redoubtable Philip Sheridan held a variety of commands under Republican Presidents and succeeded Sherman as commander in chief during the Arthur administration. Though the Democrats attracted a few former Union generals, notably Winfield Scott Hancock and the ill-fated George Armstrong Custer, there was a pervasive feeling among Union veterans that support for the Republican party represented an extension of their wartime service. "Vote the way you shot!" Republican orators exhorted at reunions of the Grand Army of the Republic. The Democrats had let the nation down during its hour of trial, Republican publicists insisted, and did not deserve the trust of those who had answered their country's call. As Oliver Morton put it: "While it may be true that not every Democrat is a traitor, every traitor is a Democrat."[21]

John Logan of Illinois, who joined the Republican high command after he arrived in the Senate in 1872, was particularly skilled at identifying patriotism with Republicanism. Rooted in the "Egypt" section of southern Illinois around Cairo, where the Mississippi and the Ohio meet, "Black Jack" Logan before the war had defended slavery and performed as a loyal lieutenant in Stephen Douglas's Democratic state machine. After serving as a general in the Union army, he became a flaming Radical and converted Egypt into a Republican stronghold. In his role as national commander of the Grand Army of the Republic he fought for steady expansion of veterans' benefits and originated the celebration of Memorial Day. In 1877 a coalition of Democrats and independent Republicans ousted Logan from the Senate, replacing him with Supreme Court Justice David Davis, a political independent. (It was this maneuver that made Davis unavailable for the vote-count commission in the Hayes-Tilden election and perhaps cost Tilden the presidency.) Two years later, Logan, once more controlling the Illinois legislature, returned triumphantly to the Senate where he remained until his death in 1886. (Logan was the model for the brilliant but morally obtuse Senator Ratcliffe in Henry Adams' great novel of Washington politics, *Democracy*.)

Besides being the party of the Union, the Republicans were, in the North, the party of Protestantism. Denominations that before 1860 had divided about evenly or leaned toward the Democrats became overwhelmingly Republican. Paul Kleppner estimates that between the Civil War and the election of 1896 northern Methodists were about 75 percent Republican; various kinds of northern Baptists, between 65 and 80 percent; Norwegian Lutherans, 80 percent; and Swedish Lutherans, 85 percent. These groups joined politically with Congregationalists, Presbyterians, Episcopalians, and Quakers who in the Jacksonian era had been principally aligned with the Whigs.[22]

The Republicans supported the Whig program of moral reform on such issues as temperance, Sunday-closing laws, and opposition to gambling but managed to avoid being identified with the elitist image that had limited the Whigs' appeal among the more plebeian Protestant denominations. As Kleppner puts it, from the Civil War to the 1890s, "the Republican party was above all else the party of morality." In Iowa, according to Samuel P. Hays, "economic issues . . . seem to have been almost irrelevant in the face of a range of social and cultural differences . . . which centered primarily on prohibition and Sunday observance." In most states Republicans backed the maintenance of Protestant devotional exercises such as morning prayers and reading from the King James Bible in the public schools, which the Supreme Court then regarded as entirely a state matter. Even in New York, where association with moral puritanism had definite political costs in the metropolitan areas, the Republicans as late as 1896 supported a Sunday-closing law and Republican state boss Thomas Platt paid a Protestant publicist to tour upstate counties on behalf of the Republican ticket. (Pragmatic Republican politicians, however, tried not to offend other groups in the party coalition. "Prohibitionists and liquor men alike are crotchety and sensitive," Rutherford Hayes wrote to his official campaign biographer, William Dean Howells, the budding novelist, in 1876. *"Keep all on that score out of the book. . . .* I am a liberal on that subject [pro-temperance], but it is not to be blabbed.")[23]

While aiding Protestant moral causes, the Republicans resisted efforts by the Catholic church, often backed by the Democrats, to channel public funds to Catholic schools. In 1875 Blaine, at the behest of the Grant administration, introduced and guided to easy passage in the House a constitutional amendment that prohibited the use of public funds to support sectarian schools but specifically permitted "reading of the Bible in any school or institution." Early in the 1876 campaign, Hayes privately concluded that the Republicans' most effective issue was to "rebuke the Democracy by defeat for subservience to Roman Catholic demands."[24]

Protestant ministers reciprocated by urging their flocks to vote the straight Republican ticket. "Let us pray for His coming, and vote as we pray!" urged a Baptist minister in Illinois. The Republican party, declared a Congregationist clergyman in New England, was "the *party* of God, the *party* of Jesus Christ," while the Democrats were "the party of iniquity." In the 1880s, a Protestant divine warned that it would be morally inconsistent to go "to the Lord's table on Sunday and vote for Cleveland on Tuesday."[25]

In some midwestern farm states, where Catholics were relatively few and the real political competition was between Yankee Protestants and Protestants with non-Calvinist origins, many German Lutherans remained aligned with the Democrats. But in the East, where the chief ethnocultural division was between Protestants and Catholics, German Lutherans tended to be Republicans.

Identification of the Republicans with business, though it had some political liabilities, was on the whole a political plus. Republican state organizations in the 1870s and 1880s were not controlled, in the sense of being dictated to, by business or business establishments. The large sums raised by state party machines through assessments levied on federal and state jobholders, and from kickbacks from companies doing business with the state, made them to a considerable degree financially independent. But the campaign contributions made by business certainly helped swell the Republicans' coffers. Beyond that, Republican support for business expansion, through tariffs and publicly financed internal improvements, was in tune with the preferences, most of the time, of a majority of voters. Even after the panic of 1873, economic optimism among most Americans remained strong and rapid economic growth soon resumed. "Big business," as an abstract entity, was already unpopular, particularly in the South and West. But the entrepreneur, the inventor, and the self-made businessman were American heroes, as was shown by the phenomenal success of the Horatio Alger novels. The party that promised to give free rein to "luck and pluck" was bound to attract a large constituency.

Blacks were drawn to the Republicans in both the South and North as the party that had ended slavery and fitfully continued to defend civil rights. But most blacks seem also to have supported the republican ideology of individual enterprise. Frederick Douglass, the great black Republican leader of the period, wrote: "All that any man has a right to expect, ask, give, or receive in this world, is fair play. When society has secured this to its members, and the humblest citizen of the republic is put into the undisturbed possession of the natural fruits of his own exertions, there is really very little left for society and government to do."[26]

THE PENNSYLVANIA MODEL

Finally, the Republicans were able to retain their dominance in most of the North in part because of the operational superiority of their state organizations. After the election of Hayes, the shrewder Republican bosses recognized a need to retool their machines. The closeness of the result in 1876 put them on notice that they might soon lose access to federal patronage.

Hayes as President, moreover, proved not nearly as amenable as Grant had been to political control by the Senate bosses. He filled his cabinet with reformers and former Liberal Republicans, including the hated Carl Schurz as secretary of the interior. Worse than that, he often ignored the bosses' directives in his distribution of patronage. The worst brawl over patronage during the Hayes administration came when the President, despite vehement objection by Roscoe Conkling, nominated Theodore Roosevelt, Sr., a patrician businessman without previous political experience, to be collector of the port of New York, with control of the New York Customs House, traditionally the richest source of political plums in the federal orchard. After a stiff fight in the Senate, in which Conkling used every resource at his command, the President's nominee was rejected, a blow that contributed directly to Roosevelt's death a few weeks later from peritonitis—or so his son always believed.[27]

In 1880, over fierce Stalwart resistance, the Republican national convention nominated Representative James Garfield of Ohio to succeed Hayes (who had decided not to seek a second term). Chester Arthur of New York, an affable functionary of the Conkling machine (he had been the New York port collector whom Hayes had dismissed to make way for Roosevelt), was nominated for Vice President as a sop to the Stalwarts. When Garfield became President in 1881, the battle over patronage resumed. Again the New York Customs House became the center of contention. Again Conkling demanded that the Senate reject the President's nominee for collector of the port of New York, a prominent reformer. But Garfield, backed by Blaine, who had become secretary of state, proved a tougher nut than Hayes. Facing defeat in the Senate, Conkling suddenly resigned and returned to New York to seek vindication through reelection by the state legislature—taking with him the recently elected junior senator from New York, Thomas Platt, his principal henchman, who also resigned. The battle was transferred to the New York legislature. There Blaine's New York supporters, led by Whitelaw Reid, editor of the *Tribune,* Greeley's old paper, joined the Democrats to urge rejection of Conkling and Platt. As the struggle neared its climax, Garfield, strolling through Union Station in Washington with Blaine on his way to a train that was to take him on a vacation trip to New England, was shot down by Charles Guiteau, a political jobseeker gone mad. "I am a Stalwart," Guiteau shouted, "and Arthur is President now!"

After 79 agonizing days, Garfield, who had seemed to represent a fresh departure for the Republicans, died. Arthur, as the assassin had said, was President. But Conkling's political career was finished (he died seven years later on the streets of New York, frozen in the famous blizzard of 1888). Garfield's death produced a wave of public disgust with the spoils system. Even President Arthur, a product of the machine, was converted, whether by prudence or by conscience, to the need for civil service reform. The first proposal for a system of competitive examinations and protected tenure for the federal civil service, based on the British model (a product of British liberalism), had been introduced in Congress in 1865. Civil service reform had become a favorite cause of Liberal Republicanism. In 1883 Congress passed and Arthur signed the Pendleton Act, which established a merit system for a substantial part of the federal service.

Although the bosses continued to have a say in the hiring and firing of many federal employees, the days when the federal payroll could be counted on to supply a reliable army of party workers were over. The bosses needed new sources for both manpower and campaign contributions. Some had already found them in the rapidly growing work forces of their state governments.

When Simon Cameron retired from the Senate in 1877, he had persuaded the Pennsylvania state legislature to elect his son Donald to his seat. Within a few years, however, real power in the state's Republican machine had passed to Matthew Stanley Quay, who was elected as Pennsylvania's junior senator in 1887. Thin and tubercular (he could never purchase life insurance), Quay had begun his political career as secretary to Pennsylvania's wartime governor, Andrew Curtin. While serving in the Union army, he had won the Congressional Medal of Honor for heroism at the battle of Fredericksburg.

On his return to Pennsylvania after the war, Quay had correctly judged the likely winner in the ongoing struggle between Curtin and Simon Cameron for control of the state Republican party. He entered Cameron's service as editor of a paper called the *Radical*. In this role, he wrote scathing editorials attacking the Republicans' retreat from the protection of black civil rights in the South. He jabbed at the Pennsylvania Railroad as "the great monopoly of our state." (The Camerons owned a small railroad that competed with the Pennsylvania.) But he defended the spoils system. "If office holders should not pay the necessary expenses of political campaigns," the *Radical* asked, "who ought to pay them?" When the old boss retired, Quay, without ever quite supplanting Donald Cameron, who preferred foreign travel with his friend Henry Adams to the details of politics, became effective leader of the machine.[28]

Even before passage of the Pendleton Act, Quay had recognized that in the future the state government would have to be the machine's principal base. Systematically assessing state employees and extracting contributions from businesses affected by state government, including the Pennsylvania Railroad, Quay built a larger and more efficient organization than the somewhat informal and loosely structured machines that had been run by bosses like Conkling and the Camerons. "Both businessmen and social agencies welcomed a leader who could end the chronic discord that disrupted the flow of legislation and appropriations in which they were vitally interested," writes Quay's biographer, James Kehl. "They looked with satisfaction on the appearance of a central source to which they could turn to receive a desired franchise, amend a limiting charter, push an added appropriation, initiate a preferential bill, or energize a recalcitrant committee chairman."[29]

Every year, state employees received a letter from the Republican state committee: "Two percent of your salary is ———. Please remit promptly. At the close of the campaign we shall place a list of those who have not paid in the hands of the head of the department you are in." Banks receiving deposits of state funds were required to pay kickbacks to the machine, "with a conservative yield of $150,000 annually." Railroads, utilities, traction companies, and other corporate interests made regular contributions to the party, "actually relieved that there was an efficient and effective broker to receive their money, distribute it judiciously, and assure the desired results."[30]

With the money so raised, Quay financed a state organization with an annual budget that Kehl estimates "competed favorably with the budgets of several railroads (Reading, Lehigh, and B&O), but was not as large as that of the Pennsylvania." The Republican state committee maintained a payroll of 20,000 full-time or part-time party workers, at an annual cost of about $24 million. What did all these workers do? Some performed staff jobs, preparing mailings, organizing rallies, soliciting funds. But most were in the field, doing political favors for residents of city precincts, small towns, and rural counties, and mobilizing the faithful on election day. Through the services of this army, the Republican machine usually controlled not only the state government but also most county and local governments, including those of the state's two major cities, Philadelphia and Pittsburgh. (Leaders of the Philadelphia and Pittsburgh organizations, backed by disgruntled business interests, sometimes challenged the state machine, but their need for state jobs for their workers normally gave Quay the upper hand.)[31]

In New York, Thomas Platt (known as the "easy boss," apparently because he was less domineering and arrogant than Conkling had been) assembled an organization similar to Quay's, though on a somewhat smaller scale: 10,000 workers at an annual cost of about $20 million. Platt's power was limited by the presence of a strong reform faction in the Republican party led by young Theodore Roosevelt, Jr., Tammany's continued domination in New York City, and support by many businessmen for moderate Democrats like Cleveland, which kept the Democrats competitive in state elections. Not until 1897 was Platt's control over the legislature sufficiently firm to send him back to the Senate. Other Quay-type Republican state machines were established in Ohio, Illinois, Michigan, and Wisconsin. Somewhat less robust variants formed in some of the newer states of the Great Plains.[32]

The Republican national organization returned to the more usual pattern of a federation of state parties that got together every four years to run a national ticket. State bosses were still usually senators, partly because many state constitutions prohibited governors from serving more than a single term or required them to run for reelection every two years.

The national Republican party, nevertheless, was still more tightly organized than its Democratic opposition. In 1888, after the Democrats had held the White House for four years and a majority in the House of Representatives for six, Quay took a turn as chairman of the Republican national committee. The Republican candidate for President was former Senator Benjamin Harrison of Indiana (grandson of William Henry Harrison). Like Hayes and Garfield, Harrison was no friend of the bosses, but they accepted him for his clean record and because he was expected to carry Indiana, one of the keys to every presidential election during the period.

Quay took personal command of the canvass in New York which, with Indiana, was expected to determine the outcome. Early in the campaign, he financed a private census of every household in New York City in order to block Tammany's practice of inflating Democratic totals through massive vote fraud.[33]

Harrison ran behind Cleveland, the incumbent Democratic President, in the national popular vote, but by carrying New York and Indiana he achieved a comfortable majority in the electoral college. The Republicans picked up 19 House seats in the former Confederacy and the Border states, thereby winning a House majority. After the election Harrison met with Quay and other party leaders. "Providence," said the pious President-elect, "has been good to us." Quay later complained to a journalistic crony: "Think of the man! He ought to know that Providence hadn't a damned thing to do with it. We put him in."[34]

There is something to be said for Quay's view of the matter. The Republican state machines helped maintain the party's hegemony in most northeastern and midwestern states and helped keep the party competitive in national elections. Following a common ideology on national policy issues, they helped produce exceptionally high levels of Republican party unity in Congress.

The role of the Republican party organization should not be exaggerated, however. The main reason the Republicans usually won in most non-southern states and more often than not at the national level, and that Republicans in Congress generally voted together, was that majorities among both the non-southern public and Republican officeholders continued to subscribe to the Republican ideology: nationalist, Protestant moralist, and free-enterprise capitalist. Indeed, the effectiveness of the Republican organizations probably resulted to a great extent from the attractiveness of the party's ideology to the more able politicians or prospective politicians. "Early in life," Tom Platt wrote, "I became a believer in the Hamiltonian theory of politics. From that time I have held consistently to the doctrine of government by party, and rule of the party by the regular organization."[35]

Like the Jacksonians in the 1830s and the New Dealers of a later time, the Republicans of the 1870s and 1880s seem to have felt they had the wind of history at their back. Providence, Benjamin Harrison might have said, gave them ample reason: their party had ended slavery and won the Civil War; after the setback of the mid-1870s, the national economy resumed growth at an unprecedented rate; the great trans-Mississippi West, though with tragic results for American Indians, was opened to settlement and economic use; the United States was becoming a power to be reckoned with in world affairs. True, governmental corruption and concern over economic concentration were beginning to cause political stress. And a farmer revolt, triggered by drought and falling prices for agricultural commodities, was building in the supposedly safely Republican states of the Great Plains and Far West. But for the majority of Americans the ideology that Lincoln and other Republicans had introduced to national power in the 1860s was still producing good results.

8

THIRD-PARTY CHALLENGE

Populist Uprising

FROM THE END OF THE CIVIL WAR through the early 1890s the chief economic issue dividing the Democrats from the Republicans at the national level was the protective tariff. The Republicans, even most of the so-called mugwumps who defected to vote for Cleveland against Blaine on the corruption issue in 1884, generally favored keeping tariffs high to protect developing American industry. The Democrats, responding to the interests of their farmer and working-class constituencies, and to advice and pressure from part of the financial community, called for tariff reduction. On broader fiscal and monetary issues, there was little difference between the major parties. On some economic issues, under the leadership of Grover Cleveland, the Democrats were even a shade more conservative than the Republicans.

As a result, when economic conditions were bad, as they were in the mid-1870s and the early 1890s, there was a sense among many of the economically hard pressed that the two-party system was not responding to their grievances and needs.

Right after the Civil War, the Democrats had flirted with the option of becoming the "soft money" party in national politics, presumably in the hope of appealing to debtors who would get to repay their loans in depreciated currency. In 1868, the Democratic platform endorsed the greenback idea, proposed the year before by Representative George Pendleton of Ohio (later author of federal civil service reform), under which Civil War bonds would be paid off in depreciated paper dollars, known as greenbacks, instead of gold, as had been promised when the bonds were issued. But the Democratic presidential candidate in 1868, Governor Horatio Seymour of New York, was a hard-money man who steered as far away as possible from the greenback proposal. After the election, which he lost decisively to Grant, Seymour complained that the greenback plank had frightened not only bondholders but "all creditors and businessmen" and had created the impression that the party was "putting out to sea and sailing away from land."[1]

Disenchanted with the Democrats, some of those favoring the greenback proposal formed their own party, hoping to break through the two-party system as the Republicans had done in the 1850s. In 1876, the Greenback party nominated Peter

Cooper, a wealthy philanthropist, as its candidate for President. The party's platform promised not only to pay off the national debt in paper money but also to restore silver, which had been demonetized with little fuss in 1873, as a national currency. Cooper attracted only 82,000 votes. In 1878, however, candidates running for Congress with Greenbacker support, often on fusion tickets with the Democrats, received more than a million votes—close to 15 percent of the national total. When the new Congress met, the Greenbacker candidate for Speaker of the House received 14 votes—close to a balance of power between the candidates of the major parties.[2]

In 1880 the Greenbacker candidate for President, Representative James Weaver of Iowa, a former Union army general, received 300,000 votes—eight times Garfield's plurality in the popular vote. Two years later the Greenbackers infusion with the Democrats elected Ben Butler governor of Massachusetts. As it turned out, this was the party's undoing (though the party probably was already in decline).

Butler, a Balzacian character with a boundless zest for political conflict, had begun in the 1850s as a Jacksonian Democrat in Whig Massachusetts, had gone on to become a political general in the Union army whose brutal treatment of civilians in occupied New Orleans provoked international protest, and had then become a Radical Republican congressman who outdid even Thaddeus Stevens in his vengefulness toward the South. (Lincoln once said that Butler was "as full of poison gas as a dead dog.")[3] Taking up the greenback idea and the Greenback party, Butler infused both with his personality and ambition. Inevitably nominated by the Greenbackers for President in 1884, he received only 175,000 votes. Having violated the rule that in order to survive a new party must increase its vote in each succeeding election, the Greenbackers soon expired.

The idea that a new party founded on economic discontent could win national power, however, remained alive in the minds of many citizens dissatisfied with the economic policies supported by the Republicans and Democrats. When the economic skies again darkened in the late 1880s, a new political movement, based mainly on the West and South, launched a formidable challenge to the existing party system.

"LESS CORN AND MORE HELL"

In the decade and a half after the Civil War, the United States Army, directed by Sherman and Sheridan, had won decisive victories over tribes of American Indians in the trans-Mississippi West. Enterprising settlers poured onto the virgin lands of the Great Plains. Starting with small homesteads, many soon took out expensive mortgages that enabled them to buy larger farms. Unusual rainfall in the West from 1877 through 1886 produced abundant crops, encouraging farmers to acquire more and more land. Then, in 1887, a decade of drought set in. When the national economy turned down at the end of the 1880s, prices for wheat and other farm commodities resumed the downward trend they had generally followed since the end of the Civil War. Farmers who had bet on continued rain and stable or rising prices faced bankruptcy. Particularly on the more marginal lands of the western Great Plains—the so-called Middle Border—farms were seized by banks and other lenders, often headquartered in the East. In Kansas alone, 11,000 mortgages were foreclosed in four years.[4]

Many farmers concluded that the market system put them at a hopeless disadvantage against the "money power," the eastern banks and industrial monopolies that financed their mortgages, determined the rates railroads charged to carry their produce to market, and then largely dictated the prices at which it was sold. When weather was good and the economy strong, the money power claimed an unfair share of the profit created through their labor. When the rain stopped or the economy weakened, the money power took their land. "Everywhere I came in contact with the *discontented*," wrote the novelist Hamlin Garland, himself "a son of the Middle Border," after traveling across the Great Plains in the early 1890s. "I saw only those whose lives seemed about to end in failure. . . . Why should our great new land fall into this slough of discouragement?"[5]

As they had in Jackson's time, economically threatened farmers looked to the national government to take their side against the money power. Among the forms of federal intervention demanded by various farm leaders were inflation of the currency, regulation of railroad rates, and provision of credits on produce held in storage until prices rose. Farmers' Alliances, first organized in Texas in 1878, and then in Illinois in 1880, became vehicles for political action. Farmers, said Mary Elizabeth Lease, a young Kansas lawyer who barnstormed across the prairie, orating at political rallies that resembled camp meeting revivals, should "raise less corn and more HELL." She made clear the targets she had in mind for damnation: "bloodhounds of money," "government of Wall Street, by Wall Street, and for Wall Street," and proprietors of the "accursed foreclosure system."[6]

Most of the western farmers were Republicans—members of the party of Protestantism, to which most of them at least nominally subscribed. But the national Republican party, they believed, had in its later days become subservient to the money power, either directly, or indirectly through the control of state bosses like Platt, Quay, and Logan. The Democrats were little better—in some cases worse. The party of Jefferson and Jackson was dominated at its national level by New York politicians who were themselves tools of the money power, and in many of the states by corrupt big-city machines. The Democrats, moreover, were still tainted by association with the Confederacy, and by softness on Catholicism.

In the local Farmers' Alliances, talk grew, as it had in the 1870s, of a new third party—a purifying force that would bring the Republic back to the ideals of Jefferson and Jackson—a republic of virtue, based on Christian values and the moral strength natural to independent yeoman farmers. "It was an era of fervent meetings and fulminating resolutions," Hamlin Garland later recalled. Earlier protests had been moderate in expression. "The Farmers Alliance came as a revolt."[7]

In 1889 the local Alliance in Cowley County, Kansas, ran its own slate of candidates for county offices, and, in fusion with the Democrats, won a landslide victory over the entrenched Republican organization. Building on the Cowley County model, Kansas farm groups in 1890 formed a new party which they called the People's party. After a hastily organized campaign, the People's party won 36 percent of the vote for its candidate for governor, just behind the winning Republican's share of 39 percent, and elected five members to the federal House of Representatives, in some cases with Democratic endorsements. Gaining control of the Kansas legislature, the new party elected William Peffer as its first United States senator. In Nebraska and South Dakota similar parties formed by state Alliances made strong races for statewide offices and elected numerous state legislators. Talk quickened of a great national party of productive workers, industrial laborers as well as farmers.[8]

Pacification of the trans-Mississippi West had also opened the way for mining operations in the Rocky Mountains and the desert that lay beyond. Since parts of this region were rich in silver, the region acquired a direct economic interest in the coinage of silver as an authorized national currency. This goal fitted neatly with the conviction among farmer radicals that expansion of the money supply would ease their economic problems. By the end of the 1880s most agrarian radicals had added "free and unlimited coinage of silver" to their agenda of demands.[9]

In the South, farmer unrest had proceeded along a somewhat different track. In most southern states after Reconstruction members of the old planter class regained political, economic, and social dominance. Small farmers in the upland regions, some of whom had for a time during Reconstruction supported the Republicans, were excluded from political power Agriculture was generally depressed, not so much because of weather as because of inefficient farming methods and low prices for cotton. The patricians who controlled the state governments kept taxes low and state services starved. For a time, the patrician leaders—known to their political enemies as "Bourbons"—were able to maintain a united Democratic party, warning that any sign of defection to the Republicans would undermine white supremacy.[10]

By the 1880s, however, the old Jacksonian strain in the southern Democracy had begun to chafe under this domination by a conservative elite. If collaboration with the Republicans was out of bounds, since that would mean recognizing the rights of blacks, why should not poor white farmers through force of numbers take over the Democratic party? Beginning in Georgia in 1886, rural equalitarians introduced primary elections (at first for the election of pledged delegates to Democratic state conventions) as a means of challenging patrician control in what had become effectively one-party states. Southern Farmers' Alliances were organized similar to those being formed in the West, though at first with the avowed purpose of being "strictly white man's non-political, secret, business" associations.

In the 1890 elections, equalitarians broke through in several southern states to take control of Democratic parties and therefore of state governments. In Georgia, fiery young Thomas G. Watson led a campaign that won him a seat in Congress and gave his faction the governorship and majorities in both houses of the state legislature. In South Carolina, Benjamin Tillman, "Pitchfork Ben," a one-eyed farmer, won the governorship over a candidate put forward by the planter establishment. In Texas, James Hogg was elected governor on a platform that promised regulation of railroads.

Tom Watson, the most brilliant, and among the most vitriolic, of the equalitarians, went so far as to propose an alliance between poor whites and poor blacks, arguing that enmity between the two groups was benefiting nobody but the Bourbons. "You are kept apart," he told farmers of both races, "that you may be separately fleeced of your earnings. You are made to hate each other because upon that hatred is rested the keystone of the arch of financial despotism which enslaves you both."[11]

Fresh from their triumphs in the fall elections, representatives of western and southern Alliances gathered in Ocala, Florida, in December 1890. Following Watson's advice, organizers of the meeting invited representatives of the Colored Farmers' Alliance. A delegation from Kansas proposed that a call be issued for a convention to form a national People's party. Some southern equalitarians hung back. They were hesitant, they acknowledged, to give up the power they had begun to acquire through participation in southern Democratic parties. The meeting ended inconclusively, with agreement only that a convention should be held to consider third-party prospects in St. Louis in 1892.[12]

In May 1891, the Kansans and some others who shared their determination to form a third party gathered in Cincinnati and launched a national People's party, complete with a national chairman and an executive committee. By the time the scheduled St. Louis convention met on Washington's birthday, 1892, Grover Cleveland, anathema to rural equalitarians, was the clear front runner for nomination by the Democrats for another term in the White House. Finding President Harrison equally unacceptable, the assembled delegates agreed to give their support to the recently founded People's party. That summer General James Weaver—who had led the Greenbackers in 1880—was chosen as the People's party candidate for President.[13] The party became known as the Populists—a term apparently coined in 1892 by a writer for the Columbus, Ohio, *Dispatch*.

THE PARTY OF HARD TIMES

Thinking to establish unbreakable control of both the electoral college and the Senate, the Republicans during Harrison's term had hurried to statehood the sparsely settled, but supposedly impregnably Republican, western territories of North Dakota, South Dakota, Wyoming, Idaho, Montana, and Washington. In the very next election, the Populist candidate, Weaver, carried two of the new states, Idaho and North Dakota, and came in second in South Dakota and Wyoming. Weaver also carried the western states of Kansas, Colorado, and Wyoming, for a total of 22 electoral votes. The South, however, was solid for Cleveland—only in Texas and Alabama did Weaver win more than 20 percent of the popular vote. In the Northeast and the Great Lakes states, the People's party simply did not exist. In no state east of the Mississippi and north of the Mason-Dixon line (the boundary between Pennsylvania and Maryland) did the Populist candidate win as much as 5 percent of the popular vote.

With Cleveland's return to the White House for a second term, the Democrats for the first time since the Civil War simultaneously controlled both the presidency and both houses of Congress. The nation promptly entered the worst economic depression up to that time—fixing indelibly in the minds of many voters an association between the Democratic party and economic hard times that was to last for more than 30 years. By the end of 1893, almost 600 banks had failed, more than 15,000 businesses had gone bankrupt, and "perhaps as much as a quarter of the country's nonagricultural work force had experienced unemployment." In 1894 production dropped to 75 percent of capacity, wages fell 10 percent, and more than 40 percent of nonagricultural workers at one time or another were unemployed.[14]

Economic hard times helped set off a series of bitterly contested strikes against mining and manufacturing companies. In the coalfields of Pennsylvania, Illinois, Ohio, and Indiana, strikes by miners led to "bloody skirmishes," causing Governors William McKinley of Ohio and John Peter Altgeld of Illinois to call out their state militias. A strike at the Pullman works outside Chicago culminated in riots in July 1894 that were put down with the help of 2,000 federal troops dispatched by Cleveland (Over Altgeld's angry protest).

Cleveland's response to the depression was not exactly indecisive. Believing that the economic collapse had been caused by the Silver Purchase Act and the McKinley tariff, both enacted by the Republicans in 1890, he wielded federal patronage to persuade the Democratic majorities in Congress to repeal the Silver Purchase Act and to make some adjustments in tariff rates (though the final tariff bill was such a mixed bag that he allowed it to become law without his signature). But he did nothing to bring direct help to the unemployed.

The 1894 midterm elections were a disaster for the Democrats. In the House, the Democrats lost 113 seats, producing a switch from a Democratic majority of 91 to a Republican majority of 139. In the Senate, where only one-third of the 88 seats were at stake, the Democrats lost only five seats, but that was enough to restore Republican control.

Clearly no Democrat remotely associated with Grover Cleveland would have any chance of winning the presidency in 1896. But it was by no means certain that the Republicans would be the chief beneficiaries of the social and economic turmoil. In the 1894 congressional elections, the Populists' share of the total vote rose to 12 percent, compared to 9 percent in 1892. There were six Populists in the Senate and seven in the House, as well as others in both bodies elected with Populist support. If economic hard times drove the nation in a radical direction, might not

Populism, particularly if it found a charismatic leader, rather than Republicanism be the wave of the future?

The economy recovered somewhat in 1895 but then plunged again in the early months of 1896, producing more bank failures, more bankruptcies, and more layoffs. As the 1896 Democratic convention approached, support for "free silver" swept through the party, not only in the silver-producing states but among all who adhered to the traditional Jacksonian remedy of inflation as an economic restorative. Only a few redoubts in Democratic state parties in the Northeast and around the Great Lakes held out in favor of Cleveland's hard-money policy. There was, Cleveland complained, "not a single man in the Senate with whom I can be on terms of absolute confidence." Governor Altgeld of Illinois, who in 1892 had broken the Republicans' monopoly on political power in that state, predicted: "If our party takes a firm position on [the silver issue] and the Republican party straddles the question, as it will be obliged to do, we will sweep the country and achieve a greater victory than we ever have." Altgeld threw down the gauntlet to the gold-bugs: "The continuation of the single gold standard means the permanent degradation of the great toiling and producing masses of this country."[15]

THE CANDIDATE OF SOUND MONEY

The Republican party leaders who gathered in St. Louis in early June 1896, and their business supporters, clearly recognized both the seriousness of the Populist challenge and their own party's opportunity to reclaim the White House by capitalizing on voter reaction against Cleveland. As their candidate for President, they nominated William McKinley, the one-term governor of Ohio.

McKinley, a quiet man, had served six terms in Congress, representing the largely rural district that included Canton. He had acquired a reputation as a good listener and a superb political tactician. His major accomplishment in the House had been steering to enactment the highly protectionist McKinley tariff of 1890. For this triumph he had won the title "Napoleon of Protection"—more, one guesses, for cunning and determination than for dramatic flair. Though he had served in the Civil War, he was not part of the military elite that included Grant, Hayes, Garfield, and Harrison. (Toward the end of the war, he had been an aide to Hayes.) In Ohio politics he stayed outside the orbit of the Quay-type machine built by Governor, later Senator, Joseph Foraker. He made his base in the older establishment of moderate politicians and businessmen formed by Hayes and Senator John Sherman.[16]

Like Lincoln and Seward in the 1850s McKinley fought against making the Republican party the instrument of Protestant hegemony. As governor, he had appointed Catholics to important posts in state government, thereby incurring the wrath of the anti-Catholic American Protective Association. (He did not, however, as young Theodore Roosevelt was doing in New York, publicly attack the A.P.A.)

Like his friend and supporter, Mark Hanna, a Cleveland businessman, McKinley sought to stay on good terms with the emerging force of organized labor. He called up the state militia to maintain order during the coal-mine strike of 1894 but was credited by labor with having been at least as restrained in his use of troops as the radical Altgeld in Illinois.[17]

McKinley's bid for the Republican presidential nomination had been skillfully planned and managed by Mark Hanna. Though widely identified as a boss, Hanna was a different kind of politician than the type exemplified by Quay, Platt, and Foraker. Having devoted his early years to converting the family wholesale grocery into a flourishing coal and iron company, Hanna had come to active politics relatively late in life—at first to protect his investment in a Cleveland streetcar line. Unlike reformers like Roosevelt, his interest in politics was directly functional, but the function he had in mind was not the enrichment of a political machine.[18]

Like his fellow millionaire businessmen in the booming industrial heartland of western Pennsylvania and northeastern Ohio, John D. Rockefeller and Andrew Carnegie, who also dabbled in Republican politics, Hanna believed devoutly in the benevolent effects of American business. The primary purpose of government, as he conceived it, was to provide a favorable climate for business which when operating smoothly would produce a rising standard of living for almost everybody. Hanna believed, he said, in a "business state." He was rather more candid than Rockefeller, Carnegie, and the rest about the use of money in politics to protect business interests. He accepted that workers were entitled to a fair share of the income produced by business enterprise—his companies were among the first to sign contracts with organized labor. But businessmen must have the authority to make major economic decisions. "Some men must own," he said, and "the great mass of men must work for those who own." It would not be correct to say that Hanna served the Republican party as he might have worked for a church or a fraternal order—he expected his companies to profit directly from the relationship. But his chief concern was with an entire economy, indeed an entire social order, rather than with a quick personal return.

In 1888 Hanna had supported John Sherman for the Republican nomination for President. When Harrison and Sherman seemed to deadlock, Foraker, though pledged to Sherman, had tried to swing the nomination to Blaine, in hopes of getting the second spot on the ticket for himself. McKinley, in contrast, when a group of delegates proposed him as a dark horse for the presidential nomination, had insisted on remaining loyal to Sherman. Hanna was impressed. "You might have been President," he told McKinley. When Harrison was nominated and elected, Hanna resolved that at some future convention McKinley should have his chance.

Hostile journalists and cartoonists of the day liked to depict Hanna pulling the strings on his obedient puppet, McKinley. Those who observed the relationship closely found it quite otherwise. The partnership somewhat recalled that of Seward and Weed, but it was less equal. McKinley was the dominant ego, and Hanna the faithful technician. William Allen White, the journalist, who knew them both well and rather preferred Hanna, conceded that Hanna in McKinley's presence was always "just a shade obsequious."[19]

Looking toward the 1896 convention, Hanna established a firm base for McKinley in the Midwest and developed broad support among the southern delegations, which since the time of Hayes and Garfield had taken their cues from the dominant faction in the Ohio organization. Both McKinley and Hanna preferred to play down the monetary issue and base the fall campaign on the promise of higher tariffs. The eastern financial interests who were expected to pay a large share of the campaign costs did not agree. Senator Henry Cabot Lodge of Massachusetts, who like his friend Roosevelt traced his political lineage to the reform strain in the party initiated by Charles Sumner, is reported to have carried their demand that the platform include specific advocacy of gold to Hanna at the Republican convention in St. Louis. Tom Platt of New York was on hand to reinforce the message. Foraker, employed as an attorney by the Morgan bank while he waited a chance to be elected to the Senate, applied leverage from inside the Ohio delegation.[20]

Hanna at first resisted. But when pressure mounted from the easterners, backed by some business allies in Chicago and Cincinnati, Hanna, with McKinley's approval, agreed to an unequivocal pledge to maintain the "existing gold standard," rather than the "existing standard" as originally drafted. The plank was hammered out in a hotel room by a knot of party leaders (with Melville Stone, president of the Associated Press, present because he knew how to spell "inviolably"). As a sop to the Republican silverites, an escape clause was added holding out the possibility of "free coinage of silver" upon "international agreement with the leading commercial nations of the world, which we pledge ourselves to promote." It was not enough. Senator Henry Teller of Colorado, one of the founders of the Republican party in the West, led the delegations of five silver-producing states out of the convention. Hanna joined the majority in chanting: "Good-by! Good-by! . . . Go to Chicago! Take the Democratic train!" In the press section, young William Jennings Bryan, covering the convention for the Omaha *World-Herald*, was seen to look on with a "smile of satisfaction."[21]

"A CROSS OF GOLD"

When the Democrats met in Chicago in July, the silverites were not only in a clear majority but appeared to possess the two-thirds still needed to nominate a candidate for President. A resolution commending the Cleveland administration was voted down 564 to 357. There was no doubt that the convention would adopt a strong platform plank calling for unlimited coinage of silver. But the silverites had not yet found a presidential candidate who could dramatize their cause. Altgeld, their natural leader, was constitutionally disqualified because he had been born in Prussia a few months before his parents had emigrated to the United States in 1847. Former Senator Richard Bland of Missouri, "Silver Dick," who had made a career of single-mindedly advocating the cause of silver, appeared to be the front runner. But many delegates doubted that Bland had the political gifts to capture the tide of public sentiment that seemed to be flowing toward the Populists, who were scheduled to meet the following week in St. Louis.

What was needed, Democratic strategists figured, was not simply an economic argument but a leader who could draw on social discontent that went beyond economic hardship. Populism as it had developed by the summer of 1896 had taken on strong tones of cultural nativism, even religious bigotry. The Populists were reacting not simply against the money power but against the whole world of cities and alien customs and loose living they felt was challenging the agrarian way of life. Agriculture, while still a mighty political force, was, they must have recognized, a declining factor in the national economy. Farmers, who in Jackson's day had comprised about 70 percent of the national work force, now made up only about one-third. White Protestants living on farms or in small towns were still a substantial majority of the nation's population, but their hegemony was slipping. America had been the Promised Land of evangelical Protestantism. Now, even in good times, evangelical Protestants had to share the national legacy with other groups.[22]

Spurred by economic loss, many within the Populist movement began to blame their troubles not only on bankers and monopolists but also on alien cultural forces. In California the rabidly anti-Catholic American Protective Association (A.P.A.) was influential within the Populist leadership. Anti-Semitism, formerly not a significant factor in the United States (the large immigration of Jews from eastern Europe started only in the 1880s), began showing up in Populist discourse. Noting the presence of August Belmont, Jr., American agent of the Rothschilds, among Cleveland's economic advisers, Populist leaders charged that America was slipping under the control of international "Shylocks." As Associated Press dispatch from the Populist convention in St. Louis reported "extraordinary hatred of the Jewish race" among the delegates. "It is not possible to go into any hotel in the city without hearing the most bitter denunciation of the Jews as a class and of particular Jews who happened to have prospered in the world."[23]

On the night of July 8, William Jennings Bryan, former congressman from Nebraska, loser in a race for the Senate in 1894, still only 36 years old, addressed the by now tumultuous Democratic convention as final advocate for the proposed platform plank promising free coinage of silver. Bryan had perfected the rhetorical devices in his speech through long experience on the small-town lecture circuit. With his mighty voice, a major asset in the days before electronic amplification, he immediately gripped the crowd.

The silver plank, he said, was not anti-business, as the gold Democrats claimed. Their trouble was that they defined business too narrowly. "The man who is employed for wages is as much a businessman as his employer. The attorney in a country town . . . as much . . . as the corporation counsel in a great metropolis. The merchant at the crossroads store . . . as much . . . as the merchant of New York.

The farmer who goes forth in the morning and toils all day, begins in the spring and toils all summer, . . . is as much a businessman as the man who goes upon the Board of Trade and bets upon the price of grain. . . ."[24]

Bryan invoked the names of Jefferson and Jackson. What the Democratic party now needed, he said, was "an Andrew Jackson to stand as Jackson stood, against the encroachments of concentrated wealth." The convention must decide whether the party was "upon the side of the idle holders of idle capital, or upon the side of the struggling masses. . . ."

The great cities, he acknowledged, were said to favor the gold standard. But "the great cities rest upon these broad and fertile prairies. Burn down your cities and leave our farms, and your cities will spring up again as if by magic. But destroy our farms and the grass will grow in the streets of every city in this country."

The throng, now hushed, hung on every syllable of Bryan's great peroration: ". . . We shall answer their demands for a gold standard by saying to them, *you shall not press down upon the brow of labor this crown of thorns. You shall not crucify mankind upon a cross of gold.*"

The crowd exploded with a roar that must have rivaled the roar that had heralded Lincoln's nomination in 1860. "Hell," cabled a correspondent for a London newspaper, "was broken loose in Chicago." The silver plank carried by a vote of better than two to one. The next day Bryan was nominated on the fifth ballot for President, with delegations from several eastern states and Wisconsin abstaining.[25]

The Populists, meeting in St. Louis the following week, were caught in a dilemma. Should they endorse Bryan, thereby risking the loss of their party identity at the very moment when the country seemed to be turning in their direction? Or should they run their own candidate, thereby splitting the vote of the discontented and assuring victory for the conservative Republicans? Most of the party leadership, including General Weaver, seeing a chance for real power at last, urged endorsement of Bryan. Mary Elizabeth Lease, the Kansas firebrand, "nearly burst a blood vessel" in her enthusiasm for Bryan's candidacy.[26]

A few urban radicals who had attached themselves to Populism warned that Bryan would have little appeal for industrial workers in the cities. And some southern Populists, who had cast their lot against the southern Democracy, resisted losing their new party's autonomy. For the Populists simply to fuse with the Democrats, said Tom Watson of Georgia, would be to "return as the hog did to its wallow." In the end, a compromise was worked out through which the Populists endorsed Bryan for President but substituted Watson as their candidate for Vice President in place of the Democratic choice, a banker who had declared for free silver. Henry Demarest Lloyd, a radical publicist, wrote what he took to be the epitaph of the Populist party: "The Free Silver movement is a fake. Free Silver is the cowbird of the Reform movement. It waited until the nest had been built by the sacrifices and labour of others, and then it laid its eggs in it. . . . The People's party has been betrayed."[27]

THE CLEAR MAJORITY PARTY

Despite Cleveland's evident unpopularity, McKinley made no effort to identify Bryan with the administration. After Bryan's nomination, Democratic supporters of the administration met, with Cleveland's approval, to form a "National Democratic" party pledged to maintain the gold standard. The new party nominated John Palmer of Illinois as its candidate for President. The National Democrats, financed by Democratic businessmen like August Belmont, Jr., and former Democratic national chairman Abram Hewitt, concentrated on draining off enough votes for Palmer in Indiana, Michigan, Minnesota, Kentucky, and Kansas to make sure that McKinley would carry those states. (They succeeded in Kentucky and failed in Kansas; the other three states ultimately went for McKinley by absolute majorities.)

Bryan stumped the nation in a railroad "whistle stop" campaign (still a rare practice for presidential candidates). He made some gestures toward organized labor and ethnic working-class voters, whom he urged to join a coalition of the "toiling masses." But his primary strategy was to rally the agrarian base of the old Jacksonian majority. Unlike Cleveland, he made no attempt to accommodate the Republican ideology, but rather offered rural voters the Jeffersonian–Jacksonian faith in undiluted form. His attacks were directed not merely at the money power that made its headquarters in big cities, but at the cities themselves, with their inherent tendency to corruption. By identifying with traditional rural values—an identification that no doubt was entirely sincere—he hoped to bring back to the Democratic party the mass of evangelical Protestants, who had been predominantly Jacksonian. He tried to drive a line of political cleavage between the Northeast and the rest of the country. This meant sacrificing not only New England, which in 1828 had opposed Jackson, but also New York and Pennsylvania, which had been Jacksonian strongholds. By holding the South, attracting disgruntled farmers and silverites in the Great Plains and the Far West, and combining an increased share of the farm vote with the normal Democratic city vote in Illinois, Ohio, Indiana, Michigan, and Wisconsin, he could, he was convinced, win the election.

During September and October, Hanna pulled out all the stops to restore the nation's voters to what he regarded as their political and economic senses. The Republican campaign was waged nationwide, not just in states that seemed doubtful. Hanna's propaganda machine turned out almost 200 pamphlets, many of them targeted at particular groups and translated into a dozen languages. About 200 million pieces of campaign literature were distributed before election day.

The business community, except for the owners of silver mines, gave almost united support for McKinley. Hanna levied fixed assessments on corporations, which they for the most part dutifully paid. (Finding cash left over after the election, Hanna, to the astonishment of corporate executives, sent back proportionate shares of their contributions.) Beyond providing funds that helped pay for enormous mailings and subsidized party workers, businessmen communicated directly with their employees, customers, and clients. Mill owners warned their workers that if Bryan won on Tuesday, "the whistle will not blow on Wednesday morning." Some contracts were made contingent on a Republican victory. A few days before the election, tens of thousands of businessmen representing a wide range of industries and financial interests paraded in New York City wearing chrysanthemums and carrying golden oranges.[28]

The fervor that developed among McKinley's supporters, however, grew from more than economic fear or party enthusiasm. Many Protestant voters came to regard Bryan's campaign as a direct challenge to the very Christian values that he claimed to personify. Bryan's attempt, through bold use of Christian imagery and emphasis on equalitarian themes, to reclaim northern evangelical Protestants for the Democracy was blunted by his identification with economic nostrums that seemed to violate the Protestant work ethic. Early in the campaign, some evangelical clerics rallied to Bryan's side. "He is undoubtedly," said one, "to lead [us] out of the sin-cursed land of gold-bugs. . . ." A midwestern Methodist magazine, while doubting the economic wisdom of free silver, extolled Bryan's opposition to "the syndicated powers which have had their way for so many decades." For the most part, however, northern Protestant clergymen and publicists rejected Bryan's assertion that his program was biblically inspired. "That platform," said a prominent Baptist minister, "was made in hell." A Chicago evangelist criticized Bryan's invocation of "the Crown of Thorns and the Cross of the Nazarene" to justify "the unholy spectres of dishonour and revolution." A widely read Episcopal magazine warned that Bryan's election would cause "the ruin of national fiscal morality." In all the country, Bryan's managers could find only four prominent clergymen who were willing to endorse him. On the Sunday before election, many Protestant pastors preached against Bryanism with the text, "Thou Shalt Not Steal."[29]

As James Sundquist has shown, Bryan actually ran *behind* the combined 1892 Democratic and Populist vote in every county of Illinois, Indiana, Iowa, and Wisconsin, including many counties where evangelicals were numerous. Paul Kleppner has found some correlation in rural counties of Ohio and Michigan between support for Bryan and the dry vote in prohibition referenda in other years. But even in five Ohio counties cited by Kleppner for their evangelical characteristics, Bryan got no better than 45.5 percent of the vote, compared with 45.2 for Cleveland in 1892. In the states of the Middle Border, Bryan ran well ahead of the normal Democratic vote, carrying Kansas, Nebraska, and South Dakota. But this probably had more to do with populist economics than with evangelical morality.[30]

While failing to exert much attraction for evangelicals outside the Great Plains, Bryan's campaign managed to chill many normally Democratic working-class voters in the major cities of the Northeast and around the Great Lakes. Many of them were no doubt persuaded by the Republicans' argument that free silver would further undermine the economy, costing industrial workers their jobs as well as hurting corporate managers and stockholders. Samuel Gompers, head of the American Federation of Labor, steered his part of the union movement away from collaboration with the populists. "Cooperation or amalgamation of the wageworkers' organization with the People's party," he had said in 1892, was "impossible, because it is unnatural." The Knights of Labor, which had been more inclined to coalesce with the populists, had almost vanished by 1896. But the distrust felt among many urban workers toward Bryan was cultural as well as economic. Bryan's evangelical style and emphasis on Protestant moral values were jarring to the sensibilities of many working-class Catholics. And his appeal to class antagonism ran counter to Catholic social conservatism. Archbishop John Ireland of St. Paul, a leading Catholic prelate of the time, warned that the populists were "lighting torches which, borne in the hands of reckless men, may light up in our country the lurid fires of a commune." McKinley's inclusion of Catholics in his state administration in Ohio, and his refusal to be bullied by the A.P.A., also probably won him some points with Catholic voters.[31]

Even the weather in 1896 seemed to turn Republican. The drought ended and the fall harvest was bountiful. Some of the economic pressure felt by farmers receded. In the old Northwest, many farmers, whose livestock consumed grain produced on the Great Plains, believed that farmers farther west were at least partly to blame for problems that had resulted from earlier overexpansion.

In the final weeks before the election, enthusiasm became feverish on both sides. Bryan's crusade for free silver and relief for the "toiling masses" was met by McKinley's no less impassioned campaign for sound money and the "full dinner pail." Bryan could not stop talking—he set new world records for the number of speeches on a single day; on the day before election he spoke 27 times. In Canton, Ohio, meanwhile, throngs of the Republican faithful arrived daily by railroad and marched to McKinley's home, where the candidate appeared regularly on his front porch to respond to their questions (which he insisted on editing in advance). Railroad records show that during the fall of 1896 about 750,000 people made the journey to Canton—*more than 12 percent of McKinley's total vote in November.*[32]

As Figure 8–1 shows, Bryan's strategy did not wholly fail. He swept the South and carried the new western states admitted during Harrison's term (except North Dakota), plus Colorado, Missouri, Nevada, Nebraska, Kansas, and Utah (admitted to the union in 1896 after the Mormon church proscribed polygamy), for an electoral vote total of 176. In the Northeast, Bryan was crushed as expected, losing every county in New England and all but one in New York (including New York City and Brooklyn). For the first time since 1872, the Republicans successfully invaded the Border states, carrying Maryland, Delaware, West Virginia, and Kentucky. In the states of the old Northwest, which both sides regarded as crucial, McKinley achieved a clean sweep, with majorities ranging from 51 percent in Indiana to 60 percent in Wisconsin.

McKinley's vote in the electoral college was 271, a margin of 95. The nationwide popular vote was fairly close, McKinley winning about 7 million votes to about 6.5 million for Bryan, on an 80 percent turnout. But for the first time since 1876, the winner in the popular vote had an absolute majority, 51 percent, rather than only a plurality. The Republicans won large majorities in both houses of Con-

Figure 8–1   Electoral vote by states, 1896

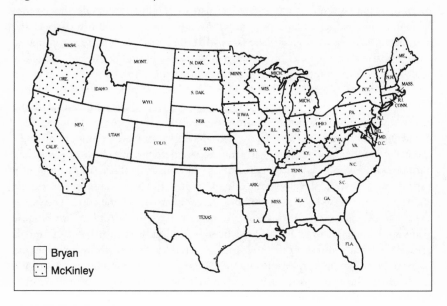

Source: Historical Statistics of the United States, Bureau of the Census, 1961

gress. The Republican party had emerged, once again, as the clear majority party in the country.

THE SYSTEM REINFORCED

The outcome of the populist uprising of the 1890s showed among other things the durability of the two-party system that had come out of the Civil War. Populism had expressed deeply felt social and economic discontents and had gathered a sizable constituency among a still numerous social class, small farmers in the West and South. Under a different electoral system, such as proportional representation or one including a second round in the general election, or even at a different time in American history, it might well have provided the basis for an effective and enduring national party. But the institutions of the electoral college and first-past-the-post elections, and the still compelling loyalties holding most northern Protestants to the Republican party and most white southerners to the Democratic party, combined to prevent the survival of the People's party, if not of populism as a social force.

The political outcome of the populist uprising illuminated a quality of the post–Civil War party system that had not much characterized the party system before 1860: when a powerful social force developed, it was likely to be taken up by one of the two major parties rather than to produce a durable third party. Whether the Democrats took over populism in 1896 or populism took over the Democrats is perhaps arguable. The fact is that the Democratic party continued to exist, its basic constituencies little changed, while populism became an ideological strain expressed by interest groups working within the party.

Why did the Populists fail to endure as a significant independent party while the Republicans of the 1850s and 1860s succeeded? In part because the underlying political system, rooted in the Constitution and the natural competition between the republican and liberal traditions, had grown more mature. Important social groups and individual politicians had acquired weighty interests in maintaining their parties. Both Republican and Democratic politicians had taken pains to put legal barriers in the way of development of new parties. In part because the economic and social troubles of the 1890s, though severe, did not match the controversy over slavery as a force capable of smashing an entire party system. And in part because populism was related organically to the liberal tradition that normally had found its primary political expression through the party that descended from Jefferson and Jackson. Populism, in fact, by infusing the Democratic party with its grievances and ideals, drew the party back to its roots and renewed the vigor of competition between the liberal and republican traditions.

The Republican party came out of the 1896 election stronger than it had been since the years right after the Civil War. Though both major parties made gains in some areas and among some groups formerly dominated by the other, the advances achieved by Bryan in the Great Plains and Rocky Mountain states proved to be short-lived, while some of the Republican gains in urban and suburban areas of the Northeast and Midwest were to be of long duration.

By 1900, six of the western states that had voted for Bryan were back in the Republican column. Four years later, as the West went wild for Theodore Roosevelt, the Republican ticket achieved a regional clean sweep.

Among the formerly Democratic major cities that voted for McKinley in 1896, in contrast, several, including Milwaukee, Indianapolis, and Columbus, Ohio, became firmly Republican. Detroit, New Haven, and Cleveland, all former Democratic strongholds, became marginal in local, state, and national elections. Chicago, which had leaned Democratic, was closely contested between the two parties until the onset of the Great Depression in the 1930s. Only New York, Boston, Jersey City, and St. Paul quickly swung back to the Democratic column. In cities that had traditionally been Republican, including Philadelphia, Pittsburgh, and Cincinnati, Republican majorities became overwhelming—in Philadelphia ranging around three to one.[33]

The 1896 election witnessed for the first time the emergence of a solidly Republican vote in newly developing suburbs—bosky communities on the borders of great cities, largely populated by families in which the breadwinner commuted each day to work in the city. Before the 1890s, the counties in which these communities were located had been largely rural and often, for historic reasons, Democratic. Bergen County, New Jersey, just across the Hudson River from New York City, had voted Democratic in every presidential election from the Civil War through 1892. In 1896 it voted almost two to one for McKinley. Westchester County, New York, just north of New York City, heavily Democratic since the days of the Regency, voted 60 percent for McKinley. Montgomery and Bucks Counties, Pennsylvania, outside Philadelphia, both marginally Democratic since

Figure 8–2   California vote by counties, 1896

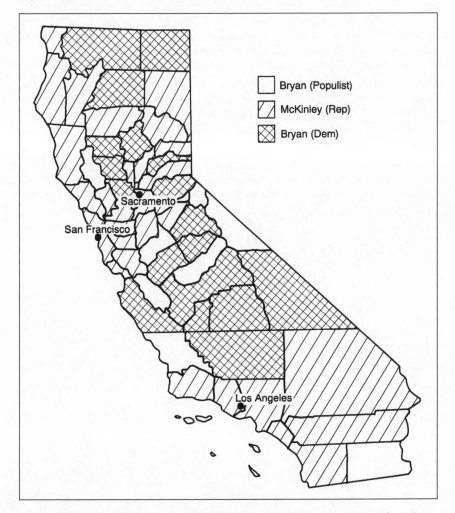

Bryan (Populist)

McKinley (Rep)

Bryan (Dem)

Source: Edgar Eugene Robinson, *The Presidential Vote, 1896–1932,* Octagon, New York, 1947

the Civil War, each went for McKinley over Bryan by margins of about three to two. All these suburban bailiwicks, growing rapidly in population and influence, and others like them in New England and the Midwest, were to be Republican strongholds during most of the twentieth century.

California, which was still casting only nine electoral votes (fewer than 19 other states, including Alabama and Kansas), voted narrowly for McKinley in 1896 in patterns substantially different from those it had displayed in voting even more narrowly for Lincoln in 1860, as shown in Figure 8–2. As in 1860, San Francisco and the counties surrounding San Francisco Bay were Republican, and most of the agricultural counties in the great Central Valley were Democratic or Populist. But the southern counties, including Los Angeles, Orange, and San Diego, largely settled after 1870 from the Republican Midwest and still accounting for only about 20 percent of the state's total vote, had shifted from Democrat to Republican, with fateful consequences for the state's political future.

The 1896 election, beyond its immediate effects on national policy, represented a reinvigoration of the competition between the republican and liberal traditions within the structure of the party system that had come out of the Civil War. As Sundquist writes, the party system of 1860, "rather than being weakened by the new upheaval, was reinforced."[34] But the content of political conflict carried on through the system had been changed. The liberal tradition, which during the 1870s and 1880s had been confined to limited expression through city machines and associations of rural radicals, had been restored as the dominant force within the national Democratic party. It was from the battle lines laid down in 1896 that much of the political struggle and discourse of the twentieth century was to rise.

9

REACTION AGAINST PARTIES

The Progressive Era

THE POPULISTS OF THE EARLY 1890s had aimed to form a party capable of break-ing through the existing party system. But they had no particular objection to the party as a political institution. In contrast, the progressives, their successors as advocates and agents of political reform, set out not only to supplant one of the major parties but to reduce drastically the role and power of party institutions.

The progressives, who won control of many state and local governments around the turn of the century and established broad influence in Congress and in several national administrations, had almost as low a view of parties as the Founders. Governmental inefficiency and political corruption, they argued, grew almost inevitably from the party system. Parties of the kind that had evolved by the end of the nineteenth century, Herbert Croly, a leading progressive ideologist and publi-cist, claimed, were concerned chiefly with the pursuit of patronage, which pro-duced "enfeeblement" of government. "Overthrow of the two-party system," Croly wrote, was "indispensable to successful progressive democracy."[1]

The progressives concentrated mainly on institutional reform, rather than, like the populists, on economic redistribution. Among their principal targets were exist-ing party structures. Where the progressives won power, particularly in the West, they passed laws that shackled party operations and undermined party discipline. The effects of these changes on the political system were profound, and they con-tinue to be felt to the present day.

THE BEST OF TIMES

After McKinley's victory in 1896, the Republicans entered a period of political dominance at the national level. Prosperity returned, just as McKinley had said it would. Some economists today argue that discoveries of large gold deposits in Alaska and South Africa were more responsible than McKinley's policies for the economic boom. But most voters were not inclined to haggle. The Republicans had offered an economic approach they promised would bring good times. When good times in fact followed, most of the electorate were prepared to credit the physician whose remedy had been tried.

Matched a second time against Bryan in 1900, McKinley won by a landslide margin of more than 6 percentage points in the popular vote and 292 to 155 in the electoral college. In 1904 Theodore Roosevelt, who had succeeded to the presidency after McKinley's assassination by an anarchist in 1901, achieved a truly massive popular vote majority of almost 20 percentage points over the Democratic candidate, Judge Alton B. Parker of New York, a moderate conservative in the tradition of Tilden and Cleveland. Roosevelt carried every state outside the former Confederacy except Maryland and Kentucky.

What Roosevelt called the "normal Republican majority" appeared to have become an enduring reality in the nation's political life. Republicans maintained seemingly unassailable majorities in both houses of Congress. Even in midterm congressional elections, which almost always produce gains for the party that does not hold the White House, Republican majorities suffered little erosion. In the midterm election of 1902, with Roosevelt freshly in office and the economy buoyant, the Republicans actually won seats formerly held by Populists in both houses of Congress.

Financial panics in 1903 and 1907, with some spillover effects on the general economy, did little to dent Republican dominance. In 1908 the Democrats returned to Bryan, still the ardent champion of economic and cultural populism. Though national unemployment, in the wake of the 1907 panic, had risen above 8 percent, Bryan lost to William Howard Taft, Roosevelt's chosen successor, by more than a million votes.

In one region of the country, the South, the Republican tide did not run— indeed quite the opposite. The Democratic national ticket carried every state of the former Confederacy, except Tennessee in 1920, in every election between 1896 and 1928. Democrats virtually monopolized southern state and local offices and representation in Congress.

Hegemony in one region, however, could not by itself make the Democrats serious contenders for national power. At the national level in the early years of the new century, the Republican majority appeared almost impregnable.

Yet there were factors in the objective situation that were bound, eventually, to produce political discord. The Republican national majority after McKinley's reelection seemed so secure against external challenge that it was almost certain to spawn internal conflict. Party factions that had hung together while populism seemed a genuine threat now felt free to pursue their particular, sometimes clashing, agendas. Competing personal ambitions came into play.

The nation, moreover, despite the general glow of optimism that greeted the new century, faced difficult—some intellectual critics said potentially fatal—underlying social problems. Growing concentration of wealth in the hands of a relatively few financiers, corporate tycoons, and rich families seemed to many Americans, including some who rejected the economic nostrums of populism, a menace to the social foundations of democracy.

Industrialization, while producing a generally rising material standard of living, required many workers to labor under conditions that were unhealthy, dangerous, or demoralizing and disrupted ancient ties of working people to land, craft, community, and even family. Rapidly growing cities in the East and Midwest fostered crime, political corruption, crowded and unsanitary living conditions, and a sense of social atomism. Vast migrations from southern and eastern Europe brought new hands to support economic growth and enriched the variety of American life. But they also introduced religious, cultural, and moral differences that offended or frightened many descendants of earlier settlers, including German and Irish Catholics and German Jews. Pursuit of material things, encouraged by the very productivity of the American economy and incited by the newly created industry of mass advertising, conflicted with traditional virtues of thrift, modesty, sharing, and temperance. Social freedom opened new opportunities for women and youth and enlarged the range of available recreations and pleasures but inevitably caused tension within families and communities.

Populism had represented, in part, an attempt to deal with some of these problems through a return to the social and economic conditions of an earlier time. It had grown up as a challenge to the dominant Republican ideology and had been embraced by the opposition Democratic party. The progressive movement, which began to develop in the latter part of the 1890s, was, in contrast, an extension of the dominant ideology. It built on the assumptions of that ideology and tried to cure some of its operational flaws.

SOURCES OF PROGRESSIVISM

The root source of the progressive movement may have been the tendency that Gunnar Myrdal discerned among ordinary Americans, when they "see something wrong," to feel "not only that there should be a law against it, but also that an organization should be formed to combat it."[2] Its more immediate sources were diverse, sometimes overlapping, and sometimes in conflict. They included:

The Federalist Tradition. The Liberal Republicans of the 1870s and the "mugwump" Republicans who broke with the party in 1884 to vote for Cleveland against Blaine, had passed on the Federalist tradition of public service descended from John Adams, John Marshall, and John Jay. (Party regulars at the time said that a mugwump was one who "sat on the fence with his mug on one side and his wump on the other.") Federalist Republicans fully subscribed to the basic principles of the Republican ideology but believed it had been corrupted by machine bosses like Quay and Platt. They also were critical of business-oriented politicians like Hanna, who they thought placed too much emphasis on the economic aspect of Republicanism while neglecting the moral idealism Republicans inherited from Lincoln, Charles Sumner, and other reformers of the 1860s.

Politicians and publicists in the Federalist tradition tended to be moderate free traders who reflected the interests of finance capitalism and the internationalist vision of the east coast intelligentsia, rather than orthodox Republican protectionists. Their number included Theodore Roosevelt in New York, Henry Cabot Lodge in Massachusetts, Philander Knox (McKinley's Attorney General) in Pennsylvania, William Howard Taft in Ohio, and a host of young lawyers, businessmen, and journalists, like Elihu Root, Henry Stimson, and George Perkins, clustered around Roosevelt's banner in New York (some of whom also had other motives for becoming progressives, as I will mention below).

The Social Gospel Movement. Toward the end of the nineteenth century Protestant denominations later designated "mainline" (Methodists, Presbyterians, Episcopalians, Lutherans, and Congregationalists, among others) produced a body of social and political activists espousing the "Social Gospel." Inspired by eloquent preachers like Washington Gladden, Josiah Strong, and Walter Rauschenbusch, and by lay militants like Frances Willard and Jane Addams, the Social Gospellers held that Christian values were affronted by the economic suffering and social corruption associated with industrialization and urbanization. "The keener moral insight created by Christianity," Rauschenbusch declared, "should lend its help in scrutinizing all claims to property and power in order to detect latent public rights and to recall the recreant stewards to their duty." Some of the Social Gospellers advocated a vague kind of socialism as the ultimate cure to the problems of modern society, but most of them concentrated on attacking immediate social evils such as drunkenness, gambling, political corruption, slum housing, interference with workers' right to organize, denial of legal equality to women, and economic exploitation of children.[3]

Many Social Gospellers were active in the Republican party, the political home of most northern mainline Protestants. A study of leading progressive Republicans in California found that almost all were "urban, native-born, high-status Protestants from the old independent middle class."[4]

As with the populists, there was an element of reaction against cultural and ethnic displacement in the indignation that moved the Social Gospellers. "I am," Frances Willard said, "first a Christian, then I am a Saxon, then I am an American." Most Social Gospellers felt genuine sympathy for the urban poor of all ethnic groups who were, as Rauschenbusch observed in his parish in the Hell's Kitchen section of New York, "out of work, out of clothes, out of shoes, and out of hope." But cultural pride sometimes produced moral arrogance. Many progressives, complained Brand Whitlock, himself a veteran of many reform campaigns, believed "that there were no social problems that the Anti-Saloon League could not solve in a week."[5]

The Municipal Reform Movement. Another batch of progressives concentrated on rationalizing and cleaning up city governments. The party machines that had taken hold in most large cities not only were exacting tribute in the form of payoffs and graft but were failing to deliver municipal services with anything approaching acceptable efficiency. The spectacular growth of many eastern and midwestern cities had created enormous problems in meeting needs for new schools, protection against crime and fire, public transportation, water, sewage disposal, and other public services. When city governments did badly at coping with these problems, it was natural to blame a political system that filled government jobs with party workers and that demanded campaign contributions or outright bribes as conditions for obtaining city contracts.

Business executives and middle-class citizens, most of whom still lived inside city limits, felt united with the moral reformers by practical need. "The professional politician must be ousted," said a reform leader in Des Moines in 1906, "and in his place capable businessmen chosen to conduct the affairs of the city." The reform drive in Los Angeles, said one of its organizers, was "unquestionably a movement on behalf of the businessman, the taxpayer, and decent government." In the middle-to-late 1890s and the first years of the new century, reform administrations took over city halls in New York, Jersey City, Chicago, Detroit, Cleveland, and Toledo, among other municipalities.[6]

The municipal reform movement gave new currency to the view that most problems of government are technical problems of administration. Politics should not be a battle over spoils, or a struggle between groups defined by religion or ethnicity or class or memories of ancient wars, but a means for gaining public support for scientifically constructed systems of taxation, management of services, and budget control. To help formulate scientific solutions to governmental problems, city reformers and their business allies set up privately financed municipal research agencies in many large cities. The first of these was the Bureau of Municipal Research of New York City, launched in 1906 with funds largely supplied by Andrew Carnegie and John D. Rockefeller.[7]

Reformers decided that the political parties, Republican as well as Democratic, were standing in the way of the application of scientific administrative techniques to city problems. Municipal reformers of the Progressive Era liked to say there was "no Republican or Democratic way to clean the streets." As a practical matter, reformers found that loyalty to national parties was an obstacle to their getting control of city governments. If voters stuck to their national parties in city elections, forces supporting reform in both parties were likely to be divided and defeated by the locally dominant party machine.[8]

In 1909 municipal reformers in Boston, allied with Republicans in the Massachusetts legislature, made Boston one of the first major cities to adopt nonpartisan city government. This example was soon followed by other cities, particularly in the West and South. By 1929, 26 of the nation's 36 largest cities held nonpartisan elections for local offices.[9]

City reformers were bound to be drawn eventually into conflict with state machines, Republican or (in states like New Jersey and Indiana) Democratic. If reform was needed at the municipal level, why should not its principles be applied to state government as well? Cities, moreover, were dependent on the states for much of their income and were subject to extensive state regulation. Reform mayors raised their sights to state capitals. In Michigan, Hazen S. Pingree, reform mayor of Detroit, a Republican, took on the Republican state machine led by Senator James McMilland and in 1896 was elected governor. In Ohio, Tom Johnson, mayor of Cleveland, a Democrat, who attacked not only machine politics but business corruption, ran for governor in 1902 but lost to his conservative Republican opponent.

Trust-busting. A new kind of "muckraking" journalism, commissioned by recently launched mass-circulation magazines, helped stir up anger against the business trusts and their corrupting effects on government. Series of articles by Ida Tarbell on the formation of Standard Oil, Lincoln Steffens on collusion between corporations and corrupt politicians, and Upton Sinclair on ruthless practices in the meat-packing industry, among others, aroused public indignation and demand for reform.

After Bryan's defeat in 1896, the fight against the trusts was mainly championed by progressive Republican governors at the state level, including Robert LaFollette in Wisconsin, Albert Cummins in Iowa, and Hiram Johnson in California. Opposition to big business had a regional aspect, expressing resistance of the western "periphery" against the eastern "metropole," in the terminology of W. D. Burnham and Paul Kleppner. But it also was taken up by some politicians in the Northeast and eventually attracted the partial support of Theodore Roosevelt.

The populists also had attacked big business. But they had concentrated on providing more economic leverage for small farmers and other members of the "toiling masses" in the marketplace. The progressive Republicans emphasized the threat to democratic institutions posed by unchecked business power. In 1897 the Wisconsin Progressive Republicans, led by LaFollette, issued a platform of eleven planks, eight of which were primarily political or governmental, including promises to "nominate candidates by Australian ballot at a primary election"; to "enact and enforce laws to punish bribery in every form by the lobby"; to "prohibit the acceptance by public officials of railroad passes" (a standard means through which the railroads won favor with state legislators); and to "enact and enforce laws making character and competency the requisite for service in our penal and charitable institutions." Of the three planks that were primarily economic, two dealt with foreign trade, calling, ambiguously, for both "reciprocity" and "protection for the products of the factory and the farm"; the third forthrightly endorsed conservative Republican monetary policy: "Sound money, a dollar's worth of dollar."[10]

Progressives at the state level fought against patronage-based state machines, whose coffers were filled by unreported contributions from corporations. Like the municipal reformers, many of the state progressives came to feel that organized parties were impediments to democratic government.

The anti-party measures instituted by Hiram Johnson in California to help break the power of the Southern Pacific Railroad epitomized the remedies to which many state progressives were drawn. In the early years of the twentieth century the Southern Pacific controlled both California party organizations and "secretly fostered new factions to keep the old ones in check." The railroad's money, according to Abe Rueff, Republican boss of San Francisco, "was the power behind almost every political throne and behind almost every insurgent revolt." The Southern Pacific's Political Bureau maintained "a railroad political manager in every county in the state. This manager might be a Republican boss in a Republican county, or a Democratic boss in a Democratic county; in important or doubtful counties he was merely the railroad boss, with whom both Republican and Democratic bosses had to deal." The state was usually competitive in national elections, but in Sacramento, the state capital, the Southern Pacific was king.[11]

In 1910, Hiram Johnson (whose father was a Republican state legislator and a stalwart defender of the railroad) entered the Republican primary for governor. Running on the slogan "Kick the Southern Pacific out of politics," he won a sweeping victory. Johnson received some support in the primary from urban liberals in the San Francisco Bay area, but his strongest backing came from socially conservative middle-class Protestants in southern California, particularly Los Angeles and Orange counties, apparently attracted in part by his identification with puritanical moral reform. In the general election, Johnson again swept the south but was closely contested by his Democratic opponent in the north.[12]

As governor, Johnson persuaded the legislature to establish a public utility commission which subjected the Southern Pacific and other railroads to fairly strict regulation. Johnson's main legislative effort, however, was devoted to enacting a far-reaching program of electoral and party reform, including the introduction of the referendum, initiative, and recall, which he claimed would assure popular control of government. The parties were reduced to little more than shells. Johnson also secured passage of a cross-filing law, which permitted candidates for state and congressional offices to enter primaries of both parties without naming their own party on the ballot. The cross-filing law not only helped wreck California parties but contributed to the development of an almost totally candidate-oriented brand of state electoral politics.

The "New Nationalism." America's quick victory in the Spanish–American War of 1898 produced a wave of enthusiastic support for an expanded role for the United States in world affairs. Theodore Roosevelt, who had been assistant secretary of the navy when the war began, and others drew on the expansionist doctrines of Admiral Alfred Thayer Mahan, who called for an enlarged navy and the acquisition of bases and colonies all over the globe, particularly in Latin America and on the Pacific rim. "God has not been preparing the English-speaking and Teutonic peoples for a thousand years for nothing but vain and idle self-contemplation and self-admiration," Republican Senator Albert Beveridge of Indiana declaimed in 1900. "No! He has made us the master organizers of the world to establish system where chaos reigns. . . . And of all our race He has marked the American people as his chosen nation to finally lead in the regeneration of the world. This is the divine mission of America, and it holds for us all the profit, all the glory, all the happiness possible to man. . . ."[13]

Aggressive pursuit of America's national interest abroad was to be accompanied by rededication to "national purpose" at home. "The promise of American life," Herbert Croly wrote in 1909, "is to be fulfilled not merely by a maximum amount of economic freedom but by a certain measure of discipline; not merely by the abundant satisfaction of individual desires but by a large measure of individual subordination and self-denial." American capitalism was to be brought more into the service of national destiny. "The true friend of property, the true conservative," Roosevelt said in a widely acclaimed speech he called "The New Nationalism" in 1910, "is he who insists that the creature of man's making shall be the servant and not the master of the man who made it. The citizens of the United States must effectively control the mighty commercial forces which they themselves have called into being."[14]

Many businessmen were alarmed by the degree of government regulation of the economy that Roosevelt's program seemed to envision. But some leaders of the business community, as Gabriel Kolko and other historians have shown, welcomed the new nationalism, in both its international and domestic aspects, with open arms. The Republican ideology had never required complete nonintervention by government in the economy. The protective tariff, which most Republicans supported, was after all a massive intrusion by government into the "natural" operation of the market. And Republicans carried on the Hamiltonian and Whig traditions, calling for federally financed internal improvements to promote economic growth.

By the first decade of the twentieth century some American businessmen with broad horizons, particularly among Wall Street financiers, had concluded that unrestrained competition was undercutting maximization of profits. Private efforts to control competition were coming unstuck, and in any case such efforts might now be subject to prosecution under the Sherman Anti-trust Act, which had been enacted in 1890. The financial panics of 1903 and 1907 persuaded growing numbers of businessmen that the federal government should take a hand in stabilizing and rationalizing markets. Observing the effects of cutthroat price competition in the steel industry, Andrew Carnegie commented in 1908: "It always comes back to me that Government control, and that alone, will properly solve the problem." Carnegie was in many ways an exceptional businessman, and his view cannot be taken as representative. But his opinion was echoed by so hardbitten an entrepreneur as Judge Elbert Gary, chief executive of U.S. Steel, who in 1911 told a congressional committee: "I believe we must come to enforced publicity and governmental control . . . even as to prices."[15]

Gabriel Kolko has identified George Perkins, partner in the Morgan bank and close adviser to Roosevelt, as the principal pointman in bringing a portion of the business elite into the progressive movement. "Federal regulation is feasible," Perkins told an audience of businessmen in 1909, "and if we unite and work for it now we may be able to secure it; whereas, if we continue our fight against it much longer, the incoming tide may sweep the question along to either government ownership or socialism."[16]

The sources feeding progressivism pursued differing, in some cases incompatible, social goals. But they had in common certain assumptions and themes: government should play an active role in promoting the public good; political life is best seen as a moral struggle between good and evil; public confidence requires honest elections and effective government; the existing party system is a major barrier to political reform; and government should serve the public interest rather than advancing particular interests to the exclusion of others or acting chiefly as broker between competing special interests. All these themes came together in the pronouncements and personality of the charismatic leader who became the progressive movement's virtual embodiment: Theodore Roosevelt.

THE ROOSEVELT FACTOR

Through most of his career, except during his third-party campaign for the presidency in 1912, Roosevelt described himself as a "conservative." Looking back in 1916 on his leadership of the progressive movement, he claimed that his approach had represented "not wild radicalism . . . [but] the highest and wisest form of conservatism."[17]

Roosevelt was drawn to politics as a young man in the early 1880s by ambition and an itch for public service—and perhaps by a desire to settle scores with machine bosses like Tom Platt whom he held responsible for his father's humiliation in the fight over the New York collectorship in 1877. He began attending meetings of his local Republican organization in midtown Manhattan, which he found manned by "cheap lawyers, saloon keepers, and horsecar conductors. . . ." Asked by friends in the social elite why he was associating with such dreadful people, he replied "that the people I knew did not belong to the governing class, and that the other people did—and that I intended to be one of the governing class; and if they proved too hard-bit for me I supposed I would have to quit, but that I certainly would not quit until I had made the effort and found out whether I really was too weak to hold my own in the rough and tumble."[18]

Though a reformer from the start, Roosevelt resolved to operate within the structure of the Republican party. His fellow delegates to his first Republican national convention, in 1884, he observed, included "some scoundrels, but for the most part good, ordinary men, who do not do very much thinking, who are pretty honest themselves, but who are callous to any but very flagrant wrongdoing in others, unless it is brought home to them forcibly." Under pressure to join the mugwumps who were deserting Blaine to vote for Cleveland in 1884, he denounced the bolters as suffering "from a species of moral myopia, complicated by intellectual strabismus." He took over leadership of the municipal reform movement in New York but had nothing but scorn for "ultra independents" who refused to work within the limits set by political reality. "The Goo-Goo and Mugwump idiots," he said, "are quite as potent forces for evil as the most corrupt politicians." In his dislike for economic and social radicals he at times exhibited an almost Tory sensibility: he once declined to be introduced to the radical Governor John Altgeld of Illinois because he thought he might someday have to "meet him at the head of troops."[19]

Returning from the Spanish–American War in the fall of 1898 a highly publicized hero, Roosevelt, obeying his sense of what was practical, went to Tom Platt's "Sunday School"—the sessions the boss held in New York's Fifth Avenue Hotel to confer party endorsements and other political favors. Following his own sense of what was practical, Platt backed Roosevelt for the governorship. This alliance of convenience proved unhappy. Before becoming governor, Roosevelt had viewed reform as a matter of throwing out corrupt politicians and installing leaders motivated by dedication to public service. "We were still accustomed," he later recalled, "to talking of the 'machine' as if it were something merely political, with which business had nothing to do." But experience in Albany convinced him that support from big business was "the most important element" in Platt's "strength." Roosevelt concluded that the political system was permeated by the influence of irresponsible corporate wealth. He set out to break the power that the alliance of big business and machine politicians exercised over the state legislature. Unlike LaFollette and Hiram Johnson, however, he sought not to dismantle the parties but to make the Republican party the instrument of reform.[20]

Platt dealt with the problem by proposing that the Republicans nominate Roosevelt for Vice President in 1900. Mark Hanna, elected to the Senate from Ohio in 1897, was appalled. Roosevelt, he believed, represented forces within the Republican party that threatened to negate the victory won at such cost in 1896. But McKinley, to Hanna's dismay, would do nothing to block the move, and Platt, with help from Quay, secured Roosevelt's nomination. "Don't any of you realize," Hanna asked, "that there's only one life between that madman and the presidency?"[21]

Roosevelt proved a zestful campaigner, as McKinley had expected, stumping the country with energy and eloquence that matched Bryan's. The Republican ticket won an easy victory in November. In less than a year McKinley was dead. Hanna, sunk in grief over the loss of his friend, shuddered at the thought of "that cowboy" in the White House.

As President, Roosevelt worked closely with the Republican leadership in Congress to achieve passage of a moderate economic reform program. He never gave up his dislike for Platt and his relations with Hanna remained cool. But he got on well with Quay, whom he privately described as "worth a hundred men like

Miller of the *New York Times,* [or] Villard and Ogden of the *Evening Post* [journalists whom Roosevelt placed among the 'goo-goos']."[22]

After Hanna's death in 1904, leadership of the business-oriented Republicans in Congress passed to Senate Majority Leader Nelson Aldrich of Rhode Island and House Speaker Joseph Cannon of Illinois. During Roosevelt's second term, the congressional Old Guard, as it came to be called, was increasingly challenged by progressive Republicans like LaFollette of Wisconsin, elected to the Senate in 1905, and George Norris of Nebraska, elected to the House in 1902. Though Roosevelt looked on the progressives as part of his natural constituency, he took pains to remain on good terms with the conservative leadership. When LaFollette urged him to hold out for a tougher act regulating railroads in 1906, Roosevelt objected, "But you can't get any such bill as that through Congress." LaFollette replied, "That is not the first consideration, Mr. President." Roosevelt was adamant: "I want to get something through." His reward was the Hepburn Act, which gave the Interstate Commerce Commission limited but effective powers to protect consumers.[23]

Roosevelt made clear to leaders of the business community that, while he aimed to eliminate what he regarded as abuses in the economic system, he did not plan to attempt fundamental change of the system itself. Elihu Root, grand vizier of New York's legal establishment and Roosevelt's secretary of state after 1905, told friends on Wall Street, "I say to you that [Roosevelt] has been . . . the greatest conservative force for protection of property and our institutions in the city of Washington." When the panic of 1907 struck, Roosevelt, following George Perkins' advice, agreed, as a gesture to restore business confidence, to allow J. P. Morgan to consummate the acquisition by U.S. Steel of Tennessee Coal and Iron, the major steel producer of the South.[24]

Deciding not to run for reelection in 1908, Roosevelt engineered the nomination and election of his secretary of war and close personal friend, William Howard Taft of Ohio. Taft, from a well-established family in Cincinnati (his father had been Grant's Attorney General), had strong school and family ties to New England and was at least as thoroughly imbued as Roosevelt with the Federalist creed of public service. He had thoroughly approved Roosevelt's program of economic and political reform, and he gave every indication of intending to carry it on. As has often been noted, Taft's Department of Justice actually brought more antitrust actions than Roosevelt's had—even to the extent of questioning the propriety of Roosevelt's approval of U.S. Steel's acquisition of Tennessee Coal and Iron. Taft, however, drew closer to the Old Guard leaders, Aldrich and Cannon, than Roosevelt had been perceived to be—following, he thought, Roosevelt's counsel that to be effective a President must have the support of his party in Congress.

Aldrich and Cannon represented the almost completely negative and pessimistic brand of conservatism that had grown stronger on one side of the Republican party while progressivism was advancing on the other. The Old Guard's dour humor was exemplified by Cannon's lament to Taft, as they rode one day down

Pennsylvania Avenue in the back seat of the White House's first open motor car, that he was "damned tired of this everlasting yielding to popular outcry against wealth" and "that unless we put a check to it . . . there is no telling where it will lead." Taft, wrote his military aide, Archie Butt, after a presidential trip to the Midwest, "simply hates Speaker Cannon and expresses his contempt for him whenever he can do so, yet he openly flattered him on the trip down the Mississippi, was photographed with his arms around his neck, and appeared to endorse him whenever they spoke together." Toward Aldrich, a fellow patrician, Taft felt genuine respect. But, as Archie Butt wrote to his sister: "Whether Senator Aldrich is a horse thief or not, the entire West and South so regard him, and to the former section, especially, he is regarded as the one man who is at enmity with their interests."[25]

Progressive strength among congressional Republicans continued to grow. LaFollette, Beveridge, and Albert Cummins, elected to the Senate from Iowa in 1908, regularly picked fights with Aldrich. In March 1910, George Norris led almost forty House Republicans to join the Democratic minority in a successful revolt against Cannon (and "Cannonism"). The insurgent coalition changed the House rules, drastically reducing the powers of the Speaker. Cannon offered to resign, but the majority voted to keep him on in his weakened office.[26]

Taft backed Aldrich in an effort to purge incumbent progressives in the Senate. In the 1910 Republican primaries, progressive forces won victories in Indiana, Wisconsin, Minnesota, Idaho, California, Washington, and New Hampshire. In November, the Democrats, profiting from Republican division and a moderate downturn in the economy, made sweeping gains in House races; with 56 added seats, they were able to form the majority for the first time since 1894. In the Senate, the Republicans retained control but with a greatly reduced majority.

Roosevelt, moved by some combination of animal restlessness, disapproval of the kind of conservatism represented by Aldrich and Cannon (whom he had begun referring to as "the enemy"), and disappointment with Taft's performance, openly criticized the administration. As the 1912 presidential election approached, Roosevelt showed clear signs of wishing to return to the White House. The new device of primaries to elect national convention delegates, adopted in 15 states by 1912, gave him the means for tapping his continuing popularity among the public. But first he had to dispose of LaFollette.[27]

BULL MOOSE PROGRESSIVES

In 1874 Robert LaFollette, then a young student at the University of Wisconsin in Madison, had listened to a talk by Chief Justice Edward Ryan of the Wisconsin Supreme Court. "A new and dark power" the Chief Justice warned, was "looming up" in American life. "Vast corporate combinations of unexampled capital" were "boldly marching, not for economic conquests only, but for political power. . . . The question will arise, and arise in your day, though perhaps not fully in mine,

'Which shall rule—wealth or man; which shall lead—money or intellect; who shall fill public stations—educated or patriotic free men, or feudal serfs of corporate capital?'" Young LaFollette took the message to heart and resolved to place himself on the side of "intellect" and political leadership by "educated or patriotic free men" (a constituency substantially different from that to which Bryan appealed).[28]

A few years later, LaFollette ran successfully for district attorney in Dane County, which includes Madison. Apparently without hesitation, he identified himself with the Republican party, which he regarded as "one of the most powerful and unified party organizations that ever existed, I suppose, anywhere in the world . . . the party of Lincoln and Grant and Sherman. . . ." His hero at the time was James Garfield, who he felt was "facing forward instead of backward." But he soon was challenging the state Republican machine led by Senator Philetus Sawyer, a wealthy timber baron who had made himself the political agent of the state's railroad and lumber interests.[29]

After several failures, LaFollette in 1900 fought his way up through the old convention system to win control of the Wisconsin Republican party. Elected governor of Wisconsin in 1900, and then elected to the United States Senate in 1905, he became the acknowledged leader of western progressives.

In 1911 LaFollette formed the National Progressive Republican League and indicated his intention of seeking the Republican presidential nomination against Taft. Like the platform of the Wisconsin progressives in 1897, the platform of the National Progressive Republican League concentrated on political and governmental reforms: direct election of United States senators; direct primaries for the nomination of all elective officials; adoption at the state level of initiative, referendum, and recall; and enactment of a "thoroughgoing corrupt practices act."[30]

Roosevelt at first presented himself as a centrist on the Republican spectrum, positioned between the passivity of Taft and the supposed radicalism of LaFollette. In a speech before Kansas Republicans, Roosevelt lambasted men "who make promises before elections that they do not intend to keep" (clearly meaning Taft) and men "whose eyes are a little too wild to make it safe to trust them" (LaFollette.)[31]

Feeling leadership of the progressive movement slipping away from him, LaFollette became vituperative on the stump. In a long, rambling speech before the Periodical Publishers Association in Philadelphia in February 1912, LaFollette self-destructed. "He kept repeating himself, endlessly and angrily, until the hour grew late and restless diners left the banquet hall or cried, without pity 'Sit down!' while the flow of words went on." Roosevelt's people put out word that the Senator from Wisconsin had suffered a nervous breakdown. LaFollette sank into a miasma of bitterness from which he never fully recovered.[32]

In a speech in Cleveland late in February, Roosevelt dramatically declared: "My hat is in the ring." In the primaries that followed, he won 236 delegates to 41 for LaFollette (mostly from Wisconsin) and only 34 for Taft. But only about 20 percent of the convention delegates were chosen through primaries.

During the course of the primary campaign, Roosevelt came out for the one genuinely radical cause he embraced in the course of his career: recall of judicial decisions. "When a judge decides a constitutional question," he said in a speech in Columbus, "when he decides what the people as a whole can or can not do, the people should have the right to recall the decision if they think it is wrong. A judge, Roosevelt declared, "is as much a servant of the people as any other official." Speaking with Rousseauian disdain for established norms, he averred that "legalistic justice is a dead thing."[33]

Root, Lodge, and Stimson immediately turned against Roosevelt on the judicial recall issue. So did his son-in-law, Nicholas Longworth, Republican congressman from Ohio, husband of the famous Alice. But militant advocates of participatory democracy were thrilled by Roosevelt's stand. It is of course possible that Roosevelt, in the course of his ruminations on government, had concluded that recalling judicial decisions would serve progressive values. But it seems fair to speculate that he was also opportunistically anxious to nail down support from Social Gospellers and Progressive Leaguers who might otherwise have backed LaFollette.

The Republican national convention gathered amidst great excitement in Chicago in the middle of June. Root, in the chair, gaveled through approval of Taft delegates for all disputed seats. Each side charged the other with bribery and theft. Roosevelt supporters controlled delegations, mostly elected through primaries, from Pennsylvania, Illinois, California, New Jersey, Minnesota—and even Ohio. Among the larger states, only New York, where the machine had delivered against its old nemesis, was solidly for Taft. On key procedural votes, the Taft forces had a majority of about 50 in a total of more than 1,000 delegates. More than one-third of Taft's delegates came from southern states that were sure to vote Democratic in November. If the small body of delegates pledged to LaFollette had supported the Roosevelt forces on procedural votes, enough Roosevelt delegates probably would have been seated to form a majority. LaFollette refused.[34]

When it became apparent that Taft would be renominated, many Roosevelt delegates left the convention hall and reassembled at two o'clock in the morning in the Congressional Hotel. Hiram Johnson jumped up on a table and announced that a new Progressive party would be formed the next day. Roosevelt hesitated. Was he really prepared to lead a bolt that might destroy the Republican party he had served and led for so long? If he was, could he command the resources that would enable him to wage a serious campaign? George Perkins and Frank Munsey, one of the great press lords of the day, joined Roosevelt in his hotel room and gave their assurance: "Colonel, we will see you through." (Later, some of Perkins' associates in the Morgan bank objected to his role in Roosevelt's campaign. Perkins replied: "Much that I am advocating would be decidedly to every corporation's advantage in a perfectly proper way. . . . I [therefore] can see no harm and much possible good in what I am doing.") Roosevelt announced his willingness to lead the Progressive cause.[35]

The new party's national convention met early in August, also in Chicago. It was, as one historian has observed, "less a convention than a revival." Veterans of scores of insurgent campaigns, dating back to the 1890s, converged on the convention hall. Delegates marched through the aisles singing hymns and wildly cheering every mention of Roosevelt's name. Their leader declared that he entered the campaign feeling "strong as a bull moose"—giving the Progressives their nickname, the Bull Moose party. Hiram Johnson was nominated for Vice President.[36]

The Progressive platform included planks calling for women's suffrage, direct election of United States senators, ratification of a constitutional amendment permitting a federal income tax, prohibition of child labor, a minimum wage for working women, and recall of judicial decisions. Jane Addams, the pioneer social worker and founder of Chicago's Hull House, said the platform's social welfare planks contained "all I have been fighting for for a decade." The plank on "Commercial Development," dictated by Perkins, pledged "strong national regulation of interstate commerce" but went on to affirm: "The corporation is an essential part of modern business. The concentration of modern business, in some degree, is both inevitable and necessary for national and international business efficiency."[37]

Roosevelt's acceptance speech was a scorching indictment of the existing party system. "Our fight," he said, "is a fundamental fight against both of the old party machines, for both are under the dominion of the plunder league of the professional politicians who are controlled and sustained by the great beneficiaries of privilege and reaction." But the way to overcome "privilege and reaction" was through government regulation rather than through trust-busting. The Sherman Act, he proposed, should be revised to permit utilization of "those forms of industrial organization that are indispensable to the highest productivity and efficiency." With the crowd roaring its approval, he proclaimed: "We stand at Armageddon, and we battle for the Lord!" The speech was, Frank Munsey wrote, "splendidly progressive" but "at the same time, amply conservative and sound."[38]

The national campaign that followed was the climax and in some ways the conclusion of the Progressive Era. The division in the Republican party assured the election of the Democratic candidate, Woodrow Wilson, as President, and helped the Democrats achieve majorities in both houses of Congress. Wilson included some ideas borrowed from the progressives in his administration's program and is himself identified by some historians as a progressive.[39] But he also represented newer forces at work in the polity and pointed toward the next era of social reform.

The Progressive party lingered in a withered condition until 1916 and then rejoined the Republicans. LaFollette finally ran for President in 1924 on a ticket he called Progressive, though it had little organized party support outside Wisconsin. He won 17 percent of the popular vote and the electoral votes of one state, Wisconsin.

10

THE PROGRESSIVE LEGACY, CITY
MACHINES, AND THE SOLID SOUTH

THOUGH THE PROGRESSIVES failed to win the presidency in 1912 and swiftly declined as a political party thereafter, the cumulative effects of the reforms enacted during the Progressive Era tremendously altered the nature of American politics. The weakening of parties was a principal result of progressivism—setting in motion a process that is still underway.

Yet some major political institutions that the progressives attacked came through the Progressive Era essentially unshaken. In the West, the progressives practically eradicated state and city machines based on patronage. But in most states of the Northeast and the lower Great Lakes region, the machines actually increased their efficiency and power. And in the South, the overwhelming dominance of the all-white Democratic party, based on the exclusion of blacks from participation in the political system, became even more secure.

CHANGES IN THE RULES OF THE GAME

Among the most consequential of the effects flowing from the Progressive Era were major changes in the laws, and even the constitutional provisions, that set the rules of electoral politics. The first big change in electoral rules began before the progressive movement really got started and probably helped lift it off the ground. The so-called Australian ballot—a method of election, named for the country of its origin, under which the state prints and makes available at the polling place ballots containing the names of all duly nominated candidates, to be cast in secret—received its first American use in Louisville, Kentucky, in 1880. Its use spread rapidly, and by 1892 the Australian ballot was required by three-quarters of the states containing 72 percent of the people. Four years later, after its adoption by New York, the Australian ballot was used by nine-tenths of the states with 92 percent of the people. (Its use did not become universal until 1950, when it was finally adopted by South Carolina.)[1]

Early in the nineteenth century voice voting—announcing one's choice audibly at the polls—had been a common form of suffrage. This method gradually gave way to the use of paper ballots printed by the parties, with each party's ballot containing only the names of its own candidates. Party workers distributed the ballots to voters they had reason to expect would support their party's ticket. Opportunities for vote-buying were obviously large. Even voters who did not sell their vote were under considerable pressure to vote a straight party line to stay in the good graces of the locally dominant party. The role of the party, not simply in the electoral process but in the actual business of casting a ballot, was crucial. A shift in public sentiment from one party to another was likely to have an effect right down through state and local offices.

As with many such procedural changes, the introduction of the Australian ballot did not immediately produce major changes in behavior. Party machines, where they existed, retained or even, for other reasons, increased their strength. Most voters continued to cast a straight party ticket. In New York straight party voting actually increased slightly during the first few years after adoption of the Australian ballot. But over time the effects of this new voting procedure were immense. Political organizations that still bought votes made sure they got what they paid for through such devices as the "floating ballot": they gave the voter a ballot already marked for the party slate and paid him only when he turned over the unmarked ballot he got at the polling place, ready for another round. But their hold over the great majority of voters was loosened. Voters might still vote a straight party ticket, but splitting a ticket eventually became more common.[2]

In time, ticket-splitting became routine for many voters and straight party voting became hardly respectable. Many states made it impossible to vote for the party slate by checking the party box on the ballot or by pulling a single lever. The party box was removed from the ballot and the voter was required to make a separate choice for each office up for election. (In 1988 only 20 states, mostly in the South and Midwest, still permitted voters to vote a straight ticket with one mark on the ballot or one pull of the lever.)[3]

The spread of nonpartisan elections for local offices further weakened the hold of parties on the voting process. Minnesota in 1913 went further and established nonpartisan elections for the state legislature; Nebraska did the same in 1934. Minnesota returned to partisan elections for the legislature in 1973; but Nebraska maintains nonpartisan elections for the nation's only unicameral legislature to the present day.

The swift adoption of the Australian ballot was a symptom of deep public discontent with the political process in the closing years of the nineteenth century, and specifically with the role of parties. Other reforms quickly followed. The one that had the most critical effect on parties was the introduction of the direct party primary. As early as 1842 parties in Crawford County, Pennsylvania, a rural county in the state's northwest corner, were selecting candidates for public office through secret balloting by party members. After the end of Reconstruction in the South, as real electoral choices increasingly were made inside the Democratic party, some states introduced primaries to give voters a chance to participate in the process (or more concretely to enable populists to consolidate their position after they got control of party machinery).[4]

Robert LaFollette saw the primary as the real key to revitalizing the political system. "Under our form of government," he wrote in 1898, "the entire structure rests upon the nomination of candidates for office. . . . With the nominations of all candidates absolutely in control of the people . . . the public official who desires denomination will not dare to seek it if he has served the machine and the lobby and betrayed the public trust." Under LaFollette's leadership, Wisconsin adopted the direct primary in 1903. Other states quickly followed. By 1912 a majority of the states had passed laws requiring primaries for nominations for at least some state offices. For the progressives, V. O. Key wrote, "the direct primary constituted a means by which an enlightened people might cut through the mesh of organized and privileged power and grasp control of government. They had a faith that the people, once equipped with the proper weapons, would throw from office the rascals in possession of the city halls and state houses."[5]

Some states, mainly those in the Northeast and Midwest with strong party organizations, adopted the "closed" primary under which voters can participate only in the primary of the party in which they are registered members. Other states, beginning with Wisconsin, established the "open" primary, under which voters can vote in either primary regardless of their party registration. The state of Washington in 1935 went further and introduced the "blanket" primary (sometimes called the "jungle" primary), under which all voters receive a ballot containing the names of all the nominees of all the parties and can vote for the candidates of one party for some offices and for the candidates of other parties for other offices. Alaska adopted the same practice when it became a state in 1959. Louisiana has gone even further, establishing a "nonpartisan" primary in which all candidates appear on the ballot without party designation. If no candidate wins a majority in the first round, there is a runoff between the candidates who finish first or second, even though they may both be of the same party.

In 1905 Wisconsin authorized the first primary for the selection of delegates to a national party convention. (A delegation from Wisconsin led by LaFollette had been denied seating at the 1904 Republican national convention.) In 1910 Oregon authorized the first presidential preferential primary, enabling voters to choose among candidates for a party's presidential nomination. By 1912, 15 states were holding some form of presidential primary—partly as a result of efforts by backers of LaFollette or Roosevelt who saw the primary as the best means for their candidate to win that year's Republican nomination. By 1916 the number had risen to 26. After 1920 interest in presidential primaries waned for a time and eight states repealed their primary laws. But the device remained an electoral option—available when political pressures so dictated in the 1970s.

"The primary system," Austin Ranney has written, "freed forces driving toward the disintegration of party organizations and facilitated the construction of factions and cliques attached to the ambitions of individual leaders." David Truman agrees: "The direct primary has been the most potent in a complex of forces pushing toward the disintegration of the party."[6]

There can be no doubt that the direct primary, over time, deeply eroded the cohesion of parties. Though party organizations, particularly in states with histories of strong party machines, were still often able to control nominations for offices with relatively low visibility, such as the city council and the state legislature and even the federal House of Representatives and the state judiciary, they became increasingly vulnerable to challenge from insurgent or independent candidates for such high-visibility offices as mayor, governor, and United States senator. In some states, running against the party organization in the primary, and therefore being seen as "unbossed," even came to be perceived as an advantage.

Oddly, nomination for the most visible office of all, the presidency, for some time continued to be influenced substantially by state and city party organizations, which still played important roles at national conventions. But the explosion of presidential primaries in the 1970s, along with other factors, took care of that.

One effect of the primary, even for lesser offices, Joseph Schlesinger has pointed out, was to strengthen the position of incumbent officeholders, with or without party organization endorsement. The incumbent, with opportunities to do favors directly for constituents and to get his name in the newspaper (and later his or her face on the television screen), could develop a personal following that enabled him, if necessary, to defeat a primary opponent put up by the organization. This could make him more "independent," in the way that LaFollette intended, and the Founders would have applauded. But as campaign costs rose, officeholders without roots in a party organization often came to rely on direct contributions from "the lobby." And officeholders unable to fall back on a strong party machine were open to intimidation by special-interest groups that could pour activists and resources into a primary.[7]

Loss of control over nominations greatly reduced the ability of the party organization—in some cases the "boss," but often simply the inner core of regulars who took responsibility for keeping the party running—to maintain a degree of harmony between branches and levels of government. If the organization could not punish dissidents, its capacity to achieve party unity on a given issue became, at most, advisory.

THE ATTACK ON PARTIES

Party organizations were further weakened by the enactment in 1913 of the Seventeenth Amendment, which provided for the direct election of federal senators, rather than election by state legislatures, as previously. Needing to attract mass support from the public, senators and senatorial candidates were motivated to build personal organizations, sometimes related to state party organizations, but focused mainly on the interests of the individual officeholder or candidate.

The Nineteenth Amendment, enacted in 1919, which gave women the right to vote, was chiefly propelled by the demand of women for political equality. But progressives also supported it with the argument that when women got the vote they would see to it that corrupt party machines would soon be demolished.

The chief immediate effect of women's suffrage was a sharp decline in electoral turnout as figured in percentage terms. Since women at first voted in smaller proportions than men, and since the size of the potential electorate had been approximately doubled, the percentage of turnout fell (though there were also other causes)—from 62 percent in the 1916 presidential election to 49 percent in 1920. The actual number of people voting, however, went up by more than 8 million, creating a great new reservoir of political power.

The progressives in some states enacted other measures aimed at extending democracy. The device of referendum, authorized first by South Dakota in 1898, enabled voters to act directly on legislation placed on the ballot by the state legislature or through public petition. Initiative, introduced by Oregon in 1902, empowered voters to require action on specific legislative items. And recall, introduced by Los Angeles in 1902 and at the state level by Oregon in 1908, permitted voters to depose elected officials in special elections before the end of their terms. These tools of direct democracy were most popular in the West, where the progressives were strongest, but varying mixes of them were adopted by more than two-thirds of the states. All three devices were instituted by California, Michigan, Colorado, Arizona, Idaho, Nevada, North Dakota, Oregon, and Washington (joined by Alaska in 1959). Their political effect in states where they were widely used, such as California, was to strengthen special-interest groups that could mobilize resources around a particular issue and to undermine parties.

LIMITING THE ELECTORATE

Many of the progressive reforms of the electoral process were aimed at broadening democratic participation. But some were aimed at driving corruption out of the system, even if it meant some contraction of democracy.

Since early in the nineteenth century, reformers had thought of requiring that lists of eligible voters be compiled some time before an election as a means for combating multiple voting and other forms of election fraud being practiced by party machines. Conservatives had recognized that voter registration would hold down the size of the electorate and would probably skew it toward the educated and well-to-do. Some Whigs in New York in the 1840s had called for voter registration, but the proposal was rejected by Seward, who argued that identifying the Whigs with such a measure would antagonize the poor and the foreign-born.[8]

By the time of the Civil War 11 states had adopted some kind of pre-election voter enrollment. By 1880 the number had grown to 28. Before 1890 most states that required registration had election officers compile the rolls of eligible voters. The individual voter had no responsibility in the process. Many states exempted rural counties from registration requirements, on the grounds that election fraud was not a problem outside the cities (a dubious supposition, as was shown by later prosecutions of vote fraud in rural counties, particularly in the Border states and the South).[9]

In the 1890s some states began to require that individual voters appear personally at the county courthouse or a municipal registration office to register before a cut-off date in advance of the election. Registration once accomplished generally did not have to be renewed. In the South registration became linked to the drive to disenfranchise black voters. Outside the South personal voter registration was required in 1900 by about 30 percent of the counties, and enrollment by election officials was maintained by an additional 24 percent. Twenty years later these figures had risen to 45 percent requiring personal registration and an additional 22 percent with state-maintained enrollment—a total of 67 percent of non-southern counties with some kind of voter registration.[10]

The progressives were genuinely outraged and alarmed by vote fraud—if for no other reason than that the machines were making effective use of fraud against them. Also, however, as Paul Kleppner has pointed out, many of the reformers were not displeased that stringent registration laws tended to discourage participation by voters who had little education, were relatively recent immigrants, or might be disposed to sell their votes. The inclination of some progressives to limit the electorate was motivated in part by the practical calculation that poor immigrants in the cities, usually controlled by the machines, were likely to vote against them. Also, however, many progressives shared the view of most of the Founders that republican government would be unworkable without well-informed, independent voters who cast their ballots for what is best for the nation as a whole. Voters who lack awareness, public-spiritedness, or economic means, they believed, might better be kept out of the electorate. They dismissed the idea that a poor, uneducated individual with little command of English might have enough sense and drive to vote his own best interest.

In some states, as Kleppner has shown, reformers with motives not much different from those of white southerners passed poll taxes and literacy requirements to limit voter eligibility. Massachusetts and Connecticut had required proof of literacy to vote since before the Civil War. They were joined between 1900 and 1926 by 11 other non-southern states, including New York. In that same period, seven non-southern states, including Wisconsin, Minnesota, and Michigan, lengthened their residency requirements for voting, in some cases to as much as one year. Between 1894 and 1920, 12 non-southern states, including Wisconsin, Nebraska, Michigan, and Minnesota, repealed laws that had given aliens the right to vote.[11]

REFORMING CAMPAIGN FINANCE

One reform aimed at purifying the election process that did not involve limiting the electorate was the effort to curtail campaign spending by business. Exposures by the press in 1904 of Mark Hanna's methods of assessing contributions for McKinley's campaigns from corporations in 1896 and 1900, and of the huge sums being raised to support Roosevelt's reelection, strengthened the demand for such reform. Charles Evans Hughes, elected governor of New York in 1906, intensified public indignation with an investigation revealing that major insurance companies subject to state regulation had for years been making large contributions to the state Republican party.[12]

Roosevelt, though himself the beneficiary of large contributions from business, proposed, and Congress in 1907 enacted, a law prohibiting campaign contributions by banks or corporations in elections for federal offices. (The prohibition was not extended to labor unions until 1944.) In 1910 Congress passed the first law requiring disclosure of campaign contributions in federal elections, and in 1911 placed limits on the amounts that could be spent by candidates for the Senate and the House, though not for President. About two-thirds of the states passed laws prohibiting corporations from making campaign contributions. (Such contributions remain legal in California, Indiana, Georgia, Virginia, Kentucky, Louisiana, Maryland, and about a dozen smaller states.)

The laws forbidding corporate spending in campaigns probably inhibited the flow of business money into politics somewhat, but they were easily evaded. Many corporations simply increased their executives' salaries by amounts that it was understood would be used for political purposes.

Among his proposals for campaign finance reform, Roosevelt recommended that campaigns for federal office be subsidized by the federal government. Congress took no action.

THE PRICE OF REFORM

Many of the electoral reforms instituted by the progressives weakened political parties, as they were intended to. The progressives believed that parties by their very nature develop material interests and emotional fixations that distract both elected officials and voters from the real needs of society and government.

The progressives were not wholly wrong. In the early years of the twentieth century, party organizations had in many instances become instruments of corruption. Even a century later, at a time when parties have been substantially weakened, partisan interests sometimes complicate or delay solutions to governmental problems.

What the progressives, like the Founders, overlooked was that democracy without strong parties, particularly when governmental authority is constitutionally divided, is likely to be short on means to pose significant policy choices to the voters, to coordinate governmental decision-making, or to implement ideological or policy shifts among the electorate. If there is no ready means to subordinate the particular interest of officeholders to some broader vision (or visions) of the public good, the result is likely to be institutional chaos, or political horse-trading even more cynical than that carried on by the old-time party machines.

CITY MACHINES

The Progressive Era derived much of its character from the fight for municipal reform. And yet, paradoxically, it was a time when the city machine, defined as a party organization "that both distributes patronage to elicit support and is capable of reliably centralizing power with its organization," began its fullest development. The Democratic machines in many eastern and midwestern cities were shaken by the McKinley avalanche in 1896, and many cities elected reform mayors for a term or two. In general, however, the reformers turned out to be, as George Washington Plunkitt, the sage of Tammany Hall, put it, "morning glories" who "looked lovely in the mornin' [but] withered up in a short time, while the regular machines went on flourishin' forever, like fine old oaks."[13]

From 1890 to 1910, about 75 percent of major American cities were governed most of the time by machines. These machines were more varied than legend suggests. Though "hegemonic" machines of the classic Tammany type, with a single city boss and tight central administration, included the machines in Baltimore, Kansas City, and San Francisco, they were relatively rare. More common were machines controlled by shifting coalitions of ward or aldermanic district leaders, such as those in Boston, Philadelphia, and, in this period, Chicago. Most city machines were Democratic, but some, including those in Philadelphia, Pittsburgh, Cincinnati, and San Francisco, were Republican. Many machines were anti-union, but some, like Tammany, collaborated with the emerging trade unions to support liberal labor legislation in state legislatures and Congress.[14]

At the most primitive level, the machines simply bought votes with cash or alcohol—sometimes for multiple appearances at the polls. As they matured, their ward organizations became combination welfare agencies, legal aid societies, and employment bureaus. Machines distributed turkeys to the poor at Christmas and saw to it that low-income families had a "ton of coal in the cellar" during the winter months. The ward party club became a focus of social life: "picnics, boat rides on the river or lake, and a ready purse at the mention of any charitable collection. . . ."[15]

Richard Croker, John Kelly's successor as grand sachem of Tammany Hall, proudly defended the machine's public service role: "Think what New York is and what the people of New York are. One half, more than one half, are of foreign birth. . . . They do not speak our language, they do not know our laws, they are the raw material with which we have to build up the state. . . . There is no denying the service which Tammany has rendered to the Republic. There is no such organization for taking hold of the untrained, friendless man and converting him into a citizen. Who else would do it if we did not? . . . There is not a mugwump in the city who would shake hands with him."[16]

Tammany under Croker's leadership, Martin Shefter has written, was "a model for would-be city bosses . . . much as the France of Louis XIV was a 'pattern-state' for aspiring absolute monarchs in Europe during the seventeenth century." Croker "got his political start as a bully to intimidate possible Republican voters and as a repeater, voting seventeen times in one election." In 1874 "he was arrested for murdering one opponent at the polls," but charges were dropped for insufficient evidence. Working his way up through the ranks, Croker became Kelly's chief lieutenant and took over as leader when the old boss was incapacitated by illness in 1886.

Croker further centralized and rationalized the machine's fund-raising operations. Corporations, from which "legislators had [previously] extorted money *during* the legislative session by threatening to pass bills that threatened their pecuniary interest," were assured that "a single payment *before* the election" would guarantee protection for their interests "while the legislature sat." Croker "negotiated an arrangement with the liquor dealers' associations" under which direct contributions to Tammany were substituted for payoffs to individual police officers. By controlling the distribution of political money, Croker was able to impose his will on elected city officials and so to "determine precisely which party loyalists" would be appointed to public offices. With expanded resources, Tammany enlarged its army of political workers. Croker's machine aimed to assign one worker to every 15 voters.[17]

Lincoln Steffens, the muckraking journalist, asked Croker, "Why must there be a boss, when we've got a mayor and a council?" The boss replied: "That's why. . . . It's because there's a mayor *and* a council *and* judges—a hundred other men to deal with. . . . A business man wants to do business with one man and one who is always there to remember to carry out the business." Croker regarded himself as a businessman whose business happened to be politics: "Like a business man in business, I work for my own pocket all the time." (Retiring from politics in 1902, Croker bought an estate in Ireland and, like an earlier New York expatriate, James DeLancey, devoted himself to breeding thoroughbred racehorses.)[18]

The machines had admiring defenders, then and later, among both politicians and political commentators. George Washington Plunkitt's celebrated memoir has become a favorite source of aphorisms expressing the social philosophy of the machine politician: "I seen my opportunities and I took 'em"; "To learn real human nature you have to go among the people, see them and be seen"; "Most of the Anarchists in this city today are men who ran up against civil service examinations"; and "What's the constitution among friends?"[19]

Plunkitt's observations do indeed capture some of the flavor of machine politics around the turn of the century. But they smack a little of the vaudeville one-

liner—are a bit too literary. (*Plunkitt of Tammany Hall* was put on paper by a journalist, William Riordan, who claimed he simply took down the politician's words,
delivered at his "office," Graziano's bootblack stand in the New York County
Count House off Foley Square.)[20]

We get a better sense of the grit of city politics and a clearer insight into why
the machines were so formidable from the remarks of Martin Lomasney, the
"Mahatma," Democratic leader of Boston's Ward Eight, a power in Boston and
Massachusetts politics for more than 30 years, though never boss of the whole city.
"Don't write when you can talk," Lomasney advised, "don't talk when you can
nod your head." He explained the public's distrust of reformers: "One of the
strongest of human cravings is to be left alone and the uplifter is never liked." His
view of democratic processes was not Jeffersonian: "Ballot boxes are never stuffed,
unless it's absolutely necessary." His description of the function of the ward leader
is the best moral justification for the machine ever made: "I think there's got to be
in every ward somebody that any bloke can come to—no matter what he's done—
and get help. Help, you understand; none of your law and your justice, but help."[21]

Some activists and commentators among the reformers found qualities to
respect in the machines. Jane Addams observed in 1902: "On the whole, the gifts
[from the machine] are taken quite simply as an evidence of genuine loving kind-
ness. The alderman is really elected because he is a good friend and neighbor."
Brand Whitlock, looking back on the struggle between reformers and machine
politicians in Chicago, concluded: "Perhaps Bathhouse John [Coughlin] and Hinky
Dink [Kenna, bosses of Chicago's notorious "tenderloin" district] were more nearly
right after all than the cold and formal and precise gentlemen who denounced their
records in the council. For they were human and the great problem is to make the
government of a city human." Young Walter Lippmann counseled reformers in
New York: "You can beat Tammany Hall permanently in only one way, by making the government of a city as human, as kindly, as jolly as Tammany Hall."[22]

Besides humanizing city government, the machines gave opportunities for
upward mobility to able and ambitious young non–Anglo-Saxons who were being
systematically excluded from other career paths. As Oscar Handlin observed, the
sign "Irish need not apply" did not hang over the door of the local political club-
house. "The perspicacious boss could become the familiar of the banker and the
traction magnate, be taken to lunch in a good club (though not made a member),
and puff his chest in the company of the financially mighty."[23]

It is easy, however, to exaggerate the virtues of the machines and to overlook
the corrosive damage they did (and do) to public life. The machines corrupted electoral processes, protected criminals, practiced extortion on small shopowners and
tradesmen, accepted bribes from landlords to permit violations of building codes,
allowed shoddy construction in schools and other public buildings, usually (except
in New York) starved public services to avoid conflict with corporations and the
well-to-do, and planted some of the seeds of the moral rot that now, at the beginning of the twenty-first century, threatens to consume entire cities.

URBAN POPULISM

City machines fought such governmental reforms as the introduction of civil service, restrictions on political fundraising, and the substitution of the direct primary
for nominating by caucus or convention. After around 1900, however, some city
machines began to support liberal social and economic legislation, particularly legislation affecting labor, sometimes in collaboration with Republican progressives.
Bosses like Croker had taken little interest in state or national issues that did not
directly affect the welfare of the machine. "What do I care who is President," a
machine sub-boss in Philadelphia asked Lincoln Steffens, "so long as I carry my
ward?" But Charles F. Murphy, Croker's successor as leader of Tammany, guided
the machine toward selective backing of social and economic liberalism. Murphy,
said Alfred E. Smith, himself a product of Tammany, "took a keen interest in bills
embodying social legislation." Ed Flynn, a later New York boss who became a
mainstay of the New Deal, recalled that Murphy "adjusted his thinking to a real
belief that government might, through an expansion of its functions, serve the people in new and helpful ways." State legislators chosen by Murphy worked for the
enactment of health and safety regulations on New York industries. After Smith
was elected governor in 1918, the machine supported his legislative program,
which expanded public health facilities, increased state aid to education, and provided more generous workmen's compensation.[24]

In New Jersey, the Hudson County delegation in the state legislature, which
was controlled by the Jersey City Democratic machine, played a leading part in
1911 in the enactment of a comprehensive workmen's compensation law (cautiously supported by the newly elected Democratic governor, Woodrow Wilson).
In Massachusetts, Martin Lomasney, as floor leader of the Democrats in the lower
house of the legislature, led the fight in 1911 for a bill limiting the use of injunc-
tions against strikers and requiring a jury trial for violators of court orders. In Ohio,
legislators from Cleveland's Democratic machine took the lead in 1913 in the
enactment of legislation providing state support for indigent mothers with dependent children and regulating conditions of child labor.[25]

Republican city machines, too, were sometimes socially liberal. The Rueff
machine in San Francisco worked closely with local labor unions. In Philadelphia
the Republican faction led by the Vare brothers promoted school reform and
sought increased state aid for education.[26]

Some machines began to express and work for a kind of urban populism, par-
allel to the agrarian populism of the People's party and Bryan in its emphasis on
improving the economic lot of have-nots and have-littles; in its dislike, often
amounting to hatred, for both the "money power" and "ivory tower" intellectuals; in its celebration of the tastes and judgment of the common man; in its fraternal spirit; and, too, in its tolerance of petty political corruption. Urban populism
differed from its agrarian counterpart, however, in its enthusiastic acceptance of
industrialization and its delight in big-city life; in its resistance to changes in the

rules of the political game and its commitment to the existing party system; in its hostility to the moral legacy of puritanism; and, of course, in its role as defender of, rather than combatant against, the Catholic church and the immigrant masses in the cities.

Democratic city machines produced some effective political leaders, including Al Smith and Robert Wagner in New York, and David I. Walsh in Massachusetts, who helped promote emergence of liberalism as the dominant force in the national Democratic party. At the 1912 Democratic national convention, several machine delegations (not including Tammany) played crucial roles in swinging the presidential nomination to Woodrow Wilson.

THE SOLID SOUTH

The other party bastion that was little touched by the Progressive Era was the Democratic "solid South." From the end of Reconstruction through the election of 1896, the states of the former Confederacy had been solidly Democratic in presidential elections, though the Republican party had continued to be a significant political force in several southern states and a visible presence in all. After 1896, the Republican party in the South, except in the mountain counties of eastern Tennessee, western North Carolina, and western Virginia, and a few hill counties in southern Texas, became little more than a repository for federal patronage when Republicans controlled the White House.

The willingness of some southern populists in the 1890s to collaborate with Republicans, even black Republicans, convinced leaders of the southern Democracy that as long as blacks could vote there was a possibility that a two-party system would emerge, giving blacks the balance of power. Southern state legislatures in the 1890s began enacting poll taxes and literacy tests for voting that effectively disenfranchised most blacks. In several states literacy tests were accompanied by "grandfather clauses," which provided the literacy test should not apply to voters whose grandfathers had been eligible voters and thus preserved suffrage for many illiterate poor whites. Table 10–1 gives the years in which these devices were first used.

Voter turnout in the South, already declining, promptly plummeted. In 1896 turnout had been 58 percent; by 1904 it had fallen to 29 percent. It did not rise above 50 percent again until after passage of the federal voting rights act in 1965.[27]

The South became a virtual one-party preserve, with almost all elections decided in the Democratic primary, from which blacks were excluded. Louisiana, which had given Republican James Blaine 42 percent of its vote for President in 1884, voted only 10 percent for Roosevelt in 1904; Georgia went from 34 percent for Blaine to 18 percent for Roosevelt; South Carolina, 23 percent for Blaine to 5 percent for Roosevelt; Mississippi, 36 percent for Blaine to 6 percent for Roosevelt.

In several southern states, the Democratic line on the general election ballot

Table 10–1   Federal Elections in Which Suffrage Limitations Were First Used in States of the Former Confederacy

	Poll Tax	Literacy Test
Alabama	1902	1902★
Arkansas	1894	—
Florida	1890	—
Georgia	1802	1908★
Louisiana	1898	1898★
Mississippi	1890	1892
North Carolina	1900	1902★
South Carolina	1896	1896
Tennessee	1890	—
Texas	1904	—
Virginia	1904	1902★

★With grandfather clause.
Source: Jerrold G. Rusk and John J. Stucker, "Effect of Southern Election Laws on Voting," in Joel H. Silbey, Allan G. Bogue, and Wiliam H. Flanigan, eds., The History of American Electoral Behavior (Princeton U. Press, Princeton, NJ, 1978), p. 209.

was headed by the symbol of a rooster and the slogan, "Defend White Supremacy." The "predominant consideration in the architecture of southern political institutions," V. O. Key wrote, was to assure locally a subordination of the Negro population and, externally, to block threatened interferences from the outside with these local arrangements."[28]

White populists discovered that the easiest way to gain and hold power was to be even more aggressive than the Bourbons in driving blacks out of the political system. In South Carolina, "Pitchfork Ben" Tillman in 1895 took the lead in altering the state constitution "with the avowed purpose of disfranchising the Negro." In North Carolina, Charles Brantley Aycock, champion of increased state effort for education, campaigned successfully for governor in 1898 on a pledge to "remove the Negro from politics." In Mississippi, James K. Vardaman, idol of hill-country "redneck" populists, was elected governor in 1902 on a platform promising "white supremacy" and restrictions on corporate wealth. In Georgia, Tom Watson completely reversed his prior position on race and in 1904 proposed "a change in our Constitution which will perpetuate white supremacy in Georgia." Watson went on to become among the most virulent and vituperative of southern race-baiters, defending the need for periodic lynchings and shortly adding Catholics and Jews to his targets for defamation.[29]

Within the Democratic party, politics in several southern states was structured by a struggle between populists and Bourbons, with populists often coming out on top. Only in Virginia—which Key in the 1940s described as "a political museum piece"—did the old-line oligarchy of lawyers and country gentlemen retain firm control of the Democratic party and state government. The Virginia oligarchy, Key wrote, was characterized by "a sense of honor, an aversion to open venality, a degree of sensitivity to public opinion, a concern for efficiency in administration, and, so long as it [did] not cost much, a feeling of social responsibility."[30]

Elsewhere in the South, populists, or politicians who claimed to be populists, were often in power. In Georgia, Watson, though he held no elective office from 1892 until he was finally elected to the United States Senate in 1920, maintained "his hold on underprivileged white farmers" and "was able to exert powerful and sometimes decisive influence in state primaries until his death in 1922." His role in provoking the nationally condemned lynching of Leo Frank, a Jewish mill operator accused of murdering one of his female employees in 1915, apparently increased his popularity among state voters.[31]

In Mississippi, J. K. Vardaman, a colorful demagogue who combined economic populism with race-baiting and vicious personal attacks on his opponents, was opposed for election to the Senate in 1910 by LeRoy Percy, head of an upper-class planter family from the Mississippi delta. "The undeclared issue," wrote the patrician's son, William Alexander Percy (cousin and foster father of the novelist, Walker Percy), was "the unanswerable charge against Father that he was a prosperous plantation-owner, a corporation lawyer, and unmistakably a gentleman." Despite these handicaps, Percy was narrowly victorious. Three years later in a rematch, Vardaman, supported by the even more demagogic Theodore Bilbo, ousted Percy from the Senate. "A man of honor," the younger Percy wrote, "was hounded by men without honor—not unusual perhaps, but the man was my Father."[32]

In Texas, James E. Ferguson was elected governor in 1914 after a campaign that was populist at least in style. When Ferguson was impeached for taking a bribe from a brewery, he persuaded the voters to elect his wife, Miriam, in his place. "Pa" and "Ma" Ferguson dominated Texas politics for a generation, drawing mainly on their ability to entertain and establish cultural solidarity with rural constituents.[33]

In Louisiana, politics was complicated by the division between the Anglo-Protestant north and the French–Catholic south. Before the advent of Huey Long in the late 1920s, the New Orleans machine, similar to the machines in northern cities, normally dominated state politics by allying itself with enough of the courthouse gangs in both regions to carry Democratic primaries and control a majority in the state legislature.[34]

After winning office some populists actually increased and improved state services as they had promised. Georgia raised annual per capita expenditures for education, for example, from 89 cents in 1900 to $3.13 in 1920; South Carolina in the same period from 67 cents to $3.94; Louisiana from 82 cents to $6.32; North Carolina from 50 cents to $4.75. Even Vardaman in Mississippi and the Fergusons in Texas increased state spending for education—though Vardaman limited the raise to schools attended by whites because, he said, the effect of educating blacks was "to spoil a good field hand and make an insolent cook." The *rate* of increase in state effort for services by southern states during this period was greater than in most northern industrial states: New York raised annual per capita expenditures for education from $4.60 in 1900 to $10.21 in 1920; Massachusetts from $4.93 to $10.62; even progressive California from $4.65 to $14.29. But the low tax base of the South still kept all southern states far below the national average in per capita expenditures for services.[35]

After 1920 candidates using populist rhetoric still won elections, particularly in the deep South, but the rate of improvement in state services slowed. V. O. Key's verdict on most southern populist politicians in this period, before the coming of Huey Long, seems just: "Sooner or later they sold out to the interests they attacked or became moderate with experience and success. They mouthed a humbuggery to capture the loyalties of the gullible and ignorant. They had no sincerity in their promises. . . ." In many states, particularly Alabama, Louisiana, Arkansas, South Carolina, Texas, Mississippi, and Florida, politics degenerated into a competition between shifting coalitions of courthouse gangs and candidates who campaigned with hillbilly bands, pursuing little beyond patronage, opportunities to obtain graft, and personal ambition.[36]

The close identification of the Democratic party in the South with "white supremacy" made it difficult for northern Democrats to appeal to the gradually increasing constituency of northern blacks, some of whom were growing restless with the Republican loyalty that blacks had maintained since the Civil War. Most leaders of the national Democratic party were more than willing to accept this handicap in return for almost solidly Democratic delegations from the South in Congress and for reliable support from the states of the former Confederacy in presidential elections.

11

THE PRESIDENT AS PARTY LEADER

Woodrow Wilson

WOODROW WILSON, more than Abraham Lincoln or Theodore Roosevelt, deserves credit (or blame) for creating the modern presidency. In Wilson's hands, the presidency became the chief initiator and coordinator, as well as administrator, of both domestic and foreign policy in the federal government. When Wilson's Democratic party lost control of both houses of Congress in the final two years of his second term, his continued insistence on claiming a dominant role for the presidency led to virtual governmental deadlock, with tragic results in the debate over the proposed entry of the United States into the League of Nations. But the strengthened presidency, within the executive branch as well as in relation to Congress, remained his most important legacy.

The President's party had an important part to play in Wilson's conception of effective national government. He was, however, deeply dissatisfied with the American party institution as it had evolved during the nineteenth century.

As a young political scientist—one of the founders of the discipline in the United States—Wilson in the 1880s had extolled the British party system, under which he believed the parties represented competing principles of government. The American parties, in contrast, he charged, paid lip service to "worn out principles" and were "without definite policies." In their present condition, he said, they were "unmitigated nuisances." The "two great parties" were "dying for want of unifying and vitalizing principles." The key to renewal of the parties, Wilson argued, was the emergence of strong leaders dedicated to meaningful political principles. "Eight words contain the sum of the present degradation of our political parties: No leaders, no principles; no principles, no parties."[1]

What Wilson really had in mind for the parties, as James Ceaser has shown, was that they should serve as instruments of mobilization and communication for principled leaders. He had little use for patronage-based party organizations of the kind that had developed in the United States. Such parties, he believed, stood between the voters and their natural leaders. "Among a free people," he wrote, "there can be no other method of government than such as permits an undictated choice of leaders and a strong, unhampered making up of bodies of active men to give them active support." Unlike the Founders, Wilson believed that parties can play a useful role in democracy. But he was closer to the Founders than to Van Buren and the actual practice of nineteenth-century American parties in that he conceived of the party, in Ceaser's explication, as "a temporary organization—perhaps under a traditional party label—that is 'owned' by a particular leader and that exists to promote the leader's interest." Wilson thus formulated a view of party that many commentators now maintain came close to actuality in the candidate-oriented American politics of the final decade of the twentieth century.[2]

A SCHOLAR IN POLITICS

Wilson grew up in the South during the Civil War and Reconstruction, the son of a highly regarded Presbyterian minister who served churches in middle-sized communities in Virginia, Georgia, and South Carolina. Political attitudes among his father's congregations were set by patrician planters and lawyers who venerated Jefferson but had no time for extremes of participatory democracy.

Study of political philosophy and government at Princeton and at the new graduate school at Johns Hopkins in Baltimore (both schools with close ties to the South) attracted the young Wilson to nineteenth-century British liberalism. This creed, like the southern patrician tradition, valued personal and intellectual freedom but rejected sudden social or political change.

Political attitudes acquired from such sources made Wilson feel entirely at home in the Democratic party of Samuel Tilden and Grover Cleveland. (He probably regarded the kind of conservatism represented by McKinley and Hanna as a bit vulgar.) The Democratic party of William Jennings Bryan was another matter. Though not politically active in the 1890s, he lamented the swing of the Democracy to Bryanism. Speaking to a group of Virginia expatriates in New York in 1904, he declared that the Democratic party should cut loose from "populists and radical theorists, contemptuous alike of principle and of experience." The country, he said, needed "a party of conservative reform acting in the spirit of law and ancient institutions," but it "needs and will tolerate no party of discontent or radical experiment." Earlier he had written with almost nativist disdain of the immigrant masses from which the Democratic city machines drew their strength. The countries of eastern and southern Europe, he complained, were "disburdening themselves of the more sordid and hapless elements of their populations."[3]

Toward the end of Roosevelt's second term conservative Democrats of the Cleveland stamp began speaking of Wilson, who had become president of Princeton in 1902, as a possible deliverer to rescue the party from the clutches of Bryanism. George Harvey, publisher of *Harper's Weekly,* ran editorials proposing Wilson for the national presidency from 1906 onward. Wilson entered active politics in 1910 when Harvey persuaded former Senator Jim Smith, boss of the New Jersey Democratic state machine, to make him the Democratic candidate for gov-

ernor. Wilson, who had been viewed as a conservative on economic matters, suddenly took up progressive proposals for the regulation of corporations. He also campaigned for elimination of the political "boss-system." He attracted enough support from progressive Republicans to win the governorship by a landslide.

As governor, Wilson immediately broke with Smith and prevented his election to a new term in the Senate. He at first seemed to feel more comfortable working with moderate Republicans in the legislature than with the more labor-oriented
Democrats, but eventually he went along with the program of labor reform sponsored by the Democrats.[4]

During his brief tenure as governor Wilson became responsive to the new
urban populism expressed by some of the labor unions and some products of the
city machines. His sensitivity to the interests of working-class city dwellers was
apparently sharpened by his secretary, Joseph Tumulty, a youthful veteran of Jersey City politics, who argued that the concerns of urban voters "lay even more in
social than political democracy."[5]

THE NEW FREEDOM

From the time of his election as governor, Wilson, urged on by Tumulty and others (Harvey having been dropped), regarded himself as a prime candidate for the
Democratic nomination for President in 1912. He was therefore somewhat surprised when Speaker of the House Champ Clark of Missouri, a moderate populist,
emerged as the early front runner for the nomination. Wilson's hopes for a solid
bloc of support from the South were thwarted when Tom Watson of Georgia and
J. K. Vardaman of Mississippi, who had not forgiven Wilson his attacks on
Bryanism, gave their backing to Representative Oscar Underwood of Alabama.
With help from newspapers published by William Randolph Hearst and some local
machines, Champ Clark decisively defeated Wilson in presidential primaries in Illinois, Massachusetts, and California.

At the raucous Democratic national convention in Baltimore, Bryan, a delegate from Nebraska, caused a sensation by demanding that all presidential candidates renounce any connection with Wall Street financiers like J. P. Morgan and
August Belmont. (Belmont was a member of the New York delegation.) Wilson
met Bryan's terms; Clark hedged. Clark led on the early ballots, with Wilson a distant second and Underwood third. On the tenth ballot, Tammany swung the New
York delegation to Clark. This gave Clark a majority, but still less than the required
two-thirds. Wilson, aware that in every convention since 1844 candidates who
passed the majority mark had gone on to win the nomination, telegraphed instructions to his floor managers, William McCombs and William Gibbs McAdoo, that
his name should be withdrawn. McAdoo decided to ignore the telegram. As the
balloting continued, Clark began to slip. On the 14th ballot, Bryan announced he
could not support a candidate affiliated with Wall Street and Tammany and deliv-

ered his vote to Wilson. What really put Wilson over, however, were switches to him on crucial ballots by the Indiana machine led by Thomas Taggart and the Chicago machine led by Roger Sullivan. On the 46th ballot, Wilson was nominated. Tammany stuck by Clark to the end.[6]

Early in the general election campaign Wilson made a great show of refusing to have his picture taken with Charles Murphy, leader of Tammany Hall. He also went out of his way to snub Taggart and Sullivan. Meeting with McCombs, a professional politician who had signed on early with Wilson, and whom the candidate now grudgingly approved for selection as Democratic national chairman, Wilson made clear that he believed he owed the nomination to nobody. "Remember," he later told McCombs, "that God ordained that I should be the next President of the United States."[7]

Wilson quickly recognized that his only real opponent was Roosevelt. Deprived of support from the progressive wing of the Republican party, Taft had no chance of being elected and did little campaigning. Advised by Louis Brandeis, a Boston attorney who had developed a reputation as "the people's lawyer" by representing consumer groups against the trusts, Wilson presented a program that he called the "New Freedom," to contrast with Roosevelt's "New Nationalism." The New Freedom, he claimed, would promote the vitality of "independent enterprises still unabsorbed by the great economic combinations," while Roosevelt's kind of progressivism represented "a consummation of the partnership between monopoly and government." Unlike orthodox Republican *laissez-faire,* the New Freedom would use government to help the enterprising individual who was getting started rather than to prop up the rich: "What this country needs above all else is a body of laws which will look after the men who are on the make rather than the men who are already made."[8]

After an exciting campaign, the election returns indicated little shift among the voters—except that the Republican camp was divided almost evenly in two. Wilson did no better than hold the Democratic core. He won 42 percent of the popular vote—actually 1 percent less than Bryan had received against Taft four years before. He achieved a landslide majority in the electoral college of 435 votes of a total 531— but outside the South he failed to reach an actual majority in a single state.

Roosevelt came in second with 27 percent of the popular vote and with the electoral votes of Pennsylvania, California, Michigan, Minnesota, South Dakota, and Washington. The Progressive ticket almost carried Illinois and was second in 23 other states. Taft came in last among the three main contenders, winning 23 percent of the popular vote and the electoral votes of only Vermont and Utah—eastern and western bulwarks of orthodox Republican conservatism. (The remaining 8 percent of the popular vote was won by Eugene Debs, the Socialist candidate, and a scattering of minor candidates. Debs received between 10 and 17 percent of the vote in California, Arizona, Idaho, Montana, Nevada, Washington, and Oklahoma.)

Examination of the geographic distribution of the vote within the major states shows that Wilson carried the normally Democratic areas and was able, because of the Republican split, to win pluralities in some normally Republican counties, while Roosevelt and Taft competed for the Republican vote. In New York, Wilson swept New York City and won pluralities in some normally Republican Hudson Valley and western counties. The Republican organization held most upstate counties for Taft, with Roosevelt, the former governor, carrying only two counties (Figure 11–1). In Illinois, where much of the leadership of the Republican organization went over to Roosevelt, the Bull Moose ticket carried Cook County and most of the normally Republican northern counties; Wilson swept the normally Democratic counties of southern Illinois; and Taft carried only "Egypt" and three other counties (Figure 11–2). In California, which Roosevelt carried with the help of Hiram Johnson, the Progressives were triumphant in the populous counties of southern California and the San Francisco Bay area, while Wilson held the normally Democratic Central Valley (Figure 11–3).

Accompanying Wilson's victory, the Democrats won large majorities in both houses of Congress, chiefly because the Progressives entered candidates in many congressional races, thereby splitting the Republican vote and allowing Democrats to win with pluralities. In Illinois, for example, in only 7 of the 27 House districts

Figure 11–1 New York vote by counties, 1912

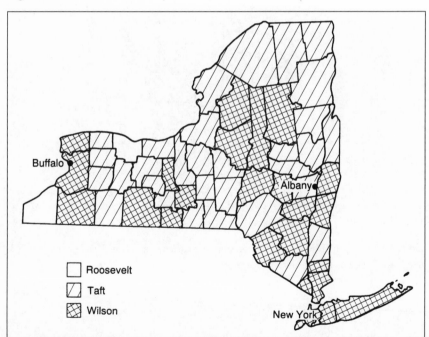

Source: Edgar Eugene Robinson, *The Presidential Vote, 1896–1932,* Octagon, New York, 1947

Figure 11–2   Illinois vote by counties, 1912

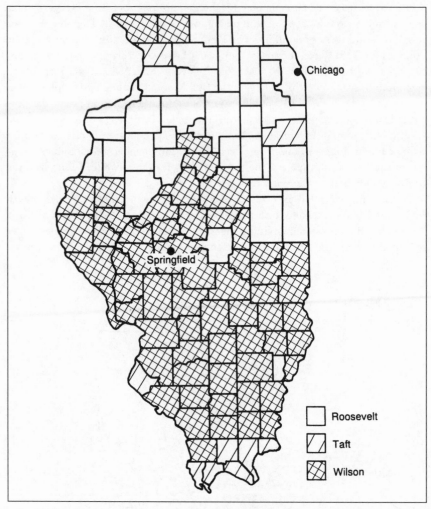

Source: Edgar Eugene Robinson, *The Presidential Vote, 1896–1932,* Octagon, New York, 1947

did the winning candidate receive an actual majority; in New York, only 9 of 43; in Ohio, 7 of 22; in Michigan, none of 13.

AN ECLECTIC PROGRAM

Wilson promptly put into practice his theory that the majority party in Congress should be mobilized to support the President's program. He was greatly aided by

Figure 11–3 California vote by counties, 1912

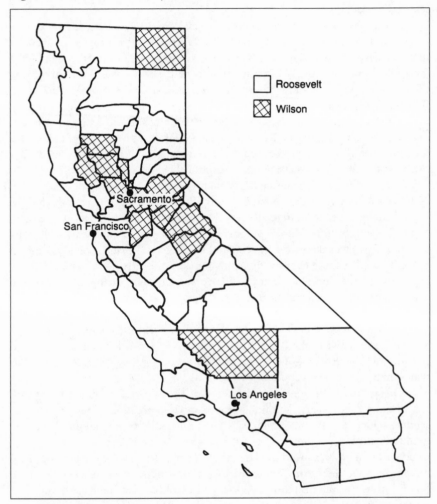

Source: Edgar Eugene Robinson, *The Presidential Vote, 1896–1932,* Octagon, New York, 1947

the fact that the congressional Democrats, having been in the minority most of the time for the last 18 years, recognized their stake in having their party identified with a successful President. In April 1913 Wilson became the first President since John Adams to deliver his State of the Union message personally to Congress—an opportunity that Roosevelt must have kicked himself for overlooking while he was President. Using federal patronage effectively, Wilson made himself, rather than Champ Clark, who stayed on as Speaker, the effective leader of Democrats in the House.

Senate Democrats, too, were responsive to the reform program the administration sent to Capitol Hill.

In the next four years the Democratic majority in Congress, helped by the handful of Progressives elected to the House and some of the progressive Republicans, enacted the most significant body of legislation since that put through by the Republicans in the early 1860s: reduction in tariff rates; a tougher antitrust law, with an exemption for labor unions (largely nullified by the courts); the Federal Reserve Act, providing a federally supervised national banking system, with participation by private banks; the Federal Trade Commission, charged with preserving business competition; the Farm Loan and Good Roads Act; an eight-hour day for railroad workers; and prohibition of shipment of goods produced by child labor in interstate commerce (declared unconstitutional by the Supreme Court in 1918).

Wilson's program, as enacted, seemed to contain elements from the "New Nationalism" as well as the "New Freedom." It included aspects of both agrarian and urban populism, the latter still pressed by Tumulty, now secretary to the President. The effects of the Wilson program were moderate, in some ways even conservative. The Federal Reserve System, for instance, could be interpreted as a means for backstopping the power of the major private banks. Brandeis, whom Wilson appointed to the Supreme Court in 1916, was privately disappointed that the administration had not acted more forcefully against the trusts. Wilson, he later said, "did not understand the importance of bigness."[9]

Wilson's program of domestic legislation, however, offered the beginnings of a genuine alternative to the Republican ideology, as Cleveland's had not. It moved toward using the federal government directly to meet public welfare needs rather than simply to promote economic growth.

On race issues, Wilson's record, expressing the values of southern paternalism, was distinctly reactionary. Wilson approved racial segregation of the federal civil service, which the Republicans and Cleveland had kept unsegregated, on the ground that it was "in the interest of the Negroes"—thereby reversing the drift of some northern blacks toward the Democratic party. Blacks were fired from federal jobs throughout the South. "There are no government positions for Negroes in the South," said the administration's appointee as Collector of Internal Revenue in Georgia. "A Negro's place is in the cornfield." Wilson described The Birth of a Nation, D. W. Griffith's classic film glorifying the Ku Klux Klan, as "history written in lightning."[10]

Wilson made Bryan his secretary of state, in part because he needed Bryan's help with western and southern populists in Congress, but also probably because he admired the Nebraskan's crusading spirit and believed it would help vitalize his administration. At first they got on well. Bryan used the State Department to promote his belief in peaceful arbitration of differences among nations and took care to give Wilson opportunities to make moral declarations on world problems. But when war broke out in Europe in 1914, friction soon developed between them. Bryan sought to maintain strict neutrality, aimed at insulating the United States against any form of involvement. Wilson gradually moved toward support for the Allies, particularly Britain. When a German submarine in 1915 sank the *Lusitania*, a British liner, taking the lives of almost 1,200 noncombatant passengers, including 128 Americans, Bryan pleaded for only a mild protest, but Wilson insisted on taking a relatively tough stand. (Not nearly tough enough, however, to satisfy Theodore Roosevelt, who was demanding that the United States assert itself more aggressively.) Bryan resigned. Wilson put in his place Robert Lansing, an international lawyer with well-known pro-British sympathies.

Seeking reelection in 1916, Wilson was keenly aware that he had won with much less than a majority of the popular vote four years before and that the Democratic party still had almost no organization in many parts of the country. He set out to present himself as a national leader who had maintained prosperity and kept the country out of war. Sensitive to the charge, by Roosevelt and others, that avoidance of conflict reflected a lack of patriotic ardor, Wilson sent instructions to the Democratic national convention that "'Americanism' should be the key note of the convention and that frequent demonstrations should attest the Democratic loyalty to the flag." Though not the first to employ mass advertising techniques in electoral politics, Wilson's 1916 campaign went well beyond earlier instances in carrying out what Walter Dean Burnham has called the "mercantilist" approach. The focus was on publicizing the candidate's personality and accomplishments rather than on rallying the party faithful.[11]

The Republican candidate was Charles Evans Hughes, reform governor of New York from 1907 to 1910, elected with progressive support but never a great favorite with Roosevelt (who privately referred to him as "Woodrow Wilson with whiskers"). Appointed to the Supreme Court by Taft in 1910, Hughes had avoided involvement on either side in the intraparty bloodletting of 1912. A remnant of Progressives nominated Roosevelt, but he immediately declined and campaigned actively—in the view of some Republicans, too actively—for Hughes.[12]

Wilson won a narrow majority of 23 in the electoral college, with 49 percent of the popular vote. The incumbent President carried, in addition to the South, most of the old populist strongholds in the Great Plains and the Rocky Mountains, and California and Washington on the west coast. Hughes achieved substantial majorities in most of the urban and industrial states stretching from New England to the west end of the Great Lakes. The 1916 election is in fact the one case that neatly fits the model pitting the "periphery" against the "metropole." A shift of fewer than 2,000 votes in California would have given Hughes victory in the state and a majority in the electoral college, though he would still have been about 500,000 votes behind Wilson in the popular vote. (Hiram Johnson had not campaigned for Hughes in California, reportedly because he believed Hughes had snubbed him during a campaign visit to the state.)

The Democrats, having lost 61 seats in the House of Representatives in 1914, lost 14 more in 1916. Nationwide, 7,810,000 votes were cast for Republican candidates for the House, compared to 7,468,000 votes for Democratic candidates. The

Democrats had four more members than the Republicans in the House in 1917, but they needed the help of six independent or minor party members to organize the body. In the Senate the Democrats lost three seats but retained a majority of 11.

Most of the voters who had supported the Progressives in 1912 had returned to the Republicans. But the "normal Republican majority" was not yet firmly reestablished. Wilson had offered a distinctive alternative to Republican rule. Whether it would become the basis for a new electoral majority remained to be seen.

DIVISION ON FOREIGN POLICY

America's foreign wars in the nineteenth century—the War of 1812, the Mexican War, and the Spanish-American War—were all politically controversial, but none left much enduring impact on divisions in national politics. The effect of the First World War, which the United States entered in April 1917, was different.

Wilson's call for a declaration of war against Germany, "to make the world safe for democracy," was approved by votes of 82 to 6 in the Senate, and 373 to 50 in the House. Most of those voting in the negative were progressive Republicans, such as LaFollette and George Norris, elected to the Senate in 1912, or Bryanite Democrats, such as House Majority Leader Claude Kitchin of North Carolina.

Midwestern progressives like LaFollette and Norris had supported much of Wilson's domestic program but had passionately criticized administration policies they believed were leading toward war. The progressives argued that, while the United States should play a benevolent role in world affairs, its main function should be to set an example of liberal democracy for other nations to follow. Involvement in foreign conflicts, they maintained, would inevitably weaken the impulse for reform at home and draw the United States into collaboration with imperialist regimes like those of Britain and czarist Russia. The fact that many of the midwestern progressives had among their constituents large numbers of German-Americans, most of whom believed the Allies were at least as morally responsible as Germany for the carnage in Europe, no doubt played some part in their insistence on noninvolvement.

Roosevelt and others who had been calling for intervention on the side of the Allies enthusiastically supported the declaration of war. But Wilson's subsequent rejection of Roosevelt's offer to lead a division of volunteers to the battlefield in France produced predictable hard feelings. By the summer of 1917, Roosevelt was denouncing the administration for the condition of "complete unpreparedness" in which the United States had entered the war. Conservatives like Lodge and Philander Knox, elected to the Senate from Pennsylvania in 1916, supported the war effort but made no secret of their distrust of Wilson's leadership.[13]

In the fall of 1918, with the war nearing conclusion, Wilson pleaded for the election of solid Democratic majorities in Congress to support his policies. The voters responded by returning the Republicans to control of both chambers, with majorities of 50 in the House and two in the Senate. Roosevelt, who had led the Republican midterm campaign, appeared the likely Republican candidate for President in 1920.

After the armistice was signed on November 11, 1918, Roosevelt wrote his friend Lord Bryce, the former British ambassador to the United States, that "at the Peace Conference England and France can get what they wish" if, "while treating Wilson with politeness, they openly and frankly throw themselves on the American people for support in any vital matter." In the first week of January 1919, Roosevelt, aged 60, died without warning in his sleep.[14]

At the Paris peace conference Wilson was outmaneuvered on some issues by the wily and experienced leaders of Britain, France, and Italy. But he won approval by the Allies for inclusion in the peace treaty of his cherished project for a League of Nations to prevent future wars. Returning to the United States in July 1919, Wilson called the League "the only hope for mankind" and asked the Senate: "Dare we reject it and break the heart of the world?" Three months later, while barnstorming through the West in an attempt to whip up support for the League, Wilson suffered a disabling stroke. Though he recovered partially, his political skill and judgment seemed severely impaired during the struggle over ratification of the peace treaty that followed.[15]

A bloc of isolationist senators, led by LaFollette and Hiram Johnson, elected to the Senate from California in 1916, were opposed to American participation in the League under any circumstance. A somewhat larger bloc of conservatives, led by Lodge, who had become chairman of the Senate Foreign Relations Committee, were prepared to accept the League if the treaty included reservations they claimed were necessary to protect American sovereignty. Wilson insisted these reservations would cripple the League and ordered Democratic senators loyal to his leadership to vote against the treaty if they were adopted. It thus became impossible to assemble the required two-thirds majority for a treaty authorizing American participation in the League, with or without reservations.

The controversies over America's entry into the war and proposed adherence to the league are often described as having been between "internationalists" and "isolationists." But this classification obscures important differences within both groups. There were, in reality, four distinguishable positions rather than two. These positions continued to attract advocates during the 1920s and 1930s and have recurred in all the debates on foreign policy that have raged within the political community, and sometimes the larger electorate, from 1945 to the present.

The four positions can be distinguished diagrammatically through two axes, one ranging from readiness to intervene economically, politically, and, if necessary and feasible, militarily in world affairs, to extreme reluctance to attempt such intervention; and the other ranging from concentration on America's national interest as almost the sole value to be pursued in the conduct of foreign policy, to emphasis on more altruistic concerns, such as spreading democracy or achieving a fairer distribution of the world's goods. There are, of course, few if any pure types. *All*

American administrations and participants in the foreign-policy debate are to some extent concerned with *both* the advancement of national interest and the extension of democracy; all under some circumstances will intervene in foreign matters, and all will at least claim to be prudent about when intervention is appropriate. Advocates for each position, moreover, tend to argue that their preferred strategy is really the best way to achieve the goals sought by all the others (as in the contention that the rational pursuit of America's national interest *requires* promotion of a fairer distribution of goods among peoples). Nevertheless, the four general positions shown in Figure 11–4 are recognizable.

In the foreign-policy debate before, during, and just after America's participation in the First World War, Roosevelt (though he died less than two months after the war ended) best represented the position of national-interest interventionism, and Wilson of altruistic interventionism (though Roosevelt also expressed altruistic goals, and Wilson of course pursued his conception of national interest). LaFollette exemplified altruistic isolationism (as did Norris, Hiram Johnson, and Bryan). In the 1890s Lodge had been an interventionist, supporting Roosevelt's expansionist aims. At that time the position of national-interest isolationism was ably expressed by Thomas B. Reed of Maine, the crusty Speaker of the House, and Senator George Hoar of Massachusetts, who led the opposition, along with Bryan,

Figure 11–4　Foreign policy positions in American politics

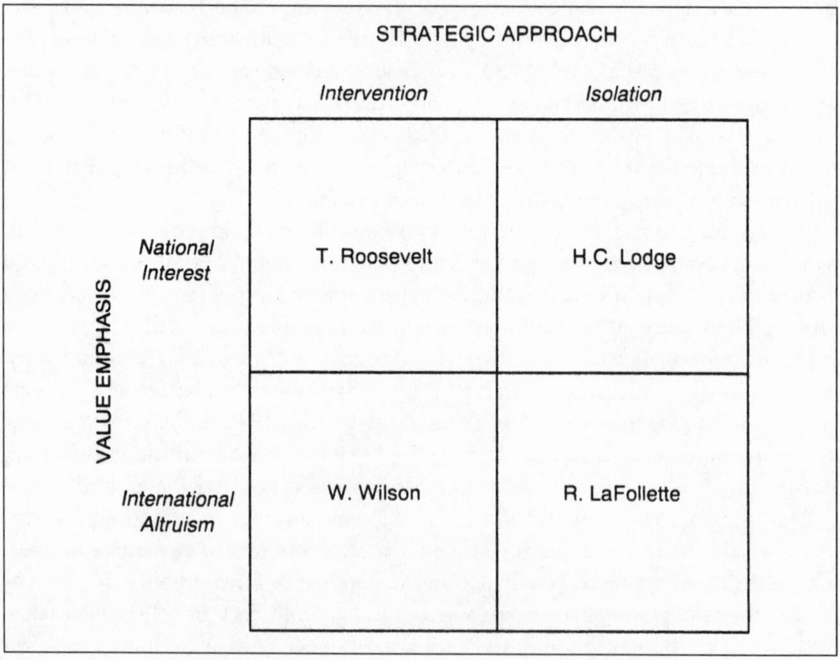

	STRATEGIC APPROACH	
	Intervention	*Isolation*
National Interest	T. Roosevelt	H.C. Lodge
International Altruism	W. Wilson	R. LaFollette

VALUE EMPHASIS

to America's acquisition of the Philippine Islands. As the years advanced, however, Lodge became increasingly critical of foreign entanglements; and in the postwar debate, after Roosevelt's death, he exemplified the national-interest isolationist position.

The foreign-policy matrix can be superimposed on the division between republican and liberal ideological traditions. Those emphasizing national interest in foreign policy, whether isolationists or interventionists, have tended, though not always, to subscribe to the republican ideology of ordered liberty. Those emphasizing altruism in foreign policy have tended, with somewhat greater consistency, to be equalitarian liberals in ideology.

In the 1920s the difference between interventionists and isolationists among domestic equalitarians deeply divided the liberal camp, preventing resumption of the alliance that had developed before the war between LaFollette progressives and Wilsonian Democrats. The difference between interventionists and isolationists among domestic conservatives was not at first so divisive. But in the years leading up to the Second World War it deeply split American conservatives and became the principal issue in the bitter struggle that tore the Republican party from 1947 to 1952. During the years of Eisenhower tranquility and consensus in the 1950s, foreign policy became a less pressing issue in national politics. But then, with the rise of the militant anti-Communist right in the Republican party and the resurgence of isolationism among liberals, it again in the 1960s and 1970s became an important basis for highly charged political division.

A NEW KIND OF PARTY CHAIRMAN

During Wilson's second term, the Republicans, perhaps shocked by the experience of losing two consecutive presidential elections for the first time since the Civil War, took steps to make their national party organization a continuing institution with a full-time professional staff—the seed of the massive party committees and squads of free-lance political consultants that now flourish in Washington.

The Democratic National Committee had been founded in 1848 and the Republican National Committee in 1854. During the nineteenth and early twentieth centuries, however, both national committees had virtually gone out of business during the years between presidential campaigns.

In 1918 Will Hays, a live-wire Indiana politician who had become Republican national chairman after Wilson's second election, established the first permanent national party headquarters in Washington and hired a staff of publicists and fundraisers. Short of stature but with a booming voice, Hays made frequent tours around the country giving speeches to party workers and interviews to local newspapers. After Congress approved the Nineteenth Amendment giving women the vote in 1919, he formed a women's division at the national committee and a National Council of Republican Women, which in 1920 helped the Republican ticket win an even larger majority among women than it did among men. He also sponsored special functions for young Republicans.[16]

As the 1920 election approached, Hays organized an Advisory Committee on Policies and Platforms, including former President Taft, leading Republicans in the Senate and House, women, and representatives of all party factions. The advisory committee was divided into sub-committees assigned to issue areas. Most of them met several times and thrashed out policy issues in advance of the national convention.

Hays was himself mentioned as a possible presidential candidate. Though he did not pursue the nomination, he was present in the "smoke-filled room" in the Blackstone Hotel in Chicago where party elders picked Warren Harding as the Republican candidate for President.

THE REPUBLICAN MAJORITY RESTORED

Wilson, still a partial invalid but vigorous to the end of his presidency, called in 1920 for election of the Democratic national ticket—Governor James Cox of Ohio for President and Assistant Secretary of the Navy Franklin Delano Roosevelt of New York for Vice President—as an expression of national approval of his administration's policies in general and the League in particular. (Franklin Roosevelt, 38 years old, with no experience in elective office beyond the New York state legislature, was the cousin of T.R. and had married T.R.'s niece, Eleanor. He had been included on the ticket for the transparent purpose of attracting progressive voters through name association.)

The voters responded with a massive victory for the Republican ticket of Senator Warren Harding of Ohio for President and Governor Calvin Coolidge of Massachusetts for Vice President. The Harding-Coolidge ticket won 60 percent of the popular vote, carried every state outside the former Confederacy except Kentucky, and cracked the solid South by carrying Tennessee. Republican majorities in Congress rose to 170 in the House and 22 in the Senate.

A number of factors contributed to the Democratic debacle. Voters were working off their resentment against the restrictions and sacrifices of wartime—against rationing of sugar and flour, against military conscription, against shortages, against government intrusion into private life. Already there was a sense that the war had been fought for nothing—that the politicians of Europe were up to their old tricks, that the world, far from having been made "safe for democracy," was naked to exploitation by old empires and new fanaticisms. Progressive isolationists like LaFollette and Johnson warmly supported the Republican ticket as a means of killing off any chance of American participation in the League. Conservatives called for restoration of a foreign policy that put America's national interest first. "Americanism," said Senator Boies Penrose of Pennsylvania, successor to Quay as boss of the state Republican machine, was the key issue of the 1920 election. What did it mean? "Damned if I know, but you will find it a damned good issue to get votes on. . . ."[17] Many German-Americans, resentful over the abuse they had received during the war, felt they had a score to settle with the Democrats. Even Irish-Americans were angry with Wilson for having failed to stand up for the Irish Republic against Britain.

Yet the rejection of the Democrats also represented a turning away from reform, a wish to be done for a while with social experiment, a belief that government had taken on too much, not just during the war but before—a will to return to conditions of what now seemed the halcyon years from 1896 to 1912. The Eighteenth Amendment, which established national prohibition of the sale of liquor on its ratification in 1919, was a spectacular triumph of the Social Gospel side of progressivism and an expression of longing for the restoration of a more homogeneous culture. "The radicalism," Calvin Coolidge later wrote, "which had tinged our whole political life from soon after 1900 to the World War period was passed. There were still echoes of it and some of its votaries remained, but its power was gone."[18]

After Harding's election Will Hays resigned as Republican national chairman to become postmaster general, a post that enabled him to distribute patronage to the Republican faithful. (In 1922 Hayes moved on to become the first president of the Motion Picture Producers and Distributors of America. In this office he administered the famous "Hays Code," a system of voluntary censorship through which the movie industry sought to fend off criticism by conservative groups of what were then regarded as "racy" films.)

Wilson remained in Washington, commenting in private with wry irony on the cavortings of the Harding administration. He died in 1924. His vision of the role of the federal government in national affairs and of the part to be played by the President's party in supporting a reform program would find new life when the Democrats returned to the White House in 1933.

THE NEW DEAL ERA

12

A FUNCTIONING MAJORITY PARTY

The New Deal

FRANKLIN ROOSEVELT'S IDEA of the proper role of a national political party was much like that of Woodrow Wilson, in whose administration he had served: When the party holds the White House, it should work to secure passage of the President's program and mobilize public support to assure his reelection or the election of his chosen successor; when it is in opposition, it should probe the weaknesses of the incumbent administration and develop an organization that will help bring victory to its national ticket in the next election.[1]

In the political environment created by the Great Depression of the 1930s, Roosevelt was able not only to restore the Democrats to the majority party status they had not held for more than 70 years, but also, for a time at least, to use the Democratic party as an effective instrument of government in reshaping large aspects of the nation's economic and social life.

TROUBLED NORMALCY

During the 1920s the Republicans, credited by many voters for having maintained generally favorable economic conditions, rolled to three straight presidential landslide victories. In 1924, Coolidge, despite the exposure of widespread corruption in the administration of Warren Harding, who had died in 1923, won easy election to a full term over John W. Davis of West Virginia, a conservative Democrat, and Robert LaFollette, who ran on an independent Progressive ticket. In 1928, Herbert Hoover, Coolidge's secretary of commerce, piled up 58 percent of the popular vote against his Democratic opponent, Governor Alfred E. Smith of New York. Smith's identification as a Roman Catholic, the first ever nominated by a major party for President, and as a "wet" on the issue of prohibition, enabled Hoover to carry even four states in the "rim South": Virginia, North Carolina, Texas, and Tennessee.

Beneath the surface of what Harding had called "normalcy" (a term apparently coined by his young speechwriter, Arthur Vandenberg), however, lay growing social, economic, and cultural discontents. Even while losing the 1928 election by a landslide, Al Smith had substantially increased the Democratic vote in many northern cities, including New York, Boston, and Chicago. Strong showings by third parties in several state elections during the 1920s, mainly in the Northwest, showed that some voters were dissatisfied with both major parties. The sharp decline in electoral turnout, though partly due to women's suffrage and other changes in the rules of the game, reflected the existence of a large pool of voters who were not motivated by political appeals but who possessed the capacity, if mobilized, to alter the balance of national politics. Turnout was slightly under 50 percent in both 1920 and 1924; even in 1928, despite the mobilizing effect of the religious issue, it rose only to 57 percent—still far below the levels of the 1890s.

The agricultural depression that set in after the First World War and continued through most of the 1920s deeply split the Republican party, pitting western Republicans, who favored passage of the proposed McNary-Haugen bill that would require the federal government to support prices of basic farm commodities by buying up surpluses, against Republican administrations and majorities in Congress that opposed market intervention. Disaffection among western farmers had caused the Republicans to lose congressional seats in the midterm elections of 1922 and 1926, though those seats were partly reclaimed in the presidential landslides of 1924 and 1928.

Rapid social and technological changes shook the moral and emotional composure of the public and undermined the dominant political coalition of social traditionalists and economic modernizers. Prohibition, while reducing consumption of liquor in its early years and perhaps diminishing poverty, turned millions of normally law-abiding Americans into habitual law-breakers and produced a huge bootlegging industry that greatly expanded the wealth and political influence of organized crime. (In Chicago, political control of the downtown "tenderloin" district passed from Hinky Dink and Bathhouse John to Al Capone.) Mass production of recently invented consumer goods, particularly the automobile, the movies, and radio, made life more agreeable and interesting for many but further eroded the traditional structures of family, church, and community. The dizzying pace of economic expansion encouraged a get-rich-quick state of mind that scoffed at conventional restraints. The "lost generation" of writers and artists, though including only a sliver of American society (often living in Europe), expressed a wider tendency to debunk and reject middle-class values.

So long as the economy continued to grow, these tensions could be kept in check. But if prosperity faltered, the Republican majority could no longer count on the bonds of social cohesion that had seen it through earlier economic crises.

ECONOMIC TRAUMA

Despite the continuing depression in agriculture, economic optimism ran high during the first few months after Hoover's inauguration as President in March 1929. By midsummer, however, there were signs that the boom might be coming to an end. Industrial production, which in June had hit a record high, went into decline. Homebuilding continued in the slump it had entered in the latter part of the Coolidge administration.[2]

On October 24, 1929, the stock market crashed, setting off a panic that cut the value of stocks almost in half. Within a few months stocks had regained some lost ground and stock prices were still far above the level at which the great bull market of the 1920s had begun. Many experienced financial operators believed that growth would soon resume. In 1930, however, unemployment began to rise. By fall, four million workers were without jobs. Gross national product dropped to a level in constant dollars lower than any year since 1925. The stock market fell below its 1929 low.

In the 1930 midterm elections economic discontent boiled over, producing a gain of 53 seats in the House of Representatives for the Democrats. For the first time since 1918, the Democrats, with a narrow majority of six, were able to organize the House. John Nance Garner, a homespun pragmatic populist from south Texas, was installed as Speaker. In the Senate the Democrats gained eight seats but were still one short of a majority.

During the first few months of 1931 the economy improved somewhat, and the Hoover administration claimed that recovery had begun. But in early spring there was another downward lurch. The Depression had begun in earnest. Unemployment doubled. The prices farmers received for their products were lower than in 1910, while expenses were 25 percent higher. "Every farmer," wrote the Kansas editor and social commentator, William Allen White, "whether his farm is under mortgage or not, knows that with farm product prices as they are today, sooner or later he must go under."[3]

Compared to Grant and Cleveland, Hoover was relatively activist in his response to economic depression. Federal expenditures for public works were repeatedly increased. In 1932 the administration and Congress launched the Reconstruction Finance Corporation to make loans to endangered banks. But Hoover's basic cure for the Depression was to let the economic cycle run its course. Large-scale government intervention, he believed, would delay recovery. The first imperative, the President argued, was that the federal government should maintain a balanced budget as "the foundation of all public and private financial stability"— a view that at the time was fully shared by Franklin Roosevelt, who had been elected governor of New York in 1928.[4]

Economic conditions in 1932 grew steadily worse. Stocks fell to only one-quarter of their value at the lowest point immediately after the crash. Unemployment rose to 24 percent—representing 12 million workers without jobs. Only about one-fourth of the unemployed were receiving any kind of relief. Workers who did have jobs faced steeply reduced wages. "The people who are exploiting the workers," warned William Green, the normally cautious and conservative president of the American Federation of Labor, "are taking no account of the history of nations in which governments have been overturned. Revolutions grow out of the depths of hunger."[5]

The Hoover administration seemed unable to cope with the growing crisis. Ordinary citizens took out their fear and outrage on the Republicans, who for so long had been the majority party. The Democrats entered the 1932 presidential campaign with an excellent prospect for victory—and perhaps for the kind of enduring political turnaround that Wilson had not quite achieved.

"THE BEARER OF LIBERALISM"

As governor of New York, Franklin Roosevelt had a clear head start for the Democratic presidential nomination. "I do not see how Mr. Roosevelt can escape becoming the next presidential nominee of his party," said James Farley, New York Democratic state chairman, the day after Roosevelt's reelection as governor in 1930, "even if no one should raise a finger to bring it about."[6]

Roosevelt's great advantage, besides his name and the attention he received as governor of the nation's most populous state, was that he seemed at least passably acceptable to most elements in the party. Though identified with urban liberals and "wets" on the prohibition issue, he excited nothing like the ire roused by Al Smith among rural populists and "drys." A favorite among reformers, he also was the choice of machine politicians like Ed Flynn, boss of the Democratic machine in the Bronx, and James Michael Curley, the rambunctious mayor of Boston. In the South, Roosevelt attracted support from both Bourbons and populists. Huey Long signed on for Roosevelt, he told Farley, because he had "met the other candidates."

Stricken by polio in 1922, and partially paralyzed thereafter, Roosevelt, according to legend, acquired from his experience deepened compassion and understanding for people with trouble. What he certainly gained from his long and painful struggle to regain some functional mobility was immense confidence in his ability to achieve whatever ends he set himself. Having aimed for the presidency at least since his sophomore year at Harvard, and goaded on by the example of his cousin Ted, Roosevelt projected an upper-class ebullience that captured the public's imagination and seemed to carry him above the internal quarrels that had torn the Democratic party in the 1920s.[7]

Farley, a skilled political technician who had learned his trade in Rockland County, an old Regency stronghold in the Hudson Valley, and Louis Howe, an asthmatic former newspaperman who had spotted Roosevelt as a future President 20 years before in the New York legislature, put together a rudimentary national organization. Roosevelt won most of the early state primaries. But in the Massachusetts primary, Al Smith, seeking a comeback after his humiliating loss to Hoover in 1928 and still a great favorite with the state's large Irish Catholic population, defeated the Roosevelt slate by a wide margin. Despite Roosevelt's control of New York state patronage, Tammany and most of the other New York Democratic city machines (except Flynn's organization in the Bronx) rallied behind Smith. Mayor Frank Hague of Jersey City, who dominated the New Jersey Democratic party, partly through terror, put his state's entire delegation in Smith's camp. In the California primary, a slate pledged to Speaker Garner and sponsored by William Randolph Hearst, the press tycoon, easily defeated the Roosevelt slate.[8]

Criticized for being vague on the issues, Roosevelt delivered a radio address in which he chided the Hoover administration for neglecting the "little fellow" while trying to bail out "the large banks and corporations." The time had come, he said, to give relief to "the forgotten man at the bottom of the economic pyramid." Smith immediately attacked Roosevelt from the right. "I will take off my coat," he declared at a dinner sponsored by the Democratic National Committee, "and fight to the end against any candidate who persists in any demagogic appeal to the masses of the working people of this country to destroy themselves by setting class against class and rich against poor!"[9]

The Democrats who assembled in Chicago in June were haunted by memories of the party's national convention in New York's Madison Square Garden in 1924. That year it had taken 107 ballots in the sweltering heat to nominate John W. Davis, who had gone down to landslide defeat by Coolidge in the fall.

On the first ballot in Chicago Roosevelt was far ahead, with Smith second, and Garner, supported by the delegations from California and Texas, third. After three ballots, Roosevelt had failed to make significant headway. Huey Long warned that several southern delegations supporting Roosevelt might not hold for another ballot. Garner was beginning to gain. Reports circulated that many delegates were ready to shift to a dark horse—perhaps to Newton D. Baker, former mayor of Cleveland and Wilson's secretary of war. Roosevelt's strength on the next ballot seemed likely to decline—probably fatally.[10]

Hearst, following events at his California estate, San Simeon, concluded that a deadlock would lead to the nomination of either Smith or Baker, both of whom he detested. He sent word to his lieutenants in Washington and Chicago that the California and Texas delegations should be shifted to Roosevelt. "Say to Mr. Hearst," Garner told the publisher's emissary to the Speaker's office in the capitol, "that I fully agree with him. He is right . . . I will carry out his suggestion and release my delegates to Roosevelt."[11]

Roosevelt was nominated by a large majority on the fourth ballot. Delegations from Massachusetts and New Jersey, and two-thirds of the delegates from Roosevelt's own state of New York, refused to shift from Smith to make the nomination unanimous. The next day Garner was nominated for Vice President.[12]

Roosevelt, breaking precedent, flew from Albany to Chicago to deliver his acceptance speech in person. The Democratic party, he said, must be "the bearer of liberalism. . . ." As President, he promised, he would bring "a new deal for the American people." (The label was apparently suggested by a currently popular book, *A New Deal,* by Stuart Chase, a liberal economist.) As the delegates celebrated, the band played a song called for by Louis Howe when he grew tired of the endless repetition of "Anchors Aweigh" as Roosevelt's theme song: "Happy Days Are Here Again!"[13]

The fall campaign proceeded in an atmosphere of growing economic panic. Roosevelt called for increased federal spending on public works and assumption by the federal government of responsibility for relief. The federal government, he said, should undertake "regularization and planning for balance among industries. . . ." At the same time, he promised to balance the federal budget and called for a 25 percent reduction in federal spending. Hoover, renominated by the Republicans, charged that Roosevelt was "proposing changes and so-called new deals which would destroy the very foundations of our American system."[14]

The election produced a landslide victory for the Democrats. Roosevelt won 57 percent of the popular vote—almost the reverse of the margin by which Hoover had defeated Smith four years before—and carried every state except Pennsylvania, Delaware, Connecticut, and the three states of upper New England (Figure 12–1). The Democrats gained 90 seats in the House and 13 in the Senate, giving them comfortable majorities in both bodies.

The 1932 Roosevelt majority included all but one of the elements in the New Deal coalition that was to dominate presidential politics for the next 36 years. The South and the Border states provided a firm base of 177 electoral votes—only 89 votes short of the 266 majority needed to elect a President. The Rocky Mountain states, second only to the South in their support for the Democrats, added 30 more electoral votes.

Big-city Democratic machines, including those that had held out at the con-

Figure 12–1   Electoral vote by states, 1932

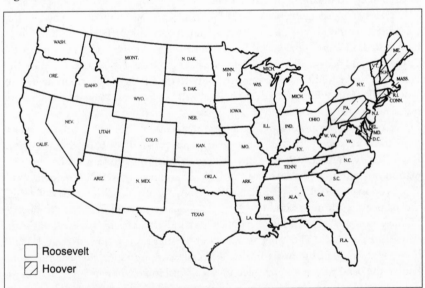

Source: *Historical Statistics of the United States,* Bureau of the Census, 1961

vention for Al Smith, helped produce huge Democratic majorities in metropolitan areas that enabled Roosevelt to carry every industrial state except Pennsylvania and Connecticut (both to be added to the Democratic phalanx in 1936). Organized labor, though not yet the political force it was to become later in the 1930s, gave both manpower and money to the Democratic cause. Catholics seem to have voted even more heavily for Roosevelt in 1932 than they had for Smith in 1928. Jews, continuing the swing away from their traditional Republican allegiance that had begun in 1928, voted more than 80 percent for Roosevelt.

Ethnic voters from southern and eastern Europe, who had been only marginally Democratic from 1918 to 1928, voted overwhelmingly for Roosevelt. In Chicago, as Kristi Anderson has shown, the Democratic percentage of the major party presidential vote in the wards with the largest percentages of foreign-born residents went from 60 percent in 1928 to 71 percent in 1932.[15]

In Boston Roosevelt carried 19 out of 22 wards, the exceptions being two Yankee bastions in Back Bay and semi-suburban Chestnut Hill. In Pittsburgh, which was carried by the Democratic ticket in a national election for the first time since the Civil War, Roosevelt piled up large majorities in the wards along the Allegheny and Monongahela rivers inhabited by steelworkers of Irish, Italian, Polish, Czech, Italian, Lithuanian, and other eastern European stocks (Figure 12–2a, b, and c).

Economically hard-pressed farmers in the Midwest and Far West swung traditionally Republican rural counties into the Democratic column. Liberal activists—including former Progressives like George Norris and Harold Ickes, social reformers like Harry Hopkins and Frances Perkins, and political theorists like Raymond Moley and Rexford Tugwell—provided tactical advice, ideas on issues, public advocacy, and, in many suburban or non-metropolitan communities where regular Democratic party structures were almost nonexistent, organized grassroots support.

The one group eventually to be a pillar of the New Deal coalition that stuck by the Republicans in 1932 was the great majority of the nation's blacks. In the South, blacks remained virtually disenfranchised in most states. But in many northern industrial states, particularly in the cities, they were an increasingly important political force. In 1932, as Nancy Weiss has shown, black districts in Chicago voted 75 percent for Hoover, in Cincinnati 71 percent, in Cleveland 82 percent, in Detroit 67 percent, and in Philadelphia 71 percent. In many of these cities Hoover received larger majorities among blacks in 1932 than he had in 1928.[16]

Northern blacks were held to the Republicans in part by tradition, in part by their ties to Republican state or city machines, and in part by their knowledge that the Democratic party in the South remained the enforcer of racial segregation and discrimination. Some blacks seem also to have distrusted Roosevelt because of his connection with Wilson, whose record on civil rights had been regressive. The one major exception to the overall pattern of black voters was in New York City, where blacks gave a narrow majority to Roosevelt. Weiss attributes Roosevelt's relatively

Figure 12–2   Pittsburgh wards voting Democratic for President, 1928–1936

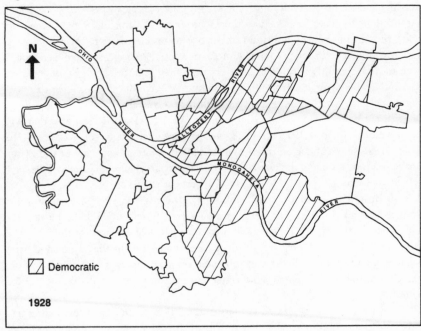

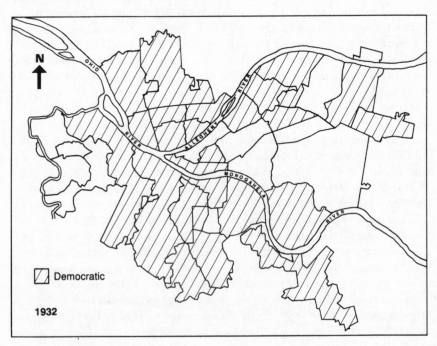

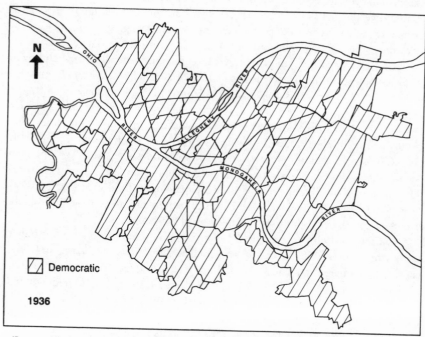

(Source: Allegheny County, Pennsylvania, Bureau of Elections)

strong showing among blacks in New York City to "more than a decade of local Democratic efforts to court black voters" in Harlem, the city's principal black community.[17]

NEW DEAL IDEOLOGY

Roosevelt had promised in his acceptance speech that the Democratic party would be "the bearer of liberalism." What he had in mind was a set of political attitudes and governmental approaches that was related to, but significantly different from, the ideology that during the nineteenth and early twentieth centuries had generally been known by that name.

Before the 1920s the term "liberal" in American political discourse usually represented, as it still does in Europe, opposition to all forms of collectivism. Liberals defended civil liberties, opposed an established church, favored limited and decentralized government, and championed the market as the fairest and most efficient means of organizing the economy. In the political struggles from the 1890s to the 1920s, progressives and liberals, though allied on some issues, were politically distinct.

Progressives were governmental activists, though the goals of their activism were often conservative. Liberals, in contrast, argued that government, because of its inherent inefficiency, intrusiveness into private life, resistance to change, and tendency to reinforce the socially strong against the weak, should be turned to only as a last resort, except for a few specified purposes such as keeping up national defense and maintaining a stable national currency. Jefferson, John Stuart Mill, and William Ewart Gladstone were the patron saints of liberalism, as Hamilton and Lincoln were of progressivism. In the great debate of 1912 Wilson and Brandeis were liberals and Theodore Roosevelt and Croly were progressives. These differences were by no means clearcut or consistently applied, but they were meaningful within the political community.

Wilson's drawing on progressive and populist doctrines, as well as on liberalism, for his administration's program tended to blur the meanings of these terms. The differences over foreign policy that developed during and after the First World War caused further confusion. Was an altruistic interventionist a liberal? If so, what had become of liberalism's preference for small government?

During the 1920s "progressive" became a somewhat tainted term for some of those who favored a degree of governmental activism, particularly among Democrats. On the one hand, it had an old-fashioned ring, was identified historically with the Republican party, and through its Social Gospel aspect was associated with militant Protestantism. On the other, after the Progressive label was taken over by LaFollette in his independent campaign for President in 1924, it came to connote a level of radicalism rejected by moderate activists like Al Smith and Franklin Roosevelt. Increasingly, therefore, liberal became the designation of choice among governmental activists, particularly Democrats, who did not believe in the desirability or inevitability of a fully collectivized economy.

In the 1930s and 1940s the older meaning of liberalism did not wholly disappear. Robert Taft, for instance, known in the 1940s as "Mr. Republican," always identified himself as a liberal. Within the New Deal itself, the civil liberties side of traditional liberalism remained an important factor.

By the end of the 1930s, however, the term liberal had come to stand for almost the reverse of its former meaning on many important governmental matters. Liberalism, put simply, was what the New Deal did: It extended government regulation over the economy; accepted some federal responsibility for the public welfare, particularly among the unemployed and the aged; undertook federal development of resource projects (public power) that seemed beyond the reach or interest of private capital; championed the cause of organized labor; sought to redistribute wealth through progressive taxation of corporate and personal income; built up the powers of the presidency; and broadened the authority of the federal government at the expense of the states. When the Second World War began in Europe in 1939, most liberals favored all possible steps by the United States, short of actual war, to support Britain and France, and later the Soviet Union, against Nazi Germany. Looking toward Asia, liberals promoted measures, again short of war, to halt the military expansion of Japan.

In the early days of the New Deal liberals sought accommodation with business through the National Recovery Administration (NRA), which encouraged collusion between major corporations in the interest of reviving the economy. But by 1935 liberalism had acquired as one of its defining characteristics an adversarial attitude toward business, at least toward big business. This anti-business attitude would be played down during periods of economic and political placidity, like the early 1950s and the 1980s, but it would always be called on when the economic or political weather got rough. In liberalism's view of the social universe, big business would always possess the resources to make it the nation's strongest single political force. The political mission of liberalism then, through its instrument, the Democratic party, would be to organize all other major interests (labor unions, small farmers, intellectuals, small businessmen, minority ethnic and religious groups, patronage-oriented political machines bearing the Democratic label, and even, until the middle of the 1940s, southern segregationists) into a political coalition that would normally outweigh the political power of business. Government dominated by the liberal coalition would, in the phrase of John Kenneth Galbraith, serve as a "countervailing power" to business, enabling society to gain the economic benefits of a market system while distributing those benefits with approximate equality through a welfare state.[18]

A somewhat less advertised aspect of liberalism was its tie to secularism—the view that religion should be strictly excluded from all aspects of public life (except perhaps to serve as cheerleader for liberalism). Some religious leaders, particularly in the mainline Protestant denominations, were enthusiastic liberals. But the core body of liberalism was almost as suspicious and hostile toward organized religion, particularly Catholicism and fundamentalist Protestantism, as toward big business.

Within the New Deal there were individuals and groups, ranging from gradualist socialists to outright Communists, including a few Soviet agents, who scoffed at liberalism. The programs of the New Deal, they believed, were no more than temporary palliatives to ease the suffering caused by the Depression, or movements toward a fully collectivized economy and perhaps society. But these were always minority voices, little represented among elective politicians. As the New Deal continued, left-wing critics of liberalism were gradually removed from positions of power within the administration, the Democratic party, and the major labor unions.

Liberalism was attacked from the right within the Democratic coalition by representatives of various forms of conservatism, including southern Bourbons like Senators Harry Flood Byrd of Virginia and Walter George of Georgia, some of the city machines, and businessmen and corporation lawyers like Bernard Baruch and Dean Acheson, who carried on the tradition of Grover Cleveland. Some aspects of populism, such as that expressed by Huey P. Long, elected governor of Louisiana in 1928 and to the Senate in 1930, also were never fully submerged in liberalism.

For a time, however, liberalism became the integrating principle, the moral inspiration, and the strategic guide around which government programs and

Democratic political campaigns were organized. Like the Federalist, Jeffersonian, and republican ideologies in earlier times, liberalism was the ideological lodestar by which the majority party set its course.

Liberalism was formulated, refined, clarified, and articulated by platoons of social philosophers, political theorists, economists, journalists, and even artists and writers of fiction. Defining liberalism became a kind of cottage industry for American academicians and intellectuals. But liberalism, true to its American roots, was—and is—to a great extent a pragmatic ideology. It evolved not so much from theoretic rationalization as from the practical application to unfolding events of the values and social assumptions of politicians and government administrators.[19]

THE PARTY IN GOVERNMENT

By the time Roosevelt was inaugurated as President on March 4, 1933, the nation seemed on the edge of economic and social chaos. Banks were failing all over the country, and many previously middle-class as well as working-class families faced destitution. "The only thing we have to fear is fear itself," Roosevelt declared in his inaugural address, seeking to restore public confidence.

During the next 14 weeks—the famous "hundred days"—Roosevelt proposed and Congress enacted a series of measures designed to deal with the immediate emergency and to start the economy toward recovery. These included: restructuring the national banking system; federal subsidies to agriculture; regulation of the securities industry; authorization of a huge public power and conservation project to be carried out under the auspices of the federally created Tennessee Valley Authority (TVA); and establishment of the National Recovery Administration (NRA), intended to facilitate collaboration between the federal government, big business, and big labor to prevent "unfair competition and disastrous overproduction."

The "first New Deal" was followed at a more deliberate pace by laws and programs aimed at producing what liberals believed would be a more equitable society. Among major items in the "second New Deal" were: the Wagner Act, designed to protect labor unions against employer coercion; the Works Progress Administration (WPA), a vast national public employment program; the rural electrification program, to bring electricity to rural areas not served by private power companies; the National Youth Administration (NYA), which offered vocational training to unemployed youth; and the Public Utility Holding Company Act, aimed at breaking up the giant power utilities. The crowning achievement of Roosevelt's first term was the Social Security Act of 1935, which provided non-means-tested benefits for retired workers, was financed through a payroll tax (because it was sold to Congress as an insurance program), and gave federal aid to state welfare programs. Though the federal budget ran what was for that time a substantial deficit, the administration's rapid expansion of federal government activities was in part financed by steep increases in graduated tax rates on personal and corporate incomes and by taxes on inheritance. "Great accumulations of wealth," Roosevelt told Congress in his 1935 message calling for higher tax rates, "cannot be justified on the basis of personal and family security."

The New Deal programs that were in place by the end of 1935 represented a critical shift in the direction of federal government policy. The shift did not amount to a sharp or definitive break with the national past. Roosevelt by no means rejected or abandoned capitalism as the underlying framework for the nation's economic system. In fact, by mitigating some of the harsher effects of a market economy, and by increasing the economic leverage of industrial workers, small farmers, and retired persons, the New Deal may well have saved capitalism in the United States from political overthrow. But after more than 70 years during which the ideology of the republican tradition had normally guided national policy, the ideology of what we now know as the liberal tradition again had become uppermost.

In the heat of the national crisis at the start of the new administration, Roosevelt's early proposals received almost united support from Democrats in Congress and broad support from Republicans as well. "The house is burning down," said Representative Bertrand Snell of New York, Republican leader in the House, "and the President of the United States says this is the way to put out the fire." As the sense of emergency slackened, some opposition developed within Democratic ranks, particularly against the administration's effort to break up the giant utility holding companies and against the tax act of 1935, but Democratic unity in Congress remained high throughout Roosevelt's first term. After 1933, however, the Republican minority in Congress generally opposed the New Deal.

In the Congresses elected in 1932 and 1934, both with large Democratic majorities in both houses, Democrats in the House of Representatives maintained party unity averaging more than 85 percent on key New Deal measures. As Barbara Sinclair has shown, House Democrats from the South and the Border states were the *most* consistent supporters of key New Deal legislation among Democratic regional groups; Democrats from the Northeast were the least supportive—mainly on farm legislation. The differences in support among regional groups were not large, however. Even in the Senate, where southern Bourbons like Carter Glass of Virginia, Walter George of Georgia, and Millard Tydings of Maryland, joined in 1933 by the redoubtable Harry Byrd of Virginia, held positions of power, the great majority of Democrats supported key New Deal measures.[20]

Democratic unity in Congress during Roosevelt's first term sprang from several sources. The President's persuasive personality, his political skill, and his popularity with the public certainly helped. Other factors, however, were clearly at work. As James Patterson has pointed out, "In 1937 . . . Roosevelt had larger congressional majorities, no less charm, a great deal more experience, and even greater popularity with the people, yet Congress gave him next to nothing in a long and bitter session."[21]

Federal patronage, most plentiful at the beginning of a new administration, helped sway wavering Democrats in 1933 and 1934. Roosevelt's "relations to Congress," Pendleton Herring has written, "were to the very end of the [first] session tinged with a shade of expectancy which is the best part of young love." The sense among congressional Democrats, out of power for so long, that they had a large stake in the perceived success of the new Democratic President also promoted party unity.[22]

Most of all, perhaps, the severity of the crisis, and the conviction among Democrats that the New Deal offered a possible solution, held the majority party together behind the administration's program. Southern Democrats strongly backed the New Deal during Roosevelt's first term, Barbara Sinclair writes, because "the South as the poorest section of the country was especially hard hit by the Depression and southern congressmen were quick to demand federal relief." The impact of "the Great Depression . . . above all," Patterson concludes, "helped make the Congresses of 1933 and 1934 the most cooperative in recent American history."[23]

A NATIONAL PARTY MACHINE

Roosevelt had long been interested in building the strength of the national Democratic party organization. His experience running as Democratic candidate for Vice President in 1920 had convinced him, he wrote in 1921, that "the party's [national] machinery was archaic" and "something [should] be done." Finding the party's congressional leadership unresponsive to his concern, he sent a letter in 1924 to 3,000 local Democratic party leaders in which he asked for advice on how the national organization might be improved. In 1925, after the Democrats had lost another presidential election, Roosevelt proposed publicly that the party's national organization should be put on a "business-like financial basis" and that a permanent national headquarters should be opened in Washington to function "every day in every year."[24]

Not until 1929, however, did the Democrats follow the example set by the Republicans under Will Hays and establish a continuing national organization. John Raskob, the business tycoon and General Motors executive whom Al Smith had persuaded to become Democratic national chairman, stayed on after Smith's defeat and set up the first permanent Democratic national headquarters in Washington. Raskob hired Charley Michelson, a witty, cynical former Hearst reporter of the *Front Page* school, to handle public relations for the national committee. Michelson's taunting press releases attacking the Hoover administration during the early years of the Depression helped keep the Republicans off balance and warmed the cockles of Democratic hearts. In 1932 Raskob openly employed the machinery he had put in place at the national committee (largely financed through loans from himself and Bernard Baruch) to resist Roosevelt's nomination.[25]

After Roosevelt was nominated, Jim Farley took over as Democratic national chairman and made productive use during the fall campaign of the national committee's new resources. Farley became postmaster general in the Roosevelt administration, but, unlike Hays in the Harding administration, he did not give up his party office.

In his combined governmental and party roles, Farley supervised the distribution of federal patronage to deserving Democrats, many of whom were sponsored by Democratic members of Congress or by state or local party organizations. In the summer of 1933, Farley complained that he had "only 150,000 jobs" exempt from civil service protection in a federal work force of 2,750,000 to fill applications from "at least 1,500,000 men and women." Preference for top positions was given to members of the "FRBC club"—For Roosevelt Before Chicago.[26]

While Farley channeled jobs to regular Democratic organizations, Roosevelt on another track encouraged Harry Hopkins, director of WPA, to develop a separate political structure by distributing federal patronage to programmatic liberals, whether or not they had ties to regular party organizations. "I thought at first I could be completely non-political," Hopkins, a former social worker, later said. "Then they told me I had to be part non-political and part political. I found that was impossible, at least for me. I finally realized there was nothing for it but to be all-political."[27]

Hopkins used his control of WPA to build his own political network among local Democratic machines as well as among liberal activists. A retrospective study of 103 Pittsburgh Democratic committeemen in the 1930s found that almost one-third had held jobs with WPA. A majority of them had been foremen or supervisors. A former committeeman from the thirteenth ward recalled: "I was laid off from my job as a printer. I got a job as a foreman on WPA. The ward chairman got you the good jobs. Anyone could be a laborer; politics was only needed in the key jobs." Political connections were also useful in renting a truck to WPA. A former committeeman from the eighteenth ward, overlooking the Monongahela River, remembered: "I got my truck on through politics. I had to go to the ward chairman to get the truck on because 20 other men wanted to do the same."[28]

The two structures of political appointees, though often on bad terms with each other, were united in support of Roosevelt. At the 1936 Democratic national convention that nominated Roosevelt for a second term, about half the 1,100 delegates were federal jobholders.[29]

CITY MACHINES UNDER THE NEW DEAL

The decline of patronage-based city machines is often traced, at least in part, to the displacement of the machines' traditional welfare function by federal government programs instituted by the New Deal. During the 1930s, however, many city machines wearing the Democratic label actually thrived on the new federal programs. The Hague machine in Jersey City, the Kelly-Nash machine in Chicago, the Pendergast machine in Kansas City, the Crump machine in Memphis, the O'Connell machine in Albany—all fattened on the jobs and dollars the federal government poured into their cities. In Pittsburgh, after the old Republican machine was overthrown in the early 1930s, it was swiftly replaced by a Democratic counterpart that used all the familiar techniques and incentives.[30]

Tammany, the great-grandfather of all city machines, it is true, came on hard times in the 1930s. After the death in 1924 of Charles Murphy, who had run a relatively tight ship, corruption in city government had got out of hand. Tammany in the early 1930s "owned 64 of the 65 aldermen, all five district attorneys, and most of the judges, while it collected its take from the more than 40,000 speakeasies and the thousands of gamblers, and swelled the public payroll with . . . hacks whose sole function was to pick up their weekly checks."[31]

During an investigation of governmental corruption in New York City sponsored by the state in 1932, Mayor James J. Walker, the celebrated "night mayor of Broadway," resigned and fled to Europe. Taking advantage of a split in the Democratic city organization in 1933, Fiorello LaGuardia ran for mayor on both Republican and independent reform tickets and was elected. During the next 12 years, LaGuardia maintained shifting coalitions that included regular Republicans, independent reformers, the Communist-infiltrated American Labor party (ALP), and the Liberal party (formed as an anti-Communist breakaway from the ALP). He was thereby able to keep a demoralized Tammany at bay and operate his own kind of benevolent autocracy in city hall.[32]

Tammany's experience in the years following Roosevelt's election, however, was far from typical. Most of the machines had opposed Roosevelt's nomination at the Democratic convention in 1932, partly because of the nostalgic loyalty some Irish Catholic bosses felt for Al Smith. After the convention, however, Roosevelt quickly made his peace with the bosses.

At the invitation of Frank Hague, mayor of Jersey City and boss of the Democratic party in New Jersey, Roosevelt had opened his general election campaign at a giant rally of machine regulars at Sea Girt on the Jersey shore. Soon after Roosevelt's election, Hague expressed gratitude for the patronage that flowed to the machine: "Your recognition of our state organization has been substantially manifested and in return I feel we owe you this pledge of loyalty." When local citizens called on Roosevelt for help against Hague's strong-arm methods and suppression of civil liberties in Jersey City, the President turned a deaf ear. "Of course there is nothing we can do about the New Jersey situation," Farley wrote in a memo to the President's secretary. "Hague is going to run it his own way. He has been reelected for four years and there is nothing we can do."[33]

The machine that came to be regarded as a model of political efficiency, the Chicago Democratic organization, led in the 1930s by Mayor Edward Kelly and Cook County Democratic chairman Patrick Nash, did not achieve real dominance in local politics until the New Deal years. Since the middle of the nineteenth century there had been a Democratic machine in Chicago run by an oligarchy of mostly Irish ward bosses. But it sometimes lost city elections to reformers or to the rival Republican machine, led in the 1920s by Mayor William Hale Thompson, "Big Bill," a demagogue who manipulated antagonisms among the city's ethnic groups and gave free rein to the crime empire ruled by Al Capone.[34]

The Democratic machine's rise to domination began with the victory of Anton Cermak over Thompson in the mayoralty election of 1931. Cermak built a Democratic organization based on working-class and lower-middle-class Chicagoans, with the exception of blacks. He was aided in this endeavor by the Depression, which hit Chicago harder than any other large city except Detroit. Though Cermak himself had ties to the underworld, the leaders of the city's business community were so disturbed by the level that corruption had reached under Thompson that they switched their support to the Democrats.[35]

In 1932 Chicago produced a margin of 250,000 for Roosevelt. At a public function in Miami with Roosevelt after the election, Cermak was killed by an assassin who apparently had intended to murder the President-elect (though rumors persisted that the shooting had been commissioned by the Chicago mob and that Cermak was the target). After Cermak's death, the machine was run by Kelly and Nash, who loyally supported the New Deal and were rewarded with a steady supply of federal dollars and jobs.

Harold Gosnell, in a classic 1937 study, found that the machines most important resource was the patronage army it was able to deploy throughout the city's wards and precincts. Among the city's 50 Democratic ward leaders, 43 held jobs with the city, county, state, or federal governments—all controlled by the Democrats. Below these were arrayed more than 3,000 precinct committeemen, more than three-fourths of whom had government jobs. Each ward leader was given a share of the approximately 30,000 patronage jobs that were distributed through the Cook County Democratic organization.[36]

The precinct captains, working under the supervision of the ward leaders, were primarily responsible for turning out the Democratic vote on election day. The ideal captain, Gosnell concluded, was "one who makes friends easily, who works hard and steadily, who gives absolute obedience, who is intelligent but satisfied with a subordinate role, who is not too demanding for himself, and who does not ask too many questions."[37]

Why did ordinary citizens follow the electoral directives of their precinct captains? Some scholars have maintained that the tie binding the individual voter to the machine was mainly material. "The relationship," in this view, was "built around the exchange of specific material incentives for votes. Because of his lack of resources the voter values the bucket of coal or other small favor he receives. . . . The machine voter is materially motivated and responds to material incentives." Others, notably Edward Banfield and James Q. Wilson, have argued that the precinct captain provided, in addition to material incentives, a sense of community amid the bewildering turmoil of big-city life. "The voter is the one contributor to the machine's system of activity who is usually given non-material inducements, especially 'friendship.'" The bucket of coal, in this appraisal, was valued not only for its own sake but as a symbol of community and social inclusion. The voters of the old city neighborhoods, Banfield and Wilson observed, recognized that the machine was, by abstract civic standards, corrupt. But they did not care, or did not care very much, because the machine seemed to serve the interests of their neighborhoods and they were not inclined by experience or culture to attach much value to a more broadly conceived view of the "public interest."[38]

Gosnell found that precinct captains in Chicago in the 1930s used both direct material incentives and more general expressions of mutuality and friendship to secure the loyalty of their constituents. Among the 300 committeemen whom he interviewed, 70 percent said they sometimes provided food for families in their precincts; 32 percent, coal; 39 percent, Christmas baskets; 37 percent sometimes helped out with rent money; 51 percent found government jobs for their constituents and 47 percent jobs in private industry; 53 percent helped constituents in trouble with the law; 27 percent admitted interceding for constituents with traffic tickets; 62 percent regularly attended funerals; 52 percent made a practice of going to weddings; and 25 percent "adjusted domestic difficulties." Gosnell noted, however, that in comparison with a study done in 1928, "the 1936 precinct committeeman in the city of Chicago was less of an employment broker, less of a tax-fixer, less of a traffic-slip adjuster, but more of a go-between for the relief agencies and the various branches of the federal government"—signifying the growing role of the welfare state.[39]

POLITICAL SUCCESS, ECONOMIC DEADLOCK

Building on Roosevelt's personal popularity, general approval of New Deal programs, and traditional use of patronage, the Democrats had clearly emerged by the end of 1934 as the national majority party. In the midterm elections, the Democrats actually added seats to their already huge majorities in the House and Senate—the only time from 1902 to 1998 that the party holding the White House did not suffer some loss of seats in the midterm congressional elections.

The Depression, however, did not go away. Though economic conditions improved somewhat, unemployment in 1935 averaged 20 percent and gross national product in constant dollars was only three-quarters of what it had been in 1929. Many Americans continued to believe that the New Deal might turn out to be only the prelude to far more fundamental changes in the nation's social, economic, and perhaps even constitutional systems.

13

VEHICLES OF OPPOSITION

THE LAST NATIONAL TRAUMA strong enough to transform the national party system fundamentally had destroyed one major party and created a new one. Many politicians and political commentators in the early 1930s believed that the anger and desperation generated by the Depression would ultimately cause at least as thorough a political change—and might lead to the abandonment of party competition altogether.

Democracy itself seemed to many to be on thin ice during the early 1930s. Roosevelt in his inaugural address expressed hope that the nation's economic troubles could be dealt with through the normal constitutional system. But if the crisis deepened, he said, he would ask Congress for "the one remaining instrument— broad Executive power to wage a war against the economic emergency, as great as the power that would be given to me if [the country] were in fact invaded by a foreign foe." Moderate conservatives like Governor Alfred Landon of Kansas and Senator Arthur Vandenberg of Michigan, both Republicans, privately suggested that some kind of temporary dictatorship might be needed. "Even the iron hand of a national dictator," Landon wrote, "is in preference to a paralytic stroke. . . ."[1]

In Europe democracy was being overthrown in many of the countries where it had been launched as a frail experiment after 1918. Authoritarian systems, of both left and right, were on the march. Many socialists and some liberals hailed Stalin's Russia as proof that Communism was a realizable goal for social equalitarians rather than a utopian hoax. For authoritarians who found Communism too materialistic, or too universalistic in its definition of the relevant "people" or "folk," or simply too threatening to their own interests, Mussolini's Italy and Hitler's Germany offered models of totalitarian nationalism.

Even many whose ideological orientations remained primarily democratic concluded that the existing American parties were too cumbersome or too compromised by venality to mobilize the political system to deal with the national emergency. For many voters the chief recommendation of the Democrats in 1932 had been that they were not Republicans. The negligible increase in turnout over 1928 showed that there was little mass rallying to the Democrats by the discontented.

Roosevelt's dramatic actions during his first few months in office undoubtedly stirred renewed hope. The President's patrician style gave a lift to public

219

morale. But the New Deal, as Roosevelt always insisted, operated within the broad structures set by existing social and economic institutions. Roosevelt sought to reform the system, not to replace it. In time he would be regarded by some who shared his social background as "a traitor to his class." But most of the millions of union laborers, sharecroppers, unemployed workers, and disgruntled intellectuals who loyally supported him at the polls could hardly have imagined that he would lead the way to any kind of social revolution. His evident roots in the establishment offered reassurance that the system might yet be made to work for most of those who now felt economically threatened or socially dispossessed. But if the ideological climate were to shift, the New Deal might be interpreted as a sham to protect the old order, the Democratic party might be consumed by its internal contradictions, and Roosevelt might be cast as the Mirabeau or Kerensky of the second American revolution.

FIRE ON THE LEFT

The American Socialist party, founded in 1901 by a coalition of leftist union leaders and intellectuals, was resolutely committed to democratic evolution toward a collectivist society. In 1932, it had more than tripled the vote for its presidential candidate, Norman Thomas, a cheery product of the Social Gospel side of progressivism, over his showing on his first try in 1928. But Thomas still polled only a little more than 2 percent of the national popular vote. Socialism, at least by that name, appeared to hold little attraction for the great majority of workers, farmers, or even intellectuals. This was partly because socialism, in its Marxist form, had been indelibly shaped by nineteenth-century European experience, which most Americans still wished to put behind them. Also, however, socialism, with its emphasis on equal shares for all, seemed too static, too preoccupied with dividing the pie and not enough with making the pie bigger, too out of touch with the underlying social optimism that most Americans never lost, even at the bottom of the Depression. In 1936, though real economic conditions had not greatly improved, the vote for Thomas, who was running a third time for President, dropped back to less than 1 percent of the national total.[2]

The American Communist party, founded in 1921, was tightly controlled by a leadership cadre that slavishly followed the party line dictated from Comintern headquarters in Moscow. It was even less successful than the Socialists as an electoral force. Communism during the 1930s became a fighting faith for a numerically small but socially significant and influential body of American writers, artists, scholars, and students. Communists gained power in some major labor unions and in sectors of the publishing and entertainment industries, and a few Communists found their way to positions of authority in the federal government under the New Deal. But the Communist party as a competitor in elections was always negligible: less than one-third of 1 percent of the national vote at its peak in 1932.

If an electorally formidable radical third party were to rise in the United States in the 1930s, most commentators recognized, it would have to grow out of some kind of populism or progressivism that had roots in the American experience. At the state level, several such parties seemed to be taking hold during Roosevelt's first term.

In Minnesota, Governor Floyd Olson, a charismatic spellbinder, led the Farmer-Labor party, an offshoot of populism that denounced both Republicans and Democrats as too conservative, into control of state government in 1930. After the 1932 election, one of Minnesota's senators and five of its nine House members were Farmer-Laborites. "I am not a liberal," Olson declared. "I am what I want to be— a radical." If the Depression continued, he proclaimed, "the Government ought to take and operate the key industries in the country." Those who resisted the radical program "because they happen to possess considerable wealth will be brought in by the provost guard." In 1934 the state Farmer-Labor convention resolved that "capitalism has failed and . . . immediate steps must be taken by the people to abolish capitalism in a peaceful and lawful manner. . . ." Under the new order that was to replace capitalism, "all the natural resources, machinery of production, transportation, and communication, shall be owned by the government."[3]

In Wisconsin, Robert LaFollette, Jr., and his younger brother, Phil, in 1934 launched yet another Progressive party. Running on the new party's ticket, "Young Bob," reserved and thoughtful, was reelected to the Senate; and Phil, who inherited more of their father's fire, was elected governor. Six of Wisconsin's ten House members were Progressives. Though less radical in his utterances than Floyd Olson, Phil LaFollette proposed consolidation of the Wisconsin Progressives and the Minnesota Farmer-Laborites with insurgencies in other states to form "a national third party—a real leftist party."[4]

In California, Upton Sinclair, the old muckraker, created the End Poverty in California movement (EPIC), aimed at replacing private enterprise with "production units manned by workers under charter from the state." Changing his party registration from Socialist to Democrat, Sinclair in 1934 entered the Democratic primary for governor and trounced the candidate supported by the party's established leaders. Sinclair set forth his program for restructuring the economy around worker collectives in his best-selling book, *I, Governor of California and How I Ended Poverty*. Roosevelt, alarmed by the prospect of a take-over of California government by left-wing radicals, virtually endorsed Sinclair's conservative Republican opponent (who promised in return not to claim that his election was a repudiation of the New Deal).

The campaign against Sinclair, Arthur M. Schlesinger, Jr., has pointed out, was notable as "the first all-out public relations *Blitzkrieg* in American politics." The team of Clem Whitaker and Leone Baxter, beginning their long and fabulously successful careers as political consultants, perhaps the first of their breed, churned out propaganda designed to discredit Sinclair personally as well as politically. The movie industry and major newspapers pitched in with newsreel pictures and still photographs of migrant vagabonds rushing to California in anticipation of a Sinclair victory (actually left-over film from the Warner Brothers movie, *Wild Boys on the Road*) and man-in-the-street "interviews" with heavily bearded characters including one who explained he was voting for Sinclair because, "Vell, his system worked vell in Russia, vy can't it work here?" Defeated in a landslide, Sinclair promptly wrote another book: *I, Candidate for Governor: And How I Got Licked.*[5]

Beyond elected officials and candidates, a number of self-selected prophets pitching economic and political nostrums assembled followings that might offer grassroots support for a new party. The most visible of these were Dr. Francis Townsend, formulator of the famed "Townsend plan," and Father Charles Coughlin, whose weekly radio broadcasts had an audience of many millions.

Townsend, a retired physician in Long Beach, California, had thought up the Townsend plan after looking out his bathroom window one morning in 1933 and being shocked to see three elderly women poking in his garbage can for food. Under the plan, which Townsend first published in a local newspaper, the federal government would provide everyone over 60 years of age with a pension of $200 a month "on condition that they spend the money as they got it." Older Americans would thereby be saved from poverty and removed from competition in the work force, and the money pumped into the economy would revive business. The pensions were to be paid for by a "transaction tax"—much like what we now call a value-added tax. The campaign to enact the plan, promoted by its founder in collaboration with some shrewd public relations specialists, gave rise to a nationwide network of Townsend clubs. The clubs were particularly strong among older Protestants in California and the Midwest. Rebuffed by Congress and the administration, Townsend in 1935 began to talk of turning the Townsend clubs into the organization for a new party.[6]

Attracting a following even larger than Townsend's, Father Coughlin, a priest of the Shrine of the Little Flower in Royal Oak, Michigan, used his nationally broadcast radio program to condemn, with fine impartiality, "godless capitalists, the Jews, Communists, international bankers, and plutocrats." The way out of the Depression, and in fact out of all social ills, Coughlin prescribed, was establishment of a "corporate state" that would manage the national economy in accordance with Christian principles. Though Coughlin's largest audience was among Catholics, he also appealed to many Protestants alarmed by the Depression and by the growing secularization of American life. In the early 1930s his Sunday afternoon broadcast was the most popular program on the airwaves—more popular even than Amos 'n' Andy or Ed Winn. Coughlin at first supported Roosevelt. "The New Deal," he said, "is Christ's deal." But by 1935 he had concluded that the Roosevelt administration "protects plutocrats and comforts Communists." He, too, began speaking of forming a new political party.[7]

THE KINGFISH

For all their national popularity, however, neither Townsend nor Coughlin had the political gifts to lead an effective third party. Floyd Olson and Phil LaFollette were not national figures. Upton Sinclair pretty much dropped out of politics after his defeat in California and in any case was never a serious national politician. The one national political leader who seemed to have the potential for bringing together various strands of economic and social protest into a formidable third political force was the junior senator from Louisiana, Huey P. Long.

When Long began his rise to political power in Louisiana in the 1920s, there was no reason to regard him, as V. O. Key wrote, as anything more than "just another southern heir of Populism: an anti-corporation man, a politician skilled in identifying himself with the poor farmer, a rabble-rouser in the familiar southern pattern." Long, to be sure, seemed more ingenious than most other populist demagogues of the period—men like Senators Theodore Bilbo of Mississippi and Tom Heflin of Alabama.[8]

Stories abound of Long's inspired knavery. My own favorite is one told by T. Harry Williams at the beginning of his definitive biography of Long:

> [Campaigning for the first time in rural, Catholic southern Louisiana, Long began each speech] by saying: "When I was a boy, I would get up at six o'clock in the morning on Sunday, and I would hitch our old horse up to the buggy and I would take my Catholic grandparents to mass. I would bring them home, and at ten o'clock I would hitch the old horse up again, and I would take my Baptist grandparents to church." The effect of the anecdote on the audiences was obvious, and on the way back to Baton Rouge that night the local leader said admiringly: "Why, Huey, you've been holding out on us. I didn't know you had any Catholic grandparents." "Don't be a damn fool," replied Huey. "We didn't even have a horse."[9]

Standard Oil in the 1920s held a more privileged position in Louisiana, probably, than that held by a business corporation in any other state. When the governor considered proposing legislation that might affect Standard, he felt obliged to submit it for approval to the corporation's headquarters in New York. Long, running for governor in 1928, presented himself as the David who dared to take on the corporate Goliath. (He had been impressed by Theodore Bilbo, who always began a speech in a Mississippi town "by denouncing in violent language the wealthiest citizen or citizens.") Long also attacked the New Orleans machine, known as the Old Regulars, and some of the more notoriously corrupt county courthouse rings. Probably few of his listeners, who had been fooled so often and for so long, believed him. But they voted for him anyhow, no doubt finding his clownish style more engaging than that of his rivals.[10]

After he became governor in 1929 at the age of 35, Long, to the surprise of everyone, perhaps including himself, "broke completely with the established pattern of leaders of his type—the promising demagogue who forgot his promises or the idealistic liberal or progressive governor who permitted reactionary elements to stall and then sabotage his program. He put through the whole of his program and even added to it as he went along."[11]

Louisiana state expenditures per capita, which before Long became governor were well below the national average and about average for the South, were by 1932 twice the national average—greater than New York or California, three times those of Virginia or Georgia, almost four times those of Mississippi. A fair amount of this increased state spending probably ended up in politicians' pockets. But state services visibly increased and improved. ("Sure, I got a bunch of crooks around here," says Willie Stark, the character modeled on Long in Robert Penn Warren's great novel, *All the King's Men,* "but they're too lily-livered to get very crooked. I got my eye on 'em. And do I deliver the state something? I damned well do.") For the first time, free textbooks were made available to school children. School teachers' salaries became the highest in the South. The state university was greatly expanded. Far more miles of state highway were laid in Louisiana in 1931 than in any other southern state—even Texas. New state hospitals were opened. Public welfare payments per case became the most generous in the south. Much of this increase in services was financed through borrowing—Louisiana's state debt per capita in 1932 was about twice the national average. But Long also pushed through a "separation tax" on the oil industry.[12]

To get this program enacted, and also, it would seem, to serve the drives of his egomaniacal personality, Long created what remains the most powerful state political machine in American history. Williams writes:

> He was the first southern leader, and very possibly the first American leader, to set out not to contain the opposition or to impose certain conditions on it, but to force it out of existence. Deliberately, he grasped the control of all existing boards and other agencies, and then just as deliberately, by creating new agencies to perform new functions, he continually enlarged the patronage at his disposal. His control of patronage gave him control of the legislature, and his control of the legislature enabled him to have laws enacted that invested him with imperial authority over every level of local government. He became so powerful finally that he could deny the opposition almost all political sustenance, and if he wished, destroy it.[13]

Long—the "Kingfish," as he liked to be called (after a leading character in the Amos 'n' Andy radio serial)—broke the power of the Old Regulars in New Orleans by sending the National Guard into the city as a virtual army of occupation. When members of the state's old-line gentry, including Hodding Carter, editor of the widely respected *Hammond Courier,* tried to organize a political opposition, he harassed them with the state militia. Accused of copying European fascists, Long joked: "Mussolini gave them castor oil; I'll give them tabasco, and then they'll like Louisiana." Elected to the Senate in 1930, he delayed taking his seat for one year while he consolidated his hold on state and local government. After giving up the governorship, he continued to run the state through his puppet successor, Governor O.K. Allen.[14]

Long played an important part in getting the presidential nomination for Roosevelt in 1932, but by the end of 1933 he was feuding with the New Deal. He compared the Republicans and Democrats to two bottles of patent medicine, "High Popalorum and Low Papahirum," one made by taking the bark off the tree from the ground up and the other by taking the bark off the tree from the top down. "The Republican leaders are skinning the people from the ankle up, and the Democratic leaders are taking off the hide from the ear down. Skin 'em up or skin 'em down, but skin 'em."[15]

In the summer of 1935 Long seemed on the verge of putting himself at the head of a vaguely populist national third-party movement. His Share-the-Wealth program, calling for seizure of all fortunes to provide every American family with a "homestead allowance" of $5,000, followed by generous welfare state benefits, appeared to be catching on with voters. His slogan, "Every man a king"—to which he quickly added, "And every women a queen"—captured the slack side of the American dream: a vision of total social equality mixed with fantasies of unlimited individual privilege. Most Americans probably recognized that Long was at one level simply a con man. But he evoked the widely held American folk-belief, also expressed by popular humorists like Mark Twain, Will Rogers, and James Thurber, that life itself is a con and only the great con artist can set it right. Long was confident that he could defeat Roosevelt at the polls: "I can take him. He's a phony. . . . He's scared of me. I can outpromise him, and he knows it. People will believe me and they won't believe him."[16]

Then, on a warm night in September 1935, in Baton Rouge, fresh from bullying the last items of his program through the Louisiana legislature, Long stepped into the rotunda of the skyscraper state capitol he had built and was shot down by a young physician, Carl Weiss, for reasons never fully determined. Weiss was immediately killed by Long's bodyguard, who riddled his body with more than sixty bullets. Long lingered for a few hours and then died.

If Long had lived, would he have been able to organize a strongly competitive third party in 1936, let alone have beaten Roosevelt? Probably not. The old obstacle of the electoral college still stood in the way of third-party movements. After the Australian ballot came into use, the two major parties had taken pains to enact ballot-access and other election laws that made it even more difficult for a third party to pose a serious electoral challenge. Roosevelt's popularity with the public was probably higher than the third-party advocates imagined, and the New Deal coalition was firmly in place. Long himself, as the public saw more of him, might have fizzled. The very emotions he aroused would have hardened resistance against him. The national press would certainly have done its best to discredit him, as the press had helped undermine Sinclair in California. The Kingfish might have ended as another ranting fanatic, the cruel fate that overtook Tom Watson and to some extent Bryan.

But what if he had succeeded? What if he had somehow overcome the forces arrayed against him and won the presidency? Would he then have been able to establish at the national level virtually dictatorial rule comparable to the rule he imposed on Louisiana? Again, probably not—at least not unless conditions had become a good deal worse than they were even in the darkest days of the Depression. American institutions of constitutional democracy, far more deeply implanted than they had been in Germany or Italy or even France, would probably have withstood even so cunning and talented a demagogue as Huey Long.

Yet Long's career stands as a cautionary example of the latent dangers to democracy posed by one-party or no-party systems, perhaps even more applicable to our time than to his. It is significant that Long rose to power in a state that in the 1930s had no party opposition and little regular party organization beyond the Old Regulars' machine in New Orleans. Floyd Olson, who also had autocratic tendencies, though probably more respect for civil liberties, did not get nearly so far in Minnesota, where he was fought by both Republican and Democratic organizations. Roosevelt himself, when during his second term he tried to break through restraint by the Supreme Court, encountered stiff and successful resistance in Congress, based in part on a campaign against the President's court-packing scheme promoted and financed by the Republican party. Thirty-five years later, Richard Nixon's abuse of presidential power was brought to light in part by the partisan opposition of Democrats in Congress. The democratic spirit of the American people and the entire system of constitutional checks and balances provide effective barriers against the emergence of dictatorship in a national crisis. But party competition has given strong, perhaps indispensable, institutional support to the health of republican government.

A RAMSHACKLE COALITION

The chance for a strong third-party movement, authoritarian or democratic, expired with Long's death. In 1936, Coughlin, Townsend, and some remnants of Long's machine formed a ramshackle organization they called the Union party. As its candidate for President the party nominated Congressman William Lemke of North Dakota, a product of the state's radical populist Nonpartisan League. Lemke received just under 2 percent of the national popular vote. After the election, Coughlin continued his radio broadcasts, which became increasingly vitriolic and anti-Semitic—and increasingly offensive and embarrassing to the Catholic hierarchy. He was finally forced off the air through government pressure after the United States entered the Second World War.[17]

Floyd Olson, stricken by pancreatic cancer during his third term as governor, endorsed Roosevelt in 1936 and died before the election. The Minnesota Farmer–Labor party, after its leadership had been infiltrated by Communists, was ousted from control of state government in 1938 by resurgent Republicans (led by Harold Stassen, elected governor at the age of 32). In 1944 what was left of the Farmer–Labor party merged with the Minnesota Democrats to form the present

Democratic Farmer–Labor party (DFL). The LaFollette brothers also backed Roosevelt in 1936. Phil was defeated for reelection as governor in 1938. "Young Bob" continued in the Senate until 1946, when, after leading the Wisconsin Progressives back into the Republican party, he was defeated in the Republican primary by an ambitious young veteran of the Second World War, Joseph R. McCarthy.

Alternatives to the New Deal, it was clear after 1936, would have to be developed within the framework of the existing two-party system.

THE COURT-PACKING FIGHT

In 1936 Roosevelt won reelection to a second term over Governor Alfred Landon of Kansas, the Republican candidate, by a landslide majority of 61 percent of the popular vote—the largest margin in a contested presidential election up to that time. Jim Farley confirmed his reputation as a political seer by correctly predicting that Roosevelt would carry every state except Maine and Vermont. Voter turnout, which had increased only slightly in 1932, surged to 61 percent—outside the South to 71 percent, its highest level since 1908.[18]

Northern blacks finally gave up their allegiance to "the party of Lincoln" and in most cities voted by large majorities for Roosevelt. Democratic majorities in Congress rose to almost four-to-one in the House and almost five-to-one in the Senate. Many within the political community predicted that the Republican party would soon go the way of the Federalists and the Whigs.

The very vastness of the Democratic majorities in Congress, however, almost guaranteed (it can be seen in hindsight) that Democratic party unity would soon decline. The New Deal coalition had come to include highly disparate elements: blacks and white segregationists, unions and anti-union economic interests, internationalists and isolationists, liberal reformers and machine politicians. Like the Republicans after McKinley's victory in 1896, the Democratic factions could now afford the luxury of fighting each other.

Roosevelt lost no time in coming up with the issue that would divide his party and unite the opposition. During 1935 and 1936 the conservative majority on the Supreme Court had repeatedly knocked down New Deal legislation. The climax came in May 1935, when a unanimous Court, including Brandeis and the moderate Chief Justice, Charles Evans Hughes, as well as the five conservative justices, ruled that the NRA, the flagship of the administration's economic recovery program, was an unconstitutional invasion of states' rights. ("This is the end of this business of centralization," Brandeis told one of Roosevelt's young aides, "and I want you to go back and tell the President that we're not going to let this government centralize everything. It's come to an end.")[19]

Only two weeks after his second inauguration, in 1937 (the date of inauguration had been moved to January 20 by the Twentieth Amendment), Roosevelt called for legislation that would permit him to appoint one Supreme Court justice for every sitting justice who did not retire within six months of his seventieth birthday, up to a total of six—thereby enabling him to pack the Court with a liberal majority. When the chairman of the House Judiciary Committee, a conservative Texan, announced his opposition, the administration had the bill embodying the President's proposal introduced in the Senate.

Roosevelt's court-packing bill produced the small miracle, James Patterson has written, of uniting "Senate Republicans for the first time in three decades." Both progressives and Old Guard Republicans denounced the proposal as a threat to constitutional government. The Republicans were immediately joined by the handful of Bourbon Democrats in the Senate, including Byrd and Glass of Virginia, George of Georgia, and Tydings of Maryland, who had regularly opposed the New Deal during Roosevelt's first term. More surprisingly, some moderate Democrats like Senator Bennett Champ Clark of Missouri (son of the former Speaker), and even a few liberals like Senator Burton K. Wheeler of Montana, who had run for Vice President on the Progressive ticket with Robert LaFollette, Sr., in 1924, announced they would vote against the bill.[20]

The Republicans, a minority of only 16 in the Senate, shrewdly decided to "let the revolting Democrats" lead the fight. Wheeler was persuaded to head an informal steering committee that included many of his old enemies among conservative Republicans and Bourbon Democrats. ("Wheeler," Arthur Vandenberg of Michigan, the chief Republican strategist, noted in his journal, "is absolutely *essential*. . . .") Once committed, Wheeler did not hesitate to make use of all the resources his new allies placed at his disposal. The senatorial steering committee drew on funds supplied by the Republican National Committee to help swing public opinion against Roosevelt's plan. Wheeler and Vandenberg worked closely with the National Committee to Uphold Constitutional Government, an umbrella organization of conservative and good-government groups put together by Frank Gannett, publisher of a string of conservative newspapers. The opposition successfully defined the court-packing plan as a step toward elected dictatorship.[21]

Roosevelt held the support of the Senate Democratic leadership, including such powerful southerners as Majority Leader Joseph Robinson of Arkansas, Pat Harrison of Mississippi, and James Byrnes of South Carolina, all of whom disliked the plan but felt compelled by their positions in the party to stick with the administration. Vice President Garner, though privately critical, also remained loyal. Roosevelt used Democratic party machinery at the national, state, and city levels, Patterson writes, to apply "utmost pressure on wavering senators."[22]

Wheeler, through Brandeis, induced Chief Justice Hughes to set forth his objections to the court-packing scheme in a letter to the Senate Judiciary Committee. The white-bearded Chief Justice, who himself had sided with the liberal minority on some of the New Deal cases, seemed the perfect symbol of constitutional, as opposed to purely majoritarian, government.

In April the Supreme Court, by a vote of 5 to 4, declared the Wagner Labor Relations Act constitutional. Justice Owen Roberts, who had previously voted with the conservatives, provided the swing vote—"the switch in time," it was later said, "that saved nine." Justice Willis Van Devanter, one of the most intransigent of the conservatives, announced his retirement, enabling Roosevelt to appoint a new justice, who presumably would further tip the balance of the Court toward the liberal side.[23]

Roosevelt still pressed for passage of his proposal to permit enlargement of the Court. As a vote neared in the Senate, Majority Leader Robinson, who, despite his own reservations, had held some members in line through appeals to personal and party loyalty, suddenly died of a heart attack. Garner told Roosevelt: "You are beat. You haven't got the votes." Roosevelt agreed to throw in the towel. Garner approached Wheeler: "For God's sake and the sake of our party, be reasonable." Wheeler's only concession was to agree that the bill should be recommitted to the Senate Judiciary Committee and thereby killed.[24]

THE CONSERVATIVE COALITION

The alliance that formed against Roosevelt's court-packing plan provided the basis for what later was known as the "conservative coalition"—a loose, informal association of conservative Republicans and Democrats in Congress that from 1939 to the end of 1958 usually held the power to block any legislation it opposed and has continued as a factor in congressional politics to the present day. Not all who came out against the court-packing plan joined the conservative coalition. Roosevelt was still able to count on support from a substantial majority of Democrats in both houses on most legislation. The court-packing fight, nevertheless, was a watershed. It showed that Roosevelt was, after all, politically vulnerable.[25]

Senate Republicans, having achieved unity on the court-packing issue, continued to act together as a party more often than they had for years. Old Guard and progressive Republicans still differed on some issues, but both groups were determined to resist what they regarded as the authoritarian tendencies of the Roosevelt administration. Some of the moderate Democrats who had opposed Roosevelt on the court-packing issue were emboldened to go against the administration on other matters. Even Wheeler, formerly a reliable liberal, voted increasingly with the conservatives.

The close division of Senate Democrats on the choice of a successor to Robinson as majority leader showed how much Roosevelt's influence had slipped. Roosevelt's candidate, Alben Barkley of Kentucky, defeated Pat Harrison of Mississippi by only one vote. (Harrison could have won if he had agreed to speak to the other senator from Mississippi, his blood enemy, Theodore Bilbo. "Tell the son of a bitch," Harrison is reported to have said, "I wouldn't speak to him if it means the presidency of the United States.") Harrison, who had held the Mississippi delegation together for Roosevelt at the Democratic convention in 1932 and had loyally supported most New Deal legislation, thereafter often used his formidable influence as chairman of the Senate Finance Committee on behalf of the conservative coalition.[26]

The White House exerted intense pressure on local Democratic machines to bring about Barkley's victory. The crucial vote came from Senator William Dieterich of Illinois, who had been so strongly committed to Harrison that he had promised to second his nomination. Dieterich switched on orders from the Chicago machine when Harry Hopkins threatened Mayor Edward Kelly with the loss of WPA funds. Similar pressure applied through Kansas City boss Tom Pendergast on newly elected Senator Harry Truman of Missouri did not work. "I can't do it, Tom," Truman reportedly said. "I've given my word to Pat Harrison."

In the House the conservative coalition at first concentrated more on exerting influence on major committees, particularly the House Rules Committee, through which bills are cleared for floor action, than on winning roll-call votes on the floor. The chairman of the Rules Committee, John O'Connor of New York, a Tammany Democrat, had generally supported the New Deal during Roosevelt's first term, but after the 1936 election he often joined Republicans on the committee and two conservative southern Democrats, Eugene Cox of Georgia and Howard Smith of Virginia, in bottling up liberal economic and social legislation. Even when O'Connor supported the administration, as on bills favored by organized labor, Cox, Smith, and the Republicans were sometimes able, with the help of some southern moderates on the committee, to maintain control.[27]

Smarting from frustration with Congress, and confident that he still held the support of a large majority among the voters, Roosevelt set out in 1938 to purge Democrats whom he considered disloyal to the New Deal in Democratic primaries. His particular targets were Senators George, Tydings, and "Cotton Ed" Smith of South Carolina, and Representative O'Connor. George, Tydings, and Smith easily defeated the New Deal loyalists whom Roosevelt persuaded to run against them. Only O'Connor lost to his loyalist opponent. O'Connor's successor as head of the Rules Committee was Adolph Sabath of Illinois, a product of the Chicago machine, who turned out to be a weak chairman. The practical effect of O'Connor's removal was to establish the two southern conservatives, Eugene Cox and Howard Smith, as the real powers on the committee. For more than twenty years the Rules Committee, of which Smith became chairman in 1955, remained a burying ground for liberal bills.

The general election of 1938 produced even more damaging results for the administration. In the fall of 1937 the modest economic recovery that had been achieved during Roosevelt's first term seemed to expire. Unemployment, which had fallen to 17 percent in 1936, returned to 19 percent in 1938. Stock prices plunged and business failures increased. Economic discontent and fear that the New Deal was making the federal government too powerful led many voters, particularly in rural areas and smaller cities of the Northeast and Midwest, to vote Republican.

The Republicans gained 75 seats in the House and seven in the Senate. Though the Democrats still maintained large party majorities in both houses, the coalition of conservative Republicans and Democrats that had begun to form in 1937 and 1938 was greatly strengthened. Among the Republicans who ousted incumbent Democrats in the Senate was Robert Taft of Ohio (son of the former President), already regarded as a forceful intellectual spokesman for conservatism. Republicans regained governorships the party had lost during the heyday of the New Deal in 15 states, including Pennsylvania, Ohio, Michigan, Kansas, Massachusetts, Connecticut, and Rhode Island. Some of the Republicans who won governorships, like Leverett Saltonstall of Massachusetts, had called for acceptance of New Deal reforms, but others, like John Bricker of Ohio, remained hard-line conservatives. In New York, young Thomas Dewey, who had established a reputation as a crime-fighting Republican district attorney in Manhattan, narrowly lost the governorship to the incumbent liberal Democrat, Herbert Lehman.

WHY SOUTHERNERS REMAINED DEMOCRATS

In 1939 Congress, reacting to political scandals in the WPA and moved by the spirit of rebellion against Roosevelt, passed the Hatch Act, which prohibited most federal employees from participating in political campaigns or even expressing political opinions in public speeches. Roosevelt fought the Hatch Act but in the end signed it out of fear that a veto would undermine his "good government" image.[28]

The "hatching" of most federal jobholders struck a mortal blow at Roosevelt's attempt, through Farley and Hopkins, to build a national political machine based in part on federal patronage. Farley, who had argued against the attempted purge of conservative Democrats in the 1938 primaries, was in any case losing favor with his leader.

Roosevelt never again enjoyed secure working control of Congress. Republican representation edged up in succeeding elections. By the second half of Roosevelt's third term, the Democrats' party majority in the House was only 20. Though the Democrats still had a majority of 21 in the much smaller Senate, the proportionately greater representation of the South and the Border states among the Senate Democrats made conservatives almost as powerful in that body as they were in the House.

An analysis of congressional roll-call votes by John Manley shows that the conservative coalition, defined as a majority of Republicans and a majority of southern Democrats opposing a majority of northern Democrats, formed on between 20 and 30 percent of the roll-call votes in most sessions of the House between 1938 and 1958 and on about 20 percent in most sessions of the Senate in the same period. The votes on which the coalition formed, Manley found, "regularly included many of the most consequential issues decided by Congress." When the coalition formed, it won more than 80 percent of the roll calls in the House in every Congress between 1938 and 1956 and in the Senate between 1945 and 1958. Moreover, as Manley points out, the coalition was even more effective at amending bills to suit its requirements in committee and in preventing bills that it opposed from reaching the floor than it was on roll-call votes.[29]

Though the coalition had no formal structure, Republican and southern conservative leaders developed close working relationships. "We did not meet publicly," Howard Smith recalled in 1970, after his retirement. "The meetings were not formal. Our group met in one building and the conservative Republicans in another. . . . Then Eugene Cox, or Bill Colmer [of Mississippi] or I would go over to speak with the Republicans, or the Republican leaders might come to see us. It was very informal." Representative Joseph Martin of Massachusetts, who became Republican leader in the House in 1939, recalled: "In any case when an issue of spending or of new powers for the President came along, I would go to Representative Howard Smith of Virginia, for example, and say, 'Howard, see if you can't get me a few Democratic votes here.' Or I would seek out Representative Eugene Cox of Georgia, and ask, 'Gene, why don't you and John Rankin [of Mississippi] and some of your men get me some votes on this?' " No formal meetings were needed, Smith said, because "I'd see Joe Martin every half hour on the floor." Relations became so close that Representative John Taber of New York, ranking Republican on the House Appropriations Committee, at one point assigned a member of his staff to assist "Judge" Smith (as he was always known after a minor judicial post he had once held) in "finding ways of reducing federal expenditures."[30]

In the early years of the conservative coalition some of its most active participants, including Representative O'Connor and Senators Royal Copeland of New York and Peter Gerry of Rhode Island, were northern Democrats in the line of Grover Cleveland. But most of these northern conservative Democrats had by the middle of the 1940s been replaced in Congress by liberal Democrats or Republicans. As James Sundquist has written, conservatives "no longer rose to leadership in the Democratic party . . . of the industrial North." The Democratic wing of the conservative coalition, which had always been mostly southern, became almost exclusively so. (Senator Frank Lausche of Ohio in the 1950s was an exception.)[31]

Most southern members of Congress during Roosevelt's first term had been strong supporters of the New Deal. But by 1939 a majority of southerners in both houses were collaborating with the Republicans against the administration on key economic and social issues. Powerful southern committee chairmen who had helped steer the early New Deal program to enactment, like Harrison and Byrnes, often joined southerners who had opposed the New Deal from the start, like Byrd and George, to block administration measures. What caused the South—or at least many southern Democrats in Congress—to change?[32]

Liberals sometimes charged that the conservative coalition was based on a cold-blooded deal—an "unholy alliance"—under which Republicans gave up their traditional support for civil rights and helped southerners block passage of liberal legislation on race-related issues, in return for which southern Democrats voted against New Deal economic programs. In the 1930s, at least, there is no evidence that such a deal existed—at least not as a simple quid pro quo of the kind that some liberals suspected. Barbara Sinclair found that in the Congress elected in 1936, 95 percent of Republicans voted with 96 percent of northeastern Democrats in the

House on roll-call votes to pass anti-lynching legislation, the chief priority of the civil rights community, against almost unanimous opposition by southern Democrats. This record supports insistence by Republican leaders that they never bartered Republican votes against civil rights in exchange for southern votes on other issues. "[Eugene] Cox," Minority Leader Martin later said, "was the real leader of the southerners in the House. . . . His opposition to the New Deal was much more ingrown than mine, and he was ready to fight to any lengths to keep further power out of the hands of Franklin Roosevelt. In these circumstances, therefore, it was unnecessary for me to offer any quid pro quo for conservative southern support. It was simply a matter of finding issues on which we saw alike."[33]

The shift of southern Democrat leaders against the New Deal after the 1936 election in part reflected continued adherence by most of them to the Jeffersonian tradition of limited government and states' rights. During Roosevelt's first term most southerners had welcomed the inpouring of federal funds to bring relief to the unemployed and to save older people from poverty. The Tennessee Valley Authority (TVA), using federal resources and legal authority to vitalize a previously poor and undeveloped region of the South, was popular in areas that benefited from its projects. But the court-packing fight reminded many southerners, including some who publicly supported Roosevelt's proposal, of their traditional resistance to centralized national government. Fear that a strong federal government would eventually take action against racial segregation in the South certainly was an underlying source of this resistance. But quite apart from issues of race, many southerners remained liberals in the old sense, convinced of the inherent conflict between programmatic, centralized government and personal freedom.

The changing distribution of power within the national Democratic party also convinced many southern Democrats that they should look elsewhere for allies. Repeal of the two-thirds rule for nominating Presidents at the Democratic national convention in 1936 deprived the South of an important check it had held within the party. In Congress, the seniority system enabled southerners like Harrison, Byrnes, and George to hold on to chairmanships of major committees. But southerners were no longer numerically dominant among Democratic members in either legislative body. In the Senate, southerners, who as recently as 1930 had made up more than half the Democratic caucus, in 1937 comprised only 29 percent. In the House, the southern share of the Democratic caucus declined from two-thirds in 1930 to just over one-third in 1937.

Some of the groups that were coming to power through participation in the New Deal coalition were viewed antagonistically by most white southerners. John L. Lewis's Congress of Industrial Organizations (CIO), a militant breakaway from the old American Federation of Labor (AFofL), had played a major role in mobilizing union support for the Democratic ticket in 1936. When Roosevelt refused to take a stand against the sitdown strikes being staged by the CIO in 1937, southern political and business leaders, who shared Vice President Garner's view that the sitdown strikes represented "mass lawlessness," were sure the President was paying off a political debt. James Byrnes, who feared the CIO would soon attempt to unionize textile mills in South Carolina, proposed legislation in the Senate to make participation in a sitdown strike a federal crime. Byrnes's move was warmly supported by Garner and other southerners—and also by Harry Truman of Missouri. In the heavily Democratic Senate of 1937 the administration was able to defeat Byrnes's effort, but only at the cost of antagonizing some southerners formerly loyal to the New Deal.[34]

Northern blacks, too, had in 1936 voted heavily for Roosevelt. Though the administration remained largely passive on civil rights, white southerners in Congress sensed that the shift of blacks to the Democratic party would eventually produce pressure for federal action against racial segregation in the South. "The South," wrote Senator Carter Glass of Virginia in 1938, "would better begin thinking whether it will continue to cast its 152 electoral votes according to the memories of the Reconstruction era of 1865 and thereafter, or will have spirit and courage enough to face the new Reconstruction era that northern so-called Democrats are menacing us with."[35]

Why then did southern conservatives not change parties? In part because of the traditional loyalty forged during the Civil War and Reconstruction that still linked most white southerners to the Democratic party. In part because there were still issues on which most Republicans and most southerners still did not "see alike"—beyond civil rights, many national defense issues, and federal support for agriculture and other southern interests. In part because southern leaders in Congress were anxious to retain the committee chairmanships they held as senior members of the majority party. Though a mass shift by conservative southern Democrats to the Republican side might have produced a Republican majority in the House after 1938, and in the Senate after 1942, coordinating such a shift would have been difficult, and negotiating a division of spoils with the Republicans might well have left the southern leaders with less power than they already had.

Finally, and probably decisively, most southern conservatives continued to regard the maintenance of a one-party system in the South as an essential means for shutting off blacks from political power. Since it was inconceivable that the Democratic party in the South would be reduced to virtual impotence, as the Republican party in most southern states had been since the 1890s, the only practical way to preserve a one-party system was for conservatives to stay inside the Democratic party. Roosevelt's attempt to purge conservative southerners in the 1938 Democratic primaries had further alienated the conservatives, but it also had shown them that the administration had little ability to act against them within the southern Democratic party. However much conservative southerners might find themselves ideologically at odds with the national Democratic party, therefore, they had strong practical as well as emotional reasons for remaining at least nominally loyal to the party of their fathers.

14

FISSION OF PARTY COALITIONS

B Y THE END OF THE 1930s, the majority party coalition that Roosevelt had constructed with help from Farley and Hopkins had lost some of its effectiveness. After the United States entered the Second World War following the Japanese bombing of Pearl Harbor on December 7, 1941, Roosevelt played down his identification with the Democratic party and attempted to govern as a national leader pretty much above party. Challenged by Thomas Dewey and the resurgent Republicans in the 1944 presidential election, however, Roosevelt fell back on the Democratic party to achieve reelection (by a surprisingly close margin) and to maintain support for his policies in Congress.

After Roosevelt's death early in 1945 and the end of the war a few months later, splits began to appear in the majority Democratic coalition and in the Republican opposition as well. During the presidency of Harry S Truman, Roosevelt's successor, alignments in national politics that had continued with little change since the Civil War began to come unstuck, and the two-party system through which the nation's politics had largely been managed for almost a century showed signs of strain.

REPUBLICAN REVIVAL

As they had while out of power at the national level during the Wilson administration, the Republicans in the 1930s took steps to strengthen their national party organization. In 1936, John D. M. Hamilton, a Kansas lawyer and a political ally of Governor Landon, became the first full-time salaried national chairman in either party. (Most previous chairmen had been either officeholders, usually senators, or wealthy men who took the job out of ambition, a sense of civic duty, or friendship for a President or presidential candidate.)

While serving as general counsel to the Republican National Committee (RNC) in 1935, Hamilton had helped found the Young Republican National Federation and the first National Committee research division. As party chairman during the 1936 campaign, he took the party into the electronic age with spot radio announcements and propaganda films. After Landon's landslide defeat, Hamilton in 1937 traveled to Britain where he studied the organization of the British Conservative party (a frequent model for later Republican chairmen). Campaign management as a distinct profession was at that time much more advanced in Britain than in the United States. Upon his return, Hamilton applied what he had learned to the bureaucratization of the structure and techniques of the RNC.[1]

While opposition to the New Deal grew among the public and in Congress during the late 1930s, calamitous events abroad further scrambled alignments in national politics. Roosevelt had early become convinced of the need to check the aggressive behavior of Nazi Germany and Japan. But he felt constrained by the overwhelming weight of public opinion against any steps that might lead to further involvement by the United States in foreign conflicts. Revelations by a congressional inquiry of the role played by munitions manufacturers and New York banks in getting America into war on the side of the Allies in 1917 had strengthened isolationist inclinations. The Neutrality Act of 1936, reluctantly signed by Roosevelt, Robert Sherwood later wrote sardonically, was "carefully designed to prevent us from getting into war in 1917."[2]

When Hitler's legions stormed into Poland in August 1939, producing declarations of war against Germany by Britain and France, a Roper poll found that 30 percent of a national sample "would have nothing to do with any warring country—not even trade with them on a cash-and-carry basis"; an additional 36 percent took the only slightly less isolationist position that the United States should "take no sides and stay out of the war entirely, but offer to sell to anyone on a cash-and-carry basis."[3] Those holding isolationist views included a small number of people who actually favored a German victory and a somewhat larger group of Communists and their sympathizers who after the Russo-German pact of 1939 followed the Moscow line of non-opposition to Hitler. Beyond that were numerous peace groups, including descendants of the Social Gospel movement; some German-Americans and Irish-Americans who were not pro-Nazi but remained anti-British; some Catholics influenced by the Vatican's collaboration with fascist regimes in Italy and Spain; and a large body of Americans, concentrated in the Midwest but found everywhere, who continued to believe in following George Washington's counsel that the United States should "steer clear" of political or military entanglements "with any portion of the foreign world." Isolationist attitudes were militantly fostered by the Hearst press and by Colonel Robert McCormick's *Chicago Tribune*.

A few days after the war in Europe began, Roosevelt announced that he had "no thought in any shape, manner, or form, of putting the Nation, either in its defenses or in its internal economy on a war basis." Gradually, however, as German armies swept across Europe and as Japan's actions became more warlike, Roosevelt began doing what he could to build up the nation's military capacities and to help Britain "short of war."[4]

In Congress conservative (national interest) isolationists, led by Arthur Vandenberg and Robert Taft, joined liberal (altruistic) isolationists, led by Burton

Wheeler, Hiram Johnson, and Robert LaFollette, Jr., in resisting the President's policies. Roosevelt drew support from most southern Democrats, many of whom were by now fighting the administration on domestic issues but who maintained the South's traditional internationalist approach to world affairs; from most northern urban Democrats, whose constituencies included many ethnic groups with roots in lands being overrun by German armies; and from a small bloc of internationalist Republicans, mostly from the Northeast.

Germany's stunning successes in the spring of 1940 in conquering the Netherlands and Belgium in a few days and knocking France out of the war, leaving Britain almost alone, actually strengthened Roosevelt's position in domestic politics. As the Republican national convention prepared to meet in Philadelphia in June, the President announced that Henry Stimson, Taft's secretary of war and Hoover's secretary of state, and Frank Knox, publisher at the *Chicago Daily News* and the Republican candidate for Vice President in 1936, had agreed to enter his cabinet as secretary of war and secretary of the navy, respectively—presenting the image of a coalition government formed to deal with the international emergency. Republican national chairman Hamilton promptly "read Stimson and Knox out of the party"—enhancing the impression that Roosevelt had sought to convey of an almost nonpartisan national leader faced with a narrowly partisan opposition. (Roosevelt's reason for recruiting Stimson and Knox were by no means purely political. Stimson, exemplar of the old Federalist-progressive ethos, was in particular a superbly effective public executive.)[5]

No President had ever sought, much less been elected to, a third term. Theodore Roosevelt had run in 1912 for what would have been his third term, counting the almost full term he had served after McKinley's assassination. But T.R. had been out of office for four years and in any case was rejected by the voters at the polls. The "two term tradition" had become a hallowed rule of American politics. Some Democratic leaders, including Farley and Garner, both of whom aspired to lead the Democratic ticket in 1940, argued that Roosevelt should stick to the tradition. The President himself seems to have been genuinely drawn in early 1940 to retire at the end of his second term to his Hyde Park estate in the Hudson Valley. But by midsummer the state of world affairs was such that Roosevelt could plausibly, and probably to some extent truthfully, say to Farley that he preferred not to run but "Jim, if nominated and elected, I could not in these times refuse to take the inaugural oath, even if I knew I would be dead in thirty days."[6]

Republican gains in the 1938 midterm elections had whetted Republican hopes of regaining the White House in 1940 and had produced a spirited contest for the nomination for President. The party was deeply divided between an isolationist wing, including both conservative and progressive Republicans in Congress; and an internationalist wing, little represented in Congress, but carrying on the Theodore Roosevelt tradition of pursuit of national interest through active involvement in world affairs, and including many of the party's supporters in the business community, particularly on Wall Street, and among east coast newspaper and magazine publishers. Unfortunately for the isolationists, their two most effective congressional leaders, Vandenberg and Taft, both decided to run for President, and their strength was therefore divided in the competition for delegates.

The internationalists seemed at first to have settled on supporting Thomas Dewey, who in the early polls led all other Republicans. If Dewey had won the close race he lost in 1938 for the New York governorship he probably would have been nominated. But, not wishing to antagonize the isolationist wing, he was cautious about committing himself to the internationalist position; moreover, the coldness of personality that later was to do him much harm in national politics was already perceived as a handicap. Henry Luce, publisher of *Time* and *Fortune* and among the most ardent of the internationalists, began using his magazines to promote Wendell Willkie, a corporation lawyer from Indiana, until recently a Democrat, who had won favorable attention on Wall Street for his aggressive representation of southern utilities against TVA. During the spring of 1940 "Willkie clubs" sprang up in many parts of the country—the first successful use in presidential nomination politics of a grassroots movement outside regular party organizations. Willkie began to rise in the polls.[7]

At the Republican convention Dewey led on the first few ballots but was soon overtaken by Willkie and Taft. Willkie's supporters in the galleries (many of whom had been packed into the hall by the Dewey organization but had been coverted after taking their seats) kept up a rhythmic chant of "We want Willkie." Apparently they had an effect on delegates on the floor, who perhaps were pleased to find a Republican leader who stirred genuine emotion. When Vandenberg dropped out on the sixth ballot, the Michigan delegation switched, not to Taft, who was ideologically closer to Vandenberg, but to Willkie—probably to some extent influenced by the close financial relationship that has always existed between Wall Street and the Detroit automobile manufacturers but also swept along by the euphoria of the moment. Michigan's move set off an avalanche that produced Willkie's nomination before the ballot was over.

"DR. WIN-THE-WAR"

Roosevelt's command of the Democratic party was by now so complete that he was able to notify the Democratic convention, through a message read by Alben Barkley, that his personal inclination was not to run, without the least disturbing the certainty that he would be renominated. Details of arranging the nomination were left to leaders of the old-line city machines, most of whom had opposed Roosevelt at the 1932 convention but were now his reliable supporters. ("They did not support Roosevelt out of any motive of affection," Ed Flynn, who replaced Farley as Democratic national chairman, later wrote, "or because of any political issues involved, but rather they knew that opposing him would be harmful to their local organizations. The Roosevelt name would help more than it could hurt, and for that reason these city leaders went along on the third-term candidacy.")[8]

Southern leaders like Byrnes of South Carolina and Sam Rayburn of Texas (who was to become Speaker of the House at the end of 1940) might have opposed Roosevelt on domestic issues or to honor the two-term tradition. But they were held to him by the conviction that he was the indispensable man to lead the nation in the war they saw ahead.

On the first and only ballot, Farley and Garner each received a handful of votes. Roosevelt was renominated with the support of more than four-fifths of the delegates. Among the Farley supporters who held out against making Roosevelt's nomination unanimous was a Massachusetts delegate, Joseph Kennedy, Jr., son of the financier Joseph Kennedy, Sr., who had held several federal posts under Roosevelt, including wartime ambassador to Britain, but who had now joined the conservative isolationists. For Vice President, Roosevelt insisted on replacing the faithless Garner with his fervently liberal secretary of agriculture, Henry Wallace. In the balloting for Vice President, southern delegations revolted and gave almost all their votes to Speaker of the House William Bankhead of Alabama. The city machines and the unions provided the votes needed to put Wallace over.[9]

The fall campaign proceeded against the backdrop of Britain's desperate struggle to survive against all-out attack by the German Luftwaffe. In September, Roosevelt persuaded Congress to approve Selective Service—America's first peacetime draft.

Willkie presented himself, accurately, as an amateur at politics. This stance appealed to the strain in American folk belief that regards a career devoted to the pursuit of public office as a sign of defective character. But in the setting of 1940 it also contributed to his undoing. Most voters were easily persuaded that the tumultuous international situation made it "no time to change horses in the middle of the stream." When the public enthusiasm that had greeted Willkie's nomination seemed to subside, he played down his internationalism and courted isolationist sentiment. Roosevelt responded with assurance that American "boys are not going to be sent into any foreign wars." Roosevelt won with 55 percent of the popular vote, down significantly from 1936 but still a sizable mandate.[10]

On December 7, 1941, the Japanese attack on Pearl Harbor ended the isolationist resistance that had remained strong in Congress and among much of the public. (Four months before Pearl Harbor, Roosevelt's request for renewal of the draft had passed the House of Representatives by only one vote.)

Soon after the United States entered the war, Roosevelt announced: "Politics is out." For the duration of the war, he said, "Dr. New Deal" had been replaced by "Dr. Win-the-War."

Thinking to avoid Wilson's mistake in 1918, Roosevelt took no part in the 1942 midterm elections. The Democrats lost 50 seats in the House and eight in the Senate—about twice the losses they had suffered in 1918. But they still had at least nominal majorities in both bodies. The Democrats' congressional reverses probably resulted in part from a tendency among voters to take out wartime frustrations and anxieties on the President's party in midterm elections even while continuing to support the war—as had occurred in 1862 and 1918, and would later in 1950 and 1966. Also, public support for liberalism continued to erode. In Nebraska, the venerable George Norris, who since the early 1930s had called himself an independent, was defeated for reelection to the Senate by a conservative Republican.

In 1944 Willkie, now unreservedly an internationalist, tried for a second shot at the Republican nomination. But Dewey, elected governor of New York in 1942, had assumed full control of what later came to be known as the eastern establishment, and through it of a financially related network of middle-sized and small city bankers, lawyers, and newspaper editors in the Northeast, Midwest, and Far West who produced delegates to Republican national conventions. Defeated decisively by Dewey in the Wisconsin primary in April, Willkie dropped out of the race. Soon he was approaching Roosevelt through intermediaries with the proposal that they join in forming a new third party, a liberal party (presumably to be led by Willkie after Roosevelt's retirement), leaving conservative Republicans and Democrats to come together in an opposing conservative party. Roosevelt, who hoped to obtain Willkie's endorsement for reelection, expressed interest in the idea. Willkie suggested they get together after the election. But in the middle of October, Willkie, only 52, without having endorsed anyone for President, died of a heart attack.[11]

At the Republican convention, Dewey easily won the nomination over Governor Bricker of Ohio, who had been left to carry the Old Guard conservative banner. Following the fairly common practice of giving the vice-presidential nomination to a leader of the ideological opposition within the party, Dewey took Bricker as his running mate.

Roosevelt, who was dying and probably knew it, but who was determined to stay the course at least to the end of the war, accepted the Democratic nomination for a fourth term. Over bitter protest by liberal and left-wing sections of the party, he acceded to demands by southern and city machine leaders that Henry Wallace be dropped from the ticket. (He may also have developed his own doubts about Wallace's fitness to become President.) As Wallace's replacement, Roosevelt signaled his preference for Senator Truman of Missouri, who appeared to be a moderate populist in the line of Champ Clark, Garner, and Jimmy Byrnes. (Truman had regarded Byrnes as his mentor in the Senate and had planned to nominate the South Carolinian for Vice President at the 1944 convention before himself being pressured by Roosevelt to join the ticket.)[12]

Despite the advantage of running as commander-in-chief during wartime, Roosevelt was reelected with a majority of only 53 percent of the popular vote. Dewey carried ten midwestern and Rocky Mountain states, including Ohio, Indiana, Wisconsin, and Colorado, plus the reliably Republican New England states of Maine and Vermont.

On April 12, 1945, twelve weeks into his fourth term, and less than a month before the end of the war in Europe, Roosevelt died of a stroke at his southern retreat in Warm Springs, Georgia. Truman, who knew almost nothing about Roosevelt's recently completed secret negotiations with Churchill and Stalin at Yalta, or of the far advanced development of the atomic bomb, succeeded to the presidency.

A SPLIT IN LIBERALISM

On July 16, 1945, the first atomic bomb was exploded in the desert near Ala-mogordo, New Mexico. "For a brief period," reported General Leslie Groves, commander of the Manhattan Project that had produced the bomb, "there was a lighting effect within a radius of 20 miles equal to several suns at midday. . . ." Less than four weeks later, American planes, carrying out Truman's orders, dropped atomic bombs on Hiroshima and Nagasaki. On August 15, Japan surrendered and the Second World War ended.

The first of the big issues that divided the Democrats in the postwar years was the resumption of the old quarrel between interventionists and isolationists, with Stalin's Soviet Union now cast in the role formerly played by Germany and Japan. Before Truman had been many months in office, Stalin had made clear his deter-mination to establish Soviet hegemony over all of eastern Europe and had given grounds for believing that he intended to foment Communist takeovers wherever possible in other parts of the world.

Roosevelt, whatever his concessions to isolationist opinion during the 1930s, had always been an internationalist in his private inclinations and after the fall of France in 1940 in his public acts. He had maintained a balance, probably more out of instinct than calculation, between the national-interest interven-tionism of his cousin Ted and the idealistic internationalism of his former leader, Woodrow Wilson.

Truman, it soon became apparent, was in foreign policy more a T.R. nation-alist than a Wilsonian internationalist. He installed Byrnes as his secretary of state and during the first year of his presidency gave his former Senate mentor an almost equal say in directing foreign policy. The new administration responded vigorously to Stalin's aggressive moves in eastern Europe. By the middle of 1946 the "cold war" between Russia and the West was in full swing.

Initially the most critical response to the Truman-Byrnes policy of checking the Soviets came not from the old national-interest isolationists like Taft, who were torn between their dislike for foreign entanglements and their hatred for Commu-nism, but from the left within the Democratic coalition, indeed within the admin-istration. Henry Wallace, after stepping down as Vice President, had taken the job of secretary of commerce in Roosevelt's fourth term and had stayed on after Tru-man's succession. While Truman and Byrnes carried on the national-interest side of Roosevelt's internationalism, Wallace extended its altruistic side.

Wallace, the son of Harding's and Coolidge's secretary of agriculture, had grown up in Iowa where he had been a Republican until the early 1920s. He had roots in the progressive tradition that had fostered the liberal isolationism of the

LaFollettes and Hiram Johnson. But he had deduced from the moral axioms of that tradition an imperative for altruistic internationalism rather than a return to isolationism. The goal of American postwar policy, he had said in 1942, "should be to make sure that everybody in the world has the privilege of drinking a quart of milk a day"—a statement often cited by conservatives of the time as a classic example of fuzzy-minded utopianism. The twentieth century, Wallace declared, "can be and must be the century of the common man" (a statement that he meant to contrast with Henry Luce's prediction that the twentieth century would be the "American century"). The Truman-Byrnes policy of resisting Stalin, Wallace believed, was undermining chances for creating a harmonious international community based on good relations between the world's two most powerful nations. Stalin's insistence on establishing Communist dictatorships in the countries of eastern Europe, he argued, grew out of a sense of the Soviet Union's vulnerability to attack and should not be interpreted as a threat to the United States.[13]

During the first year and a half of his presidency, Truman tried to keep Wallace, whom he privately distrusted, inside the administration tent. In September 1946, Wallace, speaking at a rally of left-wing Democrats in New York, warned that "the tougher we get the tougher the Russians will get" and called for recognition that "whether we like it or not the Russians will try to socialize their sphere of influence just as we try to democratize our sphere of influence." He had previously read the speech to Truman, and the President, perhaps not listening closely, had indicated approval.[14]

Byrnes, attending a meeting of European foreign ministers in Paris, threatened to resign. Arthur Vandenberg, who during the war had undergone a spectacular conversion to internationalism and was now a bulwark of support among Republicans for the administration's foreign policy, complained: "We can only cooperate with one secretary of state at a time." Truman, forced to come down decisively on one side or the other, asked Wallace for his resignation.[15]

Out of office, Wallace became the most visible spokesman for those liberals and leftists who favored maintaining good relations with the Soviet Union at almost any cost. Some of those advocating a conciliatory approach to Stalin were Communists or sympathizers with Communism who believed the Soviet Union represented the wave of the future and therefore regarded Soviet expansionism as a positive force. Many others, including Wallace himself, did not want to establish the Soviet system in the United States or welcome its spread over western Europe but were convinced that concessions to the Soviets were needed to preserve world peace and pave the way for global social progress.

Whatever their motives, all brands of "progressives" (as Wallace's supporters called themselves) were sharply critical of the administration's "containment policy"—named for George Kennen's famous recommendation in 1946 that the United States should act "to contain" the power of the Soviet Union "both militarily and politically for a long time to come."[16] The issue caused a deep split in liberalism, never fully healed. On one side were the liberal cold-war "realists," who on domestic policy continued to be liberal, sometimes very liberal, but on foreign policy championed national-interest interventionism that put them in alliance with conservatives like Dewey and Vandenberg. On the other were intellectuals, publicists, and some politicians and union leaders who claimed that liberal values led as compellingly to a conciliatory approach in foreign policy as to equalitarianism in domestic policy.

The quarrel was carried on with particular heat, not surprisingly, in New York City. On the campuses of City College, Columbia, and New York University, and in the bars and coffeehouses of Greenwich Village and the Upper West Side, cold-war realists debated angrily and at length with Wallaceite progressives. Both groups included representatives of a broad range of liberal and left-wing ideologies.

The American Labor Party (ALP) had been founded in 1936 as a means for New York trade unions and intellectuals to support Roosevelt's reelection outside the machinery of the still Tammany-dominated Democratic party. The next year it provided a structure through which liberals and leftists could back Fiorello LaGuardia, the reform Republican who had broken Tammany's control of city hall in 1933, for reelection as mayor without pulling the reviled Republican lever. From the time of its founding, the ALP had been attacked by both Democratic and Republican organizations as a front for Communists. According to Ralph Straetz and Frank Munger, "it was not infiltrated by Communists to any great extent until 1938." But by 1942, Straetz and Munger found, Communists controlled ALP organizations in four of New York's five boroughs, the Bronx being the exception. With the coming of the cold war, the ALP made attack on the Truman administration's containment policy one of its principal missions.[17]

By the mid-1940s many of the original union and intellectual sponsors of the ALP had become alarmed by the extent to which it had been taken over by Communists. In 1944 the Liberal party was founded by union leaders and intellectual activists, notably David Dubinsky of the International Ladies Garment Workers Union, Alex Rose of the hatters union, and Reinhold Niebuhr, the neo-orthodox Protestant theologian, to provide liberals and socialists with a party line on which they could vote for Roosevelt for a fourth term without pulling either the Democratic or the ALP lever. In the late 1940s, the Liberal party strongly supported Truman's anti-Communist foreign policy. New York City was thereby provided with an almost European-type multi-party system (though the local Republican party after LaGuardia's retirement became largely a receptacle for federal and state patronage).[18]

The ALP and the Liberals occasionally ran candidates of their own but mostly used their strength strategically to support nominees of one of the major parties, thereby obtaining considerable patronage in the way of judgeships and appointive offices. The ALP, suffering from its identification with Communists, expired in 1955. But the Liberal party has continued as a separate force in New York politics to the present time, usually allied with the Democrats but sometimes backing the Republicans or running its own candidates and occasionally providing the margin of victory in close elections.

COLD WAR DEBATE

The coming of peace had released pent-up frustrations and angers that seemed to produce a reaction among the national electorate similar to that which had restored the Republicans to power in 1920 (or that which in Britain in April 1945 ended 14 years of Conservative rule and brought in the Labour Party with a huge majority in the House of Commons). In the 1946 midterm elections the Republicans gained 55 seats in the House of Representatives and 13 in the Senate, achieving majorities in both bodies for the first time since the early 1930s. Many Republicans concluded that with Roosevelt gone and many voters returning to earlier political preferences the Democrats had ceased to be the majority party. Truman appeared to be floundering. Almost everyone expected that a Republican would be elected President in 1948.

Truman's hard-line policy toward the Soviet Union had at first been supported by most conservatives, Republicans as well as southern Democrats, who shared his distrust of Communists. But by the time the conservative-controlled eightieth Congress assembled in 1947, some former isolationists like Taft had begun to question the assumptions on which the administration's foreign policy was based. The Soviet Union, Taft argued, given the human and economic losses it had suffered during the Second World War, could "not want war within any reasonable time."[19]

Taft's domination of congressional Republicans, however, was not yet complete. Since the Ohio senator's first priority was to push through legislation curbing the power of labor unions (enacted over Truman's veto as the Taft-Hartley Act), he deferred on foreign policy to Vandenberg, now an outspoken internationalist. Even among midwestern Republicans with an isolationist bias, opposition to Truman's foreign policy during most of the eightieth Congress remained fairly muted. The eastern wing of the Republican party, still led by Dewey and following foreign-policy cues from Dewey's friend and adviser, John Foster Dulles, lineal descendant in the New York legal establishment of Root and Stimson, firmly supported containment.

At the beginning of 1947 the President accepted the resignation of Byrnes, who had never quite been able to bring himself to regard Truman, a very junior colleague when Jimmy Byrnes had been cock-of-the-walk in the Senate, as his equal, let alone superior. As Byrnes's successor, Truman appointed General of the Army George C. Marshall, army chief of staff during the Second World War. Dean Acheson, a principal architect of the containment policy (which he stiffened beyond what Kennan had intended), stayed on as under secretary of state. Marshall and Acheson worked closely with Vandenberg and Dulles. In May 1947, Congress approved the administration's request for a package of aid to Greece and Turkey, taking the place of military and economic support formerly supplied by the now financially exhausted Britain. Aid to Greece, Truman argued, was particularly urgent, since that nation's pro-Western government was under heavy assault from a Communist guerrilla force backed by the Soviets. Taft reluctantly went along with Vandenberg's support for Greek-Turkish aid on condition that it not be interpreted as "a commitment to any similar policy in any other section of the world."[20]

Early in 1948, after Communists had seized control of Czechoslovakia, the last country occupied by Soviet armies with a non-Communist government, Congress enacted the first phase of the Marshall plan, providing $4 billion in aid to support the economic recovery of western Europe. Vandenberg led the fight for approval of the Marshall plan in the Senate. Taft supported an amendment to reduce the appropriation but voted for the plan on final passage.[21]

Wallace denounced Greek-Turkish aid and the Marshall plan as parts of Truman's attempt to establish a "global Monroe doctrine." The Communists had taken power in Czechoslovakia, Wallace said, to protect themselves against a right-wing coup encouraged by the Truman administration. Truman responded: "I do not want and I will not accept the political support of Henry Wallace and his Communists."[22]

Wallace announced he would run for President as the candidate of a newly founded Progressive party. The new party would offer a pacific alternative to the militantly anti-Communist foreign policy supported by both major parties. "There is no real fight," Wallace said, "between a Truman and a Republican." Many analysts predicted that Wallace's party would attract enough liberal and left-wing voters to end whatever chance Truman might have had of carrying states like New York, California, and Illinois. The new party was also expected to do grievous harm to Democratic candidates further down the ballot in several industrial states. In Illinois for example the presence of the Wallace party appeared to doom the unusually strong Democratic state ticket led by Adlai Stevenson for governor and Paul Douglas for senator.[23]

SOUTHERN REBELLION

Civil rights, the second emerging issue of 1948, posed an even more serious threat to the Democratic coalition. Racial injustice had been an issue the New Deal had not dared to touch. Liberalism had always in theory supported equal rights for blacks. But Roosevelt had feared that moving against racial oppression in the South would antagonize powerful southern Democrats like Garner, Robinson, Harrison, and Byrnes whose help he needed to get his economic program through Congress. (The "racial vision that Roosevelt brought to the presidency," Nancy Weiss claims, would not in any case have motivated "him to pay particular attention to race.") In the 1930s the civil rights community made action at the federal level against lynching its highest priority. (In 1933 alone, 24 blacks were lynched in the South.) When liberals in Congress, led by Senator Robert Wagner of New York, sought enactment of a bill making lynching a federal crime, the administration withheld support. The anti-lynching bill several times passed the House but was consistently blocked by filibusters by southern Democrats in the Senate.[24]

Blacks swung politically to the Democrats during the New Deal years, in part because they supported Roosevelt's economic program, which benefited the disproportionate share of blacks who were among the poorest of the poor, and in part out of appreciation for Eleanor Roosevelt's many expressions and acts supporting racial equality which most blacks believed reflected the President's true views. Still, black alignment with the Democrats remained far from monolithic—much less, for instance, than that of Jews. A 1944 survey showed that 68 percent of blacks said they had voted for Roosevelt for a fourth term, but only 40 percent regarded themselves as Democrats. In many southern states the Democratic party continued systematically to exclude blacks.[25]

Before he became President, Truman's publicly expressed attitudes on race were not particularly liberal. "I wish to make clear," he told a meeting of the National Colored Democratic Association in Chicago in 1940, "that I am not appealing for the social equality of the Negro. The Negro himself knows better than that, and the highest type of Negro leaders say quite frankly that they prefer the company of their own people." As a senator from the Border state of Missouri, he had endorsed the anti-lynching bill but had voted against an anti–poll tax amendment to the soldiers' vote bill. When Truman succeeded to the White House, most white southern Democrats assumed that he would, at a minimum, continue Roosevelt's policy of maintaining a low profile on civil rights.[26]

Early in 1948, however, Truman, mindful of Wallace's potential appeal for black voters in northern cities, and apparently also motivated by genuine conversion to more liberal racial attitudes, called for the enactment of a far-reaching package of civil rights measures, including a federal anti-lynching law, a federal anti–poll tax law, a permanent Fair Employment Practices Commission, and a permanent Civil Rights Commission. Southern Democratic leaders reacted to Truman's civil rights program with outrage. The President's proposal, said Senator Tom Connally of Texas, amounted to "a lynching of the Constitution." Representative Eugene Cox of Georgia (a key member of the conservative coalition) charged that "Harlem is wielding more influence with the administration than the entire white South." Several southern Democratic state committees voted to withdraw from the national Democratic party unless it promised to reject "anti-Southern" laws.[27]

By the time the Democratic national convention met in Philadelphia in July, Truman was trying to play down differences with the South. His political operatives at the convention worked for approval of a vaguely worded civil rights platform plank that was acceptable to the more moderate southern leaders. But northern liberals, led by Hubert Humphrey, the young mayor of Minneapolis, won a floor fight for a plank endorsing in detail the administration's civil rights program. The Mississippi and Alabama delegations promptly walked out of the convention.

A few days later, southern "States' Rights" Democrats, commonly called "Dixiecrats," assembled in Birmingham, Alabama, and nominated Governor Strom Thurmond of South Carolina to run for President. With the New Deal coalition now split into three competing parties running candidates for President, the chances of Truman's winning election to a full term seemed minute.

"GIVE 'EM HELL, HARRY"

The Republican presidential nomination in 1948 appeared to be almost as valuable a prize as the Democratic nomination had been in 1932. A number of candidates, including Vandenberg (egged on by Henry Luce, still not fully satisfied with Dewey), Governor Earl Warren of California, and Harold Stassen, the youthful former governor of Minnesota (claiming to be the candidate of the generation that had fought in the war), took the field. But the principal contenders were clearly Dewey and Taft. Dewey, reelected governor of New York in 1946, exercised firm control over the nationwide political network that had its financial roots in Wall Street. Taft, who had stood aside for Bricker in 1944, once more placed himself at the head of the faction of small-town, middle-class, Protestant, mostly midwestern conservatives who had fought the eastern conservatives for control of the Republican party since the days of Theodore Roosevelt and William Howard Taft.

The struggle between Dewey and Taft partly reflected the clash between interventionism and isolationism. This conflict was not so salient in 1948, however, since Taft had not emphasized foreign policy in his leadership of Senate Republicans. The two candidates also differed on some aspects of domestic policy. Dewey favored accommodating most of the economic reforms of the New Deal and even proposed further modest liberalization in some areas. Taft insisted on correcting some of the bad effects he believed the New Deal had introduced into American life, particularly in the area of labor-management relations. But both men were essentially moderate conservatives on most domestic issues. Taft, indeed, more than Dewey, had given serious attention to finding public means for relieving structural poverty without undermining freedom or economic efficiency. "If the free enterprise system does not do its best to prevent hardship and poverty," Taft warned, "it will find itself superseded by a less progressive system which does." The federal government, he proposed, should maintain a system of "insurance to everyone unless he refuses to work, a minimum standard of living, but it must be held within a reasonable cost, without destroying local self-government, and without removing the incentive to work which is the very keystone to adequate production." Even Taft's reputation as an implacable foe of organized labor was not wholly deserved. When Truman in 1946 during a railroad strike that threatened to paralyze the national economy proposed legislation to draft strikers, the bill passed overwhelmingly in the House, but Taft almost singlehandedly blocked it in the Senate, arguing that such action would violate fundamental American liberties.[28]

The difference between Republicans supporting Dewey and those supporting Taft, in 1948 at least, was more cultural than anything else. Dewey represented the high-powered, cosmopolitan, modernizing, business-oriented conservatism of the

Northeast, symbolized by Wall Street; Taft represented the more cautious, insular, tradition-oriented conservatism of the Midwest, symbolized by Main Street.

In the late 1940s the rapidly growing Far West was coming to hold the balance of power within the Republican party between Wall Street and Main Street. Earl Warren, elected governor of California in 1942, sometimes advertised himself as a progressive in the mold of Hiram Johnson (who died in 1945). But Warren's "progressivism" was actually of a different kind, more pragmatic than idealistic, more akin to the permissive social mores of Hollywood than to the crusading moral absolutism of the old Bull Moosers.

At the Republican national convention in Philadelphia Dewey led on the first ballot with 434 votes; Taft had 224; Stassen had 157; and a number of favorite sons, including Warren of California and Vandenberg of Michigan, had the remaining 279. At the end of an inconclusive second ballot, Stassen proposed an alliance with Taft and the lesser candidates to prevent Dewey from achieving a majority. Warren refused to join the coalition. Without California, the stop-Dewey blockade could not succeed. Dewey swept to nomination on the third ballot (the last time, at least through 1996, a Republican convention was to go more than one ballot) and took Warren as his running mate.

Truman, nominated for a full term by a deeply pessimistic Democratic convention, also meeting in Philadelphia, set out on an extensive "whistle-stop" campaign that carried him by railroad all over the country. As President, Truman had turned out to be more a liberal than a Jimmy Byrnes–type moderate. His domestic program, later called the Fair Deal, went beyond anything Roosevelt had proposed for expanding the national welfare state. Liberalism by Truman's time had come to advocate a major role for the federal government in financing and in some cases managing a broad array of services in areas like medical care, income maintenance for the poor and aging, economic renewal of decaying cities, education, and housing. Truman flavored his programmatic liberalism with dashes of populist rancor that tickled members of two important electoral groups: organized labor and small farmers.

The unions, having got over their anger with Truman for his proposal to draft strikers in 1946, and grateful for his veto of the Taft-Hartley bill (though the veto had been overridden by Congress), had become staunch supporters of the administration. At the Democratic convention, they played an important part in forestalling an attempt by some liberals to replace Truman with a more popular candidate. (The liberals' first choice—astonishingly, in view of later developments—was General Dwight Eisenhower, the nation's most popular military commander in the Second World War. After some vacillation, Eisenhower, who had recently become president of Columbia University, announced his non-availability.)[29]

Farmers, on the other hand, were generally counted firmly in Dewey's camp. Most of the midwestern farm states had voted for Dewey in 1944, and hardly anybody—except Truman—thought any of them might go Democratic in 1948. Farm income, however, was down from its record high of 1947, and many farmers were inclined to accept Truman's argument that the Republican eightieth Congress was partly to blame. Besides, farmers generally liked Truman's style, and many found Dewey (though he had grown up in Michigan) annoyingly representative of the smug and sophisticated East.

Still, the polls showed Dewey far ahead, and the New York governor campaigned as though his election were a foregone conclusion. At the end of September the Roper polling organization decided that Dewey's victory was so certain that it stopped making surveys.

Truman pressed on. In town after town, speaking from the rear platform of his campaign train, he delivered vitriolic attacks on Dewey and the Republican Congress. The crowds seemed to enjoy the show. Scattered individuals began calling: "Give 'em hell, Harry!" Most reporters discounted the crowds as composed of Democratic faithful or people out for the fun of hearing the President, in the manner of Andrew Jackson and Bryan, lambaste the money power back East. (Ronald Reagan once told me that when Truman came to Los Angeles he and Georgie Jessel, the comedian and a Democratic fundraiser, got the President in the back seat of a limousine and asked if he thought "he had a chance to win this thing." Of course, Truman said. "Of course I'm going to win. The people are with me." Their hopes only slightly raised, Reagan and Jessel continued to raise money for the Democratic cause.)[30]

The election, as everyone knows, produced the biggest upset in American political history. Dewey carried New York, Pennsylvania, and most of the rest of the Northeast (playing for the last time its old role of banner region for a Republican national ticket), four states on the Great Plains, and Michigan, Indiana, and Oregon. Thurmond carried the Deep South states of Alabama, Louisiana, Mississippi, and South Carolina. (In all these states the States' Rights ticket was listed on the ballot under the Democratic label. In Alabama, electors for Truman were not even permitted on the ballot.) Truman won almost everywhere else. (See Figure 14–1.) Wallace's ticket failed to attract support from organized labor or blacks and won only a bit more than 2 percent of the national popular vote. Thurmond ran far behind in the rim South—the states that had voted for Hoover on the religious and prohibition issues in 1928. (Texas voted 65 percent for Truman, 25 percent for Dewey, and only 9 percent for Thurmond; Virginia, 48 percent for Truman, 41 percent for Dewey, and 10 percent for Thurmond.) Thurmond's share of the national popular vote was only 2.4 percent. Truman carried the rim South, most of the Midwest (including Iowa, Wisconsin, and Ohio, states with large farm populations that Dewey had won in 1944), and all of the Far West, including California, except Oregon. Overall, Truman won just under 50 percent of the national popular vote, compared to 45 percent for Dewey.

Truman's victory was accompanied by sweeping Democratic gains in congressional and state races. The Democrats picked up 75 seats in the House and 11 in the Senate, reestablishing majorities in both bodies. Among the Democrats replacing Republicans in the Senate were Hubert Humphrey from Minnesota and

Figure 14–1   Electoral vote by states, 1948

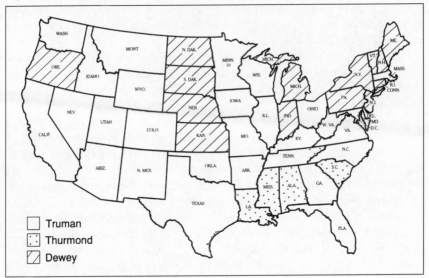

Source: *Historical Statistics of the United States,* Bureau of the Census, 1961

Paul Douglas from Illinois, both future liberal luminaries. Lyndon Johnson was elected to the Senate from Texas and Estes Kefauver from Tennessee, both winning seats formerly held by more conservative Democrats.

Outside the Northeast and the Deep South, the New Deal coalition had seemed to hold firm. But trends had been set in motion that within a few elections were to produce a strikingly different configuration of national politics.

15

DECLINE OF STATE
AND LOCAL MACHINES

D URING THE NINETEENTH CENTURY, patronage—the exchange of government jobs for political services—had been the basic material resource for the state and local machines through which the national parties carried on most of their electoral operations. Beginning with passage of the Pendleton Act in 1883, federal patronage had been greatly reduced. The machines had fallen back on state and local governments to maintain the supply of jobs for party workers.

The turn-of-the-century progressives made elimination of the patronage system in state and local government one of their principal objectives. In most of the West, they largely succeeded. But in the older industrial states of the Northeast and the lower Great Lakes region, and in a different way in the one-party South, the patronage system survived and the machines continued to function much as before.

In the 1950s, as part of the aftermath of the Second World War, a new wave of reformers renewed attack on the surviving state and local machines. Altered cultural, economic, and technological conditions made the machines increasingly vulnerable. By the end of the 1950s, they were on the defensive in most of their old strongholds.

The machines had exacted heavy prices in governmental inefficiency and social and moral corruption. But, in addition to their humanizing effects on government, they had provided much of the means through which the parties maintained internal discipline and communicated with the voters. If they vanished, the parties would have to find new bases for support.

A DECADE OF CONSENSUS

In 1952 the Republicans recaptured the White House and won narrow majorities in both houses of Congress—the last time Republicans were to achieve united control of the federal executive and legislative branches, at least through 1992. Dwight Eisenhower had discovered that he was a Republican and, after defeating Taft for his party's presidential nomination, had gone on to trounce the Democratic candidate, Governor Adlai Stevenson of Illinois, by a wide margin.

With Eisenhower the Republicans had at last found a candidate, and a President, who could bring new faces to leadership positions, improve the administration of government, and provide reassurance for groups that felt threatened by the growing power of the federal government, without raising fears that the welfare state programs established by the New Deal would be dismantled or radically changed. Eisenhower's views on domestic policy were almost as conservative as Taft's, but he did not feel obliged to upset the balance between the welfare state and the market economy that had been reached by the end of the 1930s.

On foreign policy Eisenhower's nomination and election represented a decisive victory for internationalism within the Republican party. After Taft's death at the end of 1953 most conservatives swung toward aggressive anti-Communist interventionism. This was not exactly the kind of internationalism practiced by the moderate establishment, but for the time being at least it did not represent as troublesome a challenge as that posed by traditional isolationism. The triumph of internationalism in the Republican party assured a broad internationalist consensus in the entire polity. Eisenhower could count on support on most foreign-policy issues from such moderate Democratic congressional leaders as House Speaker Sam Rayburn and Lyndon Johnson, who became Senate Democratic leader in 1953, and also from liberal cold-war "realists" like Hubert Humphrey, and John F. Kennedy, elected to the Senate from Massachusetts in 1952.

Eisenhower therefore was able to govern on the basis of a degree of consensus on both domestic and foreign policy unusual in American politics. This circumstance helped persuade many scholars and journalists that the nation, and perhaps the entire developed world, were approaching "the end of ideology"—a prediction soon refuted by events of the 1960s.

EMERGENCE OF NATIONAL PARTIES

While the ideological differences between the parties were less distinct than usual in the 1950s, the two national party committees developed more institutional resources and impact than ever before in their histories. The institutional growth of the national committees probably reflected underlying trends toward centralization and bureaucratization that are common to most extended organizations in modern industrial societies. But it also had sources that were specific to the time and to particular situations within the two parties.[1]

Eisenhower reposed great confidence in Leonard Hall, a former New York congressman and Dewey operative who became chairman of the Republican National Committee in 1953. Applying the army staff system to politics as well as to the administration of the executive branch, the President made Hall his director of political operations and gave the RNC major responsibility for managing his reelection campaign in 1956. Under Hall's leadership, the RNC expanded its staff to about 300 in presidential election years and 100 the rest of the time. Following the advice of Eisenhower's friend, DeWitt Wallace, publisher of the *Reader's Digest,* the RNC undertook the first direct-mail fundraising campaign launched by a national party.[2]

Stevenson, who despite his loss to Eisenhower had come out of the 1952 election with enhanced prestige, concurrently encouraged a growing role for the Democratic National Committee, in part to offset the fairly conservative image conveyed by the party's congressional leadership. A major factor in the expanding activity of the DNC was the innovative energy of Paul Butler of Indiana, who, with Stevenson's support, became national chairman in 1954. Through Butler's success as a fundraiser among both the party's big givers and thousands of smaller contributors, the DNC by the end of the 1950s was approaching parity in resources and staff with the RNC.[3]

The most important national party development during the 1950s was Butler's establishment of a council of policy advisers attached to the DNC. After his defeat in 1952, Stevenson had set up an informal cadre of policy specialists that became known as the "Finletter group," after Thomas Finletter, a secretary of the air force under Truman and a leader of the reform faction in Democratic politics in New York City, who took responsibility for organizing its meetings. The Finletter group, made up mostly of liberal university professors, former federal government officials, and a few politicians, prepared policy papers on a wide range of issues that became the programmatic base for Stevenson's second bid for the presidency.[4]

In 1956 Stevenson again won the Democratic presidential nomination but again lost to Eisenhower—this time by an even larger majority, and with his political prestige damaged rather than increased. A few weeks after the 1956 election, Butler received DNC approval for continuing the work of the Finletter group through a formal adjunct to the national party to be known as the Democratic Advisory Council. The purpose of the council, Butler announced, would be to shape legislative proposals that would implement the party's "progressive, forward-looking platform." Among the 20 party leaders whom Butler named to the council were Truman, Stevenson, Estes Kefauver (Stevenson's 1956 running mate), Eleanor Roosevelt, Rayburn, Lyndon Johnson, Hubert Humphrey, John Kennedy, four other members of the House and two other members of the Senate, three governors, and one mayor.[5]

Rayburn, choosing to interpret the council as an attempt to form a party body outside Congress that would prescribe policy on legislative issues, immediately announced from his home in Texas that he and the other four House members Butler had designated would not serve. Lyndon Johnson, who had earlier indicated to Butler that he favored the idea, changed course and supported Rayburn's position. Kennedy, too, for a time declined to serve. As a result of the congressional boycott instigated by Rayburn and Johnson, the council when it began to function in 1957 was heavily weighted toward the party's northern liberal wing. Only two members of Congress, Kefauver and Humphrey, were on the original council. Its deliberations were therefore much more ideologically homogeneous, and the positions it took more aggressively liberal, than would have been the case if all the persons originally named by Butler had accepted. It nevertheless was identified as "the party's official policy-making body," which, as James Sundquist has pointed out, "gave weight to its pronouncements within and outside the party."[6]

On many issues, the council simply gave its endorsement to positions that already were supported by a consensus among Democrats in Congress. But Sundquist cites two important instances where the council got out in front of the party and played a major role in shaping what came to be regarded as Democratic positions: advocacy of a liberal civil rights policy; and promotion of an expansionary fiscal policy, called for by the council's subcommittee on economic policy headed by John Kenneth Galbraith of Harvard. By forcefully attacking the Eisenhower administration from a liberal perspective, in contrast to the more accommodating approach favored by Rayburn and Johnson, the council began drawing clearer ideological distinctions between the parties toward the end of the 1950s. In November 1959, Kennedy, preparing to seek the 1960 Democratic presidential nomination, accepted membership on the council.[7]

LAST HURRAHS?

The national party organizations expanded their operations during the 1950s in part to fill the gap caused by the decline of many state and city machines. "The old boss was strong simply because he held all the cards," says a character in Edwin O'Connor's novel, *The Last Hurrah,* explaining the fall of the fictional boss, Frank Skeffington, based on Boston's Mayor and Massachusetts Governor James Michael Curley. "If anybody wanted anything—jobs, favors, cash—he could only go to the boss, the local leader. What Roosevelt did was to take the handouts out of local hands. A few little things like Social Security, Unemployment Insurance, and the like—that's what shifted the gears. . . . No need now to depend on the boss for everything; the Federal Government was getting into the act. Otherwise known as a social revolution."[8]

At the time *The Last Hurrah* appeared in 1956, old-fashioned patronage-based machines appeared reasonably strong—in some cases invincible—in many cities and some states. In New York, Carmine DeSapio had revived Tammany Hall and largely controlled distribution of city patronage during the first two terms of Mayor Robert Wagner. In Pittsburgh, Mayor David Lawrence ruled with an iron hand and was preparing the drive that took him to the governorship of Pennsylvania in 1958. In Jersey City, the Hague machine had been overthrown in 1949 when Hague tried to pass on the leadership to his nephew, but the Democratic organization that succeeded it retained many of its characteristics.

In Philadelphia, good-government reformers, led by Joseph Sill Clark and Richardson Dilworth, both members of the city's social and business establishment, had in the early 1950s at last broken the power of the old Republican machine—almost the last entrenched Republican organization in a major city. In order to oust the machine, Clark, who became mayor in 1952, and Dilworth, who succeeded him in 1956, formed an alliance with the formerly weak Democratic city organization led by Congressman William Green. By the end of the 1950s the Democratic organization, now including many of the former Republican division leaders within its ranks and using familiar machine techniques, was already crowding the reformers out of city government. This process was completed in 1962 when Dilworth resigned as mayor to run (unsuccessfully) for governor of Pennsylvania.[9]

In Chicago, Richard Daley, Democratic leader in the city's heavily Irish Bridgeport section, replaced Jacob Arvey as Democratic party chairman in the early 1950s and then got himself elected mayor in 1955. As mayor, Daley retained the party chairmanship—the first time since Anton Cermak that political and governmental power in the city had been concentrated in the hands of one man. Daley quickly set about further strengthening the already formidable Democratic city machine. He was said to pass personally on every application for the more than 30,000 jobs distributed by the Democratic organization. Democratic slate-making for city, county, and soon state offices was consolidated "under himself and a trusted few within the party."[10]

Daley made himself popular with the city's business community by launching huge construction programs and building expressways that brought millions of dollars of investment into the downtown Loop. But the bulwark of his strength remained, as under Kelly and Nash, the patronage army. In Bridgeport, where Daley continued to live in a modest dwelling, about 2,000 out of 40,000 residents held government jobs controlled by the machine.[11]

Alderman Vito Marzullo, representing an Italian and Polish ward on the near Southwest Side, explained to Mike Royko, a reporter for the *Chicago Sun-Times*, how the system worked: "I got an assistant state's attorney, and I got an assistant attorney general. I got an electrical inspector at twelve thousand dollars a year, and I got street inspectors and surveyors, and a county highway inspector. I got an administrative assistant to the zoning board and some people in the secretary of state's office. I got fifty-nine precinct captains and they all got assistants and they all got jobs. The lawyers I got in jobs don't have to work precincts, but they have to come by my ward office and give free legal advice to the people of the ward."[12]

Patronage-based Democratic machines also functioned effectively in Baltimore, St. Louis, Cleveland, Memphis, New Orleans, Albany, and many smaller cities. Republican counterparts dominated suburban bailiwicks like Nassau and Suffolk counties on Long Island, Delaware and Montgomery counties outside Philadelphia, and the "ring counties" around Chicago. Traditional machines also existed in the anthracite and bituminous coal-mining regions of Pennsylvania, the mountain counties of eastern Ohio and West Virginia, the river counties of southern Indiana, the "Egypt" section of southern Illinois, the Creole parishes of southern Louisiana, and the Mexican-American counties of south Texas.[13]

At the state level, party machines controlled government payrolls in the belt of commercial and industrial states reaching from Massachusetts to Illinois. Party turnover in most of these states had become fairly common by the 1950s. But the party holding the governorship took full advantage of state government patronage to reward party workers. As late as 1963 the governor of Pennsylvania could turn over more than 40,000 jobs without any kind of civil service protection. In West Virginia the governor controlled about 15,000 jobs. Persons appointed to jobs on a political basis were usually assessed between 1 and 3 percent of their salaries to support the machine. In Indiana the governor customarily awarded the agency for selling state license plates in each county, a lucrative enterprise, to his party's county chairman (a system that continued into the 1980s).[14]

WHY THE MACHINES FAILED

Machines that had existed at the turn of the century and had survived the assaults of the progressives seemed in many places to be carrying on much as before. Was O'Connor then wrong in diagnosing the twilight of the machines? Not really, though the trend he detected did not become fully developed until the 1960s.

Even where they remained conspicuously prominent on the political landscape, most machines had developed deep fissures. Some of the strongest Democratic machines, including that of Chicago, had been unable to check the Eisenhower tide in 1956, and patronage-based Republican machines in Pennsylvania, Ohio, and Indiana had lost their states' governorships when public sentiment turned against them. Many machines could no longer count on dominating their own party's primary—long regarded as the minimum requirement for an effective organization. Interest groups, sensing where real power lay, increasingly made their contributions directly to officeholders or candidates rather than to party organizations.

What had happened? In part, as O'Connor claimed, the welfare function of the machines was being taken over by programs at least partly financed and in some cases managed by the federal government. Low-income voters who used to depend on the precinct captain for occasional handouts or access to such government programs as existed had come to regard welfare services as rights to which they were entitled as citizens. Though the stronger machines still exercised, or strove to give the impression of exercising, some influence over the distribution of government benefits, the federal bureaucracy, particularly after passage of the Hatch Act, became largely free of domination by party organizations.

State and city governments, reacting to pressures from civic groups, public employee unions, and the press, also began to professionalize their work forces. "This trend," writes Roger Lutchin, "began to hit the police forces by the 1930s, the housing departments from the time of their creation in the thirties, and welfare from the 1930s, and continued to be important in departments such as health and education, where the trend had become significant earlier." Professional public servants, and their unions, sought "to sever the link between the ward politicians and the dispensation of [government] services."[15]

Professionalization of government work forces undermined the machines' most vital resource: the patronage system. By 1961, 52 percent of cities with over 500,000 population had "substantially all employees under civil service," and there were no cities in this category without some jobs protected by civil service. Smaller percentages of less heavily populated cities maintained full merit-system protection and 41 percent of cities from 10,000 to 100,000 had no civil service at all (Table 15–1).[16]

The trend, however, clearly was in the direction of expanding merit-system coverage. At the state level, too, the old strongholds of the patronage system began to give away. In Pennsylvania, where the state government in the 1950s had supported the largest patronage army in the nation, William Scranton, elected governor with the backing of the old Republican state machine in 1962, won enactment in 1963 of a civil service reform law that sharply reduced the number of patronage jobs.

Even where merit systems were legally in place, determined politicians could still evade their rules. Chicago, for example, according to the 1962 *Municipal Yearbook,* provided civil service protection for *all* city employees except those employed by public utilities. The Daley machine got around this impediment by hiring most city workers as "temporary" jobholders (as in a sense no doubt they were), who did not qualify for civil service protection.[17] But a system that could be maintained only through subterfuge was on a slippery footing. Eventually the courts would act against it—as indeed happened in Chicago in the 1970s.

Without patronage the machines could not go on for long in the old way. As the experience of the Republican machine in Philadelphia in the 1950s showed, political workers who have been largely motivated by government jobs, or the hope of obtaining government jobs, will not continue when the machines no longer have jobs to deliver.[18]

Table 15–1   Civil Service Coverage in Cities, Distributed by Population Groups, 1961

Population	*Percentage of Cities with*		
	Substantially All Employees under Civil Service	*Some but Not All under Civil Service*	*No Civil Serivce*
Over 500,000	52	48	0
100,000–250,000	44	41	15
10,000–100,000	26	33	41

Source: Edward C. Banfield and James Q. Wilson, *City Politics* (Harvard University Press, 1963), pp. 207–208.

Machines deprived of patronage armies were not, of course, without resources so long as they controlled or influenced the placement of government contracts or the enforcement of government regulations. As Raymond Wolfinger has written, "The New Deal did not abolish the contractor's natural desire to minimize the risks of competitive bidding, or the landlord's equally natural desire to avoid the burdens of the housing code." Wolfinger found in a study of the New Haven, Connecticut, Democratic machine in the 1960s that "it was commonplace for city or party officials to 'advise' a prime contractor about which local subcontractors, suppliers, and insurance agencies to patronize. . . . A contractor hoping to build a school would be likely to buy his performance bonds from the bond and insurance agency headed by the Democratic National Committeeman. . . . During one mayoralty campaign a party official asked a reluctant businessman, 'Look, you son of a bitch, do you want a snow-removal contract or don't you?' In the 1957 mayoralty election the biggest individual contributor, who gave $1,500 to the ruling Democratic party, was a partner in the architectural firm that designed the two new high schools. . . ."[19]

Removing the distribution of government jobs from politics did not necessarily reduce corruption. Graft and political shakedowns have survived the demise of most of the old patronage machines, as newspaper headlines almost daily testify.

What the traditional party machines had brought to the table, however, was their patronage armies. In return for a say in awarding government contracts or granting zoning variances, and in setting the general direction of government, they provided officeholders with legions of workers in the wards and precincts and with cash raised by assessing the political jobholders' salaries. Deprived of patronage, the party bosses lost much of their leverage with elected officeholders. Governors, mayors, legislators, and councilmen might still sell political favors and extort campaign contributions from businesses—as some clearly have done. But they no longer had much reason to share these opportunities with party organizations. The money they raised could more sensibly be used to finance their own campaigns—paying for expensive advertising on television and employment of the new breed of political consultants—or simply for their personal enrichment. Party organizations might have some residual value in promoting harmony in government or advancing common ideological goals. But the role of the party machine as a powerful force over state and local government was bound to decline.

A NEW KIND OF VOTER

The machines faced other problems. Television, more than newspapers or even radio ever had done, made it possible for officeholders and candidates to communicate directly with their constituents rather than relying on party workers to build their reputations and spread their messages. Even in places where neighborhood canvassers could still be mobilized for door-to-door campaigning, they were not as effective as they once had been.

Rising levels of income and education produced new generations of voters who had less need of their precinct captain's services and did not readily accept instructions, or pleas, on how to vote. Deep reduction in the flow of immigration greatly diminished the supply of foreign-born who would look to the precinct captain for help in finding jobs or dealing with government. As children and grandchildren of immigrants lost interest in ethnic attachments and moved away from old neighborhoods, the machines lost some of their function of speaking for ethnic and religious solidarity.

The movement of blacks from the South to northern cities at first reinforced the hold of Democratic city machines but ultimately put heavy strains on their cohesion. By the 1950s most northern blacks were Democrats, or at least voted Democratic, and the new arrivals at first became loyal backers of Democratic city machines. Heavy support from black wards was crucial to Daley's rise to power in Chicago. Blacks played a major role in tipping Philadelphia to the Democratic party in the early 1950s. But the large influx of blacks was perceived as threatening by many of the machines' white constituents.

American cities have always been subject to tension among differing racial, ethnic, and religious groups. In the 1840s and 1850s city politics was torn by conflict between nativist Protestants and immigrant Catholics that led to numerous riots and produced the short-lived American (Know-Nothing) party. Since the latter part of the nineteenth century, however, when non–Anglo-Saxon ethnic groups became majorities in most major northeastern and midwestern cities, the machines had been fairly successful at brokering the interests of different groups. Irish Catholics, the first of the non–Protestant groups to arrive in large numbers, had generally taken the lead in organizing Democratic machines. Members of other groups felt, with some reason, that the Irish kept for themselves a disproportionate share of the political rewards. (In New Haven in the 1930s, for example, first- and second-generation Irish made up only 13 percent of the population but held 49 percent of city government jobs.) But a sense of shared interest against old-stock Protestant establishments held most non-Protestant ethnic groups together within the Democratic party and made them willing to accept trade-offs with each other in the distribution of government benefits and services.

Blacks did not fit so easily into this pattern. Before the 1930s blacks had been predominantly Republican. As they entered Democratic ranks, and often provided Democratic candidates with margins of victory in close city and state elections, they naturally expected their share of the rewards. But many of the machines' white constituents regarded the great black migration of the 1950s as imperiling their personal security, their property, and what they had come to regard as their common American culture. They looked to the machines to protect their interests against blacks, as the machines claimed to represent working-class whites against the old-line Protestant establishments. But the machines now also represented the blacks. Most machine leaders for a time followed the course of seeking to preserve the political dominance of the white ethnic groups to which they themselves belonged while giving blacks gradually increasing shares of government jobs, benefits, and elective offices. The result was that in many cases they antagonized both sides. Many blacks continued to feel, correctly, that they were getting the shorter end of the stick. And many ethnic whites believed the machines were abandoning their interests in pursuit of black votes. At the end of the 1950s the two racial constituencies still usually hung together within the Democratic party. But the machines, already structurally weakened, were finding it difficult to serve both sides of what were perceived as conflicting racial interests.

Perhaps most damaging of all, machines had acquired an apparently unalterably bad image in American culture. This had always been true among the Protestant middle class, but now many of the machines' own traditional constituents among Catholics, Jews, blacks, and working-class white Protestants, or their children, had come to view the machines as sinister. This reputation was partly the result of first-hand acquaintance with the darker side of the machines' operations. But it was also due to impressions conveyed by the press, movies, and (later) television, in which bosses and their associates almost always were portrayed as "bad guys." An institution laboring under the burden of general condemnation in popular culture was sure to have a difficult future.

16

MOVEMENT POLITICS

The Republican Hard Right

JOHN F. KENNEDY'S ELECTION as President in 1960 restored liberal Democrats to control of the executive branch and to a leadership role in setting the direction of national policy. Though the Democrats had regained majorities in both houses of Congress in 1954, greatly augmented by the Democratic landslide of 1958 (caused by that year's deep economic recession), the narrowness of Kennedy's victory over Richard Nixon, the Republican candidate, caused the administration at first to proceed with caution. In the months before Kennedy's assassination in Dallas in November 1963, however, the dynamic young President was pressing vigorously for enactment of the liberal agenda that had been developed by Democrats in Congress and the Democratic Advisory Council during the late 1950s.

After Kennedy's death, Lyndon Johnson, the new President, utilized the wave of public emotion produced by the assassination, together with his own unequaled mastery of legislative politics, to win congressional approval for major additions to the welfare state. In his state of the union and budget messages in January 1964, Johnson called for an "unconditional war" on poverty that would deploy the resources of the federal government to eradicate "the roots of poverty in urban and rural areas." In June, Congress passed the landmark Civil Rights Act of 1964, prohibiting racial discrimination in public accommodations and employment. In August, Johnson won enactment of anti-poverty legislation providing funds for community action and job-training programs. Other important administration proposals, however, including medicare and federal aid to elementary and secondary education, were still blocked by the lingering power of the conservative coalition in Congress.[1]

The revival of liberalism in the early 1960s, and the renewal of the Democrats as the national majority party, were accompanied by the development of a new kind of politics, more devoted to ideology than to party but prepared to make a national party its political instrument. The conservative version of movement politics, zealously promoting right-wing ideology (more fully defined below), took hold in 1964 in the Republican party and won a crucial victory at that year's Republican national convention. By the summer of 1968, the emergence of a counterculture and fervid opposition to the Vietnam War had made the liberal version of movement politics a powerful force in the Democratic party.

Ideological movements and their associated special-interest groups to some extent took the place of the old patronage-based machines as mobilizers of voter participation. By their very nature, however, they were less suited than the machines had been to maintain broad coalitions within parties or to manage the pragmatic compromises needed for effective government in a country so diverse as the United States. Often they seemed more intent on making an ideological statement than on achieving attainable political goals. And the extreme positions they sometimes imposed on the parties with which they were allied further eroded the attachments of many voters to either major party.

PROGRESSIVE REPUBLICANS

At the beginning of the 1960s conservative Republicans critical of Eisenhower's willingness to accommodate most aspects of the welfare state retained major influence within the party's ranks in Congress but seemed to have little chance of playing a determining role in selecting Republican presidential nominees. Most political commentators and Republican politicians expected after the 1960 election that Nelson Rockefeller, elected governor of New York in 1958, would be the Republican party's candidate for President in 1964. Nixon, despite the closeness of the 1960 election, seemed unlikely to be given a second chance to run against Kennedy.

At the Republican national convention in Chicago in 1960, a band of mostly young conservatives had staged a brief uprising when Nixon, who had locked up the presidential nomination early, insisted on including in the platform a progressive civil rights plank called for by Rockefeller. The conservatives had put forward Senator Barry Goldwater, who had been elected to the Senate from the formerly predominantly Democratic state of Arizona on the Eisenhower tide in 1952, as their candidate for President. Goldwater had withdrawn his name in a ringing speech calling on conservatives to work to move the national party in their ideological direction. He immediately became the hero of what was coming to be known as the "conservative movement."

In 1961 a coalition of conservatives, most of whom were "amateurs" (in James Q. Wilson's sense of persons motivated primarily by ideological goals rather than by a desire to win office), set out to win the 1964 presidential nomination for Goldwater. But Goldwater's base seemed smaller than Taft's had been, and he at first appeared unlikely to break the moderate wing's dominance in the national Republican party.

Rockefeller, grandson of both John D. Rockefeller, founder of America's most famous fortune, and of Nelson Aldrich, conservative Republican leader of the Senate in the early 1900s, was not quite the political personification of the New

York establishment that Dewey had been. The Rockefeller resources were so vast that the family formed a kind of economic and social principality of its own, a bit outside the establishment and not entirely trusted by it—somewhat as the Adams family in Boston had been idiosyncratic and independent and somewhat distrusted by State Street bankers. Nelson Rockefeller had served in the state department under Franklin Roosevelt, but he seems never to have given serious thought to breaking with his family's Republican heritage. Under Eisenhower he had for a while been under secretary of the newly created department of health, education, and welfare. But he had grown dissatisfied with the kind of moderate, essentially reactive, conservatism represented by Dewey and Eisenhower.

As governor of New York he placed himself in the tradition of Theodore Roosevelt, which seemed to offer a more dynamic creed than Eisenhower's moderation or Richard Nixon's pragmatism. His faltering effort to oppose Nixon for the Republican nomination in 1960 had failed to get off the ground and had revealed a lack of empathy with grassroots Republicanism beyond the Alleghenies. The announcement in November 1961 of his divorce from his wife of 31 years clouded his standing with moral conservatives. (Polls showed that Stevenson's divorce had not affected his candidacy in 1952 but had hurt him, particularly among Catholics, in 1956.) But Rockefeller still seemed the party's natural choice to run against Kennedy in 1964.

The 1962 midterm elections appeared to bring further strength to the moderate-to-progressive wing of the Republican party. Rockefeller was easily reelected, and William Scranton and George Romney, who identified themselves as progressives, won the governorships of Pennsylvania and Michigan, respectively, replacing Democrats. In Ohio, James Rhodes, a hard-nosed pragmatist in the line of business-oriented Republican bosses like Hanna and Platt, but friendly to Rockefeller, was elected governor. Nixon, meanwhile, was losing his attempt to recover his California base by replacing Edmund ("Pat") Brown as governor (leading to a wild press conference on the morning after the election at which he promised reporters they would not "have Nixon to kick around any more").

The kind of Republican progressivism represented by Rockefeller, Scranton, and Romney, and by senators like Jacob Javits of New York, Clifford Case of New Jersey, and Thomas Kuchel of California, shared some qualities with Democratic liberalism, as right-wing Republicans never tired of pointing out, but it was also different in important ways. Like the liberals, the Republican progressives were strong advocates of federal and state legislation against racial or ethnic discrimination. Moreover, they believed the federal government had a role in meeting public needs for education, health care, housing, city renewal, and income maintenance for retired people and the poor. But, unlike liberals, and unlike many turn-of-the-century progressives, the new Republican progressives were not antagonistic toward corporate business.

Liberalism under Stevenson and Kennedy had to some extent pulled away from the anti-business stance that had often been taken by Franklin Roosevelt and

Truman. But when the economic or political going got rough, the reaction of most liberals, including Kennedy, was still to treat corporate business as an adversary. (Some liberals claimed they were responding to hostility from business. Kennedy joked that he had been only "the second choice of a majority of businessmen for the office of President. . . . Their first choice was anyone else.")[2]

Modern Republican progressives, many of whom came from business backgrounds, in contrast, generally regarded themselves as guardians of the free-enterprise system and maintained close ties with business. Rockefeller often spoke of the economic and social progress that had been achieved during the Republican party's early years through an alliance of business and government and suggested that much would be gained if that relationship were renewed with big labor as an equal partner.[3]

Another difference with liberalism was that Republican progressives emphasized the role of the states in managing government service programs—in part, no doubt, because many leading progressives were governors, but also because they believed the centralization of governmental authority favored by most liberals in the 1960s was bound to produce, in a country as large and diverse as the United States, results that were both inefficient and inequitable. On law-enforcement issues, Republican progressives were less concerned than liberals with protecting the rights of persons charged with crimes, and more concerned with maintaining public order and upholding traditional moral standards.

A final defining characteristic of Republican progressives was their fascination with administration, which they believed, probably also reflecting their background in business, to be the key to fair and effective government. As a result, they avoided contentious ideological issues and concentrated on efforts to restructure government departments, rationalize budget-making procedures, and institute new management techniques.[4]

THE HARD RIGHT

By the summer of 1963, Rockefeller's chances of winning the 1964 Republican presidential nomination had begun to slip away. His remarriage in May 1963 to the former Margarita ("Happy") Murphy, who had divorced her first husband after meeting Rockefeller, provoked far more public outrage than had his divorce from his first wife.

Eisenhower, following events from his farm outside Gettysburg and recalling criticism that Rockefeller had made of his administration in its final years, urged Henry Cabot Lodge, Jr., Nixon's running mate in 1960 and now ambassador to South Vietnam, to seek the nomination. Romney and Scranton showed signs of interest in the race.

Meanwhile Clifton White, who had been an Eisenhower operative in 1952, was putting together an extensive organization composed mainly of movement conservatives. After Rockefeller's remarriage, Goldwater began to rise in the polls: in the early spring Rockefeller had led Goldwater among Republicans by 43 percent to 26 percent; at the end of May the standing had shifted to 35 percent for Goldwater to 30 for Rockefeller.[5]

The conservative movement that began in American politics in the 1950s was not directly descended from the old Taftite wing of the Republican party. The Taftite stalwarts and the new conservatives who gathered around Goldwater's standard shared a common aversion to big government. But the Taftites tended to be isolationist, protectionist, distrustful of all kinds of change, suspicious of the military, nonintellectual, and based primarily on the Midwest and upstate regions of New York and Pennsylvania. The Goldwaterites, though they had some significant differences among themselves, were for the most part foreign-policy interventionists, free-traders, avid modernizers (delighting in the new technology and the speed of modern life—Goldwater, characteristically, was an expert pilot, flying the newest and fastest planes), pro-military, fiercely intellectual (writing books and publishing magazines), and based chiefly on New York City, the Far West, and the South. Many Goldwaterites had supported Eisenhower against Taft for the Republican nomination in 1952 on the grounds that Eisenhower was more likely to resist the advance of international Communism.[6]

Except for the Tories before the Revolution and some defenders of slavery before the Civil War, the United States had never had much of a "right" in the European sense of a political body devoted to corporate collectivism and feudal hierarchy. In Europe much of the inspiration for conservative collectivism (not to be confused with fascism, a twentieth-century hybrid of mixed ideological descent) came from the more authoritarian branch of Catholicism or from high-church Anglicanism. In the United States, Catholicism as an unestablished minority church with a largely working-class membership had generally been drawn to alignment with the more liberal party, and the high-church movement in the Episcopal church had little to do with politics.

There were, however, implicit strands of conservative collectivism in the American conception of the nation, in the generally accepted ideal of the family, and in the ideological outlooks of the more conservative religious denominations (including Orthodox Judaism). Persons strongly moved by these ideas and attitudes had for some time been dismayed by the drift of American society toward hedonism, moral relativism, and banishment of religion from the "public square." With the coming of the cold war in the late 1940s, many social conservatives had discovered, or reconfirmed, Communism as the mortal foe of all they regarded as virtuous. In Europe feudal conservatives had traditionally favored a fairly strong state (except when it challenged the church). But with the rise of socialism and the secular state in the twentieth century many had become anti-statist. This shift was naturally popular with hierarchical conservatives in the United States, where it fitted neatly with prevailing economic individualism.[7]

Thus anti-Communism and anti-statism became linked causes for a small band of conservative intellectuals and political activists, mainly Catholic and mainly concentrated in New York City, who in the early 1950s formed something approaching a traditional right. The *National Review,* founded in 1955 by William Buckley, scion of a wealthy New York Irish-Catholic family (the money having been made mostly in the Texas oilfields), provided a public voice for this kind of conservatism. In 1962 New York's multi-party system was joined by the Conservative party, organized by Daniel Mahoney, an ally of the Buckley family, as an alternative to the progressive direction the state Republican party was taking under Rockefeller.[8]

Senator Goldwater's own political roots were in a somewhat different kind of conservatism. He descended from Jewish merchants who in the nineteenth century, seeking economic opportunity and personal independence, had migrated first to California, and then to the harsh desert land of Arizona, where they founded in Phoenix what became the state's largest department store. He thus brought together the individualism of the economic entrepreneur with that of the frontiersman. Goldwater's father had married a Protestant and had converted to Christianity, and Goldwater was himself an Episcopalian (prompting the joke among Jews in 1964 that the first Jew to run for President was bound to be an Episcopalian). But he took pride in the enterprise and daring of his Jewish forebears, which he associated with the romantic legends of the western frontier.[9]

Goldwater and others like him in the West and Southwest feared and resented the growing power of the federal government to interfere with economic and social life. Expansion of governmental authority, they felt, conflicted with the desire for unrestricted personal freedom that had carried them or their ancestors west in the first place. At a more prosaic level, they were moved by the traditional dislike of small businessmen for regulation by government bureaucrats. Their economic and social attitudes were libertarian. At the same time many of them shared the view of the eastern hierarchical conservatives that Communism in general and the Soviet Union in particular posed a clear and present danger to the survival of the United States. They therefore favored a strong military—a political sentiment reinforced by the economic benefits derived from the many military bases and weapons-manufacturing industries located in the western states.

Involvement in the conservative movement seems to have filled emotional needs for many westerners as well as to have served economic or ideological interests. A new wave of migration was sweeping across the United States in the 1960s, from East to West, and particularly from Midwest to Far West. From 1960 to 1970 population in the Pacific coast states increased by 25 percent, and in the Rocky Mountain states by 21 percent (compared to a 13 percent increase nationwide). The population of suburban Orange County, southeast of Los Angeles, grew from 703,000 in 1960 to 1,420,000 in 1970. The population of Phoenix, Goldwater's hometown, rose from 664,000 to 971,000.

Such mobility, while contributing to economic growth and opening up opportunities for many, inevitably undermined social stability and produced feelings of insecurity and loneliness. Some people suffering pangs of dislocation turned to politics for emotional outlet or reassurance, or simply to make friends. Some became active on the liberal side, taking up all kinds of causes that called for increased government intervention. But many others were drawn to conservatism, directing their anger against governmental establishments they felt were unjustly taxing their incomes and expressing their yearning for community through intense national patriotism. Persons in this latter group were ready recruits for the army of volunteer activists that Clif White was putting together for Goldwater in 1963.[10]

In the Rocky Mountain states, Goldwater's own region, political conservatism was further motivated by a tendency to regard the federal government, which owned two-thirds of the land, as an oppressive absentee landlord. The federal government had come first to conquer the Indians. It had stayed primarily to help manage use of the region's scarce water supply and to preserve its spectacular natural beauty. Though few westerners wanted it to leave, many were convinced that federal policies were excessively influenced by eastern interests and eastern attitudes—thus giving too little weight to western needs and threatening western liberties.[11]

Another source of right-wing conservatism—the "hard right" as James Guth and John Green have labeled it—was the angry reaction of many white southerners against efforts by the federal government in the 1950s and 1960s to dismantle racial segregation of public schools and other public places in the South.[12] After the Supreme Court's *Brown v Board of Education* decision in 1954, which declared racial segregation of public schools unconstitutional, southern politicians led by Senator Harry Byrd of Virginia and Governor James Byrnes of South Carolina had attempted "massive resistance"—essentially a repetition of Calhoun's claim in the 1830s that state legislatures could nullify federal laws.[13] Massive resistance was struck down by the courts. But southern states, hanging on the Supreme Court's directive in 1955 that desegregation should proceed "with all deliberate speed," which seemed to suggest tolerance for a certain amount of delay, had generally found it possible to go slowly with actual integration. In the early 1960s southern blacks led by Martin Luther King, Jr., with some help from northern sympathizers, black and white, undertook nonviolent action to end racial discrimination not only in education but in employment, housing, access to public services, and most particularly voting.

The Kennedy administration at first tried to work out compromise solutions to these attacks on forms of discrimination which at the time, except for segregation of schools, violated no federal laws. In the spring of 1963, however, after King's campaign against discrimination in Birmingham, Alabama, was met with "police dogs savagely attacking Negroes, . . . fire hoses pounding them against the street . . . , burly policemen sitting on a female demonstrator . . . ," Kennedy called for broad civil rights legislation aimed at ending all forms of public segregation.[14]

After Kennedy's death, Lyndon Johnson, despite his own identification with the South (or perhaps to some degree because of it), kept up pressure for passage of the comprehensive federal civil rights law that finally was enacted in the summer of 1964.

Southern politicians, most of whom felt obliged to maintain at least a show of last-ditch resistance to integration, began to believe that fealty to the national Democratic party was no longer an effective means for insulating segregation against political change. Strom Thurmond's Dixiecrat campaign in 1948, which carried four Deep South states, had been the opening shot in the revolt of white southerners against the Democratic party. In 1960, 12 electors from Mississippi and Alabama voted in the electoral college for Harry Byrd rather than John Kennedy. Many southern white Democrats whose views on most social and economic issues were conservative decided the time had come to put aside memories of the Civil War and Reconstruction and vote in national elections with conservative Republicans—as their representatives in Congress had been doing since the late 1930s. The vested interest of state and local officeholders, and of senior southern Democrats in Congress, in maintaining a Democratic identity remained an impediment. But as the civil rights struggle quickened, with northern liberal Democrats in the vanguard of change, motivation among white southerners for breaking with the national Democracy increased.

Republicans began to win election to Congress from the formerly solid South. John Tower arrived in the Senate from Texas in 1961, taking the seat given up by Lyndon Johnson when he became Vice President. By 1963 Republicans held 11 seats in the House from the South, compared to only two (both from Tennessee) at the beginning of the 1950s. In 1964 Strom Thurmond, elected to the Senate as a Democrat in 1954, crossed over to become a Republican.

"Conservatism" in the South in the early 1960s was no doubt to some extent a code word for opposition to racial integration. But it also represented attachments to free-market economics and traditional moral standards that southerners did indeed share with northern and western conservatives like Buckley and Goldwater, and that formerly had been muted by belief that the one-party system in the South was a bulwark protecting segregation. When this bulwark began to fail, a powerful inhibition against the coming together of various kinds of conservatives to form a national right-wing political force was removed.

The state of Texas, where southern and western conservatism met, provided a particularly fertile resource for hard-right politicians. Booming economic growth had produced droves of oil-rich millionaires, like H. L. Hunt, Syd Richardson, and Clint Murchison, who were prepared to spend money freely in politics. In 1964 Lyndon Johnson, who had served the oil industry and other Texas interests faithfully during his years in Congress, was President. But many Texas millionaires found Goldwater's brand of uncompromising individualism much to their liking, and some were prepared to back their ideological choice even against their old ally in the White House. Among the Goldwater delegates from Texas to the 1964 Republican national convention was young George Bush of Houston, son of former Senator Prescott Bush of Connecticut, a staunch defender of the establishment and an Eisenhower Republican in the 1950s. The younger Bush had come to the Southwest to make his fortune in the oil business and now was trying to break into politics. He took on the ideological color of his environment—a bit awkwardly, some remember.

Taken as a whole, the modern hard right represents some aspects of the republican tradition, but also aspects of European-style feudal corporatism and indigenous American racism. It differs from the mainstream of the republican tradition in its extreme hostility toward government and its adoption of populist social attitudes that earlier had been politically allied chiefly with liberalism.

SAN FRANCISCO REPUBLICANS

The Republican party was torn in 1964 by a division even deeper than that between the forces supporting Eisenhower and Taft in 1952, with progressives and movement conservatives replacing establishment moderates and Taftite stalwarts as the principal combatants. Rockefeller, undeterred by polls showing that his remarriage had made him unacceptable to much of the public, pressed on for the nomination, assembling an enormously costly and, outside New York state, largely ineffective campaign organization. Lodge, Scranton, and Romney came under pressure to declare their candidacies. But as long as Rockefeller remained in the race, the entrance of another progressive could serve no one but Goldwater.

Clif White shrewdly concentrated on building Goldwater networks in the West, where regular party organizations had been weak since the Progressive Era, and the South, where the Eisenhower onslaught in 1952 had given hard-right conservatives control of weak state Republican parties. In most states in these regions national convention delegates were picked through caucuses or conventions. Amateur hard-right politicians achieved majorities in most of these bodies and elected Goldwater delegates.[15]

Progressive strategists recognized that Goldwater was making headway in the caucus and convention states. But they believed that national polls and voters in the primary states would convince the pragmatic politicians who controlled Republican organizations in most of the industrial states of the Northeast and Midwest that Goldwater was too far to the right to win broad support in the general election.

The first primary test came in New Hampshire early in March where Rockefeller and Goldwater were on the ballot. To the embarrassment of both, a band of enthusiastic volunteers produced a write-in victory for Henry Cabot Lodge, still ambassador to South Vietnam and not an announced candidate. Rockefeller's third-place finish in a northeastern state near New York seemed to confirm his unpopularity.

Lodge took the lead in national polls of Republican voters. Scranton won as a favorite son in the Pennsylvania primary, as did Governor Rhodes in Ohio, and Representative John Byrnes in Wisconsin. Goldwater won non-binding primaries in Illinois and Indiana that Rockefeller did not enter. But the substantial votes given to Senator Margaret Chase Smith of Maine in Illinois, and to Harold Stassen, by now a perennial presidential candidate, in Indiana, were interpreted as protests against Goldwater.

The balance of power appeared to lie with midwestern stalwarts like Senate Minority Leader Everett Dirksen of Illinois, House Minority Leader Gerald Ford of Michigan, Governor Rhodes of Ohio, Representatives Byrnes and Melvin Laird of Wisconsin, and young Representative Bob Dole of Kansas. Many of these were troubled by the radical-right direction in which Goldwater proposed to lead the party, particularly by Goldwater's opposition to federal intervention against racial segregation in the South. (Goldwater himself was not a racist but argued that federal action against segregation would violate the principle of states' rights.) Though many of the stalwarts had worked with southern conservatives in Congress on some issues, they had not forsaken the Republican party's roots in support for minority civil rights. They were, moreover, frightened by what a national ticket headed by Goldwater might do to Republican state and congressional candidates in the general election. Still, to support Rockefeller or Lodge would be to join forces with the cohorts of the eastern establishment whom the stalwarts had fought at Republican conventions since 1912.

In the Oregon primary in mid-May, Rockefeller, after an intensive personal campaign in a state where he was the only candidate who "cared enough to come" (as his slogan went), defeated both Lodge and Goldwater, effectively ending the possibility of a Lodge candidacy.

Two and a half weeks later Goldwater and Rockefeller faced each other in California's winner-take-all primary for the state's 86 delegates. California since the days of Hiram Johnson had almost always stood on the progressive or moderate side within the national Republican party. In the early 1960s, however, a strong conservative force had developed within the state, particularly in the south around Los Angeles and San Diego. So the presidential primary became a fight for control of the state party as well as a contest between the two candidates. Rockefeller's slate included much of the state's business and Republican political establishments, while Goldwater's was composed mainly of little-known but aspiring hard-right conservatives supported by a huge organization of doorbell-ringing volunteers. In Los Angeles County alone, Clif White was able to field 10,000 volunteers for Goldwater, compared to the 2,000 volunteers that were assembled for Rockefeller in the entire state.[16]

Before the Oregon primary, polls had shown Goldwater leading in California by about 10 percentage points. After Rockefeller's victory in Oregon, he immediately shot to a lead of about 10 percent in California, an advantage that he maintained going into the final weekend before the primary. On the Saturday before the primary the second Mrs. Rockefeller gave birth to a son, Nelson Rockefeller, Jr.—probably the most consequential domestic event in American politics since Martin Van Buren went calling on Peggy Eaton. Reminded of their doubts about Rockefeller's moral fitness, many voters swung back to Goldwater. The final opinion survey on Monday showed the race exactly even. Goldwater won by 68,000 votes in a total of more than two million. His margin of 207,000 in Los Angeles and Orange counties overcame Rockefeller's majority in the more progressive north.

Rockefeller folded his campaign, and for two weeks it seemed that Goldwater might be virtually unopposed in July at the Republican national convention in San Francisco. In mid-June Goldwater was one of only six Republicans to vote in the Senate against the administration's civil rights bill, going against Dirksen, who had become one of the bill's principal backers. Two days later Scranton entered the race. (I must here declare an interest: as Scranton's legislative secretary I became deeply involved in his campaign.) Scranton quickly received pledges of support from Rockefeller, Lodge (returned from Vietnam), and Romney (who for tactical reasons maintained a favorite-son candidacy in Michigan).

Goldwater's managers and many political commentators have always argued that Goldwater, regardless of the outcome of the California primary, had by the beginning of June won enough delegates from the caucus and convention states and in some primaries to lock up the nomination. Their evidence is the 874 to 409 majority won by the Goldwater forces in the convention on the only true test vote, the progressives' attempt to include a strong civil rights plank in the platform. But of this more than two-to-one majority, 86 votes came from California. If Rockefeller had won the California primary, all of those 86 votes would have been cast on the progressive side, reducing the margin to 316—and so requiring a change of only 159 more votes to produce a majority opposed to Goldwater. Under those circumstances, in my judgment, there would have been enough votes from stalwarts in states like Ohio, Illinois, Indiana, Iowa, Wisconsin, and Kansas, mindful of the preference of grassroots Republicans (Scranton led Goldwater among Republican voters in the last Gallup poll before the convention, 55 percent to 34) and fearful of the damage that Goldwater would do to other Republican candidates in November, to have prevented Goldwater's nomination. This does not mean that the nomination would necessarily have gone to Scranton, and it almost surely would not have gone to Rockefeller (who of course would have stayed in the race if he had won in California). But the nominee would probably have been someone not closely identified with the hard right—perhaps Nixon, who had remained carefully neutral. After the California primary, however, Goldwater's lead was insurmountable.[17]

When Scranton announced his candidacy, Dewey and others within the New York establishment who had hung back from helping Rockefeller entered the fight. Dewey gathered some of his old lieutenants on an afternoon in June and began making calls around the country from the boardroom of his law firm in downtown Manhattan. But the structure of the Republican party, and indeed the financial structure of the United States, had changed since the New York establishment had played a major role in bringing off Eisenhower's nomination in 1952. Banks and law firms in the South and West were no longer so responsive to calls from Wall Street, and most of the state and local politicians who at earlier critical moments had aligned themselves with the establishment were retired or dead. At the end of the afternoon, Dewey rolled down his sleeves and said, "Boys, it's not going to work. I'm going home." Dewey was right.

Why then did Scranton run? In part because he thought there was still some chance of shaking loose midwestern stalwarts like Dirksen and Rhodes. But also because, as one whose family had been active in the Republican party since the Civil War and who regarded maintaining the traditional values of the party as a kind of trust, he believed it was important that some other banner beside that of the hard right be raised at the San Francisco convention.

Goldwater swept to nomination by a majority of more than two to one. Movement conservatives, amid enormous enthusiasm (more than I have ever witnessed at a party convention except at the Democratic convention that nominated George McGovern in 1972, which I covered as a journalist), for a season at least had taken control of the Republican party.

THE TRIUMPH OF LIBERALISM

The Republicans' nomination of Goldwater directly challenged welfare-state liberalism and all its works—much as Bryan had challenged the Republicans' free-market ideology in 1896. Goldwater rejected the moderate "me-too" conservatism of Eisenhower, somewhat as Bryan had renounced Cleveland's accommodation of the republican ideology. During the general election campaign Goldwater modified his rhetoric slightly but for the most part stuck to his guns. He never backed off from proposals he had made in three books and innumerable newspaper columns for dismantling large parts of the welfare state. Even Social Security, he had suggested in New Hampshire before the primary, should "be made voluntary, that is if a person can provide better for himself, let him do it."[18]

Goldwater and his team were unusually forthright, in the context of American politics, in taking ideological positions that were in conflict with established policy. "Extremism in the defense of liberty is no vice!" Goldwater said in his acceptance speech at the Republican convention. "Moderation in the pursuit of justice is no virtue!" But they did not regard themselves as undertaking a political kamikaze. They were perhaps prepared to lose rather than to compromise their principles. But they expected to win. Hard-right conservatives for years had argued that there was in the electorate a conservative majority waiting to rally behind an ideologically pure candidate who offered "a choice not an echo," in the words of Phyllis Schlafly, the right's most pungent publicist.[19]

They turned out to be mistaken—at least for 1964. In the November election Goldwater swept Deep South states that not even Eisenhower had been able to sway from their Democratic allegiance. He carried Mississippi by 87 percent, Alabama by 70 percent, South Carolina 59 percent, Louisiana 57 percent, and Georgia 54 percent—all states where the Republican party had been almost nonexistent before 1960.

Nationally, however, Lyndon Johnson, nominated for a full term by the Democrats, won the greatest landslide majority in the popular vote, 61.1 percent, in a contested presidential election in American history (larger even than Franklin Roosevelt's majority of 60.8 percent in 1936). In the Northeast and Midwest Johnson swept not only the major cities and the metropolitan suburban counties but also small cities and rural counties that had been consistently Republican since the Civil War. Johnson carried every county in New England, every county in New York, and every county in New Jersey. In Pennsylvania he piled up large majorities in normally Republican suburban counties around Philadelphia and in the mountainous northern-tier counties, settled from New England, that had been unflaggingly Republican since the days of David Wilmot. Johnson carried all but four counties in Ohio, all but three in Michigan, all but three in Wisconsin.

Johnson won too in the Border and southern rim states that had been carried by Eisenhower in 1952 and 1956 and Nixon in 1960, though in most cases by relatively small majorities. In Virginia, traditionally conservative strongholds in the Northern Neck and the Shenandoah Valley came together with the race-conscious Southside to support Goldwater. But Johnson carried 24 of the 31 independent cities and the heavily populated suburbs around Washington to win the state by 54 percent.

Even in the Rocky Mountain states, where Goldwater's particular kind of libertarian conservatism had been born, Johnson won every state except the Republican candidate's home state of Arizona by margins ranging from 61 percent in Colorado to 51 percent in Idaho.

Johnson achieved large majorities among almost all demographic groups except southern whites. Catholics voted almost as heavily for Johnson, 76 percent, as they had for Kennedy in 1960. Jews, unimpressed by Goldwater's Jewish ancestry, voted more than 90 percent for Johnson, almost as heavily as they had voted for Roosevelt in 1944. Blacks, noting Goldwater's vote against the civil rights bill, voted 94 percent for Johnson compared to 68 percent for Kennedy in 1960—a pattern of monolithic backing for the Democratic national ticket that has continued ever since. Even northern white Protestants, the mass base of the Republican party since the Civil War, voted 57 percent for Johnson. Women were for the first time slightly more Democratic, 62 percent, than men, 60 percent.[20]

A number of factors contributed to Johnson's landslide. Some voters were moved by fear, skillfully cultivated by the Democratic campaign, that Goldwater had too reckless a personality to be trusted with control of nuclear weapons or the power to make peace-or-war decisions. Some regarded the election as a final tribute to John Kennedy. A probably significant but impossible to measure segment of northern Protestants were influenced by a sense of cultural alienation from the Republican ticket. Not only was Goldwater of Jewish descent, but his vice-presidential running mate, Representative William Miller of upstate New York, was a Roman Catholic, the first, and through 1992 still the only, non-Protestant ever included on a Republican national ticket. Miller, who had been Republican national chairman since 1961 (the first party chairman ever to make it to a national ticket), was chosen by Goldwater and his associates to appeal to urban Catholics who they believed were swinging toward social and economic conservatism. His chief effect was to make the ticket appear even more exotic to many members of the party's largest and previously most loyal ethno-cultural constituency.

The most important cause of Johnson's landslide victory, however, was the reaction of voters to the choice between unabashed welfare-state liberalism and equally unabashed libertarian conservatism. Norman Nie, Sidney Verba, and John Petrocik in their examination of American National Election Survey data for 1964 found that policy issues were more important than they had been in recent elections and that voters deciding on the basis of issues broke heavily for Johnson. In 1960, 67 percent of voters were strongly influenced in their presidential choice by party, while 62 percent were significantly motivated by their reaction to issues (the two groups obviously overlapped). In 1964 the share of voters strongly influenced by party declined slightly to 65 percent, while issue voters rose to 73 percent. Among voters influenced by issues 63 percent of Republicans favoring progressive positions and 30 percent of Republican centrists defected to Johnson, while only 28 percent of Democrats favoring conservative positions and 5 percent of Democratic centrists crossed over to vote for Goldwater.[21]

Goldwater did indeed offer "a choice not an echo"—not a moderate correction from liberalism, as Eisenhower and Nixon had done, but a truly radical effort to abolish many aspects of the welfare state. Given the choice between further expansion of the welfare state and its root-and-branch reduction, the great majority of Americans voted for expansion.

Goldwater's strong showing in the South produced the election of 16 Republican members of the House from that region—by far the largest Republican contingent since the end of Reconstruction. In the nation as a whole, however, Johnson's landslide brought net Democratic gains of 38 seats in the House and one in the Senate.

The increased Democratic majorities in Congress paved the way for passage in 1965 of most of the remaining items in what Johnson had called the Great Society program: federal support for economic development of Appalachia in March; federal aid to elementary and secondary education in April; Medicare in July; the Voting Rights Act, outlawing literacy requirements and other procedural devices that had been used to keep blacks from voting in the South, in August; and federally subsidized college scholarships in October.[22]

A STAR IS BORN

At the beginning of 1965, progressive and stalwart Republican leaders combined to sweep movement conservatives out of control of the party's national machinery. Ohio Republican chairman Ray Bliss, a pragmatic stalwart, was elected Republican national chairman, replacing Dean Burch, an Arizona conservative whom Goldwater had chosen to run the party during the 1964 campaign. Bliss instituted programs to attract college students and residents of big cities—groups among whom Goldwater had been particularly weak.[23]

Movement conservatives, however, were by no means prepared to abandon the fight. Though their candidate for President had lost badly in the general election, they had after all at the Republican convention routed the establishment that had dominated the presidential wing of the party since 1940.

The week before the 1964 election, Ronald Reagan, who during his years as a Hollywood film star had been an ardent New Deal liberal and only two years before had become a Republican, had delivered a 27-minute television address on Goldwater's behalf in which he excoriated welfare-state liberalism and identified the fight against it with America's struggle against international Communism. "The guns are silent in this war," Reagan said, "but frontiers fall while those who should be warriors prefer neutrality."[24]

Reagan's television address, though it had no effect on the outcome of the election, lifted the spirits of hard-right conservatives and made him a national political celebrity. Two years later he was persuaded by conservative southern California businessmen like Henry Salvador and Holmes Tuttle, who had helped bankroll Goldwater's campaign, to run for governor of California. Easily elected, he brought to the governorship conservative administration and rhetoric combined with a willingness to compromise on taxes and social legislation that kept California's state government among the nation's most progressive (and most expensive). Tuttle, Salvatori, and their associates were soon promoting Reagan for the Republican nomination for President in 1968. Clif White came on board to try to reconstruct the hard-right network. What ambitions Reagan himself had harbored in the depths of his soul from the beginning is difficult to fathom. But he at least shared with his supporters the determination that leadership of the Republican party should not pass back to those who had opposed Goldwater in 1964. "We will have no more of those candidates," he vowed in a speech to the Los Angeles Young Republicans, "who are pledged to use the same socialist goals as our opposition."[25]

17

REFORM POLITICS

Amateur Democrats

WHILE THE REPUBLICAN PARTY was coming under the control of the hard right in 1964, the Democrats, despite friction between President Johnson and a faction that gathered around Robert and Edward Kennedy, had seemed unusually united. By 1968, however, the extreme left, attracting converts among opponents of the Vietnam War and participants in the "youth rebellion," was gaining power within the Democratic party.

In the tumultuous politics of 1968, the Democrats ended up giving their presidential nomination to Hubert Humphrey, a mainstream liberal. But in 1972, the continuing effects of the Vietnam War and the liberal reaction against the presidency of Richard Nixon helped bring the Democratic nomination to George McGovern, the most radical candidate to lead a Democratic national ticket since William Jennings Bryan.

As Goldwater had done, McGovern failed badly at the polls in November. But the McGovern surge within the Democratic party was accompanied by procedural changes in the system of nominating presidential candidates—in both parties since the Democrats controlled most state legislatures, enacting laws governing delegate selection. The influence of television and other factors were already making the politics of presidential selection more candidate-oriented. The new nominating system carried this tendency even further. In addition, it further enhanced the power of ideological movements and special-interest groups in both parties and undermined the strength of what remained of state and local party organizations.

SWING TO THE RIGHT

The almost hegemonic domination of national politics the Democrats had achieved through the 1964 election lasted only two years. In the 1966 midterm elections they lost 47 seats in the House of Representatives and three in the Senate. In 1968 Humphrey received only 42.7 percent of the popular vote for President—a decline of 18 percentage points from Johnson's showing in 1964, almost the same as the drop in Herbert Hoover's share of the vote from 1928 to 1932.

Deep divisions in the public and in the Democratic party over the Vietnam War contributed to this precipitous fall. A majority of the public continued to support the war throughout Johnson's term. In February 1968, for example, the Gallup poll found that 61 percent backed continuation of the struggle and 23 percent favored withdrawal. But the pro-war hawks included many who were critical of Johnson's relatively cautious military strategy. Moreover, many of the more impassioned anti-war doves were liberal activists whose backing the Democratic party could not afford to lose.[1]

There were other reasons for the public's swing against Johnson and the Democratic party in the latter half of the 1960s. In August 1965, less than a week after Johnson signed the Voting Rights Act, blacks rioted for five days in the Watts section of Los Angeles, leaving 35 persons dead and $200 million in property damage. In 1966 riots broke out in black slums in many northern cities, the worst being in Newark, New Jersey (26 killed, more than 1,000 arrested), and Detroit (40 killed, 5,000 left homeless). Public support for further government action to promote civil rights declined. The percentage of citizens telling the Gallup poll that the Johnson administration was "pushing racial integration too fast" rose from 28 percent in April 1965 to 52 percent in September 1966.[2]

Johnson's attempt to finance the military buildup required by the Vietnam War without either raising taxes or cutting Great Society programs produced a federal budget deficit of $25 billion in 1968, far higher than any since the end of the Second World War. The deficit contributed to a rise in inflation, which reached 4.7 percent in 1968. That was relatively mild compared to what was to come in the 1970s, but it was higher than any since the immediate postwar years.

Public reaction against the administration's domestic policies set in, reinforced by horror stories of inefficiency and fraud in the administration of Great Society programs. The Harris poll found public support for the administration's "war on poverty" dropping from 60 percent in October 1965 to 41 percent in September 1966. The Gallup poll in August 1968 found that 46 percent of the public viewed "big government" as "the biggest threat to the country in the future," compared to 26 percent who regarded "big labor" as the biggest threat and 12 percent who most feared "big business." When the Harris poll asked in 1968 if "liberals have been running the country too long," 64 percent of *working-class whites* answered yes.[3]

When public opinion turned against the Johnson administration there was little political structure at the national level to shore it up. Thinking to eliminate any possible haven for resistance within the Democratic party, Johnson in 1965 had ruthlessly slashed the budget of the DNC and eliminated several of its programs, including the highly effective voter registration division. The national Democratic party organization, such as it was, came under direct control of the White House. As a result, most of the institutional advances that had been achieved by Paul Butler in the 1950s and maintained by the Kennedys were lost, and the DNC once more fell far behind its rival, the RNC.[4]

Under the circumstances it is not surprising that new hope arose within the party out of power. What few foresaw was the insurrection developing within the majority party itself.

DEPOSING THE KING

It had become axiomatic in the twentieth century that a sitting President could not be denied renomination for a second term by his own party. In the nineteenth century several Presidents, including Franklin Pierce and Chester Arthur, had been turned down by their parties for second terms. But the growing prestige and resources of the presidency were thought to have made the incumbent invulnerable for renomination, though not for reelection. The successes of William Howard Taft in 1912 and Herbert Hoover in 1932 in securing renomination when their popularity was at its nadir seemed to verify this assumption.

While many liberals had turned savagely hostile to Johnson by the beginning of 1968, few among the politically sophisticated believed there was a realistic possibility of preventing his renomination. Impassioned opponents of the Vietnam War, however, were determined that at least a fight should be made at the Democratic convention. The candidate most sought by the doves was Robert Kennedy, brother of the assassinated President, and formerly attorney general in the cabinets of both John Kennedy and Lyndon Johnson. Kennedy had gradually turned against Johnson's Vietnam policy after his election to the Senate from New York in 1964. But he accepted the conventional wisdom that an incumbent President could not be denied renomination and declined to lead what he was sure would be a hopeless and party-wrecking cause.

The doves turned to Senator Eugene McCarthy of Minnesota, who had come out against the war in the early fall of 1967. McCarthy, a Catholic, disliked the Kennedys, whom he regarded as lukewarm in both their liberalism and their Catholicism, and he bore a grudge against Johnson, who had publicly dangled the vice-presidential nomination before him in 1964, apparently to maintain media attention, before choosing Hubert Humphrey. Beyond these personal motives, McCarthy had become convinced that the administration was sinking more and more deeply into a war that could not be won. He agreed to run.

In January 1968, the Communist Tet offensive, which briefly penetrated downtown Saigon with suicide squads, was turned back with heavy Vietcong losses. But media coverage helped persuade a large segment of the public that the American effort in Vietnam had achieved nothing.

In the New Hampshire primary on March 12, the first electoral test of the campaign, Johnson won 50 percent of the preferential vote, but McCarthy's showing of 42 percent was hailed by the media as a sensational moral victory. (McCarthy, though second in the preferential part of the primary, won the 11 New Hampshire delegates, because Johnson's supporters had run more candidates than there were slots. Whatever the merits of Johnson's strategy in Vietnam, his campaign organization was certainly a mess.)[5]

On March 16, Robert Kennedy, urged on by advisers who now believed that Johnson could be beaten and who regarded McCarthy as a political second-rater with a personality unsuited for the presidency, announced that he would seek the nomination after all, "not . . . merely to oppose any man but to propose new policies." McCarthy refused to get out of the race.[6]

Johnson probably remained confident that he could win the nomination. He was still supported by most of the regular Democratic political structure in the South, and the machine bosses and union leaders who would control most of the delegates from the industrial states could not bring themselves to ditch an incumbent Democratic President who had delivered so much for their constituencies. Only 15 states in 1968 held presidential primaries, and in some of these the preferential part of the primary was not binding on elected delegates. Even if Johnson lost every remaining primary outside the South he was likely to command the nomination at the August convention in Chicago. But the nomination might be almost worthless, and the political fight required to obtain it would drain energies he needed to conduct the war, which had now become an obsession. On the evening of Sunday, March 31, facing almost certain and probably humiliating defeat by McCarthy in the Wisconsin primary two days later, Johnson ended a television address defending his administration with a surprise announcement: he had concluded that he "should not permit the Presidency to become involved in the partisan divisions that are developing in this political year," and therefore he would "not accept the nomination of my party for another term as your President. . . ."[7]

McCarthy commented that Johnson had been unable to "stand up against five million college kids just shouting for peace. . . ." There was some truth to McCarthy's claim. Polls showed, however, that while persons who voted for McCarthy in New Hampshire generally criticized Johnson's conduct of the war, more were critical from a hawkish perspective than from a dovish one. Many, in fact, believed that McCarthy favored stepping up the war. In November, 18 percent of those who had backed McCarthy in the primaries ended up voting for the segregationist third-party candidate, George Wallace.[8]

Five days after Johnson's withdrawal, Martin Luther King, Jr., 39 years old, was assassinated in Memphis by a white racist. Blacks, many of whom reacted to King's murder as a deliberate blow delivered by the white power structure against all their hopes, rioted in major cities. Mobs stormed through the streets of Washington within a few blocks of the White House. There was a widespread sense that the nation was rocketing out of control, approaching some kind of apocalypse.

Not only was the Democratic party divided between hawks and doves. The doves were split among themselves between those supporting McCarthy, who had taken up the fight for their cause when it seemed hopeless, and those backing

Kennedy, whom they judged to have a more realistic chance to win the presidency and end the war.

On April 27 Vice President Humphrey joined the race, declaring himself, with stunning misjudgment of the public's mood, as the candidate of the "politics of joy." Humphrey would have Johnson's blessing and would represent the cause of cold-war liberalism—the cause, as he fairly pointed out, that had been launched by Truman and carried on by John Kennedy. Though Humphrey's entry came too late for him to file in any primaries, his candidacy was identified with a number of state "favorite sons" who had been surrogates for Johnson.

In the first test on the redrawn field, the Indiana primary at the beginning of May, Kennedy won 42 percent, to 31 percent for Indiana's Governor Roger Branigan, backed by the state's Democratic machine and regarded as a stand-in for Humphrey, and 27 percent for McCarthy. In the Oregon primary at the end of May, McCarthy, gathering support from middle-class liberals who did not share the enchantment of working-class Catholics, blacks, and eastern intellectuals with Robert Kennedy, outpolled Kennedy 44 percent to 38—the first time, it was said, a Kennedy had ever lost an election.

As Oregon had set up the importance of California for the Republicans in 1964, so now it raised the stakes of the California primary, one week later, for the Democrats. Kennedy and McCarthy campaigned across the state, Kennedy hitting raw nerves of emotion among massive crowds of anti-war protesters, blacks, and Hispanics, and McCarthy delivering sarcastic taunts. Kennedy won, narrowly but solidly, receiving 46 percent of the vote to 42 percent for McCarthy. An unpledged delegation identified with Humphrey attracted only 12 percent.

Leaving the ballroom of the Ambassador Hotel in Los Angeles, where he had claimed victory before a deliriously celebrating crowd, Kennedy was shot by an Arab immigrant who believed that killing another Kennedy would somehow strike a blow against Zionism. The nation, which had reacted to the assassination of King with grief and anger mixed with some fear after the riots started, responded to this latest tragedy with emotional numbness covering bewilderment and horror. It seemed, the novelist John Updike wrote, that "God had taken away his blessing from the United States."

It became almost an article of faith among Kennedy loyalists, and more generally among liberal doves, that if Robert Kennedy had lived he would surely have won the nomination. Political scientists and commentators who have studied the question have generally concluded that the Democratic convention as constituted in 1968 would probably have nominated Humphrey even if Kennedy had been alive as an alternative. The South backed Humphrey, believing him a hawk, and the machines and unions, it is argued, would have produced enough additional delegates to put him across. The defeat of the platform plank calling for the end of the bombing in Vietnam proposed by the doves, by a vote of 1,041¼ in favor to 1,567¾ against, is offered as proof that forces loyal to the administration controlled the convention. A study by a team of British journalists at the time cited

Max Weber: "As a rule, the party organization easily succeeds in . . . castration of charisma."[9]

This analysis seems to me to underestimate the potential effects of personality and emotional momentum in so loosely structured an institution as the national party convention was in 1968. (Max Weber never attended an American political convention.) Even with Kennedy absent, the Chicago convention hovered on the brink of disintegration. Two state delegations proposed during the presidential nominating roll call that the convention recess and reconvene in another city after tempers had cooled. If Kennedy had been present, with his own power to inspire and with the magical properties of the Kennedy legacy, he would in my judgment have overwhelmed the ramparts raised against him, as unstoppably as Bryan had broken through the outriders of the Cleveland administration at the Democratic convention in 1896, or as Willkie overcame the Republican regulars in 1940. Besides possessing personal charisma, Kennedy was a bridge between the amateur Democrats of the peace movement and the professional politicians who, with their allies in the unions, comprised the regular wing of the Democratic party. Party regulars might have doubts about some of the policies that Kennedy advocated and might resent his attacking an incumbent Democratic President, but they liked him—liked his Catholicism, liked his bare-knuckles style of politics, and liked him better than Johnson, if it came to that, who often had stood against them in the past.[10]

Eugene McCarthy, though a Catholic, had none of these advantages. He reminded the regulars of the hypocritical reformers who chipped away at their political structures, of the sophisticated intellectuals who sneered at their religious and social values, of the disheveled anti-war protesters who scorned their patriotism. Mayor Daley and the Democratic bosses of Pennsylvania, New Jersey, and Ohio might in the end have gone for Robert Kennedy, particularly if they believed him a winner. But they would not have dreamed of going for McCarthy.

The Chicago convention, held in the Stockyards Arena, close by the Chicago slaughterhouses, was chaotic and at times lapsed into physical violence. Lyndon Johnson stayed in Washington, recognizing that if he appeared at the convention he was sure to be booed by about one-third of the delegates and might set off a riot on the floor. While the convention met, anti-war protesters engaged in violent demonstrations in downtown Chicago and were ruthlessly repressed by club-swinging Chicago police. Humphrey maneuvered desperately to put some distance between himself and Johnson's Vietnam policy. But he remained intimidated by Johnson's glowering oversight from the White House and by the knowledge that if the President gave the word the Texas delegation, led by Governor John Connally, and other southern delegations would desert him, leaving him with less than a majority. The image of Mayor Daley shaking his fist and shouting epithets from the floor at Senator Abraham Ribicoff of Connecticut, who had complained from the podium of "gestapo tactics in the streets of Chicago," was fixed symbolically in the minds of millions of television viewers.[11]

Humphrey was nominated by more than a two-to-one majority. But the party was in a shambles. On the last night of the convention the Chicago machine packed the galleries with city and county employees who cheered Daley more lustily than they applauded Humphrey. Later that night Chicago police raided McCarthy's headquarters in a downtown hotel and beat protesting volunteers—apparently just to show who was boss.[12]

A conviction took hold among the protesters in the streets, spreading to many activists within the Democratic party, that Humphrey had somehow "stolen" the nomination. The nominating process, it was argued, had been rigged to frustrate the will of a majority of Democrats. In some states, the defeated doves pointed out, delegates were picked by caucuses composed of party officers elected several years before the convention. In states with open primaries, like Wisconsin, Republicans could participate in primaries to select Democratic delegates. Some states with relatively strong machines, like Pennsylvania, listed candidates for delegate on the ballot without any indication of their presidential preference. Racial discrimination in the South still kept the proportion of black delegates well below the blacks' 11 percent of the national population, let alone their much larger share of the normal Democratic electorate. At the 1968 Democratic convention 6 percent of the delegates were black (compared to 2 percent at the Republican convention). The unit rule, under which a state's entire vote was given to the candidate supported by a majority of its delegates, which was followed by several southern states including Texas, was said to be inherently undemocratic.[13]

Bowing to pressure for reform of the nominating process, the convention voted to abolish the unit rule and to establish a commission charged with developing a delegate selection process for future conventions that would require state parties to make "all feasible efforts . . . to assure that delegates are elected through party primary, convention, or committee procedures open to public participation within the calendar year of the national convention." From this commission, chaired first by Senator George McGovern of South Dakota, and then by Representative Donald Fraser of Minnesota, was to flow a set of regulations which, when approved by the Democratic National Committee in 1971, would fundamentally alter the system for choosing presidential candidates by both parties and would contribute to enormous institutional changes in the parties themselves.[14]

THE CLUB MOVEMENT

In the November election, Humphrey, though his vote was down sharply from that received by Johnson in 1964, ran a much closer race than most people had expected against Richard Nixon, whom the Republicans had nominated a second time, and Governor George Wallace of Alabama, the candidate of the segregationist American Independent party. In the end, Nixon eked out a narrow plurality in the popular vote of 43.4 percent to 42.7 percent for Humphrey and a bit less than

14 percent for Wallace. Humphrey's defeat, by however small a margin, gave further impetus to groups in the Democratic party that had been working for some time to achieve basic changes in the party's internal structure and governance.

In the years after the Second World War groups of what James Q. Wilson has called "amateur Democrats" had set out in various parts of the country, mainly in big cities and college towns, to win control of local Democratic parties. In some places, these groups had organized themselves into political clubs, modeled in some ways on the neighborhood clubs maintained by the old city machines but with distinctly different objectives.

Wilson's classic study of the club movements in Los Angeles, New York, and Chicago, published in 1962, found that clubs operated by amateur Democrats in those cities were " 'purposive' organizations" in which people were active "because of the goals they feel the clubs serve rather than from any hope of material gain or because they enjoy the sociability the clubs provide." They differed in this respect from the older machine clubs, which existed first of all to acquire government jobs and favors for their members, and second to provide occasions of beer-drinking, card-playing social fellowship.[15]

The amateur clubs were devoted to promoting liberal causes. "We have to have these issues to get us to work," a club leader in California told Wilson. "We're volunteers. We have to have the feeling we are working for a cause in which we believe in order to work at all." Besides supporting liberal programmatic goals, the amateurs viewed broadening the means for democratic participation in government as an end in itself. "We plug the democratic process," said a leader of one of the Manhattan reform clubs. "This is the key part of the whole thing. Our goal is to be democratic." The Lexington Club in New York, one of the most successful reform clubs, announced on the first page of its brochure: "Basically we believe in the desirability of widespread participation in the Democratic Party. We assume that people are fundamentally good and consequently both government and politics will improve as more and more people understand and participate."[16]

The principal obstacle to participation was seen to be the hierarchically structured politics maintained by the bosses, whether old-style like Richard Daley and Carmine DeSapio, or new-style like Jesse Unruh, the speaker of the California assembly who had built a statewide machine based on money raised from business and other interest groups. "I see reform politics as a life-or-death war with the regular organization," said a leader of the Village Independent Democrats in Manhattan. "Any half-way measures are no good. . . . There can be no compromise and we cannot be unprincipled."[17]

In the late 1960s, though amateur Democrats were drawn heavily into the movement to end the Vietnam War, they did not give up their pursuit of participatory democracy as a separate and essential goal. Belief that Humphrey had been nominated through an undemocratic selection process in 1968 reinforced their determination to take control of the Democratic party away from professional politicians and place it in the hands of "the people," who they assumed, being "fundamentally good," would look for leadership to people like themselves.

A NEW NOMINATING SYSTEM

The McGovern-Fraser commission that framed the new regulations for selecting delegates to the Democratic national convention, adopted by the DNC in 1971, was dominated by leaders, including McGovern and Fraser, who shared the ideological orientation of the amateur Democrats. Not surprisingly, therefore, the commission went far beyond its mandate to make the selection process more open to public participation and prescribed rules that had the effect of greatly limiting the involvement of party organizations or even elected officeholders in the system.[18]

There are at least two views of what is meant by democratic representation. In one view, democratic representation occurs when citizens elect whatever representatives they like on the basis of some majoritarian principle. In the other, representation, to be truly democratic, must reflect proportionately the distribution of groups within the general population by such categories as race, sex, age, and income. To achieve representation that is democratic in the second sense, it may be necessary to adopt procedures that produce results different from those that would result from elections that are representative in the first sense.

The rules formulated by the McGovern-Fraser commission were based on the second view of representation. The new rules required that each state party should take "affirmative steps" before the 1972 Democratic convention to produce delegations including blacks, women, and young people in "reasonable relationship to the group's presence in the population of the state." In order to minimize the role of party organizations in the selection process, no more than 10 percent of a state's delegation were to be chosen by party committees. For future conventions, selection by party committees was to be eliminated entirely. The effect of this rule, Byron Shafer has pointed out, was to prohibit the "party caucus" system of delegate selection, under which the process began with a caucus of local party officials, "the oldest and most widely used delegate selection institution in American history."[19]

Candidates for delegate were required to indicate their preference for the presidential nomination or label themselves "uncommitted"—thereby also eliminating the traditional practice in New York and Pennsylvania of allowing candidates for delegate to appear on the ballot without signifying their presidential intentions. Systems of delegate selection were effectively limited to the "participatory convention," under which first-stage participation was open to all party members who cared to attend, and the "candidate primary," under which voters were able to choose, either directly or through designated delegates, among candidates for the presidential nomination.

The McGovern-Fraser commission was the first of a series of such rule-making bodies established by the Democratic party that over the next twelve years sought to move the national convention and the party further in the direction of participatory democracy. The Mikulski commission, chaired by Representative Barbara Mikulski of Maryland, in 1973 recommended that any presidential candidate receiving as much as 10 percent of primary or convention votes in any district should receive a proportionate share of the delegates. (The California winner-take-all state primary had already been prohibited by the 1972 convention.) The DNC adopted this recommendation, though with the threshold raised to 15 percent. "Loophole primaries" were permitted in states like New York, Pennsylvania, Illinois, and Ohio, where delegates were chosen directly by voters at the district level. In such cases the Mikulski commission recommended only that all candidates for delegate be clearly identified with a presidential preference. All delegates elected from a given district could therefore be committed to a single presidential candidate.[20]

The Winograd commission, chaired by Michigan state chairman Morley Winograd, in 1978 recommended that each state party "adopt specific goals and timetables" to carry out its affirmative action program and specified women, blacks, Hispanics, and Native Americans as objects "of remedial action to overcome the effects of past discrimination." The DNC went even further and flatly ordered that each state delegation should include an equal number of men and women. Another rule change recommended by the Winograd commission prohibited the open primary for delegate selection required by election laws in such states as Wisconsin and Michigan. When the state of Wisconsin challenged this prohibition, the Supreme Court in 1981 ruled it valid, declaring the precedence of national party rules over state election laws.[21]

These changes in Democratic party rules profoundly altered the process for nominating presidential candidates, sometimes in ways not intended or foreseen by their framers. Many state parties that formerly had selected delegates through caucuses or conventions found the affirmative action requirements so difficult to meet that they switched to choosing delegates through primaries. The number of state primaries rose from 16 in 1960, choosing 27 percent of all delegates, to 32 in 1980, electing 71 percent of delegates. Presidential candidates found it necessary to win the favor of ideological or special-interest activists who were able to turn out voters in primaries or pack the remaining caucuses. Television exposure, paid and free, in the primary states became much more important.

Imposition of affirmative action requirements in the Democratic party helped give rise to special-interest caucuses, representing, among others, feminists, blacks, Hispanics, liberal activists, and homosexuals. Many delegates identified their interests with one or more of these caucuses rather than with their state delegations. The authority of state and local party leaders was further eroded by the requirement that delegates be aligned with presidential candidates. Delegates elected on a candidate's slate naturally were more responsive to the candidate or his managers than to their party's state or local leaders.

What remained of Democratic machines in cities like Philadelphia and Cleveland did what they could to retain control of some delegates while complying with the new rules. The Chicago machine, in contrast, in 1972 put together its slate of delegates, headed by Mayor Daley, as though nothing had happened. This slate, duly elected in the the Illinois primary, was challenged at the 1972 convention by a group of Chicago insurgent reformers on the ground that it did not meet the McGovern–Fraser guidelines. The organization slate, composed of leaders of the nation's most politically effective Democratic machine, was expelled from the convention. When some of the regulars sued the insurgents whom the convention had put in their place, the Supreme Court in 1975 upheld the power of the convention to seat or unseat delegates. "The convention," the Court held, "serves the pervasive national interest in the selection of candidates for national offices and this national interest is greater than any interest of any individual state."[22]

The marked increase of state primaries and the strengthened power of the campaign organization of the presidential candidate entering the convention with the nomination locked up practically eliminated the role of the national convention as a genuine decision-making body. Under the new rules, nominations have usually been decided in the primaries, and the convention has become mainly a television spectacular for the winning candidate. By 1988 the television networks had begun to lose interest in the conventions and greatly reduced the air time allotted to them, so that even this function was being lost.

The change in rules has certainly led to many more people being involved, through primaries or caucuses, in the selection of presidential nominees. The process of picking national convention delegates officially begins, at least for the Democrats, in the year of the convention. National conventions are more demographically representative of party electorates. At the Democratic national convention in 1996, 57 percent of the delegates were women, while at the Republican convention 39 percent were women. Democratic delegates were 21 percent black (almost twice the share of blacks in the national population but about the same as in the normal Democratic electorate) and 6 percent Hispanic; Republican delegates were 2 percent black (somewhat greater than the black share of the normal Republican electorate) and 2 percent Hispanic.[23]

"COME HOME, AMERICA"

George McGovern made good use of his knowledge of how the new party rules were likely to affect future campaigns in his pursuit of the Democratic presidential nomination in 1972. The front runner for the Democratic nomination at the beginning of 1972, Senator Edmund Muskie of Maine, who had been Humphrey's running mate in 1968, went about organizing his campaign in the old way, lining up support from congressional leaders, machine bosses, and major fundraisers. McGovern, in contrast, assembled an army of grassroots volunteers, amateur Democrats, and anti-war protesters—just the kind of people who would be most valuable in mobilizing support in the increased number of primaries and the remaining caucuses. (McGovern's strategy may have been dictated in part by the fact that he had no chance of getting significant backing from the professionals.) As matters turned out, by the end of the first few primaries in March, Muskie had been virtually eliminated and McGovern was well on his way to the nomination.

McGovern's success grew out of much more than his grasp of the new party rules. His message of opposition to continuation of the Vietnam War in particular and to foreign military involvements in general well suited the anti-war activism that during the late 1960s and early 1970s produced student uprisings and riots on many college campuses and reached a kind of climax in May 1971 when tens of thousands of demonstrators thronged through the streets of Washington with the announced purpose of "shutting down the government for a day" to protest Nixon's order to pursue Vietcong forces into Cambodia. (McGovern had been a delegate to Henry Wallace's 1948 Progressive party convention in Philadelphia and was in the line of liberal isolationists like Burton Wheeler, Hiram Johnson, and the LaFollettes.)

Beyond that, McGovern's brand of liberalism came closer than any other option available in national politics to expressing the spirit of rebellion among many American youths, particularly students at elite colleges and universities, that in the late 1960s and early 1970s challenged all existing forms of authority, attacked the depersonalizing effects of modern industrial society, and extolled "liberation" from almost any kind of social restraint or norms. (The liberated person, wrote Jerry Rubin, a favorite radical publicist of the period, "can do what he wants whenever he wants to do it.") "Come home, America," the theme of McGovern's acceptance speech after he had won the presidential nomination at the Democratic national convention in Miami Beach, neatly captured the moods of both liberal isolationism and the youth rebellion.

Unfortunately for McGovern, the great majority of Americans in 1972 supported neither liberal isolationism nor the youth rebellion—in fact, viewed the latter with indignation and fear. Nixon's heavily financed campaign for reelection ground smoothly ahead—deterred only slightly by the first and fragmentary reports of the Watergate scandal that two years later was to bring Nixon down. In November, Nixon won 60.7 percent of the popular vote to 37.5 percent for McGovern— an even larger margin than that by which Johnson had defeated Goldwater eight years before.

Like the hard-right conservatives in 1964, the amateur Democrats in 1972 fell far short of winning the presidency for their preferred candidate. But also like the hard-right conservatives, they had no intention of giving up the struggle. They had made an impact on their party that continues to the present day.

CONTEMPORARY PARTIES

18

THE NEW GIANTS

National Party Organizations

DURING MOST OF THE 1970s and 1980s, erosion of support for either party in the electorate continued. This decline was caused by, among other factors: cultural change, a drastic reduction of state and local patronage, the growing role of television as communicator of political information, the increasing power of special-interest groups (both economic and ideological), and rising alienation among many citizens from all aspects of politics.

At the same time, beginning in the late 1970s, national party organizations, both the national party committees and the parties' congressional campaign committees, massively expanded their financial resources, enlarged their staffs, and became more active in campaigns than ever before in history. These highly centralized and bureaucratized national party organizations facilitated rising party unity in Congress during the 1980s and, on the Republican side, helped the Reagan administration achieve many of its policy objectives. Some political commentators even argued that the parties overall were growing stronger rather than weaker.[1]

Few practicing politicians, and few observers close to actual political life, however, believed at the end of the 1980s that the long-term decline of parties had been reversed or even stabilized. The national party organizations, despite their enormous wealth and technical sophistication, had in fact come to pose problems of their own for the underlying health of parties. By moving the direction of parties further and further from grassroots party organizations and party identifiers, and by emphasizing process over substance—trends that continued into the 1990s—they weakened the bonds of emotion and self-interest that formerly attracted most voters to one major party or the other. Without the support produced by such ties, the national party organizations themselves can hardly continue to prosper.

THE WAKE OF WATERGATE

Richard Nixon and the Republican party had little time to enjoy the fruits of their landslide victory in 1972. Within less than two years, revelations of the Watergate scandal and other abuses of executive power by the administration forced Nixon to resign on the verge of impeachment. Ten months before Nixon's resignation, Vice President Spiro Agnew, facing unrelated charges of bribery, had also left office. In the 1974 midterm elections the Republicans lost 48 seats in the House and 5 in the Senate.

Former House Minority Leader Gerald Ford of Michigan, whom Nixon had named to take Agnew's place, succeeded to the presidency in August 1974. Given the cloud of scandal that still hung over the Republican party and the painful effects of the severe 1975–76 economic recession, Ford made a surprisingly close race of his bid for election to a full term in 1976. The Democrats, still divided by intra-party quarrels over the Vietnam War (concluded by American withdrawal from South Vietnam in 1975) and civil rights, turned to a candidate for President who at the beginning of 1976 was almost unknown to the public or for that matter to most Democratic politicians: former Governor Jimmy Carter of Georgia.

Carter, in the week after his nomination by the Democrats in July, led Ford in the Gallup poll by 33 percentage points. As the fall campaign progressed, how-ever, many voters seemed to develop uneasiness over Carter's qualifications for the presidency. Ford's insistence that inflation was the number-one economic evil appeared to gain acceptance among much of the public. Ford, David Broder said after the election, "won the argument but lost the election."[2]

In the end, the continuing effects of the recession and the memory of Water-gate, combined with the still substantial lead held by the Democrats in party iden-tification among the electorate, carried Carter to victory. Carter won majorities of 50.1 percent in the popular vote and 297 to 240 in the electoral college.

The Democrats returned to united control of the federal government. The Republicans remained distant minorities in both the House and the Senate. Voters overwhelmingly indicated preference for the Democratic party in national polls. Once more there was talk that the Republican party might soon join the Federal-ists and the Whigs.

A MANAGERIAL REVOLUTION

After Ford's defeat, William Brock, who had just lost his own race for reelection to the Senate from Tennessee, was chosen Republican national chairman. Like Ray Bliss in the 1960s, Brock came in at a nadir in Republican fortunes. Some conser-vative activists were arguing that what conservatives needed was an entirely new national party. Others, less extreme, proposed that the Republican party at least change its name to escape identification with such political millstones as the Depres-sion, "country club Republicans," and Watergate. Rejecting such pessimistic counsel, Brock set out to rejuvenate the RNC.

The challenge facing Brock was even more difficult than that which had con-fronted Bliss. The campaign finance reform act of 1974, passed in response to the fundraising scandals associated with Watergate, placed narrow limits on the amounts an individual could contribute to candidates or parties. The practice of relying on a relatively few wealthy contributors (the so-called fat cats), which Nixon's fundraisers had followed in 1968 and 1972, was no longer possible. Some other means had to be found to finance party operations.

Brock's most critical decision was made during his first month as chairman in 1977. Funds not needed for current operating expenses, he determined, would be invested in a direct-mail program, much more extensive than those the RNC had used off and on since the 1950s, to build a mass base of small contributors. Some Republican leaders argued that available funds should be spent to help candidates who were planning races in the 1978 midterm elections. The decision, Brock later said, was an easy one: "There really was no other way to build an effective national party."[3]

Brock's direct-mail program was a huge success. Expenditure of $8 million in the 1977–78 cycle brought a return of $25 million—a net of $17 million. In the 1979–80 cycle, expenditure of $12 million brought $54 million—a stunning net of $42 million. After three years of operation, the overhead of the direct-mail program was, according to Xandra Kayden, "at least ten percent cheaper than all other forms of raising money."[4]

With the increased funds at his disposal, Brock expanded some of the outreach programs that had been started by Bliss and began other operations that carried the RNC into areas never before entered by a national party. In order to show the party's interest in ideas and to generate programmatic proposals that might be politically useful, Brock started publication of *Commonsense*, a moderately intellectual quarterly dealing with public policy issues. At a more popular level, the RNC published *First Monday*, a monthly magazine devoted to tabloid-style attacks on the Carter administration and the Democrats. Slick television commercials, poking fun at President Carter and House Speaker Thomas P. O'Neill and urging viewers to "vote Republican, for a change," were run nationally under RNC sponsorship.

Brock established a separate division to revive state and local party organizations and to recruit candidates for the state legislatures. Between 1977 and 1980 more than 10,000 Republicans attended campaign seminars sponsored by the local elections division. In some instances, the RNC gave support to preferred candidates in contested primaries—a degree of intervention in local politics that national parties had formerly shunned. In 1980 Brock helped pay the salaries of the executive directors of all 50 Republican state committees, and the RNC gave financial support to more than 4,000 state legislative candidates. "The Republicans," Leon Epstein observed, "have nationalized their party effort by a method analogous to the federal government's grant-in-aid system."[5]

While Brock was building up the financial resources of the RNC, Republican congressional leaders were pursuing similar courses with their campaign committees in the House and Senate: the National Republican Congressional Committee (NRCC) and the National Republican Senatorial Committee (NRSC).

Rodney Smith, finance director of the NRSC most of the time from 1977 through 1986, later explained:

> When I went to work for the senatorial campaign committee in January, 1977, the fund-raising section had only two employees and was operating out of a converted men's room. The fund-raising division was essentially an office to launder money. . . . The big change came as a result of the 1974 law which limited contributions. Before that time, there had been really no limit on contributions and relatively few large contributors could pay for the entire campaign. The new law which set a limit on contributions made it necessary to develop a large number of fairly small contributors.
>
> It was necessary to find new contributors. The best way to do that was through direct mail. We found that the best source of donors was people who had given to Republican candidates and conservative causes in the past. It's something like religious fund-raising. You go back to the same people again and again. These are true believers. It took a lot of research.[6]

A PARTY PRESIDENT

Republican fundraising was given a major lift by the emergence of Ronald Reagan as the front runner for the Republican presidential nomination in 1980. "When Ronald Reagan entered the picture," Rodney Smith recalled, "direct mail fundraising took off like a rocket."

Reagan inherited the support of the groups that had participated in the Goldwater crusade in 1964. By 1980, he had assembled some additional recruits, from whom he gained electoral and intellectual as well as financial backing:

The Religious New Right. White evangelical Protestants, comprising about 20 percent of the national electorate, had usually been predominantly Democratic in their politics, partly because they were concentrated in the South but also because they tended to be found at the lower levels of the income scale. In the early 1970s, however, evangelicals, goaded on by popular television preachers like Jerry Falwell and Pat Robertson, became concerned over the trend toward the secularization of American culture, caused in part they believed by Supreme Court decisions such as those prohibiting prayer in the public schools and establishing a constitutional right to abortion. Many evangelicals began voting on the basis of their social values rather than their perceived economic interests—"voting with God instead of voting with the unions," as one later said. In 1976 a majority of white evangelicals supported Jimmy Carter, himself a "born again" Christian. But they soon became disenchanted by Carter's failure to advance their social agenda and his backing of such liberal proposals as the women's Equal Rights Amendment (ERA). In 1980, evangelicals were at first divided among a number of conservative presidential candidates. But by early spring almost all were enthusiastically supporting Reagan. Falwell promised that he would back Reagan "even if he has the devil himself running with him" (by which he apparently meant George Bush).[7]

Right-to-Life Catholics. The overwhelming majority of American Catholics, comprising in 1980 about one-fourth the national population, had supported the Democratic party since the days of Thomas Jefferson and Andrew Jackson. During the 1960s and 1970s a substantial share of Catholics, particularly among the middle class, had developed conservative attitudes on economic and foreign policy issues. But the real break from the Democratic party for many Catholics came over the abortion issue that grew out of the 1973 Supreme Court ruling essentially establishing a constitutional right to abortion. The 1980 Democratic platform supported legalized abortion. The Republican platform, in contrast, endorsed "a constitutional amendment to restore protection of the right to life for unborn children." Polls showed that about 10 percent of Catholics were voting on the abortion issue. Most of these flocked to the support of Ronald Reagan. But the issue went deeper. The fundamental difference on abortion between the teaching of the Catholic church and the position of the Democratic party undermined the emotional bond of almost tribal loyalty that most Catholics had felt toward the Democrats. The growing share of Catholics who were becoming conservative on economic and foreign policy issues now felt perfectly free to cast Republican ballots.[8]

Neo-conservatives. In the later 1960s a group of former liberal or socialist intellectuals, including such luminaries as Irving Kristol, Norman Podhoretz, Jeane Kirkpatrick, James Q. Wilson, Ben Wattenberg, and Michael Novak, had launched a critique of many aspects of American liberalism. Some of the neo-conservatives were Jews, and their sense that a part of liberalism was distancing itself from support for Israel contributed to their ideological shift. The McGovern episode in the Democratic party and liberalism's abandonment of liberal hawks like Hubert Humphrey and Senator Henry ("Scoop") Jackson of Washington also shocked and dismayed many liberals who were militant anti-Communists. Some of the neo-conservatives continued to think of themselves as Democrats, and many felt uncomfortable allying themselves with religious right groups like the Moral Majority or the more strident hard-right politicians. But as ideological division sharpened at the beginning of the 1980s, they found themselves more and more on the conservative side. Early in 1980 some neo-conservatives supported Bush for the Republican presidential nomination. But by the time of the Republican national convention in July, most had come to regard Reagan as at least the lesser evil against Carter.

The Supply-Siders. During the late 1970s a few conservative economists, among whom Arthur Laffer was the most visible, promulgated the "supply side" doctrine that cutting taxes was the sure route to economic prosperity. This view was taken up by Representative Jack Kemp, Republican of Buffalo, and given journalistic voice by the editorial page of the *Wall Street Journal*. Conservatives of all kinds had always favored holding down or cutting taxes. But traditional conservatives, like Ford, Bush (who while running for the Republican presidential nomination in 1980 labeled the supply-side theory "voodoo economics"), and Senator Bob Dole of Kansas, had maintained that taxes could safely be cut only after reductions had been made in government spending. Otherwise, they warned, the federal budget would fall more deeply into deficit, another conservative shibboleth. This caution, some younger conservatives complained, made conservatism seem Scrooge-like and gave liberals the advantage of being associated with the expansion of popular social programs. The supply-siders argued that the real key to economic stability was not so much a balanced federal budget as the restoration of a secure currency based on gold (or some equivalent commodity). Taxes, therefore, could safely be lowered without too much concern over the size of the federal deficit. Reagan, after initial skepticism, had by the beginning of 1980 fully accepted the supply-side theory and espoused it in his campaign.

In addition to those drawn to the Reagan coalition by some aspect of hard-right conservatism, many stalwart, moderate, and even progressive Republicans joined up, particularly after Reagan's victory over Bush in the New Hampshire primary in February. They were attracted in part by the conviction that Reagan offered the best hope of restoring values and governmental approaches derived from the republican tradition to national power, and in part by the prospect of sharing the tangible rewards of victory if he was elected President.

Unlike some hard-right conservatives, Reagan was a fiercely committed Republican party man. As governor of California from 1966 through 1972, he had worked to build up the state Republican party. He had campaigned conscientiously for moderate and even progressive Republican candidates for state office as well as for fellow hard-right conservatives, thereby achieving a relatively cohesive party in a state where parties were traditionally weak.

After his nomination for President at the Republican convention in Detroit, Reagan identified his candidacy closely with Republicans of all stripes running for congressional and state offices. In September he posed on the steps of the national capitol in Washington with scores of Republican congressional candidates to symbolize his association with the entire party ticket.

The cultural groups that formed Reagan's winning coalition in November over Carter and John Anderson, the independent third-party candidate, are shown in Figure 18–1. The largest segment was made up of white mainline Protestants (including Methodists, Presbyterians, Lutherans, Episcopalians, and some smaller denominations), who, outside the South, had provided the base of the Republican party since the Civil War. To this Reagan added 60 percent of white evangelicals (Baptists and some smaller fundamentalist denominations), many of whom had sup-

Figure 18–1   Voting in the 1980 presidential election, by ethnic/religious groups

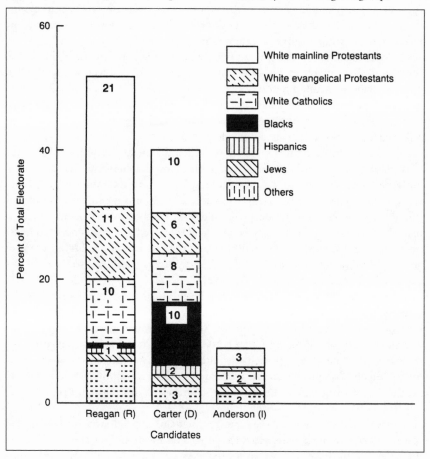

Source: American National Election Study, University of Michigan, Ann Arbor, 1980

ported Carter in 1976; and a little more than 50 percent of white Catholics, who gave majority support to a Republican candidate for President for only the second time in history. (The first time had been for Nixon against George McGovern in 1972.) Jews gave a small plurality to Carter over Reagan, but they defected to Anderson in sufficient numbers to deny a majority of their vote to the Democratic candidate for President for the first time since 1924. Blacks and Hispanics remained loyal to the New Deal coalition—though the majority among Hispanics was smaller than in earlier elections.

Even more sensational than Reagan's election as President, which by the end of the fall campaign was expected, was the Republican gain of 12 seats in the Senate, giving the Republicans control of that body for the first time since 1954. The Republicans also gained 35 seats in the House. That left them still 51 seats behind the Democrats, but they were in a position to pick off conservative or moderate Democrats to form a majority on some issues.

Carter had been weakened by a homespun presidential style that did not wear well with a majority of the electorate, and even more by the effects of double-digit inflation and anger among voters over the prolonged captivity of 52 American hostages in Iran. His unpopularity helped pull down other Democrats. The question remained whether the Republican victory had been a flash in the pan or reflected a long-term partisan and ideological shift.

As President, Reagan was swiftly rewarded for the attention he had devoted to Republican congressional candidates. With almost united Republican support in both the House and the Senate, plus backing from some conservative Democrats, Reagan during his first year in office was able to push through most of the administration's program calling for deep cuts in personal and corporate income tax rates, massive expansion of the military budget, and some reduction in federal domestic spending. Reagan and his advisers decided to put off delivering on his fourth major governmental pledge, moving the federal budget toward balance—a decision that had dire consequences for the fiscal future.

Bill Brock, who had made some enemies among the Reaganites because of his evenhandedness during the 1980 primary season, left the RNC to join the administration as chief foreign-trade negotiator. Some of the innovative programs he had introduced were abandoned. But the RNC's new leadership, closely supervised by the Reagan White House, particularly chief of staff James Baker, invested heavily in "high tech" computer technology. Money continued to flow in and the RNC played an even larger part in the 1982 midterm election campaign than it had in 1980.[9]

Figure 18–2 shows the spectacular growth of expenditures by Republican national party committees reported to the Federal Election Commission (FEC) in the early 1980s. (Expenditures on federal elections by state and local party committees are included in the totals, because the national party committees have in recent years encouraged some of their regular contributors to give directly to state and local parties, which are not subject to some of the restrictions federal law places on spending by national party committees.) Total Republican spending peaked in 1982 and then declined, but in 1988 it was still far above its 1978 level. Expenditures by Republican committees from 1977 to 1988 rose by more than twice the rate of inflation.[10]

After Reagan's election in 1980 the National Republican Congressional Committee (NRCC) attracted a huge increase in contributions to support its drive to win Republican control of the House in 1982. After that effort failed, its financial support declined. The National Republican Senatorial Committee (NRSC) suffered a similar, though less severe, falloff after the Republicans lost control of the Senate in 1986.

Figure 18–2 Expenditures by Republican party committees on federal elections, 1977–1988

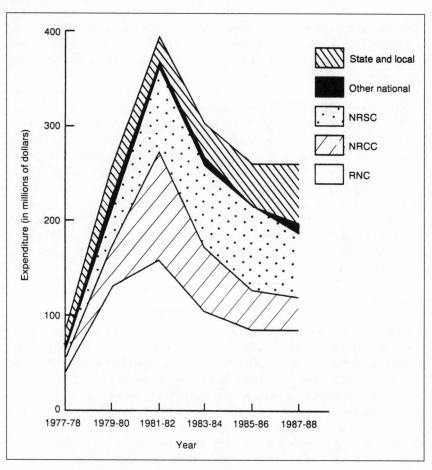

Source: Federal Election Commission

THE DEMOCRATS RESPOND

Republican party committees at the national level continued throughout the 1980s to hold a wide lead in staff and financial resources over their Democratic counterparts. But the relative size of this margin by the end of Reagan's second term was greatly reduced from what it had been ten years before. In the 1979–80 election cycle Republican committees outspent their Democratic counterparts by a ratio of 4.6 to 1. In 1987–88, though the Republicans' advantage in dollars was even larger, their relative edge was down to 2.1 to 1.[11]

Thoughtful Democrats had recognized by 1980 that the Republicans were getting far ahead of them in national fundraising and modern campaign technology. So long as many more voters regarded themselves as Democrats than as Republicans, the Republicans' financial and technological advantages did not seem particularly threatening. But after 1980, when the gap between the parties' popular support levels began to close, the Republicans' superiority in national organization became increasingly critical.

When Charles Manatt, a successful southern California lawyer with a long record of experience in Democratic politics, became chairman of the DNC in 1981, he found the national party organization in tatters. "Entering the DNC at that time," Lynn Cutler, who came in with Manatt as vice-chair, later recalled, "was like the fall of Saigon. Phones had been disconnected. Chairs literally were thrown on the floor."[12] The Democrats had lost three of the last four presidential elections, and now for the first time in more than a quarter-century they had lost control of the Senate as well.

Manatt set out as best he could to modernize the Democrats' national machinery, frankly copying some of the innovations Brock had introduced at the RNC. In 1981 he launched a direct-mail campaign aimed at broadening the party's base for fundraising. The national committee's huge debt, dating back to 1968, was refinanced, freeing up most current receipts for use on current operations. Funds taken in by national Democratic organizations gradually rose (Figure 18–3).

The DNC political division, led after 1981 by Ann Lewis, was reorganized and expanded. In 1982 the DNC invested seed money and assigned a consultant to build the institutional resources of the New Mexico state Democratic party. "Some of the state Democratic candidates in New Mexico," Brian Lunde, executive director of the DNC, recalled, "at first did not want to buy in. They felt it would interfere with their ability to control their own destinies. But they finally agreed to conduct a common mass mailing campaign, which resulted in a widespread victory for the entire Democratic ticket." In a single year this project helped the New Mexico party expand its budget by more than 600 percent. By 1984 similar party-building programs had been launched in 18 additional states.[13]

The Democratic Senatorial Campaign Committee (DSCC) and the Democratic Congressional Campaign Committee (DCCC) made some progress during the 1983–84 cycle toward catching up with their better-financed and more heavily staffed Republican counterparts. The DCCC in particular, under the chairmanship of Representative Tony Coelho of California, became an effective political instrument. Both Democratic campaign committees increased their levels of direct financial assistance to candidates and, more important, persuaded some senior members holding safe seats to share some of their surplus funds with fellow Democrats in close contests.[14]

Coelho steered business political action committees (PACs) eager to ingratiate themselves with the Democrats to races in which the need was greatest. "Tony Coelho," said Representative Barney Frank, Democrat of Massachusetts,

Figure 18–3 Expenditures by Democratic party committees on federal elections, 1977–1988

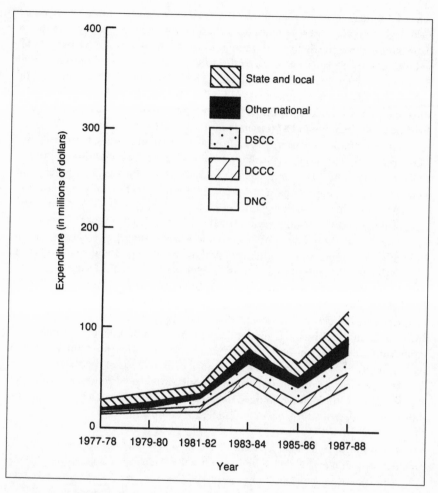

Source: Federal Election Commission

"was very good at explaining the facts of life to the PACs: if you want to talk to us later, you had better help us now. He also made clear that we did not expect them to contribute to Republican challengers where Democratic incumbents were in trouble." Coelho reportedly visited more than a hundred business and trade association PACs, making three points: "Not all Democrats are anti-business; Democrats will retain control of the House for the remainder of this century; and PACs who side with the Republicans shall pay a political price for doing so."[15]

TOO MUCH MONEY?

Since 1980 national party committees have used only a small portion of the money they have raised for direct contributions to candidates or for so-called coordinated expenditures through which party committees pay for services made available to individual House or Senate campaigns. In the 1985–86 election cycle, for example, the three major Republican committees disbursed $212 million, of which only $2.6 million went for direct contributions and $14 million for coordinated expenditures. The three major Democratic committees spent $44 million, of which $1.2 million went for direct contributions and $7.9 million for coordinated expenditures.[16]

The reason, or part of the reason, national party committees do not use more of their money for candidate contributions or coordinated expenditures is that they are restricted by the 1974 campaign finance law, which, through complicated formulas, limits the amounts parties can contribute or spend directly on individual races. Most committees in both parties in recent years have "maxed out" on expenditures for candidates whom they regarded as being in truly competitive races.

The rest of the money goes for a wide variety of purposes. These include: gathering and computerizing voter lists, polling, recruiting candidates, conducting campaign schools for candidates and their managers, researching issues, "generic" national advertising (promoting the party as a whole and therefore not counted as contributions to individual candidates), preparing media packages to be sold at cost or given as in-kind contributions to candidates, paying fees to campaign consultants, meeting the substantial administrative cost of running the committees, and contributing to state and local parties. Finally, a great deal of the money raised by national party committees is used to pay the enormous costs of fundraising itself.[17]

By 1986 the national organizations of both parties had acquired extensive and sophisticated technological resources. Thomas Hofeller, director of the RNC computer center, described the operation under his command:

> Our computer, which now contains 60 million names, is the biggest in the country in political use, We fill it with voter lists that we obtain from the states. In some cases we buy the lists from state election bureaus. In other cases, we take them from paper napkins maintained by county clerks. . . . Computer technology has been available since the late 60s and the early 70s, but the political parties only gradually became aware of its potentialities. When the Republican party finally began to use computers on a large scale in the late 1970s, that represented a quantum leap in political campaign techniques. We use computers for all kinds of purposes: for mailings, for phone banks, for demographic research, to research the opposition. . . . Parties used to be people oriented, but now they no longer have the people so the computer has to some extent filled the gap.[18]

DNC executive director Brian Lunde explained the role of the national committee in the computer age:

The DNC is a technology center. It is in a position to make maximum use of new developments in campaign technology. The DNC runs guinea pig studies of new forms of technology and the results of these are made available to Democratic candidates throughout the country. The DNC experiments with the new kinds of software.[19]

Some expenditures by party committees which are not counted, or only partly counted, against FEC limits on candidate spending directly benefit individual campaigns. In 1986, for example, Paul Herrnson reports, the NRCC made available media packages worth "nearly $100,000 on the commercial market as in-kind contributions that were valued at $2,000 or less." Under FEC regulations, polls paid for by party committees may be turned over to candidates at sharply depreciating costs as time elapses after the poll is taken—50 percent after 15 days and down to 5 percent after 60 days. This is not much help in relaying results of "tracking polls" on nightly changes in voter opinions, but it gives candidates valuable access to low-cost polling on underlying voter attitudes. Senator Gordon Humphrey of New Hampshire, for example, Herrnson found, "received the results of a statewide poll" commissioned by the NRSC "for under $100 during his 1984 bid for reelection."[20]

How much effect all this spending by national parties has had on election outcomes is difficult to judge. Some of the national party committees now maintain sizable bureaucracies, which seem to bring with them many of the same kind of operational problems and inefficiencies that afflict most large bureaucracies. The committees in addition are burdened by particular handicaps that spring from their political nature. The chief executives of all major party committees are politicians, most of whom have no special training or interest in administration and who regard the chairmanship as a temporary post in a career with larger objectives. Using the chairmanship as a stepping-stone to something else no doubt motivates performance but also may introduce conflicting interests. Turnover of professional staff on most of the committees is frequent, reflecting in part changing committee leadership.

Many of the contributors and some politician clients are critical of the high salaries received by some staff professionals and the large fees paid by the committees to consultants and pollsters. Former Senator Paul Laxalt of Nevada, outgoing general chairman of the national Republican party (a post created by the Reagan White House to oversee the activities of all national Republican party committees), said in 1987: "We've got too much money, we've got way too many political operatives, we've got far too few volunteers. . . . We are substituting contributions and high technology for volunteers in the field." After the Republicans lost control of the Senate in 1986, the NRSC promptly paid bonuses totaling $257,000 to 87 staff members—causing considerable uproar from contributors to the committee's $84 million war chest. "Most of the consultants hired by the RNC," a Republican consultant told Thomas Edsall of the *Washington Post,* "do hardly anything to earn their fees and they get picked up because they know someone."[21]

Most candidates, however, particularly those who have been in close elections, speak highly of the committees' contributions and services. Though the committees sometimes miss participating in races that turn out to be close, they often have been credited with providing crucial assistance in competitive elections. In the first half of the 1980s, when the Republicans' superiority in staff and financial resources was clear, Republican candidates won most of the close congressional elections. In the second half of the decade, in contrast, as the Democratic committees began to catch up, the record of partisan outcomes in close elections was reversed. Candidates often comment with appreciation, and sometimes with awe, on the state-of-the-art television facilities, nightly tracking polls, and computer technology that are made available to them.[22]

PAC POWER

The rise in fundraising and spending by national parties came at the same time as the rapid growth of expenditures by business, labor, and ideological political action committees—the so-called PACs. Though PACs had existed since the 1940s, they were relatively minor providers of campaign funds until after the passage of the post-Watergate campaign finance reforms in the 1970s. The new regulations limited campaign contributions by an individual to $1,000 per candidate for each campaign (primary, general, and in some states runoff primary), and $20,000 to national party committees, per year, up to a total of $25,000 by each individual per calendar year. Large contributions from individuals to candidates or for direct expenditures by campaign committees, on which both parties in the past had largely depended, were thereby practically eliminated. PACs, drawing on small contributions raised by corporations, labor unions, and interest groups, in contrast, were permitted to give $5,000 to candidates for each campaign and $15,000 to party committees, *with no limit on total contributions*. PACs inevitably became major sources of campaign revenue.

The number of PACs increased from 600 in 1974 to more than 4,100 in 1990. In 1979 successful House candidates got 17 percent of their campaign contributions from PACs, and candidates elected to the Senate got 11 percent. In 1986 these shares had risen to 42 percent for the House and 27 percent for the Senate. The steady increase in PAC contributions to Democratic and Republican candidates from 1977 through 1988 is shown in Figure 18–4.[23]

Though about two-thirds of PAC money comes from corporations and trade associations, most of whose leaders are politically conservative, PACs gave more to Democrats than to Republicans until the Republicans won control of Congress in 1994. The reason for this apparent anomaly is that PACs give most of their money to incumbents as the best means of assuring future access to lawmakers. ("I've had people who contribute to my campaigns," a senator told Brooks Jackson of the *Wall Street Journal*, "and they get access; the others get good government.") During the

Figure 18–4   PAC contributions to congressional candidates, 1977–1988

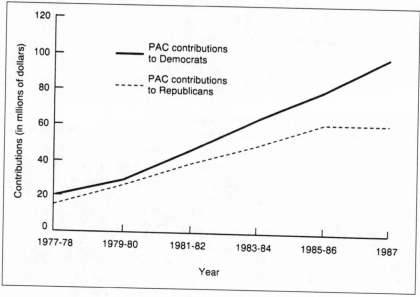

Source: Federal Election Commission

1970s and 1980s there were always more incumbent Democrats than Republicans.[24]

    The effects of PACs on national parties have been mixed. PACs make most of their contributions directly to candidates rather than to party committees and therefore are often cited as a cause of the weakening of parties. "The emergence of PACs," Bill Brock has said, "poses a serious threat to the role of parties." In the view of Robert Strauss, the Washington super-lawyer and political insider, who served as chairman of the DNC from 1972 to 1977, "The availability of PAC money has contributed to the undermining of party discipline."[25]

    Most party committees in Washington, however, maintain close working relationships with PACs. Many PAC paymasters look to party committees for guidance in determining how to distribute whatever money they give to challengers and candidates for open congressional seats. Party committees are usually candid with PACs in appraising their candidates' chances, because, as Tim Hyde, assistant director of the NRSC, said: "There's no point in lying to the PACs about the nature of a race, because the people running the PACs are pretty skillful at detecting what's going on. They're careful about what they do with their dollars."[26]

    Party committees bring candidates to Washington and introduce them to potentially interested PAC directors. The Republican committees utilize their relatively larger staffs to customize presentations by individual candidates to PACs, while the Democrats go in more for mass gatherings at which PAC operatives are encouraged to shop among the candidates. "The Democrats," a PAC operative told Paul Herrnson, "rely on the much larger Cattle Shows, while the Republicans also use the more intimate Dog and Pony Show approach."[27]

RISING PARTY UNITY

The increased activity of national party committees has probably contributed to rising party unity on roll-call vote in Congress, as shown throughout the 1998 session in Figures 18–5 and 18–6. The declining share of southern conservatives among the Democrats in Congress, the falling share of progressive Republicans, and the ideological polarization caused by the Reagan administration have all been factors in boosting congressional party unity. But most political participants and observers also credit the party campaign committees with fostering party cohesion. Senator Richard Lugar of Indiana, who chaired the NRSC in 1983–84, argues that "centralized fund-raising and the campaign support we are able to provide produces heightened camaraderie among Senate Republicans which translates into increased unity on rollcall votes." The late Kirk O'Donnell, an experienced Washington Democratic operative who served for several years in the 1980s as assistant to House Speaker O'Neill, agreed: "When party committees actively help candidates running for office, they naturally are able to exert more influence on them after they are elected." Former Representative Vin Weber of Minnesota, an influential advisor to the Republican leadership, observes: "The NRCC has been of tremendous value in building the party [in the House]. It not only gives support to Republican candidates in elections, but also helps promote party unity once they are elected." And Audrey Sheppard, political director of the DSCC during the 1980s, maintains; "Bringing incumbent [Democratic] senators together to work for the [campaign] committee has helped build party unity and cohesion. These senators are not necessarily pals, but when you put together a road show and take them to a state to raise money, that gives them the experience of working together for the party cause. And that gives them a sense of fellow feeling that carries through later on the Senate floor."[28]

Since the time of William McKinley, an incumbent President has almost always been able to dominate his party's national committee. Some Presidents, like Johnson and Nixon, have chosen for reasons of their own to maintain weak national committees. But others, including Eisenhower and Kennedy and more recently Ronald Reagan and Bill Clinton, have built up the national committee as a political arm of the administration

The Reagan administration regularly used the RNC to promote public and political support for its legislative program, beginning with the 1981 tax cut. Pamela Adkins, director of media advertising for the RNC during Reagan's second term, explained in 1986:

Figure 18–5   Average party unity score in the House, 1972–1998

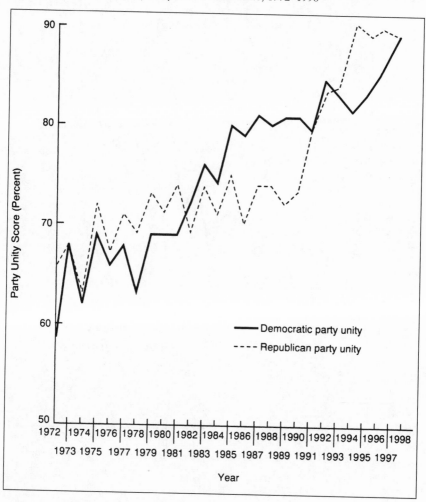

Source: Congressional Quarterly

We view it as a major part of our mission to rally support for the President's position on issues like the Contra vote [then coming up in Congress]. We did this
on the MX [missile] vote, and on the budget vote, and on many others. We produce generic advertising for use in selected media markets. We also provide
Republican spokespersons to speak for the administration position via satellite on
local television channels. Recently we made Jeane Kirkpatrick available for interviews by six stations. We also use personalities like the Vice President and Patrick
Buchanan and Alexander Haig. These interviews are targeted into districts which

Figure 18–6   Average party unity scores in the Senate, 1972–1998

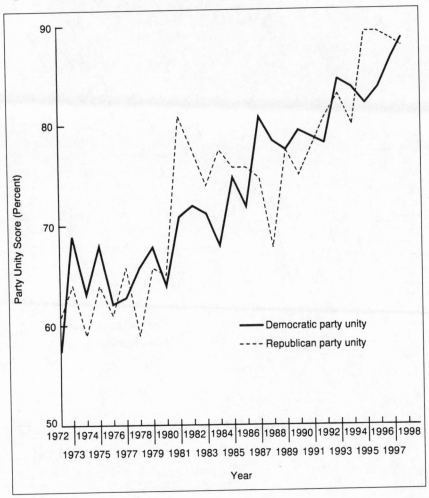

Source: Congressional Quarterly

are critical on any particular vote. More and more we are using targeted advertising for particular districts. That way you can jump right over the Washington news coverage. . . .[29]

When critical votes approached in Congress, the Reagan White House and the RNC called on state party officials to help sway Republican senators and representatives. Washington state Republican chairman Jennifer Dunn (elected to the United States House of Representatives in 1992) said in the spring of 1986:

We are doing everything we can to encourage our House members to vote for aid to the Contras. We are able to direct donations into their campaigns for reelection and there is no question this gives us some help in coming back to them on legislative matters. . . . We [also] generate mail, generate phone calls from around the state to our congressmen.[30]

An incumbent President's influence over his party's congressional campaign committees is of course more limited. The relationship between the White House, the national committee, and the congressional campaign committees is not pyramidal or hierarchical. The congressional committees raise their own funds and may follow somewhat different guiding stars of ideology or personal ambition.

During recent Republican administrations, however, the Republicans were always in the minority in the federal House and usually in the Senate. As a result, Republicans in Congress depended to a great extent on their alignment with the White House for legislative leverage. After 1994, roles were reversed, and congressional Democrats relied on support from the Clinton White House. Presidents, moreover, can be highly effective fundraisers—a task to which Presidents Reagan, Bush, and Clinton devoted much time and energy.[31]

"MORNING IN AMERICA"

In 1984 Ronald Reagan swept easily to a second term over his Democratic opponent, former Vice President Walter Mondale. Reagan amassed 59 percent of the popular vote, the fourth-largest landslide in history, and won all electoral votes except those of Minnesota, Mondale's home state, and the District of Columbia.

The composition of Reagan's victory among cultural groups is shown in Figure 18–7. The traditional Republican base among white mainline Protestants increased only slightly over its 1980 level. But among white evangelicals Reagan's margin soared to 80 percent, and among white Catholics to 59 percent. Jews, who early in 1984 had been drawn to the Republicans by the rise in the Democratic party of Jesse Jackson, whom many Jews regarded as anti-Semitic, were ultimately carried back to the Democrats by concern over the prominence of Falwell and other fundamentalists in the Reagan campaign. Jews gave Mondale about two-thirds of their vote—a fairly small majority by historical standards. Hispanics divided about as they had in 1980. Blacks, now making up 22 percent of the total Democratic vote, remained firmly loyal to the New Deal coalition.

The most important demographic change in the 1984 election was that voters under 30, who had been more Democratic than the rest of the population since polls started to be taken in the 1930s, were now the most Republican age group in the electorate. For the first time in more than 50 years, the Republicans seemed to have a realistic hope of becoming the wave of the future.[32]

James Baker, still at that time White House chief of staff, oversaw direction of

Figure 18–7   Voting in the 1984 presidential election, by ethnic/religious groups

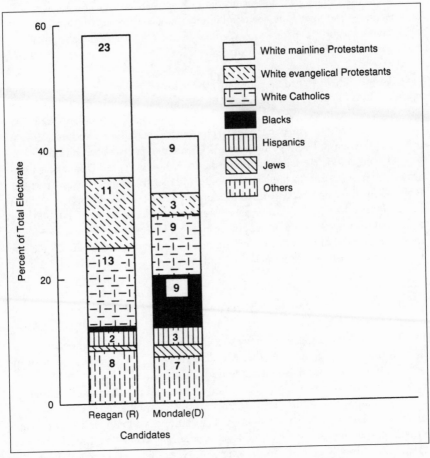

Source: American National Election Study, University of Michigan, Ann Arbor, 1984

the Reagan campaign. A series of slick television commercials, largely devoid of substance, associated the President with the cheerful theme, "Morning in America." The RNC, chaired by Frank Fahrenkopf, former state chairman in Nevada, was assigned responsibility for building up Republican voter registration, to counter Charles Manatt's announced plans for massively increasing Democratic registration, and for turning out the vote on election day.

"The federal campaign finance law," Baker later said, "that makes it possible for the national committee to give money for grassroots organization to state and local parties made it advisable for us to expand the role of the national party organization over what we had done in 1980."[33] (National contributions for "party-building" by state and local organizations—the famous "soft money"—are not counted against limits on spending for national candidates.)

Fahrenkopf concentrated the RNC's efforts on 650 key counties (or, in New England, towns), largely bypassing Republican state organizations. A staff of 40 field operators led by William Lacy, the RNC's political director, supervised local party activities in each of these counties.[34]

In the battle for new registrants, the Republicans scored a clear victory. Registration went up sharply in many areas among groups that were expected to vote Democratic. But in most places those gains were matched or exceeded by new registrants among groups favoring the Republicans. In North Carolina, for example, registration among blacks went up by 179,000, but registration among whites, many of them evangelicals, rose by 308,000. Republicans heavily outnumbered Democrats among new registrants in California and Florida and took the larger share of the 19 percent increase in registration in Texas.[35]

At the start of the 1984 campaign, Reagan had intended to do even more than he had in 1980 to help congressional and state Republican candidates, in hopes of scoring an across-the-board party sweep. But in his first debate with Mondale in early October, the 73-year-old President appeared hazy and uncertain. Though the polls did not waver much, the White House political operatives became frightened and decided to devote almost all their resources to Reagan's reelection. "By the time we got back on track," one of them later said, "it was too late to make an all-out drive for Congress." Perhaps partly as a result, the Republicans actually lost two seats in the Senate and regained a net of only 14 of the 27 seats they had lost in the House in the midterm elections of 1982.

19

STATE PARTIES

Seeking New Roles

BEFORE THE DECLINE OF state and local party organizations began in the 1950s, state parties were roughly classifiable into three main groups. In a belt of older industrial states reaching from New England to Illinois (much of the area covered by the baseball major leagues before expansion), traditional patronage-based party organizations had survived the Progressive Era and continued to operate much as they had in the nineteenth century. The party holding the governorship monopolized the bulk of state patronage, but the party currently out of power also usually controlled a fair number of jobs through the legislature and other state offices. In most of the West, beginning with the upper midwestern states of Michigan, Wisconsin, and Minnesota and extending to the Pacific coast, the progressive reforms had taken hold, most job patronage had been eliminated, and party organizations were typically weak—in some states, such as California, almost to the point of nonexistence. In most of the South and several of the Border states, state politics remained patronage-oriented, but the predominance of the Democratic party had produced a politics of faction rather than of party, and state party organizations were largely irrelevant.

During the 1970s and 1980s many state party organizations in all three groups began moving, for varying reasons, along the road earlier traveled by national party committees toward professionalization of staff, bureaucratization of structure, and functional concentration on fundraising and providing campaign services for candidates.[1]

AN INSTITUTIONAL CRISIS

During the late 1980s and early 1990s I directed a study at the Brookings Institution of representative state party organizations. Our study found that the old patronage-based state machines that used to dominate such states as Pennsylvania, Ohio, and Illinois have almost disappeared. A series of Supreme Court decisions has made old-fashioned patronage systems controlling thousands of non-policy-making government jobholders essentially illegal. In 1976 the Court ruled, in a case involving the Democratic organization of Cook County, Illinois, that government employees cannot be fired on the basis of party affiliation.[2] In 1990, the Court went further and ruled by a 5-to-4 majority, this time against the Illinois state Republican organization, that "party affiliation and support" cannot be considered in filling government jobs "unless party affiliation is an appropriate requirement for the position involved."[3] Since practically all the framers of the Constitution used patronage for political purposes, and since patronage was an integral part of politics in many states for more than two hundred years, the Court's majority can fairly be accused of ruling on the basis of personal beliefs rather than on the basis of objective constitutional doctrine.

In this case, however, the Court merely delivered a crucial (probably not quite final) blow to a system that already was dying. By the late 1980s, civil service laws, government employee unions, and the moral force of public opinion had pretty much dried up job patronage in most of the system's former strongholds.

In Pennsylvania, where the governor in the 1960s could fill more than 40,000 government jobs on a political basis, only about 2,000 jobs were still available as patronage in 1988. Tom Lamm, legislative secretary to Governor Robert Casey, a Democrat, told me: "The unions and the civil service have just about put an end to patronage. We still have a personnel office that checks with the county chairmen to fill what jobs we have. But the jobs just aren't there any more."[4]

In Ohio, where party chairmen from Mark Hanna to Ray Bliss had access to state patronage when their party controlled the governorship, the supply of political jobs also has slowed to a trickle. "Many Democratic workers and county leaders," Jim Carey, political director of the Democratic state committee, said, "were surprised after the Democratic sweep [of state offices] in 1982 to discover that there really were not many state jobs available. . . . Patronage does not really exist as a major factor in state politics." In Illinois, Democratic state chairman Calvin Sutker, who had recently moved the state party headquarters out of the offices of the Cook County organization, said: "The party no longer functions as an employment agency. More and more, we must rely on the spirit of voluntarism that moves so many other organizations in American society."[5]

A partial exception was Indiana, where the governor could still fill about 13,000 jobs on a political basis, and where the Republicans ran a tightly disciplined state machine until they lost the governorship in 1988. "The Republican organization," Republican state chairman Gordon Durnil acknowledged, "plays a part in filling many vacancies." Even in Indiana, however, the effects of the Supreme Court's 1976 ruling against politically motivated firing had reduced the value of patronage. "It is no longer possible," Durnil lamented, "to fire people from the state payroll for political reasons."[6]

The elimination of most job patronage has not removed other kinds of patronage as an important factor in state politics. In many states, politics is directly involved in the award of contracts, placement of state bank deposits, purchase of professional services, and other exercises of the state's economic power. Most governors make hundreds, and in some cases thousands, of appointments to state boards and commissions that oversee state colleges and hospitals, regulate gambling and liquor sales, license trades and professions, administer state toll roads, and represent the state in a myriad of other activities. Most of these positions on boards and commissions are non-paying, but they are nevertheless much in demand. Persons seeking such appointments may be motivated by desire to perform public service, hunger for ego-gratification—or more concrete objectives. Appointments to boards and commissions, as well as appointments of lawyers to vacant judgeships in many states, are usually made on a political basis.

These forms of patronage, however, are useful primarily in raising campaign contributions rather than in providing the manpower on which the old party machines depended. Loss of job patronage, along with other social and cultural factors, has made it impossible in most states for traditional party machines to continue in the old way.

THE SERVICE FUNCTION

Politics in most western states had been candidate-oriented since the Progressive Era. During the 1970s and 1980s, candidates and their campaign organizations, with associated bevies of PACs and consultants, increasingly became the focus of politics in the old machine states of the Northeast and Midwest as well. At the same time, a new kind of state party, which concentrated on providing campaign services, began to emerge in both the former machine and non-machine states, and also in the former one-party states of the South.

In the old machine states, many state party organizations offered their party's nominees for state offices a wide range of modern campaign services and technology. Jim Carey of the Ohio Democratic state committee said: "We have become service-oriented. [For example] the party now runs workshops where we train candidates and campaign managers." Pennsylvania Republican chair Earl Baker concurred: "The time has passed when the party in Pennsylvania was a holding company for political power. We have become a service organization. We provide phone banks, mailings, advice to local people." New Jersey Republican state chair Frank Hollman said: "We have put at least a million dollars into building our computer operation. . . . In the last gubernatorial election the state committee ran phone banks that made a million and a half phone calls in the week before election alone. We use paid supervisors for the phone banks but wherever possible we use volunteers to make the actual calls."[7]

Even in Indiana, where both parties staunchly defend the patronage system and claim its fruits when they control the governorship, the state parties were developing modern service capabilities. Republican state chair Gordon Durnil said:

In the late 1960s the leaders of the Indiana Republican organization realized that in many states the consultants were taking over. We decided to teach ourselves the new campaign technology. The Republican party developed a capacity for direct mail and handling demographics and other aspects of modern campaigning. As a result, politics in Indiana has remained party-oriented.[8]

In some of the western states where parties have been traditionally weak, state party organizations were carving out a role for themselves as providers of campaign services at lower costs than those charged by free-lance consultants. Colorado Democratic state chairman Buie Seawell said: "I see the state party organization as a sort of quartermaster corps, delivering services that achieve economies of scale. Many of the services the state party performs would cost ten times as much if the individual candidates went out and bought them on the open market." Washington Republican state chair Jennifer Dunn said: "We make extensive use of direct mail . . . send out publications carrying the Republican message. I established the new position of communications director."[9]

In the South, the new campaign technology was first adopted by the state Republican parties that began to grow after the breakthrough achieved by the Goldwater campaign in 1964. Royal Masset, political director of the Texas Republican party, said: "We have a computer file that contains eight million registered voters. We make out lists available to candidates, charging on a use basis. . . . We run candidate schools at which we train about 400 candidates in an election year." Marty Connors, executive director of the Alabama Republican party, said: "We target direct mail at voters living along the wishbone pattern formed by the interstate highway cutting across Alabama. We know that's where most of the potential Republicans are."[10]

By the middle 1980s, Democrats in many southern states had found it necessary to respond with service-oriented state party organizations of their own. Bobby Kahn, executive director of the Georgia Democratic state committee, said:

> The Democratic party in Georgia used to be pretty much of a club for county leaders. It had only a secondary interest in getting people elected. . . . This has now changed. The party now exists to serve Democratic candidates for public office. We have built a computer file of voters that contains more than two-and-a-half million names, that we make available to candidates for a small fee based on the size of the district where the candidate is running. The voter lists can really be used to do the most amazing things: to address letters, to put labels on mail, as a phone bank list, for polling. . . .[11]

LEGISLATIVE CAMPAIGN COMMITTEES

Legislative campaign committees, similar to those operated by the congressional party caucuses in Washington, have come to play a significant part in the politics of some states. Letterhead legislative campaign committees existed in some states for many years, mainly as channels through which lobbyists conveyed contributions to incumbents. In the 1960s Jesse Unruh, then speaker of the California assembly, built a new kind of legislative campaign machine. Using the broad powers of the California speakership ("like those of the Speaker of the House in Washington before the dethronement of Joe Cannon in the early years of this century," according to a California political operative), Unruh raised a huge (for that time) campaign war chest from which he distributed funds to Democratic assembly candidates.

After Unruh departed to run for governor in 1970, the campaign committee became involved in a protracted struggle between Democratic factions in the assembly. The struggle was resolved in 1981 after Willy Brown was elected speaker—at first with support from Republicans as well as from one of the Democratic factions. Brown developed the campaign committee into an instrument of his personal power and carried its fundraising capacity far beyond what even Unruh had achieved. After the next general election he obtained united backing from the Democrats and dispensed with further support from the Republicans. By 1986 Brown was able to distribute more than $5 million to Democratic candidates (compared to $2.5 million raised by the Republican assembly minority).[12]

As William Cabala, Brown's chief of staff, pointed out to me, the speaker's organization in the assembly and its Republican counterpart are "cohesive forces contending against each other for public offices, which is at least one of the traditional definitions of a political party."[13]

By the late 1980s legislative campaign committees had emerged in more than 30 states, some built on the Unruh-Brown model, others more loosely structured. "In at least twelve of these," Barbara and Steven Salmore wrote, "the amount of funds raised is enough to exert a significant effect on campaigns; in at least 14 states these funds are a source of power for the legislative leadership, which controls the caucus campaign activities."[14]

Legislative campaign committees developed in some of the former machine states when legislators discovered they could no longer depend on local patronage-based party organizations to secure their reelections. Congressmen facing the same problem formed personal organizations serviced by their staffs and fed by campaign contributions from PACs. But, as the Salmores observed, "the key difference between federal and state legislators is that members of Congress are better able to operate as independent entrepreneurs than their counterparts in the states. . . . The obvious solution to the problem state legislators have is to band together in some larger organization that will have the resources they lack."[15]

Many of the legislative campaign committees not only recruit candidates for open seats and to run against vulnerable opposition incumbents, but also, unlike most of the current official state party organizations, actively enter primaries to support their choices. Their criteria for the selection of candidates are generally highly pragmatic. As former Wisconsin Democratic House Speaker Tom Loftus, who in the late 1980s directed one of the strongest of the legislative campaign committees, put it: "Our only test is that a candidate is in a winnable seat and he or she is breathing, and those two requirements are in order of importance. . . . We don't care if this person believes in the principles of the Democratic party or if he or she belongs to the Democratic party. We know if they make it they will vote with the Democrats to organize, and that's the goal we care about."[16]

The legislative campaign committees have become adept at obtaining campaign contributions from PACs, which during the 1980s grew increasingly active at the state level. Legislative leaders in most states enjoy more institutional power than their congressional counterparts in Washington. As a result, PACs have been inclined at the state level to steer their contributions through party committees controlled by legislative leaders. "Instead of being put out of business by the PACs," political scientist John Bibby comments, "the legislative parties have learned how to maneuver them." Legislative campaign committees in some states have acquired some of the attributes of the old patronage-based party machines and have recently come under fire from reform groups like Common Cause and Ralph Nader's organization.

Control of the funds distributed by legislative campaign committees has helped legislative leaders in many states maintain a considerable degree of party unity on roll-call votes, particularly when their party controls the governorship but is in the minority in the legislature. In California the Republican minority in the legislature sustained all of Republican Governor George Deukmejian's vetoes during his two terms, from 1983 through 1990; and in Colorado the Democratic minority was successful in sustaining all but one of Democratic Governor Roy Romer's vetoes from 1987 through 1990. In Wisconsin the Republican minority in the Senate in 1987 voted unanimously as a bloc to sustain Republican Governor Tommy Thompson's vetoes of 270 items in the general appropriations bill, though some of the cuts affected projects in districts represented by Republican senators.[17]

THE PRICE OF SURVIVAL

The recovery, or in some cases the emergence, of state parties should not be exaggerated. State party organizations in many states, including California and New York, remain chronically feeble. Almost all candidates for governor and other state offices now raise their own funds and form personal campaign organizations. Though sources of campaign contributions are difficult to research in many states, there is no doubt that parties rank a distant third as contributors behind individuals and PACs. In the 1990s, candidates running as independents or on third-party tickets were elected to the governorships of Connecticut, Alaska, Maine, and Minnesota. In a few states, such as Connecticut and North Carolina, coalitions across party lines for a time took control of a house in the state legislature.

State party organizations of some kind have in most places survived the waves of cultural, economic, and technological change that have swept across American politics in the last 30 years. In some of the states where party organizations were legally hobbled during the Progressive Era, and in some states of the formerly one-party South, parties have even grown institutionally stronger. But state parties almost everywhere have lost the roots that the old patronage-based state organizations used to maintain in the day-to-day life of local communities.

With a few exceptions, such as Indiana and the state of Washington, state party organizations are no longer centers of major political power. They do not dominate their own party primaries, and most of them do not even play an important role in slating candidates for state offices. For the most part they have converted themselves into service organizations, supplying financial, technical, and managerial assistance to candidates running on their lines. Some also provide governors elected under their labels with significant help in building support for the enactment of legislative programs or for sustaining vetoes.

These functions have helped keep state party organizations on the political map. But the fledgling party organizations now showing signs of life in some states will certainly be imperiled if support for parties in the broader electorate continues to erode.

20

LOCAL PARTIES

Getting Along Without Patronage

"ALL POLITICS," House Speaker Thomas P. O'Neill used to say, "is local"—meaning that voters cast their ballots on the basis of how public issues directly affect their daily lives. Actually, all politics is *not* local: much electoral behavior is shaped by currents rising from sources far beyond local neighborhoods or voting districts. O'Neill nevertheless was right in the sense that under democracy all governmental authority and all direction of national policy are based ultimately on decisions exercised by individual voters in local polling places. For this reason major parties try to maintain organizations of their supporters in as many as possible of the nation's more than 100,000 voting districts.[1]

Some political analysts have recently argued, and some politicians have believed, that in an age when candidates are carried by television into most people's homes, and when pollsters report shifts in voters' opinions on an almost hourly basis, local party organizations no longer play an important part in either winning elections or the conduct of government. Recent experience has shown, however, that local organizations are still essential for managing some aspects of campaigns, such as carrying on registration drives, arranging rallies, setting up phone banks, facilitating use of absentee ballots, and turning out the vote on election day. "We still need local parties," a national consultant says, "to handle the ground war."

Moreover, officeholders and candidates who do not have ties to local party organizations are cut off from the kind of specific information and personal contact that even the most sophisticated polls cannot gather. "A candidate who doesn't have to deal with grassroots organizations," a California campaign manager said, "will never learn what is really going on in this country. His impressions will be formed by what he hears from the rich and powerful."

In much of the United States truly local politics, determining the direction of government in cities, counties, towns, boroughs, townships, school districts, and other local units, is officially nonpartisan. Willis Hawley found in 1968 that 64 percent of cities and towns with populations over 5,000 used nonpartisan ballots for local elections and estimated that 85 percent of all school board members were elected on a nonpartisan basis. Today the incidence of officially nonpartisan local government is probably even higher.[2]

In many places where elections for local office are legally nonpartisan, however, party organizations support slates of candidates who are identified with the party in everything but ballot designation. And even where local elections are genuinely nonpartisan, voters usually must choose between candidates running on party lines for national and state offices.

Prior to the 1960s local Republican organizations were virtually unknown in much of the South, and Democratic organizations were similarly scarce in parts of New England and the Midwest. Today, however, there are almost no states that are totally noncompetitive in national elections, and no states where the candidates of either party for state office are automatically excluded from election. (The District of Columbia remains an apparently unreachable Democratic citadel.) Both parties therefore are motivated to bring out their supporters even in places where they have little chance of winning a local majority.

Cornelius Cotter, James Gibson, John Bibby, and Robert Huckshorn, on the basis of a massive mail survey of 7,300 county-level party organizations in the late 1970s, concluded: "Local party organizations have not become less active or less organized over the past two decades. These findings do not support the thesis of party decline."[3]

My own impression, based on much less quantitative evidence but gathered through interviews with local party leaders and political observers in most of the 20 states covered by the Brookings study in the late 1980s and early 1990s, in places where patronage-based party machines used to operate at the local level, party organizations are generally weaker than they were 30 years ago—in many cases much weaker. It is true that in some places where local parties have historically been weak, mainly in the South and West, local party activity has grown. But even in many of those places local party activity is often carried on outside official party structures.

CHICAGO AND PHILADELPHIA

In the belt of states stretching from Massachusetts to Illinois where patronage used to abound, local party organizations in many places have come on hard times. Patronage remains more of a factor in the politics of some localities in these states than it does at the state level. But even before the Supreme Court's decision in 1990 that virtually outlawed traditional job patronage, the supply of positions that could be filled on a political basis in most city, county, and town governments had greatly diminished. Most local organizations that were built on patronage have not been able to fill the gap left by its removal.

Traditional party organizations have not wholly disappeared in some of their old strongholds, however. Interviews with politicians and political observers in Chicago and Philadelphia, and telephone surveys of half the ward leaders in the

Democratic and Republican parties in both cities, produced evidence of organizations that still function at the ward level, though with greatly reduced resources of job patronage and money. (Table 20–1.)

Most ward leaders we questioned in both cities and in both parties were middle-aged men—a finding confirmed by William Crotty's survey of Chicago committeemen at about the same time.[4] The Chicagoans tended to be somewhat younger than the Philadelphians, possibly reflecting more active competition for the position of ward leader. Particularly among the Chicago Democrats, many ward leaders held elective office. Even among the Republicans, whose party has not controlled the city government in either Chicago or Philadelphia for many years, a number of ward leaders held appointive government jobs. In Chicago most of the Republicans with appointive government jobs worked for the state government; in Philadelphia the Republican government jobholders worked for state legislators or in state agencies under Republican control. Practically all the ward leaders in both parties complained about their inability to find patronage jobs to reward their precinct workers.

Particularly in Chicago, ward leaders also complained about the lack of "street money" to distribute to party workers on election day. About three-fourths of Chicago Democratic ward leaders said that in recent years they had received no funds whatever from the party to pay workers. Those who did report receiving street money said they were given about $50 per election division. (Chicago wards each have about 60 divisions, containing an average of about 450 voters.) Some ward leaders said that, though they received no election-day money from the party,

Table 20–1   Survey of Ward Leaders in Chicago and Philadelphia

	Chicago		Philadelphia	
	Democratic	Republican	Democratic	Republican
Average age	46	44	51	57
Percentage female	8	16	30	17
Percentage of ward leaders holding elective office	80	0	18	8
Percentage holding appointive govt. jobs	8	36	33	14
Reported average percentage of precinct workers in ward with government jobs	36	9	9	4
Percentage maintaining a ward party headquarters	96	84	63	44
Reported average percentage of ward residents reached through door-to-door canvassing	71	67	62	60

they were given money by some of the candidates. Chicago Republican ward leaders also reported receiving either no street money or about $50 per division. In Philadelphia ward leaders did somewhat better: most ward leaders in both parties reported receiving about $100 per division for election-day expenses. (Philadelphia wards include from 20 to 30 divisions, containing an average of about 600 voters.)

Almost all the ward leaders we interviewed in both parties said they actively support slates of candidates in their party's primary, continuing the traditional practice of city machines. In recent years, however, Democratic ward leaders in both cities had often divided over which slates they backed. Republican ward leaders in Philadelphia had usually given united support to an endorsed slate in primary elections, but those in Chicago reported sometimes splitting. Most ward leaders said their organizations conduct traditional door-to-door canvasses before the general election and claimed that their workers make personal contact with surprisingly large numbers of their ward's residents (possibly inflated).

How much effect do these ward organizations have on election outcomes? Very little, most politicians concede, in general elections for highly visible offices such as President, governor, or mayor. "Television is the thing that really has the effect now on how people vote," said George Dunn, chairman of the Cook County Democratic Committee. "It brings the candidates right into the voter's parlor and the organization can't compete with that."[5]

In contested primaries for highly visible offices, politicians and political observers in Chicago and Philadelphia estimate, an effective ward leader who works hard can add about 5 percentage points to his candidate's showing. For less prominent offices, such as city council or judgeships, he can do considerably better.

Philadelphia Controller Joseph Vignola, a Democratic ward leader in South Philadelphia as his father was before him, explained:

> In a working-class community like my neighborhood . . . people who want certain city services will go to their Democratic committeeperson. They ask him for help getting the streetlight fixed up the alley and the committeeman is still sometimes able to be helpful on matters like that. The committeeman then asks them to support candidates in elections they do not much care about and they are likely to accept his recommendations. When they go to the polls they may not follow the committeeman's advice on the top of the ticket but if the committeeman is wise he will not argue about the top of the ticket but will try to get their vote for the rest of his slate. As a rule they do not know the rest of the people who are running and if the committeeperson says, "Give my guy a vote," they are likely to do it.[6]

To maintain even this level of effectiveness, traditional organizations require incentives to attract and hold the precinct committeemen who are their essential links to ordinary voters. In the past this need was largely filled through the award of jobs in city or county government—or state government, when the organization's party controlled the governorship or other state offices. All the politicians with whom I talked in Chicago and Philadelphia agreed that the combined effect of court orders, civil service, and government employee unions had pretty much killed the patronage system in local government. Even government employees who originally got their jobs through patronage no longer feel much obligation to work for the organization. Alderman Roman Pucinski, a veteran captain in the Chicago machine, said: "People holding city jobs know they can't be fired, so it's hard to keep up their interest in politics. It's not the same as when their livelihood depended on how well they were able to carry their division."[7]

Lucien Blackwell, majority leader of the Philadelphia city council and one of the city's most powerful black politicians, said:

> The patronage situation is certainly not the same as it was several years ago. There is still some patronage in the parking commission and some other commissions of that kind, but other than that the patronage system is virtually dead. . . . If we had more jobs to dispense we would have a better chance of overcoming the political chaos that threatens to engulf this city.[8]

And William Meehan, who for more than 30 years led the Republican organization in Philadelphia, said:

> Here and there are still a few jobs. The court system in Philadelphia still makes a certain number of appointments available to the political organizations. And the Board of Revision of Taxes, though it is now controlled by the Democrats, still gives us a few jobs. But the courts have now made it almost impossible to fire people [for political reasons]. Or really to hire people. As a result political organizations will soon be a thing of the past. So what will you have left? The PACs and the consultants.[9]

As at the state level, the decline of job patronage has not eliminated patronage in the form of contracts and favors. A leader of the Philadelphia Democratic organization said:

> There is no quid pro quo. But a person who does a million dollars worth of business with the city is glad to make a contribution of $50,000. He can charge up the contribution to client development. . . . But that money goes to the office-holder, not the party. He uses it to go on the tube and make direct contact with the public.

The ability of officeholders to finance their own campaigns through contributions from businesses and interest groups has further weakened the hold of the traditional party organizations. As a result, Lucien Blackwell said: "Nobody is afraid of the Democratic party. Every candidate raises his own money. Every candidate builds his own fortress."

SUBURBAN MACHINES

The most effective of the remaining traditional party organizations, based on patronage and delivery of government services, are probably not those in large cities but the machines, mostly Republican, In suburban domains like Nassau and Suffolk counties, New York; Delaware and Montgomery counties, Pennsylvania; and DuPage County, Illinois.

The Nassau County Republican organization, often cited by political scientists and journalists as a model, was said in the late 1980s to control more than 20,000 jobs in local government which could still be distributed as patronage. Persons holding these jobs provided much of the personnel for "an elaborate superstructure of ward chairpersons, precinct committee members, and block captains who turn out the vote on election day."[10] The machine in theory is governed by the Nassau County Republican executive committee, composed of 69 members (one for each of the county's local political units), most of whom hold elective or appointive office at the town, county, or state level. Operating decisions are made by an inner circle of about 30 that meets weekly in the office-building headquarters owned by the organization in Westbury, a suburban Long Island community. Within this inner circle the Republican county chairman is the unquestioned boss.

One key to the success of the Nassau Republican organization, according to Joseph Margiotta, who ruled the machine for 16 years before he was sent to jail in 1983 for extortion (obtaining campaign contributions from insurance companies doing business with the county), is that it maintains "centralized control of slating" of candidates for both county and local elective offices. By imposing a tight hierarchical structure, Margiotta explained, the organization is able to preserve the loyalty of its troops and to assure that all local governmental units provide efficient and effective services that keep it popular with Nassau County voters.[11]

Though the Nassau machine usually rolls up large majorities for national and state Republican candidates, it concentrates its attention on local elections. "The party was born on concern for local government," said the Republican leader of a Nassau town. "It's the greatest potential for patronage."[12] (In 1999, Nassau County voters, reacting against a county tax increase, elected a Democratic majority on the county council, but the Republican machine continued to control the job-rich county executive.)

Why have Republican machines in some suburban counties survived, even prospered, while their Democratic counterparts in the big cities have generally gone into deep decline? In part because the racial divisions that helped fracture many Democratic city machines in the 1980s have so far been less of a factor in the internal politics of most suburban counties. In part because business support that has sometimes helped reformers against Democratic city machines has not been as forthcoming against Republican machines in the suburbs. In part because not only middle-class but also working-class families in the suburbs have regarded Republican machines as protectors against the spread of the troubles that beset Democratic-controlled cities, including but not limited to troubles connected with race, from which many of them fled. And in part because the social and economic problems of suburban counties, though often substantial, have not been nearly as severe as those that have stricken most big cities since the 1960s. As a result, suburban machines have faced fewer problems in maintaining governmental services at a level that has been at least acceptable to most residents.

UPSTATE

In some middle-sized-city or rural "upstate" counties of historically strong-party states, patronage-based local organizations continue to operate in something like the old way. But many of these upstate machines show signs of rust and are gradually giving ground to legal, technological, and cultural change.

In Schuylkill County, Pennsylvania, a hard-coal-region bailiwick where both parties for many years maintained strong party machines that regularly contested control of the courthouse, with the Republicans usually winning, we interviewed one-third of the precinct committeepersons in both parties. Of these, 11 percent of the Republicans and 17 percent of the Democrats reported holding appointive government jobs. Significantly, 22 percent of the Republicans and 42 percent of the Democrats gave their occupation as "retired." The Republican committeemen said they had been active in politics for an average of 22 years, and the Democrats for an average of 33 years. Most committeemen in both parties reported holding party meetings in their districts at least monthly, with more toward election time. (One Democratic committeeman said he holds 200 meetings a year—in his local bar.) County elections in the 1980s, however, were becoming increasingly candidate-oriented, with most candidates for even county offices relying on their own self-generated organizations more than on the party organization.

In Delaware County, Indiana, which includes Muncie (the *Middletown* studied by several generations of sociologists), we also interviewed one-third of the committeepersons in both parties. The Democratic organization has usually been dominant in Delaware County, a stronghold of organized labor. We found that 33 percent of the Democratic committeepersons held appointive county jobs, and one Republican (6 percent) had an appointive state job. One Democratic committeeman, the county sheriff, held an elective office. The Democrats had been active in politics for an average of 20 years and the Republicans for an average of 23 years; 17 percent of the Democrats and 18 percent of the Republicans gave their occupation as retired.

Donna Ashby, recorder of deeds in Delaware County and vice chairman of the Democratic county committee, explained the operation of the patronage system and her concern for its survival:

> There are about 400 jobs in the city and county that are filled on a patronage basis. Courthouse employees who work for Democratic county officeholders belong to our one percent club, which means they pay one percent of their salaries to the Democratic party. This is entirely voluntary, but we feel that those who get their jobs through the party should pay for part of the party's upkeep. . . . [But] civil service is gradually changing the way politics operates. Every year lawsuits are filed challenging the hiring or firing of workers on a political basis. . . . We sometimes recruit people to be committeemen, but more than half the positions are contested in the Democratic primary. It is regarded as a desirable thing to be a Democratic committeeman in Delaware County.[13]

The Indiana state Democratic party assesses its county affiliates for annual contributions, but the Delaware County organization has always refused to pay the assessment. The Delaware County Democrats, in fact, refused to permit the state party even to hold fund-raising events in the county.

Jacqueline Bowen, Republican chairman in Delaware County and director of the state licensing bureau in Muncie at the time of my visit, said that neither of the county party organizations was as strong as it used to be. The Republicans, she said, benefited not only from bits of patronage they received from the state government (then under Republican control) but also from association with the state's leading political personalities: "Richard Lugar and Dan Quayle [then still a senator]," she said, "are tremendous attractions when they come to Muncie. These people are like gods!"[14]

THE SOUTH

In states where state party organizations have historically been weak, local party organizations have generally been even weaker. Perhaps in part because there have been no strong patronage-based local machines to resist them, the new technology-driven state parties in some southern and western states during the 1980s had considerable success generating organized party activities in some localities.

In most of the South the one-party system produced weak local parties. This did not, however, necessarily translate into unstructured local politics. Patronage-based courthouse machines, similar to those in the strong-party states, have traditionally dominated politics in most southern counties. Until recently, almost all of these have been nominally Democratic, but as a rule they have not operated within the structure of the official local Democratic party.

As southern states moved toward two-party competition in national and state elections, courthouse organizations still bearing the Democratic label, usually led by the sheriff or a county judge, often held on to power at the local level. Patronage remained the bond that held many of these courthouse alliances together. "It's a way of life!" J. R. Mathews, Democratic chairman in Troup County, a rural constituency in western Georgia, responded when I asked if patronage played an important part in county politics.[15]

Feeling heat from the advancing Republicans, some of these local organizations sought help from their state Democratic parties. (Others, particularly in Florida and Texas, switched to the Republican label.) Even when aligning themselves more closely with the state Democratic organization, however, the courthouse gangs often continued to play down the official local Democratic structure. The executive director of the Georgia Democratic party said: "The person who is county chairman often is not a significant political figure in the county. Sometimes the person who is county chairman has that job because he couldn't get anything else." And the district attorney of a rural county in East Texas said: "All candidates for county office file as Democrats, whether they are or not. But the party organization is very weak. Candidates form alliances among themselves without much regard for party."

While the Republican party in the South during the 1970s and 1980s grew at the state level, some southern Republican leaders recognized that the party's future would not be secure until it developed foundations in local politics. Texas Republican Chairman George Strake said: "A party that grows only at the top will be swept away when its first generation of leaders passes from the picture. We have been working at building the party's infrastructure at the county and neighborhood levels." By the middle of the 1980s significant Republican organizations had developed in some southern cities. Dallas Republican Chairman Fred Meyer (later state chairman) said in 1986: "We have now the strongest local organization in Texas, built around 41 clubs of Republican volunteers. On the weekend before election we will put a piece of literature on every doorstep in Dallas County."[16]

In the middle and late 1980s local Republican organizations began to spring up beyond the limits of metropolitan areas, where Republicanism first took hold in the South. "We're going after the courthouses," said Marty Connors, executive director of the Alabama Republican party. "The governorship is important to the Democrats, but the courthouse is where they live. If you talk about taking the courthouses, you're talking about taking away the family business." The driving force behind their local organizations, southern Republican leaders claim, is conservative ideology, often conveyed by local evangelical Protestant churches.[17]

Responding to the Republican challenge, Democratic leaders in some southern metropolitan areas, with help and encouragement from state parties, have tried to build local organizations of party activists. Often they have found it necessary to reach beyond the party's official structure. Dallas Democratic Chairman Sandy Kress said:

> When I became county chairman I expected the precinct leaders who are elected by Democratic voters in every precinct in Dallas county would be my army. I found that not to be the case. The precinct leaders are given responsibility by law

for conducting the party's primary elections, and most of them regard that as the extent of their job. For real party workers I had to go out and recruit people who are interested in advancing the goals of the Democratic party.[18]

THE WEST

The historic weakness of local party organizations in many midwestern and western states is often traced to the party-hobbling reforms of the Progressive Era. Even before those reforms were passed, however, local party organizations in most western states were weak. The success of the progressives in enacting laws restricting the role of parties in the West may in fact have reflected the circumstance that parties were weak there to begin with—possibly because of social underdevelopment or the generally more individualistic character of western life.

Elections for local offices in most midwestern and western states are nonpartisan in fact as well as in name. Local party organizations therefore have been focused mainly on state and national politics. While state parties remained weak, local parties had few outside resources or leadership on which to draw. Politics became almost wholly candidate-oriented.

In many places local party organizations still seem largely irrelevant to the political process. A midwestern county chairman said: "When I agreed to be chairman I thought I would be dealing with the great issues of the day. What the party chairman actually deals with are the annual picnic and the bingo game. The biggest decision the party chairman makes is who is to run the bingo game." A state party chairman in a western state with a history of weak local party organizations said: "Most of the county chairs are lovely, nice people, but they do not deliver much in the way of political support. . . . They are not the kingmakers of local politics."

Since 1960 three factors have contributed to the development of increased party activity in some localities of historically weak-party midwestern and western states: support from active state party organizations; the growing importance of ideology in politics; and new campaign technologies that make it advantageous for candidates to participate in a common political structure offering shared services.

I discussed the role of state parties in the preceding chapter. The part played by ideology is exemplified by the Republican organization in Orange County, California, between Los Angeles and San Diego, which until the late 1990s regularly produced huge majorities for national and state Republican candidates. Unlike the Nassau County Republican organization, the Orange County Republicans are unable to attract supporters through distribution of patronage or by taking credit for efficient local government. What they offer instead is conservative ideology.

Though politics is much more candidate-oriented in Orange County than in Nassau County, the Orange County Republican organization maintains a professional staff of political technicians and provides volunteer workers for the party slate.

In interviews with Republican district leaders in Orange County's eight assembly districts, we asked what if any issues they used to build support for the party. As Table 20–2 shows, they responded for the most part with "conservatism" or "conservative political philosophy" or broad categories of issues with conservative content. Only one Orange County Republican leader mentioned "local issues." In contrast, Democratic leaders in the same eight districts, whom we also interviewed, responded with a mixture of primarily local concerns and liberal interests.

Table 20–2   Issues Identified as Sources of Party Support by Orange County District Leaders
(Number of times mentioned in parentheses if more than once)

Republican	Democrats
conservatism (4)	traffic (3)
conservative political philosophy	crime (3)
limited government	civil rights (3)
foreign policy	environment (2)
low taxes	housing (2)
strong defense	economic issues (2)
local issues	party of people not as fortunate
	health issues
	drugs
	schools
	no issues

WESTSIDE LOS ANGELES

Ideology, in this case liberal, also played an important part in the success of the so-called Waxman-Berman alliance, which in the 1980s exerted powerful influence over the politics of several congressional districts on the Westside of Los Angeles County, an area that includes affluent communities like Beverly Hills, Malibu, and Pacific Palisades, and also "slightly tattered districts taken over by the young and the bohemian, communities populated by senior citizens on fixed incomes, and quiet middle-class backwaters." Through access to the wealth and glamour of the Hollywood movie industry, the alliance also made its presence felt in working-class districts in East Los Angeles, in other parts of California, and indeed in selected congressional races all over the United States.[19]

Led by Congressmen Henry Waxman, Howard Berman, and Mel Levine, the alliance derived its effectiveness in part from mastery of modern campaign technology and in part from ability to raise funds through identification with liberal national and international causes. It also aggressively championed support for Israel (no longer automatically associated with liberalism in all parts of the country).

Though the alliance became involved in some contests for local offices in Los Angeles County, it did not attempt to play much of a role in the administration of local services. These are not the kind of people, the *Los Angeles Times* has observed, "you call up if your garbage doesn't get picked up."[20]

The alliance got started in the 1970s as an association of liberal Democrats representing Westside districts in the California assembly. When first Waxman and then Berman and Levine were elected to Congress, they continued to maintain their local political network. Candidates whom they supported took their places in Sacramento. Though once at odds with Assembly Speaker Willy Brown (who defeated Howard Berman in the 1981 fight for the speakership), the alliance later established an entente with Brown and other San Francisco Bay area Democrats with a shared interest in preserving the apportionment gerrymanders that have contributed to Democratic supremacy in both the California congressional delegation and the state legislature.

The alliance's operational base was a Westside political consulting firm owned by Michael Berman, Howard's brother, and Carl D'Agostino—known locally as "BAD Politics." The firm specialized in direct-mail campaigning. Michael Berman, interviewed in a cluttered office exuding the atmosphere of a Raymond Chandler novel, explained its role:

> The consultant is needed to guide the candidate through the multi-variate electorate of humongous voting groups. California voters are very different from those in New York. They have been torn from their institutional roots so there is no way you can organize them on a neighborhood basis. You have to reach them in some other way. . . . I form coalitions of candidates so I can work for them more efficiently. . . . We send mailings from a candidate or slate of candidates to people with Jewish surnames, people with Hispanic surnames, people who join environmentalist groups, women who designate themselves Ms. [I asked, "Why Ms.?" and he said, "Because they can be presumed to be feminists."] Each group receives a common message, and then there is a special message directed at the group's particular interest. . . . It's a very expensive form of campaigning. But it is effective.[21]

The alliance placed little stock in grassroots organization. Door-to-door canvassing in Southern California neighborhoods with rapid population turnover, one of its strategists said, is "not cost effective."

Michael Berman and Carl D'Agostino arranged endorsements for their clients by prominent alliance leaders. John Emerson, a liberal Democratic activist who participated with them in many campaigns, described the system:

> Election to the legislature from a Westside district can cost more than a million dollars. So a candidate needs lots of money. He also needs credibility with the media. Being handled by BAD Politics gives a candidate instant credibility and

brings endorsements from leading members of the Waxman–Berman coalition. Once a candidate has these he can raise money. He may not be the best candidate. But if he has BAD Politics, endorsements, and money he may not even be challenged.[22]

Modern urban local party organizations like the Waxman–Berman alliance are based more on policy positions and less on manipulation of government favors than was that of the old machines. They appear to reach political decisions through consensus and collegial discussion—"hours and hours on the telephone," Michael Berman said. There is no "boss." But the new organizations maintain little two-way contact with most local neighborhoods and communities, and in that sense are less democratic than the machines. They operate a form of local politics designed for a society in which localities as organized communities hardly exist and in which voters are represented as identifiers with interest groups, followers of causes, practitioners of life-styles—"women who designate themselves Ms."

A NEED FOR POLITICAL WILL

As the examples above suggest, local party organizations in the United States remain enormously varied—in structure, mode of operation, motivating goals, and electoral effectiveness. The trend toward functional convergence that can be observed among state party organizations is much less apparent at the local level.

Some generalizations, however, can be made. The old city-hall and court-house patronage machines, though still operating with a fair amount of efficiency in some places, are generally playing a much smaller role in local politics. The mass parties of the nineteenth and early twentieth centuries, which performed in some localities almost as secular churches, are gone and not likely to return. Most voters take no part in local party activities. Even many of the voters who nominally identify with a party now appear to regard themselves as political consumers, selecting between party nominees as they might shop at rival supermarkets.

Yet associations of politicians at the local level continue to work together to achieve common goals, both in election campaigns and in government. Except in purely local politics, and in some places even there, these associations most often operate under the labels of one of the two great national parties. In some places, particularly in the South and West, local party groups, though sometimes outside the official party structure, are more active and effective than they were 20 or 30 years ago.

The overall health of local party organizations in the United States is best described as poor but not hopeless. Remnants of party structure remain almost everywhere, and in some places there are signs of promising growth. Institutional devices for renewing parties are available. I will describe some of these in the next, and final, chapter. But, most of all, they need to be motivated by fresh charges of political will.

21

REBUILDING THE PARTIES

M ANY OF THE SOCIAL and political trends affecting parties that developed during the 1970s and 1980s accelerated and gathered force in the 1990s. Largely candidate-oriented campaigns became more common at all levels of government. Ideological and religious interest groups increasingly shaped political behavior. Voter turnout in elections, after brief rises in 1992 and 1994, steadily declined.

Attachment among the voters to the two major parties remained at historically low levels. A national survey in 1996 found 71 percent saying they usually split their tickets (voted for candidates of different parties for different offices), compared with 42 percent in 1942. Election of Jesse Ventura, a former professional wrestler, as governor of Minnesota in 1998 on the Reform party ticket against well known candidates of the two major parties was perceived as a particularly vivid symptom of voter disenchantment with the existing two-party system.

David Broder, the dean of American political journalists, as early as 1972 had warned in his prophetic book, *The Party's Over,* that "party loyalties have been seriously eroded, the Republican and Democratic organizations weakened by years of neglect." Walter Dean Burnham in 1982 reported a "massive loss of confidence in the workings of our political institutions, especially the parties." William Keefe in 1988 found the party system "in disarray—more so than at any time in the last century."[1]

By the end of the 1990s, experience with weakened parties had convinced most political scholars, many journalists, and some in the general public that E. E. Schattschneider long ago had been right: "Political parties created democracy" and democratic renewal requires strengthening of parties. L. Sandy Maisel wrote in 1999: "For all its imperfections, so vividly described by political analysts and journalists of all types, party remains the vital linking institution. When parties are weak, the linkage role of the electoral process is not played well. When they are strong, a possibility exists that representation and accountability will follow."[2]

As the twentieth century neared its close; some political scientists found at least tentative signs of party revival. John Green and Daniel Shea wrote, also in 1999: "Signs of strength [in the party system] appear to outweigh indications of weakness. While the balance of evidence may be temporary and the illness far from cured, a new stage in party politics may be developing."[3]

THE POLITICS OF DISCONTENT

In 1988 George Bush had been elected President as Ronald Reagan's Republican successor. Though running behind his Democratic opponent, Governor Michael Dukakis of Massachusetts, during most of the summer, Bush received a lift from the Republican national convention in August that carried him through a largely issueless campaign to majorities in November of 53 percent in the popular vote and 315 in the electoral college.

Geographically, Bush's victory was based on overwhelming superiority in the entire South, the Great Plains, and the Rocky Mountains region, plus narrow majorities in California and most of the older industrial states from Connecticut to Illinois (the old Republican heartland.) Dukakis carried New York, Massachusetts, three states in the upper Midwest, the Pacific Northwest, and a scattering of smaller states and the District of Columbia. In terms of cultural groups, Bush suffered some erosion from Reagan's 1984 showing among Catholics but maintained the traditional Republican base among white mainline Protestants and kept the huge Republican lead that had developed during the 1980s among white evangelical Protestants. African Americans, Hispanics, and Jews remained faithful to the old Democratic coalition.

The Democrats, who had regained control of the Senate in 1986, preserved comfortable majorities in both houses of Congress.

Bush's approval rating among the national public, after soaring to the unprecedented level of 91 percent following America's swift victory over Saddam Hussein's Iraq in the Gulf War of 1991, declined steeply during the relatively brief recession of 1991–92. One thing that most voters remembered from the 1988 campaign was Bush's declaration, written by his speechwriter, at the Republican convention: "Read my lips: no new taxes." When he seemingly effortlessly broke this pledge in a budget deal with the Democratic Congress, voter cynicism toward politics and politicians grew. The 1992 recession, though never very deep, hit professional and white-collar workers who had generally kept their jobs in earlier economic downturns since the Second World War. As the 1992 election approached, public opinion surveys found exceptionally low levels of trust in government and satisfaction with the general level of American life.

While many voters seemed to be fed up with Bush and the Republicans, there was no corresponding surge in confidence for the Democrats whose administration of Congress was mired in petty scandals Since Bush had appeared unbeatable after his association with victory in the Gulf War, the race for the Democratic presidential nomination attracted a seemingly weak field. Governor Bill Clinton of Arkansas, though damaged by what turned out to be the first of many revelations of extramarital sexual indulgence, staged what turned out to be the first of many "comebacks" from the brink of electoral oblivion to win the Democratic nomination.

Responding to revulsion among many voters with the entire political system, Ross Perot, a multimillionaire Texas businessman, announced, then withdrew, then reannounced, his independent candidacy for President. For a time during the summer of 1992, before his temporary withdrawal from the race, Perot actually ran *first* in national polls pitting him against Bush and Clinton. Though he ultimately came in third, and did not win a single vote in the electoral college, after many voters became concerned over his appearance of erratic behavior and some hardening of loyalties to the two major parties, his showing of 19 percent of the popular vote was far higher than any independent or third-party performance since Theodore Roosevelt's achievement on the Progressive ticket in 1912. Perot ran particularly well among independents, first-time voters, and voters in the West.

Clinton in the end was elected President with 43 percent of the popular vote and 370 electoral votes, to Bush's 38 percent of the popular vote and 168 electoral votes. Clinton, however, actually ran two percentage points behind Dukakis's losing 45 percent of the popular vote in 1988, and fell behind Dukakis's showings with women, independents, younger voters, and Catholics, among other demographic groups. Clinton swept most of the West, the Midwest, the older industrial states, and a few southern states, while Bush carried most of the South, Indiana, and a few smaller states. But Clinton won absolute majorities of the popular vote only in New York, Arkansas, Maryland, and the District of Columbia,

Democratic majorities were slightly reduced in the House and increased in the Senate. Since the overwhelming majority of incumbents from both parties were reelected in congressional elections, it was apparent that incumbency, with its advantages in name recognition and attraction of campaign contributions, rather than party identification was the deciding factor in most races. Total PAC spending on congressional elections increased about 20 percent above the 1987–88 cycle, with Democrats receiving almost twice as much as Republicans.

A PARTY ELECTION

Two years later voter reaction against the governing Democrats produced the first election in many years in which party was decisive from the national to the local levels. Republicans, running on the "Contract with America," formed under the direction of House Republican Whip Newt Gingrich, offered an available instrument for voters determined to clean up moral rot and unresponsiveness that had infected American politics. Surveys found that most voters had little knowledge of the actual content of the Contract, but it became an effective symbol for a party perceived to have a program for positive change. Early missteps by President Clinton, and the failure of his fatally complicated health care plan in Congress, persuaded many voters that neither he nor his party could be expected to achieve national reform.

For the first time in 40 years, the Republicans won control of both houses of Congress, gaining 52 seats in the House and nine in the Senate. At the state level, the Republican share of governors rose from 20 to 31, with the gains including the major states of New York, Pennsylvania, and Texas. Republican advances were massive across the once solidly Democratic South. In the industrial states of the Midwest, most of which had voted for Clinton in 1992, incumbent Republican governors were reelected by staggering majorities: 72 percent in Ohio, 62 percent in Michigan, 64 percent in Illinois, 67 percent in Wisconsin, and 63 percent in Minnesota. The number of state legislative house seats under Republican control rose from 33 to 49. Among the defeated Democratic incumbents were such luminaries as House Speaker Tom Foley, and Governors Mario Cuomo of New York and Ann Richards of Texas. In most parts of the country Republicans gained down to the courthouse and townhall levels.

With their new majorities in Congress in 1955, Republicans indulged waves of triumphalism that led them to overestimate their bargaining position with Clinton. Gingrich, installed as House Speaker, dictated a belligerent stance. Senate Majority Leader Bob Dole, while preferring a more pragmatic approach, concentrated on his pursuit of the 1996 Republican presidential nomination. Republican party unity on rollcall votes in both houses rose to levels unprecedented in American history, as was shown by Figures 18–5 and 18–6. Democrats, realizing that their only hope was to stand together behind Clinton, were almost as united.

Congressional Republicans passed most of the procedural reforms promised by the Contract, and, by restraining the growth of government spending, helped lay the foundation for the seeming miracle of a federal budget surplus in 1999—also aided by the large tax increase pushed through Congress by Clinton entirely with Democratic votes in 1993. But the Republicans' attempt to make radical cuts in federal programs could not be sustained against the President's veto. After twice causing partial shutdowns of the federal government during the budget wars in the fall and winter of 1995–96, they caved to Clinton upon realization that the national public was turning against them. The Republicans' one major substantive victory was enactment of welfare reform in the summer of 1996, which Clinton, having vetoed two earlier versions, with the presidential election approaching signed to the anguish of many of his liberal supporters.

DEADLOCK

In the fall of 1996, Clinton, whom most commentators two years before had written off as doomed, won reelection against Dole, the Republican candidate, and Ross Perot, now running as the candidate of the newly launched Reform party, with 49 percent of the popular vote and 379 in the electoral college. Though still falling short of an absolute majority in the popular vote, and losing some of the Great Plains and Rocky Mountains states he had won in 1992, Clinton substantially increased his share of the vote in California and the older industrial states and added Florida to his coalition. He strongly outpolled Dole among women, younger voters, and Catholics, among others, though running slightly behind among men.

Perot's eight percent of the popular vote, though still relatively high for a third-party candidate, was less than half of what he had won in 1992. Voter turnout fell to 49 percent, its lowest level in a presidential election since 1924.

The Republicans lost eight seats in the House of Representatives and actually gained one in the Senate. PAC spending on congressional elections grew by another 14 percent over 1991–92, now favoring Republicans by almost two-to-one for Senate races, but dividing about evenly between parties for the House. Corporate givers clearly had concluded that the Senate was firmly Republican, but were still hedging their bets on the House.

The two parties settled down for four years of acrimonious conflict between the Democratic White House and the Republican controlled Congress. Levels of party unity in Congress fell back slightly, but the Republicans were able to turn back most Democratic proposals, while the Democrats prevented passage of Republican legislation by veto-proof majorities. Gingrich's prestige was badly damaged early in the 1997 session when he was reprimanded and fined by the House for ethical misconduct.

Party differences became bitter after the special prosecutor investigating various alleged Clinton administration scandals charged early in 1998 that the President had repeatedly engaged in oral sex with a young female intern, Monica Lewinsky, in the oval office. The President for many months denied this accusation to the media, the general public, members of his staff and cabinet, and his family, until evidence became irrefutable. In the early fall, the House Judiciary Committee, voting along party lines, approved articles of impeachment against Clinton, based in part on evidence that he had committed perjury in a civil law suit arising from an earlier alleged sexual transgression.

Clinton's behavior at first seemed to help the Republicans politically. But by the time the midterm elections came around in November, many voters, basking in the prolonged prosperity they credited at least in part to the administration's management of the economy, and doubting that the President's offenses warranted his removal from office, were in a mood to punish his attackers. The Republicans retained control of both houses of Congress, but failed to win the veto-proof majority they had been aiming for in the Senate, and lost seats in the House—the first time the White House out-party had not gained in midterm elections since 1934, the height of the New Deal.

Gingrich, taking responsibility for this setback, a few days after the election resigned, not only from the Speakership but from the House. The week before Christmas the House, voting mainly along party lines, approved two articles of impeachment. Early in the new year the Senate, also voting mainly on party lines, divided almost evenly on impeachment, far less than the two-thirds majority needed to convict.

Talk of major party realignment, which had been common after the Republican landslide in 1994, again gave way to predictions of *dealignment*—the trend toward loosening of ties among voters to either major party. Jesse Ventura's surprise election as governor of Minnesota on the Reform party ticket was pointed to as clear evidence of the continued weakening of the traditional parties.

While many political scholars and journalists argue that American democracy needs strong parties, some maintain that realignment may not after all be so bad, and is in any case inevitable. Parties, this contention goes, have made some valuable contributions to democracy, but the time when they were necessary or even particularly useful is now past. By contact through modern communications media and polling techniques, and representation of citizens by a wide variety of interest groups, officeholders can now respond directly to voters without cumbersome mediation by parties. As one experienced political consultant put it: "The television set has become the political party of the future." He might have added the internet and the computer.

WHY PARTIES?

It has been part of my argument in this book that parties, though not without detrimental effects, have played an essential part in maintaining a productive balance between accountability and effective operation in American government.

The traditional arguments for parties in democracy are well known:

1. Parties provide channels through which ordinary citizens can affect the course of government.
2. Parties give political leaders reliable bases on which to build support for their programs in the legislature and among the general electorate.
3. Parties offer a means for organizing dissent against the policies of an incumbent administration.
4. Parties, to protect their own rights to free expression, are natural guardians of civil liberties.
5. Parties "keep each other honest," since each party has a political interest in exposing corruption, deception, and abuses of authority by its opposition.
6. Parties perform many of the chores of democracy, such as getting voters registered and to the polls, disseminating information, and organizing public meetings for expression of opinion.
7. Parties recruit and screen candidates for public office, from local election officials to President of the United States.
8. Parties spur the development of new ideas.

Some of these functions are perhaps now less important than they once were, and some are now to some extent performed by other agencies such as news media and interest groups. But democracy still needs all of them. Without parties they would not be performed as well, and some might not be performed at all.

What is probably less familiar is the role that major American parties have played in carrying on the creative struggle between the republican and liberal traditions, as described in this book. American democracy, I have argued, has been nurtured not by one ideological tradition but by two: the republican tradition, emphasizing, along with freedom, public order and economic growth; and the liberal tradition, stressing, also along with freedom, economic and social equality.

Each tradition has at times offered approaches and programs that seemed better suited to the situation at hand. But neither has held the sole key to social progress. There is no prospect that the two will ever come together into a kind of super-ideology that permanently resolves or synthesizes the contrasting values they represent. American democracy needs both of them, and therefore needs the two major parties which have been their principal political embodiments.

The current weakness of parties can be overstated. As we have seen, heavily financed party organizations at the national level are more active than ever, and even at the state and local levels there are signs of life in places where until recently parties seemed clearly in decay. About two-thirds of the voters still profess some kind of allegiance to one major party or the other. But the inability of contemporary parties to rally support for their party tickets with anything like their former efficiency, or to provide voters with meaningful choices in many elections, can hardly be in doubt—as is shown by persistent ticket-splitting, declining voter turnout, and predominantly personality-oriented politics.

The ability of parties to continue playing their traditional functional roles, or their larger role of maintaining the ideological competition that has vitalized American democracy, is seriously endangered. Believers in the need for strong and effective parties, therefore, are well advised to consider means for restoring the health of parties and the party system.

In this final chapter I will examine some remedies recently proposed by political scientists, politicians, and interested citizens to reinvigorate parties and will make some recommendations of my own. The unforeseen effects of some of the party reforms instituted in the 1970s provide warning that proposals for party renewal should be approached with care. Some suggested changes would probably make the situation of the parties or the quality of public life a good deal worse. But others have real merit.

PATRONAGE

The current plight of the parties has led some reformers to reevaluate the job patronage system through which parties used to motivate their grassroots workers and achieve discipline among elected officeholders. The patronage system did indeed help produce governments that were in some ways more effective and responsive than the bureaucratized structures that have succeeded them. Chicago under the Daley machine partly deserved its reputation as "the city that works" (though it did not work very well for the blacks and other minority groups who were pinned into the ghettoes the machine helped perpetuate). But I doubt that many of those who are now nostalgic for the patronage system ever witnessed close-up the rampant corruption it almost inevitably bred, or the cruelties it imposed when political jobholders with few resources were swept out of office by a triumphant opposition.[4]

It may well be that many elected officeholders at the state, local, and even federal levels are now unduly hampered by civil service requirements that restrict their ability to appoint subordinates who share their political perspective. But legal and administrative changes to produce more accountable government would not restore the kind of mass patronage that used to sustain party machines.

There is virtually no public support for return to a system under which great armies of ordinary government workers obtained and kept their jobs by serving a political party. Larry Sabato found in a national poll in 1986 that only 13 percent of those questioned agreed that "more government jobs [should] be filled by workers and leaders of the winning candidate's party." So the patronage system as a means for building grassroots party organization is not coming back. Strengthening parties in the electorate will have to be achieved by other means.[5]

A MULTI-PARTY SYSTEM

Some special-interest groups, such as the National Organization for Women (NOW), have argued that what chiefly ails the party system is the failure of the two major parties to express or represent significant points of view within the electorate. This problem, they say, can be cured by opening up the system to the emergence of a third, fourth, or infinite number of parties.

Several eminent political scientists have joined this call for change to a multi-party system. Robert Dahl, for example, has charged that it is "highly unlikely. . . that the deprivation of Negro rights could have gone on so long, with so little national attention, if the United States had . . . three or four major parties, and more sources of ideological dissent." Theodore Lowi contends: "A two-party system simply cannot grapple with complex programmatic alternatives in a manner that is meaningful to large electorates." Under a multi-party system, Lowi claims, "parties could present real choices, especially after everyone begins to recognize that the compromises would take place in the legislature, after the election."[6]

As I argued in Chapter 1, elimination of the electoral college system as it now operates would go a long way toward destroying the two-party system in the United States. If third or fourth parties come to hold the balance of power in close presidential elections—as has rarely happened under the electoral college system—nonmainstream candidates like Jesse Jackson and Pat Robertson, and special-interest groups like NOW, will be strongly motivated to form parties of their own that will play powerful roles in national politics. If the two-party system crumbles at the presidential level, it will probably not long survive at the congressional or state levels.

If the two-party system somehow survived elimination of the electoral college, its demise could certainly be achieved through the more drastic constitutional changes of installing a proportional representation system of elections or going to a parliamentary system of government (both steps that are favored for other reasons by some heavy thinkers).

The two-party system, of course, has its shortcomings, of the kind pointed to by Dahl and Lowi. Minority points of view, particularly the views of relatively small minorities proposing changes that challenge current orthodoxies, do get less representation than they would under a multi-party system. The full range of ideological choices usually present in most European democratic polities has generally not been available in the United States.

The governmental disadvantages of going to a multi-party system—to say nothing of the political costs—seem to me, however, far to outweigh what would be gained. Multi-party systems have at times caused havoc in such relatively homogeneous countries as France, Italy, and the Netherlands. In a country as large and varied as the United States, a multi-party system would be likely to produce paralysis of government at the national level. (Divided control of government by *two* parties has done damage enough.) Emergence of a multi-party system in the 1850s contributed to subsequent secession and civil war. It is perhaps unfair to invoke the Nazis as an extreme example—but the Weimar republic's multi-party system did play an important part in opening the door to Hitler in the 1930s.

Moreover, as I have argued, the range of ideological choice usually offered by the American two-party system is wider than has generally been recognized. There *is* usually more than a dime's worth of difference between the Republican and Democratic parties. The two great ideological traditions represented by our major parties, while sharing many fundamental values and therefore supporting national unity in times of crisis, differ significantly on important issues. The absence of monarchists and Marxists as real choices in most American elections seems an acceptable price for the advantages of the two-party system.

Minor parties have at times played a useful and influential role in American politics by developing issues and programs that were later taken up and put into effect by one of the major parties, as in the cases of the Abolitionists of the 1840s, the Populists of the 1890s, and the Progressives of 1912; or by enabling aggrieved minorities that felt unrepresented by either major party to let off steam, as in the cases of various Socialist parties and George Wallace's American Independent party of 1968. There are good arguments, on equity grounds, for lowering some of the legal barriers that the two major parties have taken such pains to put in the way of new or minor parties. But constitutional changes that would transform third parties from useful social goads to real contenders for political power would cause far more social damage than political good.[7]

CAMPAIGN FINANCE

I will not go far into the larger issues of political campaign finance reform which have been ably and extensively dealt with by such political scientists as Herbert Alexander, Michael Malbin, David Magleby, and Candice Nelson.[8] But certain aspects of campaign finance are crucial to the future of parties and therefore require attention here.

Amendment of the federal campaign finance law in 1979 permitted state and local parties to receive unreported contributions in unlimited amounts for "party-building" expenditures that would not be counted against limits on contributions for individual candidates. During the 1980s and early 1990s these so-called soft money contributions—distinguished from hard money contributions that went directly to candidates and therefore were subject to the tight limits set after the Watergate scandals—helped pump new life into some state and local party organizations. By the mid-1990s, however, soft money was being used by both national parties as a giant loophole to undermine federal campaign finance regulation.

After the 1996 election, when extensive circumvention and some outright violations of campaign finance laws were widely publicized, soft money became a principal target for reformers. In 1996 the two major parties together raised an estimated $263 million in soft money—about twelve times as much as in 1984. Early in 1997 Senators John McCain, Republican of Arizona, and Russell Feingold, Democrat of Wisconsin, introduced legislation that would completely prohibit soft money.

By then, however, another new development in campaign financing had further complicated the picture. Interest groups, both economic and ideological, had discovered they could largely accomplish their purposes through independently placed "issue advocacy" ads, not calling directly for the election of a particular candidate, but unmistakably presenting the case for a candidate or party, sometimes including candidates' names and pictures. The Supreme Court has held, on the basis of speech and press freedoms guaranteed by the Constitution, that the sources of money raised for such ads need not be reported. A study by the Annenberg Public Policy Center estimated that between $130 and $150 million was spent on issue advocacy ads in the 1996 congressional elections. The original McCain-Feingold bill would also have restricted independent advocacy ads that could reasonably be interpreted as favoring a particular candidate for federal office within 60 days of an election.

A bi-partisan counterpart of McCain-Feingold passed in the House, over the opposition of House Republican leaders. But Senate Republicans, finding themselves by now major beneficiaries of soft money, used a filibuster to prevent it from coming to a vote in the Senate.

McCain, in an effort to attract sufficient support to cut off a filibuster, ultimately dropped restrictions on independent issue advocacy ads. But with curbs on independent issue advocacy gone, the only institutions limited would be political parties—the one type of institution whose primary purpose is to affect the outcome of elections!

Full disclosure of the sources of all money used for political purposes, whether by parties or independent groups, coupled with substantial increases in unrealistic limits on hard money contributions, would go some distance toward dealing with the problem, but of course would not solve it entirely. Whether the Supreme Court would change its mind to allow requirement of full disclosure remains doubtful. Other, more incremental, reforms therefore are in order.

Before passage of the 1986 tax reform act, individuals were permitted to take a tax credit for 50 percent of political contributions, including contributions to parties, in figuring their federal income tax. Restoration and expansion of this credit would obviously benefit parties and should be regarded as a justified public expense.

Direct subsidization of parties by government, which some have suggested and several states now provide, seems to me, on the other hand, very dubious. The value of parties to democracy derives to a great extent from their being *independent* associations pursuing political objectives they choose for themselves. Some reformers argue that making parties directly dependent on government appropriations would not necessarily jeopardize that role. But the social risks, in my view, outweigh the financial benefits that parties would gain.[9]

Using selected forms of indirect government authority to aid parties, however, would be both legitimate and wise. The extension to political parties of the same low postage rates available to nonprofit and educational organizations in 1978 helped the parties to increase their mailings. It would be good public policy to set even lower rates for one or two mass mailings each year.

Probably the greatest single reform the federal government could enact to aid parties—and to clear up the campaign finance mess as well—would be to require that every television and radio station make available to parties during each campaign season a set amount of free time in prime-time viewing hours to use as the parties see fit. The skyrocketing cost of television advertising has been the most important factor driving up campaign costs. If free time were made available to parties to distribute among their candidates or to develop issues, some of the pressure of paying for television and radio advertising would be relieved, and officeholders and candidates would be motivated to look more to their parties for support.[10]

Many commentators argue that a law requiring electronic media to give parties free viewing time can never be enacted, for two reasons: individual officeholders do not really want to give that much power to their parties, and the political clout of the television industry will effectively block such a reform. To the first, it must be said that if politicians are serious when they claim they want to strengthen parties, this is one of the best ways to do it. And if they want free media time—which most do—obtaining it through the parties is more likely to be politically palatable to the public than giving it directly to candidates. To the second, the answer should be even firmer: if officeholders do not have the backbone to stand up to the television moguls to enact a reform that will serve both the public interest and their own long-term political interests, the need to cleanse the political system is even more urgent than has been realized. The original McCain-Feingold bill would have required TV stations to give low-rate air time to candidates, but McCain also dropped this provision, which was fiercely opposed by the broadcasting industry.

DEREGULATION

Political parties, like local government, operate for the most part under state law. The states, Leon Epstein points out, have tended to regard parties as "public utilities"—bodies with mixed private and public nature. Since the Progressive Era, most states have imposed tight regulations on how parties operate and manage their internal affairs. These regulations, Sabato argues, give the United States "the dubious distinction of hosting the most governmentally fettered parties in the democratic world."[11]

Some government regulation of parties is justified to assure the fairness of the procedures by which parties nominate candidates for public office and to prevent the erection of discriminatory barriers like those that used to be maintained by Democratic parties in the South. But the states have little legitimate interest in how the parties run their internal organizations or make political decisions.[12]

Existing state laws stipulating how state and local party committees are to be selected, who may serve on such committees, how committees are to be structured, and when they must meet should be repealed. Prohibitions against elected officeholders serving as party officers, of the kind enacted in the 1980s by New York, should be rescinded. Limits on party participation in local elections should be dropped.[13]

In the second half of the 1980s the Supreme Court delivered a number of important decisions declaring unconstitutional some of the regulations through which states had hobbled their parties. In 1986 the Court ruled that Connecticut could not prevent the state Republican party from instituting an open primary. In 1989 it declared unconstitutional California and Florida laws prohibiting state parties from making endorsements in primaries. While these rulings have improved the legal environment, the states should do more themselves to clean out unnecessary regulations still in effect.[14]

THE ELECTORAL PROCESS

Most states now require that parties nominate their candidates for office through primary elections. Some advocates of stronger parties—and some who would like to make the parties more open to citizen participation whether or not they are electorally strong—propose that parties go back to the caucus and convention systems for nominating candidates.

Through deregulation, parties should be permitted to choose their nominees in any (nondiscriminating) way that suits them. But under current conditions parties in most places, in my judgment, would be unwise to use this freedom to return to systems of nominating candidates through local caucuses or district conventions.

Primaries were adopted during the Progressive Era chiefly to overcome the power of machines to pack and dominate caucuses and conventions. The machines have now grown so weak that this is no longer much of a danger. But more recent experience has shown that in states that still use caucuses the main beneficiaries are often ideological activists promoting views that are not representative of rank-and-file opinion within their parties. Such "amateurs," in Wilson's terminology, are nowadays the people who are most likely to come out for lengthy party meetings and to act as cohesive blocs. In Minnesota, where party caucuses are used to screen candidates and to make endorsements before primaries, fewer than 2 percent of the voters normally participate. As a result, both of Minnesota's major parties (the Democratic Farmer-Labor and the Independent Republican) have at times been skewed toward their ideological extremes. At the presidential nominating level, which I will discuss more fully below, the 1988 successes of Pat Robertson in the Michigan and Iowa caucuses and Jesse Jackson in the Michigan caucuses showed the vulnerability of the caucus system to takeover by groups that represent only a small minority within the party. In one way of looking at it, the activists deserve to be rewarded for their dedication and effort. But if parties become exponents of extreme views, they will inevitably lose more of their ability to mobilize popular support.

Most advocates of strong parties prefer closed primaries, in which only registered party members can participate, over the various kinds of open primary. Closed primaries, they argue, build party cohesion, make parties responsible for their choices, and prevent raids by voters from outside the party. When the Supreme Court ruled in 1986 that Connecticut could not prohibit the Republican party from opening its primary to independents, strong-party advocates were pleased that the Court had struck a blow against state regulation, but many were dismayed at the end for which deregulation in this case was to be used.[15]

The arguments in favor of closed primaries seem to me generally sound. But I do not think it would be a good thing if *all* states adopted the closed primary. It is worth recalling that the progressives opposed closed primaries because they permitted two established party machines acting in collusion to divide and conquer insurgent reformers. If each machine controlled its own primary, real choice in the general election might be eliminated. This danger, though now substantially reduced, still exists in such places as Chicago and West Virginia. Also, use of the open primary by a minority party to attract new supporters, as the Connecticut Republicans set out to do, seems a permissible political tactic. One of the advantages of a federal system is that various states can continue to experiment with different procedures. The comparative benefits and liabilities of allowing parties to keep their operations, including primaries, as open as they choose deserve further trial.

Two other proposed reforms in electoral procedures (actually reinstatements of procedures that were dropped by many states during the Progressive Era) are less ambiguous. The straight-party lever (or straight-party box in places that still use paper ballots), through which a voter can cast his or her ballot for a party's entire ticket through a single motion (or a single mark on the ballot), is now available in only 20 states. Because it promotes party cohesion and makes voting simpler without preventing the voter from selecting individually for separate offices if he or she chooses, it should be more generally adopted.

Likewise, voter registration or enrollment by party or as an independent, now required by only half the states, is a useful party-building tool, even in states with open primaries, and involves no significant invasion of the voter's right to privacy. It should be extended to states, mainly in the South and Midwest, which do not currently require it.

COMMUNITY SERVICE

Though changes in law and governmental procedures can help rebuild the parties, most of the work of party renewal must be done by the party organizations themselves.

Contemporary parties would be wise to follow the model of the old machines in making the town or neighborhood party organization a center for social activities and community functions as well as for tasks that are directly political. It is probably no longer feasible for most party organizations to provide their supporters with turkeys at Christmas time, but parties can still perform many valuable services in guiding citizens through the tangles of modern bureaucracy. In some cities, Baltimore for example, party clubhouses still seem to be focuses of neighborhood social life.[16] Some party organizations in urban areas have succeeded in attracting unattached young people by sponsoring recreational events that provide opportunities for social contact. Party organizations that offer their communities a variety of social activities, such as picnics, dances, amateur theater productions, and bingo games, may realize rich political rewards.

Parties may also become vehicles for volunteer service devoted to filling community or environmental needs. The RNC during the 1980s encouraged sponsorship by local party units of projects like cleaning up litter in the Grand Canyon, organizing food banks for the needy, and conducting job fairs. Although the DNC had no counterpart program at the national level, some local Democratic committees undertook similar projects.[17]

Parties are primarily organized to achieve political objectives, and they should keep such objectives uppermost in allocating their limited energies and resources.

But non-political activities that help parties with their primary tasks and are either fun or socially useful are certainly worth considering.

A NEW WAY TO NOMINATE PRESIDENTS

One of the most important responsibilities that our system entrusts to the major parties is that of selecting the two candidates for President. The nominating process through which parties winnow the field of presidential candidates has enormous impact on the course of national government. Moreover, it strongly influences the judgment of individual voters on which party, if either, they should regard as their political home. The quadrennial party conventions, at least in theory and to some degree in fact, are the parties' highest governing bodies.

The mixed system of delegate selection, partly through primaries and partly through choice by state party organizations, that existed from the Progressive Era through 1968 for the most part served both the nation and the parties well. Though it produced an occasional Warren Harding, most of the candidates nominated by both major parties were of high calibre. The heated battles for the presidential nomination that occurred at most conventions when the party did not have an incumbent President seeking reelection stirred up popular enthusiasm and helped persuade voters that parties were significant institutions.

The same cannot be said of the system launched early in the 1970s by the McGovern–Fraser reforms, under which candidates usually are nominated in the primaries and the conventions are little more than prolonged "photo opportunities." Conventions have become more demographically representative than they were under the old system, and certainly many more people get to participate in the selection process. But the special-interest groups and political consultants who dominate candidate organizations have become the major players in controlling the conventions. The result is that the conventions are less *politically representative* than they were under the old system. The new process of selecting presidential candidates is of course not the only reason for the decline of voters' interest in and support for parties. But the coincidence of the two phenomena in time suggests they are related.

Under the current system for nominating presidential candidates, moreover, campaigns begin too early, go on for too long, cost too much money, and are usually settled too early in the election year.

What is to be done? Many politicians and some political scientists and journalists would like to go back to the old system—"back to the smoke-filled room." But that is not possible. In a democracy it is usually not feasible to move from what is perceived to be a more democratic process to one that is perceived to be less democratic. Nor in this case is it really desirable. The old system had serious flaws. It really did, as the McGovern–Fraser commission charged, unfairly limit the representation of some groups, and the smoke-filled-room metaphor suggests a form of oligarchic control that is inconsistent with democratic values.

What is needed is a system that restores the national convention as a genuine decision-making body truly representative of the party in the electorate but at the same time retains the good effects of the McGovern–Fraser reforms. Proposals for a national primary or regional primaries through which candidates would be directly nominated would probably make the situation worse. A national primary that directly nominated candidates would further undermine the parties, increase the candidate-orientation of national politics, and heighten the influence of PACs, consultants, and interest groups. Regional primaries, proposed by some state officials, would keep most of the bad features of the present system and would exacerbate its tendency to give undue influence to the states that go first.

The late Everett Carll Ladd, reacting to defects in the present system, offered a plan under which one-third of convention delegates would be allotted to party officials and officeholders, and the other two-thirds chosen through "nationally structured primaries to be held on a single day—for example, the third Tuesday in June." Each state's delegation under Ladd's plan would be divided in proportion to the support received in the primaries by the presidential candidates, with a threshold requirement of 10 percent in the state before a candidate received any delegates.[18]

My own modification of Ladd's plan, which he conceded might be improved, is as follows: All members of Congress, all governors, party leaders in state legislatures, and all state party chairs and vice-chairs would automatically be made delegates to their party's national convention. This would achieve a certain amount of "peer group" review, one of Ladd's objectives, while improving on the somewhat arbitrary system of selecting certain officeholders as "super-delegates" that the Democrats have used since 1984. It would also give some bonus to states that elect a party's candidates to state and congressional offices. The other delegates would be elected by party members (as defined by each state party), two from each House district, in primaries held on the same day in the late spring all over the nation. Candidates for delegate could run pledged to a presidential candidate or unpledged. The first two "past the post" in each House district would be elected.

What would be the effects of this plan? In a year when one candidate was far ahead of the pack, as Ronald Reagan was for the Republican nomination in 1980, he would in effect be nominated on the primary day. But in most years support at the time of the primary would probably be divided among several candidates, and the nominating decision would be more likely to go to the convention. We could get back to something like the old system with most of the old system's undemocratic features removed.

There would be some costs. It may be dangerous, as James Ceaser has pointed out, to go so far in "nationalizing" the rules governing the nominating process—though a kind of de facto nationalization is already taking place. Whatever value there is in having presidential candidates handshake their way across Iowa and New

Hampshire—and some thoughtful observers believe there is a good deal (though Iowa and New Hampshire are hardly representative of the United States)—would be lost. And the influence of television, alas, would probably be further magnified.[19]

Whether it is worth paying these costs and embarking on yet another round of reform (reform of reform) depends on how severe one judges the flaws in the present system to be. I think they are potentially very severe. From the standpoint of the overall national interest the present system has several serious shortcomings. One is that the time and effort now required to mount an effective campaign make it very difficult for some of the most highly qualified individuals in both parties, those already holding important offices such as governorships of major states and leadership posts in Congress, to run for President, and heavily handicap those who do run. In 1988, Governor Mario Cuomo of New York was deterred from running for the Democratic nomination for President by the responsibilities of his office; and Senator Bob Dole of Kansas, minority leader in the Senate, was burdened in his pursuit of the Republican nomination by his duties in Washington. In 1992, Governor Cuomo almost surely, and House Minority Leader Richard Gephardt probably, would have launched early candidacies if the rigors of the primary schedule had not conflicted with their jobs. In 1996, Senator Dole found it necessary to give up the Senate leadership to devote full time to running for the Republican nomination for President. In 2000, the problems encountered by Governor George W. Bush in the early Republican primaries were attributable in part—though certainly not entirely—to his being held down well into the primary season by gubernatorial responsibilities in Texas. The only important office that does not seriously weigh on the time and energy needed by non-incumbent candidates to run for President under the present system is Vice President.

From the standpoint of the welfare of the parties—which in this context is my particular interest—the present system of nominating presidential candidates undermines the role and influence of state and local party organizations, weakens the effectiveness of the party in government, and reinforces other social forces that have been sapping the strength of parties in the electorate.

For both broad social reasons and reasons pertaining particularly to the interests of parties, therefore, I am convinced that the system through which parties nominate presidential candidates needs to be overhauled.

A SENSE OF PURPOSE

Skilled political technicians like Martin Van Buren, Francis Preston Blair, Thurlow Weed, Mark Hanna, Will Hays, Jim Farley, and Bill Brock, and state and local party bosses like Simon Cameron, Zachariah Chandler, Matthew Stanley Quay, Richard Croker, Martin Lomasney, and Richard Daley, in their own times helped produce vigorous and effective parties. Their like would be useful now in rebuilding party machinery, utilizing new technologies, and developing grassroots party networks.

But the basic source of the strength of successful parties in times past, as many of the technicians and bosses themselves would concede, lay not in machinery or techniques or systems of organization, but in the sense of public purpose that moved their grassroots workers and the voters who identified with them in the electorate.

National parties have been at their most effective under leaders like Andrew Jackson, Abraham Lincoln, William McKinley, Woodrow Wilson, Franklin Roosevelt, and Ronald Reagan, who have regarded parties not simply as instruments for winning elections, or for gathering the spoils of office, but as a means for achieving essential public goals. The same can be said of vigorous minority parties led by politicians like Henry Clay, William Jennings Bryan, and Robert Taft. Though those parties did not directly set the course of government, they aggressively tested the majority party and often planted seeds from which later majorities grew.

The visions pursued and the programs presented by strong majority and minority parties did not always serve the public interest well, or at least as well as the times required. But parties moved by a sense of public purpose, even at their most misguided, have met two primary needs of democracy: they provided a foundation, both electoral and programmatic, on which coherent government policies could be built; and they served public accountability by giving voters a meaningful choice in elections.

There is a continuing argument in political science over whether political parties are best regarded as vote-getting machines that take whatever policy positions are needed to win elections, or whether they are more truly described by Edmund Burke's definition of party as a body of citizens "united, for promoting by their joint endeavors the national interest, upon some particular principle in which they are all agreed." There are important distinctions between these two views, and there is some empirical evidence on both sides. But the fact is, as American political history amply shows, and as can be shown from the histories of other nations as well, that the parties that have been the most successful vote-getting machines over any prolonged period have been parties that at least in a general way fulfill Burke's definition. Parties that have done best electorally, such as the Jacksonian Democrats, the Civil War and turn-of-the-century Republicans, and the New Deal Democrats, have gained much of their dynamism from the conviction among party workers and those identifying with the party in the electorate that they were promoting "the national interest, upon some particular principle [or principles] in which they are all agreed."

To say that party renewal depends finally on a stronger sense of public purpose is not to say how such a sense, or the policy programs that embody it, are to take shape. Parties cannot produce a sense of public purpose out of thin air, nor should they. But each of the major national parties today stands in the line of a great ideological tradition, either the republican or the liberal. These traditions do not automatically suggest programs that embody purpose. But when the values they represent are applied to the opportunities and needs of our time, concrete goals and programs should be forthcoming.

Political consultants, academic experts, and journalistic pundits are of some help in developing ideas for party programs. But the major work must be done by political leaders themselves. Woodrow Wilson was right when he said that strong parties require strong leadership. Perhaps it is difficult when surveying current party luminaries, or potential luminaries now in the second or third ranks, to imagine any of them providing the kind of leadership Wilson had in mind. But observers attempting prophecy in the 1850s would have expressed similar doubts about Abraham Lincoln as would those in the 1920s about Franklin Roosevelt.

Democracies are continuously threatened by the competing demons of social atomism and authoritarianism, though the American polity has been fairly successful at keeping both pretty much at bay. At the beginning of the twenty-first century the forces promoting atomism seem to pose the graver danger to the nation's social, cultural, and political health. But if atomism were to proceed far toward social or cultural anarchy, there almost surely would be an authoritarian reaction.

It is therefore imperative that our institutions balance the needs for social order and effective government with the needs for public accountability and the protection of personal liberties. Traditionally, political parties have played a major role in maintaining that balance, and the Republic would certainly have developed along very different lines without them.

Parties at best are imperfect institutions. Some of the reservations the Founders expressed about them were justified. But by and large they have served democracy and the United States well. They should not be turned into emotional idols, conveying social hatreds or blocking rational political discourse. But they should be renewed as vibrant political institutions, capable of mobilizing voters to take up again the challenge of making good the unfolding promises of American life.

NOTES

Chapter 1. Introduction: The American Two-Party System

1. Supplement to *American Political Science Review*, vol. 44 (September, 1950), pp. 1–15; James L. Sundquist, "Strengthening the National Parties" in A. James Reichley, ed., *Elections American Style* (Brookings, Washington, DC, 1987), p. 221; Larry J. Sabato, *The Party's Just Begun* (Scott, Foresman, Glenview, IL, 1988), p. 5; Leon D. Epstein, *Political Parties in the American Mold* (U. of Wisconsin Press, Madison, 1986), p. 38.
2. E. E. Schattschneider, *Party Government* (Rinehart, New York, 1942), p. 1; Maurice Duverger, *Political Parties* (Wiley, New York, 1954), pp. 425–26.
3. The meanings I give these terms are of course almost the reverse of those recently assigned them by scholars like J. G. A. Pocock, Robert Bellah, and Gordon Wood. But it seems to me more sensible and less confusing to use terms as they are now generally understood than to give them meanings currently abandoned, at least in the United States. I will discuss in later chapters how the meanings of both terms have evolved. J. G. A. Pocock, *The Machiavellian Moment: Florentine Political Thought and the Atlantic Republican Tradition* (Princeton U. Press, Princeton, NJ, 1975); Robert N. Bellah *et al.*, *Habits of the Heart: Individualism and Commitment in American Life* (U. of California Press, Berkeley, 1985); Gordon S. Wood, *The Creation of the American Republic* (U. of North Carolina Press, Chapel Hill, 1969). For a partial refutation of the interpretation of ideological divisions in the eighteenth century propounded by Pocock and Wood, see Isaac Kramnick, *Republicanism and Bourgeois Radicalism: Political Ideology in Late Eighteenth-Century England and America* (Cornell U. Press, Ithaca, NY, 1990).
4. Arthur M. Schlesinger, Jr. *The Cycles of American History* (Houghton Mifflin, Boston, 1986).
5. V. O. Key, "A Theory of Critical Elections," *Journal of Politics,* 1955, v. 17, pp. 3–18.
6. Nikolai Kondratieff, *The Long Wave Cycle* (Richardson & Snyder, New York, 1984).

Chapter 2. Intention of the Founders: A Polity Without Parties

1. Noble E. Cunningham, Jr., *The Jeffersonian Republicans: The Formation of Party Organization, 1789–1801* (U. of North Carolina Press, Chapel Hill, 1957), p. 94.
2. Jefferson to Francis Hopkinson, March 13, 1789, quoted by Arthur M. Schlesinger, Jr., *The Cycles of American History* (Houghton Mifflin, Boston, 1986), p. 258; Hamilton and Madison quotes from *The Federalist* (Modern Library, New York, 1937), pp. 4 and 54;

Adams to Jonathan Jackson, October 2, 1780, quoted by Daniel Sisson, *The American Revolution of 1800* (Knopf, New York, 1974), p. 49.

3. Walter Berns, *The First Amendment and the Future of American Democracy* (Basic Books, New York, 1970), p. 205.

4. Sisson, *American Revolution,* p. 207; Gerald Stourzh, *Alexander Hamilton and the Idea of Republican Government* (Stanford U. Press, Stanford, CA, 1970), p. 118.

5. A. H. M. Jones, *Athenian Democracy* (Blackwell, Oxford, England, 1957); Lily Ross Taylor, *Party Politics in the Age of Caesar* (U. of California Press, Berkeley, 1949).

6. Harold Perkin, *The Origins of Modern English Society: 1780–1880* (Routledge & Kegan Paul, London, 1969), p. 50; L.B. Namier, *England in the Age of the American Revolution* (Macmillan, New York, 1930), p. 207. For discussions of Tory and Whig ideology, see J. C. D. Clark, *English Society: 1688–1832* (Cambridge U. Press, New York, 1985), pp. 74–93; and W.H. Greenleaf, *Order, Empiricism and Politics, Two Traditions of English Political Thought: 1500–1700* (Oxford U. Press, Oxford, England, 1964), pp. 80–94, 142–205.

7. David E. Ginter, *Whig Organization in the General Election of 1790* (U. of California Press, Berkeley, 1967), pp. xix–xxi; R. L. McKenzie, *British Political Parties* (St. Martin's Press, New York, 1952), p. 3.

8. Bernard Bailyn, *The Ideological Origins of the American Revolution* (Harvard U. Press, Cambridge, MA, 1967), p. 35.

9. Bailyn, *Ideological Origins,* pp. 289ff.; Gordon S. Wood, "The Democratization of the Mind in the American Revolution," in *The Moral Foundations of the American Republic* (U. Press of Virginia, Charlottesville, 1986), p. 113.

10. Jackson Turner Main, *Political Parties Before the Constitution* (U. of North Carolina Press, Chapel Hill, 1973), pp. 326–55. Main uses the labels cosmopolitans and localists to identify the groups I call conservatives and populists. Main's terms capture cultural characteristics but I think mine are better at conveying political orientation.

11. *Ibid.,* pp. 365–407.

12. Henry F. May, *The Enlightenment in America* (Oxford U. Press, New York, 1976), p. 199.

13. *Ibid.,* pp. 174–211; Gordon S. Wood, *The Creation of the American Republic* (U. of North Carolina Press, Chapel Hill, 1969), p. 233.

14. May, *Enlightenment,* p. 201.

15. Richard P. McCormick, *The Second American Party System* (Norton, New York, 1966), p. 106; Alfred F. Young, "The Clintonians of New York," in *The First Party System,* W. N. Chambers, ed. (Wiley, New York, 1972), pp. 23–25; Main, *Political Parties,* pp. 143–49.

16. *Ibid.,* pp. 244–48; J. R. Pole, "Deference Politics in Virginia," in *The First Party System,* Chambers, ed., p. 35; Rhys Isaac, *The Transformation of Virginia: 1740–1790* (U. of North Carolina Press, Chapel Hill, 1982), p. 319; David Hackett Fischer, *Albion's Seed: Four British Folkways in America* (Oxford U. Press, New York, 1989), pp. 405–10.

17. Main, *Political Parties,* pp. 115, 118.

18. *Ibid.,* pp. 104, 118.

19. Dickinson quoted by Wood, *American Republic,* pp. 430–31; Knox letter quoted in Louis Hacker, *The Triumph of American Capitalism* (Columbia U. Press, New York, 1940), p. 185; Hamilton quoted by Main, *Political Parties,* p. 151; Madison quoted by Richard K. Matthews, *The Radical Politics of Thomas Jefferson: A Revisionist View* (U. of Kansas Press, Lawrence, KS, 1984), p. 100.

20. Charles A. Beard, *An Economic Interpretation of the Constitution of the United States* (Macmillan, New York, 1935), p. 324.
21. *The Federalist*, pp. 47, 15.
22. *Ibid.*, pp. 55–56.
23. *Ibid.*, p. 58.
24. *Ibid.*, pp. 55–57, 62.
25. *Ibid.*, p. 56.
26. *Ibid.*, p. 61.
27. *Ibid.*, p. 339.
28. *Ibid.*, pp. 338–39.
29. *Ibid.*, p. 337.
30. Main, *Political Parties*, pp. 357–58.
31. Wood, *American Republic*, pp. 483–99; Jefferson quoted by Richard Hofstadter, *The Idea of a Party System* (U. of California Press, Berkeley, 1969), p. 123.
32. *Ibid.*, p. 196; Sisson, *American Revolution*, pp. 42, 43, 45, 52.
33. James L. Sundquist, "Strengthening the National Parties," in A. James Reichley, ed., *Elections American Style*, (Brookings, Washington, DC, 1987), p. 20.

Chapter 3.   The First Parties: Federalists and Republicans

1. John C. Miller, *The Federalists Era: 1789–1801* (Harper, New York, 1960), pp. 1–19.
2. Martin Van Buren, *Inquiry into the Origin and Course of Political Parties in the United States* (Kelley, New York, 1967), p. 60.
3. Drew R. McCoy, *The Elusive Republic: Political Economy in Jeffersonian America* (U. of North Carolina Press, Chapel Hill, 1980), p. 153.
4. Richard K. Matthews, *The Radical Politics of Thomas Jefferson* (U. of Kansas Press, Lawrence, KS, 1984; Russell Kirk, *The Conservative Mind: From Burke to Eliot* (Regnery, Washington, DC, 1986), p. 77.
5. Stourzh, *Alexander Hamilton and the Idea of Republican Government* (Stanford U. Press, Stanford, CA, 1970), p. 74.
6. *Ibid.*, p. 16; Matthews, *Radical Politics*, p. 114.
7. Noble E. Cunningham, *The Jeffersonian Republicans: The Formation of Party Organization, 1789–1801* (U. of North Carolina Press, Chapel Hill, 1957), pp. 8–9.
8. *Ibid.*, p. 11.
9. *Ibid.*, p. 12.
10. *Ibid.*, pp. 21, 22; Lance Banning, *The Jeffersonian Persuasion: Evolution of a Party Ideology* (Cornell U. Press, Ithaca, NY, 1978), pp. 161, 165.
11. *Ibid.*, p. 177; Cunningham, *Jeffersonian Republicans*, pp. 14–20.
12. Richard Hofstadter, *The Idea of a Party System* (U. of California Press, Berkeley, 1969), pp. 80–84.
13. *The Federalist* (Modern Library, New York, 1937), pp. 343, 371.
14. Van Buren, *Inquiry*, p. 207.
15. Thomas Jefferson, *Notes on the State of Virginia* (Norton, New York, 1972), p. 163; Madison quoted by Henry F. May, *The Enlightenment in America* (Oxford U. Press, New York, 1976), p. 100.
16. Cunningham, *Jeffersonian Republicans*, p. 48.

17. G. Adolf Koch, *Republican Religion: The American Revolution and the Cult of Reason* (Holt, New York, 1933), p. xii.

18. Donald H. Meyer, *The Democratic Enlightenment* (Putnam, New York, 1976), pp. 137, 142.

19. May, *Enlightenment*, p. 289.

20. William Nisbet Chambers, "Party Development and Party Action," in Chambers, ed., *The First Party System* (Wiley, New York, 1972), p. 52.

21. May, *Enlightenment*, pp. 244–45.

22. *Ibid.*, p. 245; Stourzh, *Hamilton*, p. 122.

23. Cunningham, *Jeffersonian Republicans*, p. 256, argues that "the Republican party was not the outgrowth of persisting state parties." It "was a new growth that sprang from the divisions in Congress and the national government. . . ." But see David Hackett Fischer, "The Revolution of American Conservatism" in *First Party System*, Chambers, ed., pp. 78–84; and Banning, *Jeffersonian Persuasion*, p. 114. See also Alfred F. Young, "The Democratic Republicans of New York," p. 96; Henry Ammon, "The Jeffersonian Republicans in Virginia," p. 111; and Paul Goodman, "The Democratic–Republicans of Massachusetts," p. 101, all in *First Party System;* Chambers, ed., and Daniel Sisson, *The American Revolution of 1800* (Knopf, New York, 1974), p. 213.

24. Van Buren, *Inquiry*, p. 182.

25. Banning, *Jeffersonian Persuasion*, p. 243.

26. *Ibid.*, p. 94; Cunningham, *Jeffersonian Republicans*, p. 71.

27. Banning, *Jeffersonian Persuasion*, p. 243; Hofstadter, *Idea*, pp. 126–27; Van Buren, *Inquiry*, p. 486.

28. Banning, *Jeffersonian Republicans*, p. 91.

29. *Annals of America*, vol. 3 (Encyclopedia Britannica, Chicago, 1968), pp. 610–11.

30. Cunningham, *Jeffersonian Republicans*, p. 91.

31. *Ibid.*, pp. 95–96.

32. *Ibid.*, pp. 106–107.

33. Hofstadter, *Idea*, p. 115.

34. May, *Enlightenment*, p. 255; Hofstadter, *Idea*, pp. 101, 107.

35. *Ibid.*, p. 106.

36. *Ibid.*, pp. 108–109.

37. *Annals*, p. 67.

38. Hofstadter, *Idea*, p. 107.

39. *Ibid.*, p. 110.

40. Cunningham, *Jeffersonian Republicans*, pp. 138–39.

41. *Ibid.*, p. 164.

42. *Ibid.*, pp. 164–65.

43. *Ibid.*, p. 146.

44. Stourzh, *Hamilton*, p. 33.

45. Cunningham, *Jeffersonian Republicans*, pp. 182–83.

46. *Ibid.*, pp. 254, 257.

47. *Ibid.*, p. 250.

48. *Ibid.*, p. 183.

49. *Ibid.*, p. 254.

50. Fischer, "Revolution," p. 81; Koch, *Republican Religion*, p. 246.

51. Van Buren, quoted in Anson Phelps Stokes, *Church and State in the United States* (Harper, New York, 1950), vol. 1, p. 675; Cunningham, *Jeffersonian Republicans,* p. 225.

52. A. James Reichley, *Religion in American Public Life* (Brookings, Washington, DC, 1985), pp. 177–82; Cunningham, *Jeffersonian Republicans,* p. 219.

53. For a discussion of the Federalists in opposition from 1800 to 1816, see David Hackett Fischer, *The Revolution of American Conservatism* (Harper, New York, 1965). Fischer argues that the Federalists in this period, though unable to win national elections, were more politically effective than is generally understood.

54. Allen Potter, "Great Britain: Opposition with a Capital 'O'," in *Political Oppositions in Western Democracies,* ed. by Robert A. Dahl (Yale U. Press, New Haven, CT, 1966), p. 7.

55. May, *Enlightenment,* p. 260; Van Buren, *Inquiry,* p. 251; Brogan, quoted in Clinton Rossiter, *Parties and Politics in America* (Cornell U. Press, Ithaca, NY, 1960), p. 77.

56. Meyer, *Enlightenment,* pp. 144, xii.

57. Stourzh, *Hamilton,* p. 40; Van Buren, *Inquiry,* p. 80.

58. *Ibid.,* p. 484.

59. A. James Reichley, *Conservatives in an Age of Change* (Brookings, Washington, DC, 1981), p. 10.

60. Hofstadter, *Idea,* pp. 102, 128.

61. *Ibid.,* p. 153; Cunningham, *Jeffersonian Republicans,* p. 142.

Chapter 4. One-Party Hegemony: The Jeffersonians

1. Daniel Sisson, *The American Revolution of 1800* (Knopf, New York, 1974), p. 11.

2. Henry Adams, *History of the United States of America during the Administrations of Thomas Jefferson* (Viking, New York, 1986), pp. 170–72.

3. Richard Buel, Jr., *Securing the Revolution: Ideology in American Politics, 1789–1815* (Cornell U. Press, Ithaca, NY, 1972); John C. Miller, *The Federalist Era* (Harper, New York, 1960), pp. 268–75.

4. Morton Borden, *The Federalism of James A. Bayard* (Columbia U. Press, New York, 1954), pp. 86–91.

5. Carl E. Prince, "The Passing of the Aristocracy" in William Nisbet Chambers, ed., *The First Party System* (Wiley, New York, 1972), p. 163.

6. *Ibid.,* p. 164.

7. Sisson, *Revolution,* p. 60.

8. Noble E. Cunningham, "An Embodiment in the House?" in Chambers, ed., *First Party System,* p. 135.

9. Richard P. McCormick, *The Second American Party System* (Norton, New York, 1966), pp. 231–31.

10. Paul Goodman, "The Democratic-Republicans of Massachusetts," in Chambers, ed., *First Party System,* p. 101.

11. Sisson, *Revolution,* p. 87; Richard K. Matthews, *The Radical Politics of Thomas Jefferson* (U. of Kansas Press, Lawrence, KS, 1984), pp. 23, 85, 86.

12. Andrew W. Foshee, "Jeffersonian Political Economy and the Classical Tradition," *History of Political Economy,* vol. 17, no. 4 (Winter, 1985), pp. 531–32; Matthews, *Jefferson,* p. 32.

13. Matthews, *Jefferson*, p. 27; Martin Van Buren, *Inquiry into the Origin and Course of Political Parties in the United States* (Kelley, New York, 1967), p. 41.
14. Matthews, *Jefferson*, p. 37.
15. Donald H. Meyer, *The Democratic Enlightenment* (Putnam, New York, 1976), p. 115.
16. Matthews, *Jefferson*, p. 23.
17. *Ibid.*, pp. 15–18.
18. Walter Dean Burnham, "The American Voter," in Thomas Ferguson and Joel Rogers, eds., *The Political Economy* (Sharpe, Armonk, NY, 1984), pp. 117–19.
19. McCormick, *Second Party System*, pp. 41, 108; William N. Chambers and Philip C. Davis, "Party, Competition, and Mass Participation: The Case of the Democratizing Party System, 1824–1852," in Joel H. Silbey, Allan G. Bogue, and William H. Flanigan, eds., *The History of American Electoral Behavior* (Princeton U. Press, Princeton, NJ, 1978), pp. 174–95.
20. Walter Dean Burnham, "The Turnout Problem," in A. James Reichley, ed., *Elections American Style* (Brookings, Washington, DC, 1987), p. 113.
21. Anson Phelps Stokes, *Church and State in the United States,* vol. 1 (Harper, New York, 1950), p. 509.
22. Adams, *History,* pp. 429–30.
23. Gerald Stourzh, *Alexander Hamilton and the Idea of Republican Government* (Stanford U. Press, Stanford, CA, 1970), pp. 39–40.
24. For a comprehensive study of Federalism in its declining years, see David Hackett Fischer, *The Revolution of American Conservatism* (Harper, New York, 1965).
25. Howard Lee McBain, *DeWitt Clinton and the Origin of the Spoils System in New York* (Columbia U. Press, New York, 1907), p. 77; McCormick, *Second Party System,* p. 109.
26. McCormick, *Second Party System,* p. 111.
27. Donald B. Cole, *Martin Van Buren and the American Political System* (Princeton U. Press, Princeton, NJ, 1984), p. 49.
28. *Ibid.*, p. 95.
29. Marvin Meyers, *The Jacksonian Persuasion: Politics and Belief* (Stanford U. Press, Stanford, CA, 1957), p. 109.
30. Noble E. Cunningham, Jr., "Presidential Leadership, Political Parties, and the Congressional Caucus, 1800–1824," in Patricia Bonomi, James MacGregor Burns, and Austin Ranney, eds., *The American Constitutional System Under Strong and Weak Parties* (Praeger, New York, 1981), pp. 11–12.
31. Richard Hofstadter, *The Idea of a Party System* (U. of California Press, Berkeley, 1969), pp. 188–293.
32. Van Buren, *Inquiry into the Origin and Course of Political Parties,* p. 3.
33. Cole, *Van Buren,* pp. 112–17.
34. Robert V. Remini, *The Life of Andrew Jackson* (Harper, New York, 1988), pp. 28–41.
35. McCormick, *Second Party System,* pp. 129, 223.
36. Martin Van Buren, *Autobiography,* vol. 1, edited by John C. Fitzpatrick (Da Capo Press, New York, 1920), p. 152.
37. Cole, *Van Buren,* p. 159.
38. Stokes, *Church and State in the United States,* vol. 1 pp. 693–98; Robert V. Remini, *Andrew Jackson and the Course of American Democracy, 1833–1845* (Harper, New York, 1985), p. 74; Ronald P. Formisano, *The Birth of Mass Political Parties: Michigan,*

1827–1861 (Princeton U. Press, Princeton, NJ, 1971), pp. 137–64; A. James Reichley, *Religion in American Public Life* (Brookings, Washington, DC, 1985), pp. 180–83.

39. Thurlow Weed, *Autobiography,* edited by Harriet A. Weed and Thurlow Weed Barned, vol. 1 (Houghton Mifflin, Boston, 1884), p. 180.

40. Cole, *Van Buren,* p. 96.

41. Ralph M. Goldman, *The National Party Chairmen and Committees: Factionalism at the Top* (Sharpe, Armonk, NY, 1990), p. 13.

Chapter 5.   Formation of Mass Parties: Democrats and Whigs

1. Marvin Meyers, *The Jacksonian Persuasion: Politics and Belief* (Stanford U. Press, Stanford, CA, 1957), p. 21.

2. Martin Van Buren, *Inquiry into the Origin and Course of Political Parties in the United States* (Kelley, New York, 1967), p. 2. For a discussion of the roots of Jacksonian ideology in pre-Revolutionary populism and Jeffersonian equalitarian agrarianism, see John Ashworth *"Agrarians" and "Aristocrats": Party Political Ideology in the United States, 1837–1846* (Cambridge U. Press, New York, 1987), pp. 7–51.

3. Martin Van Buren, *Autobiography,* vol. 1 (Da Capo, New York, 1920), pp. 341–42.

4. Richard Hofstadter, *The Idea of a Party System* (U. of California Press, Berkeley, 1969), pp. 239–52; Richard P. McCormick, *The Second American Party System* (Norton, New York, 1966), pp. 120–24.

5. William Ernest Smith, *The Francis Preston Blair Family in Politics,* vol. 1 (Macmillan, New York, 1933), p. 88.

6. Donald B. Cole, *Martin Van Buren and the American Political System* (Princeton U. Press, Princeton, NJ, 1984), pp. 95–96.

7. Van Buren letter to Thomas Ritchie, 1827, quoted by James W. Ceaser, *Presidential Selection: Theory and Development* (Princeton U. Press, Princeton, NJ, 1979), pp. 135–38.

8. Cole, *Van Buren,* p. 94. The journalist was the young James Gordon Bennett, on his way to founding the illustrious *New York Herald.*

9. Hofstadter, *Idea,* pp. 244–45.

10. Cole, *Van Buren,* p. 94.

11. Ceaser, *Presidential Selection,* p. 152.

12. Richard P. McCormick, *The Second American Party System* (Norton, New York, 1966), p. 61.

13. *Ibid.,* pp. 182–98; Cole, *Van Buren,* p. 96.

14. Van Buren, *Autobiography,* vol. 2, p. 584.

15. Richard C. Bain and Judith H. Parris, *Convention Decisions and Voting Records* (Brookings, Washington, DC, 1973), p. 18.

16. Lee Benson, *The Concept of Jacksonian Democracy: New York as a Test Case* (Princeton U. Press, Princeton, NJ, 1961), p. 94.

17. Richard L. McCormick, *The Party Period and Public Policy* (Oxford U. Press, New York, 1986), p. 160; Ronald P. Formisano, *The Transformation of Political Culture: Massachusetts Parties, 1790s–1840s* (Oxford U. Press, New York, 1983), pp. 197–220.

18. McCormick, *Second System,* p. 337.

19. Glyndon G. Van Deusen, *Thurlow Weed: Wizard of the Lobby* (Little, Brown, Boston, 1947), p. 77.

20. *Ibid.*, p. 76.

21. *Ibid.*, p. 27.

22. Smith, *Blair*, vol. 1, p. 88.

23. Robert V. Remini, *The Life of Andrew Jackson* (Harper, New York, 1988), pp. 222–27.

24. Van Buren, *Autobiography*, vol. 1, p. 625.

25. Smith, *Blair*, vol. 1, pp. 113–14.

26. *Ibid.*, pp. 115–16.

27. Robert V. Remini, *Andrew Jackson and the Course of American Democracy* (Harper, New York, 1984), pp. 101–05.

28. Cole, *Van Buren*, p. 259; Ralph M. Goldman, *The National Party Chairmen and Committees* (Sharpe, Armonk, NY, 1990), p. 35.

29. Cole, *Van Buren*, p. 259.

30. McCormick, *Second System*, pp. 210, 245–47, 310–18; Charles Cole, *The Whig Party in the South* (American Historical Association, 1914), pp. 39–63, 68–69, 327–36.

31. Daniel Walker Howe, *The Political Culture of the American Whigs* (U. of Chicago Press, Chicago, 1979), p. 31.

32. *Ibid.*, p. 210; Horace Greeley, *Recollections of a Busy Life*, vol. 1 (Kennikat, Port Washington, NY, 1971), p. 166.

33. Howe, *Political Culture*, p. 32; Benson, *Jacksonian Democracy*, p. 199.

34. Howe, *Political Culture*, pp. 208, 210. For the Whigs' condemnation of class conflict, which they claimed was fomented by the Democrats, see Ashworth, *"Agrarians" and "Aristocrats,"* pp. 62–73.

35. Ronald P. Formisano, *The Birth of Mass Political Parties: Michigan, 1827–1861* (Princeton U. Press, Princeton, NJ, 1971), pp. 137–64; William G. Shade, "Political Pluralism and Party Development," in Paul Kleppner, ed., *The Evolution of American Electoral Systems* (Greenwood Press, Westport, CN 1981), pp. 102–103.

36. Anson Phelps Stokes, *Church and State in the United States*, vol. 1 (Harper, New York, 1950), p. 826.

37. William N. Chambers and Phillip C. Davis, "Party, Competition, and Mass Participation: The Case of the Democratizing Party System: 1824–1852," in Joel H. Silbey, Allan G. Bogue, and William H. Flanigan, eds., *The History of American Electoral Behavior* (Princeton U. Press, Princeton, NJ, 1978), pp. 174–93; McCormick, *Second Party System*, p. 30.

38. *Ibid.*, p. 268.

39. Greeley, *Recollections*, vol. 1, p. 252.

40. Walter Dean Burnham, "The Turnout Problem," in A. James Reichley, ed., *Elections American Style* (Brookings, Washington, DC, 1987), p. 113.

41. Gustavus Myers, *The History of Tammany Hall* (NY: Dover, New York, 1971), pp. 73, 90–91.

42. Bain and Parris, *Convention*, p. 40; Goldman, *National Party Chairmen*, p. 23.

43. McCormick, *Second Party System*, pp. 30, 350.

44. Bain and Parris, *Convention*, pp. 37–39.

45. *Ibid.*, p. 241.

46. James Hennesey, *American Catholics* (Oxford U. Press, New York, 1981), p. 119.

47. Jeter Allen Isely, *Horace Greeley and the Republican Party* (Octagon, New York, 1965), p. 83.

48. Ray Allen Billington, *The Protestant Crusade* (Rinehart, New York, 1938), p. 389.

49. Seymour Martin Lipsett and Earl Raab, *The Politics of Unreason: Right-Wing Extremism in*

America, 1790–1970 (Harper, New York, 1970), pp. 55–61; Sydney E. Ahlstrom, *A Religious History of the American People* (Yale U. Press, New Haven, CT, 1972), pp. 564–68; Michael F. Holt, "The Politics of Impatience: The Origins of Know Nothingism," *Journal of American History,* vol. 60, no. 2 (September 1973).

50. Eric Foner, *Free Soil, Free Labor, Free Men: The Ideology of the Republican Party Before the Civil War* (Oxford U. Press, New York, 1970), pp. 237–41; Paul Kleppner, *The Third Electoral System, 1855–1893* (U. of North Carolina, Chapel Hill, 1979), pp. 57, 68–72.

51. Isley, *Greeley,* p. 114.

Chapter 6.   Party Government: The Civil War Republicans

1. Jeter Allen Isely, *Horace Greeley and the Republican Party* (Octagon, New York, 1965), p. 31; Horace Greeley, *Recollections of a Busy Life,* vol. 1 (Kennikat, Port Washington, NY, 1971), pp. 315–19.

2. George H. Mayer, *The Republican Party 1854–1964* (Oxford U. Press, New York, 1964), p. 26.

3. William Ernest Smith, *The Francis Preston Blair Family in Politics,* vol. 1 (Macmillan, New York, 1933), p. 313.

4. Mayer, *Republican Party,* p. 23; William E. Gienapp, *The Origins of the Republican Party, 1852–1856* (Oxford U. Press, New York, 1987), pp. 123–24; Ralph M. Goldman, *The National Party Chairmen and Committees* (Sharpe, Armonk, NY, 1990), p. 47.

5. For useful discussions of the relationship between the Know-Nothings and the Republicans, see Joel H. Silbey, *The Partisan Imperative: The Dynamics of American Politics Before the Civil War* (Oxford U. Press, New York, 1985), pp. 127–64; Gienapp, *Origins of the Republican Party;* and Dale Baum, *The Civil War Period: The Case of Massachusetts* (U. of North Carolina Press, Chapel Hill, 1984).

6. Smith, *Blair,* vol. 1, p. 315. Gienapp finds no record in contemporary newspapers of this story, later told by Morton.

7. *Ibid.,* p. 321; Isely, *Greeley,* p. 256.

8. Eric Foner, *Free Soil, Free Labor, Free Men: The Ideology of the Republican Party Before the Civil War* (Oxford U. Press, New York, 1970), pp. 40–64.

9. *Ibid.,* pp. 248–49; Clinton Rossiter, *Parties and Politics in America* (Cornell U. Press, Ithaca, NY, 1960), p. 79.

10. Goldman, *National Party Chairmen,* p. 49; Gienapp, *Republican Party,* pp. 375–411.

11. Gienapp, *Republican Party,* pp. 292–93; Mayer, *Republican Party,* p. 8; Frank B. Evans, *Pennsylvania Politics, 1872–1877: A Study in Political Leadership* (Pennsylvania Historical Commission, Harrisburg, PA, 1966), p. 10.

12. Isely, *Greeley,* p. 266.

13. Louis Hacker, *Triumph of American Capitalism* (Columbia U. Press, New York, 1940), p. 337.

14. Glyndon G. Van Deusen, *Thurlow Weed: Wizard of the Lobby* (Little, Brown, Boston, 1947), p. 251.

15. Goldman, *National Party Chairmen,* p. 51.

16. Malcolm Moos, *The Republicans* (Random House, New York, 1956), p. 66; Smith, *Blair,* vol. 1, p. 482.

17. J. David Greenstone, "Political Culture and American Political Development: Liberty, Union, and the Liberal Bipolarity," in *Studies in American Political Development,* vol. 1,

Karren Oren and Stephen Skowronek, eds. (Yale U. Press, New Haven, CT, 1986), pp. 36–45; Abraham Lincoln, *Speeches and Writings: 1832–1858* (Viking, New York, 1989), p. 398.

18. Eric Foner, *Reconstruction: America's Unfinished Revolution, 1863–1877* (Harper, New York, 1988), p. 24.
19. Foner, *Reconstruction*, p. 19; Moos, *Republicans*, pp. 61, 77; Hacker, *Capitalism*, p. 229.
20. Hacker, *Capitalism*, p. 279.
21. Eric L. McKitrick, "Party Politics and the Union and Confederate War Efforts," in W. W. Chambers and W. D. Burnham, eds., *The American Party Systems* (Oxford U. Press, New York, 1967), p. 130.
22. Foner, *Reconstruction*, p. 6.
23. *Ibid.*, p. 49.
24. *Ibid.*, p. 5; MeKitrick, "Party Politics," pp. 144–45.
25. *Ibid.*, p. 139.
26. *Ibid.*, p. 138.
27. *Ibid.*, p. 140.
28. *Ibid.*, p. 141.
29. *Ibid.*, p. 150.
30. Foner, *Reconstruction*, p. 177.
31. *Ibid.*, p. 180.
32. *Ibid.*, pp. 229, 250.
33. Smith, *Blair*, vol. 2, p. 361.
34. *Ibid.*, p. 360; Foner, *Reconstruction*, p. 218.
35. Foner, *Reconstruction*, p. 225.
36. Goldman, *National Party Chairmen*, pp. 109–14.
37. Foner, *Reconstruction*, p. 236.
38. Smith, *Blair*, vol. 2, p. 429.

Chapter 7.   Machine Politics: The Gilded Age

1. James Bryce, *The American Commonwealth*, vol. 2 (Macmillan, New York, 1893), p. 21.
2. Walter Dean Burnham, *Critical Elections and the Mainsprings of American Politics* (Norton, New York, 1970), p. 72; Arthur M. Schlesinger, Jr., "The Crisis in the American Party System," in Richard L. McCormick, ed., *Political Parties and the Modern State* (Rutgers U. Press, New Brunswick, NJ, 1984), p. 77. Nast seems to have created the symbols of the Republican elephant and the Tammany tiger, but the donkey was sometimes used to symbolize the Democracy as early as the 1830s.
3. Patricia A. Hurley and Rick K. Wilson, "Partisan Voting Patterns in the U.S. Senate, 1877–1986," *Legislative Studies Quarterly*, vol. 14 (May, 1989), pp. 225–50; Jerome M. Chubb and Santa A. Traugott, "Partisan Cleavage and Cohesion in the House of Representatives," *Journal of Interdisciplinary History*, vol. 7 (Winter, 1970), pp. 375–402; J. Richard Piper, "Party Realignment and Congressional Change: Issue Dimensions and Priorities in the U.S. House of Representatives," *American Politics Quarterly*, vol. 11 (October, 1983), pp. 459–90.
4. For political behavior among Jews in the nineteenth century, see Lawrence H. Fuchs, *The Political Behavior of American Jews* (Free Press, New York, 1956), p. 32.

5. Martin Shefter, "New York City's Fiscal Crisis: The Politics of Inflation and Retrenchment," *Public Interest,* no. 4 (Summer, 1977), pp. 102–103.

6. Martin Shefter, "The Emergence of the Political Machine: An Alternative View," in Willis D. Hawley *et al.,* eds., *Theoretical Perspectives on Urban Parties* (Prentice-Hall, Englewood Cliffs, NJ, 1976), pp. 22–23.

7. *Ibid.,* pp. 25–31.

8. Matthew Josephson, *The Politicos* (Harcourt, Brace, New York, 1963), p. 88.

9. Eric Foner, *Reconstruction: America's Unfinished Revolution, 1863–1877* (Harper, New York, 1988), p. 492; Earle Dudley Ross, *The Liberal Republican Movement* (Holt, New York, 1910); Dale Baum, *The Civil War Period: The Case of Massachusetts* (U. of North Carolina Press, Chapel Hill, 1984), pp. 168–82.

10. Foner, *Reconstruction,* pp. 96–97.

11. Richard C. Bain and Judith H. Parris, *Convention Decisions and Voting Records* (Brookings, Washington, DC, 1973), p. 102.

12. Foner, *Reconstruction,* pp. 568–75.

13. Josephson, *Politicos,* p. 228.

14. *Ibid.;* Leon Burr Richardson, *William E. Chandler: Republican* (Dodd, Mead, New York, 1940), p. 185. William Chandler later became a leader in the Blaine faction of the Republican party. He was appointed secretary of the navy by President Arthur in 1882 as a concession to the Blainites. In 1887 he was elected to the United States Senate from New Hampshire and served there until 1901. In the 1890s he aligned himself with what later became the progressive wing of the Republican party and became a close friend and adviser of the young governor of New York, Theodore Roosevelt.

15. Josephson, *Politicos,* pp. 228–29.

16. C. Vann Woodward, *Reunion and Reaction: The Compromise of 1877 and the End of Reconstruction* (Doubleday, New York, 1951), pp. 161–74.

17. Ralph M. Goldman, *The National Party Chairmen and Committees: Factionalism at the Top* (Sharpe, Armonk, NY, 1990), p. 89.

18. Woodward, *Reunion,* p. 20.

19. Goldman, *National Party Chairmen,* p. 97.

20. Brand Whitlock, *Forty Years of It* (Appleton, New York, 1914), p. 27.

21. Morton, quoted in Walter Dean Burnham, "The Turnout Problem," in A. James Reichley, ed., *Elections American Style* (Brookings, Washington, DC, 1987), p. 103.

22. Paul Kleppner, *Parties, Votes, and Political Cultures* (U. of North Carolina Press, Chapel Hill, 1979) pp. 182–85.

23. *Ibid.,* p. 328; Samuel P. Hays, *American Political History as Social Analysis* (U. of Tennessee Press, Knoxville, 1980), p. 80; Paul Kleppner, *The Cross of Culture: A Social Analysis of Midwestern Politics, 1850–1900* (Free Press, New York, 1970), p. 114.

24. *Ibid.,* p. 113.

25. *Ibid.,* p. 90; Kleppner, *Parties,* p. 328.

26. Frederick Douglass, *Life and Writings,* ed. by Philip S. Foner, vol. 4 (International Pubs., New York, 1975), p. 271.

27. Edmund Morris, *The Rise of Theodore Roosevelt* (Coward, McCann, & Geohegan, New York, 1979), pp. 93–96.

28. James A. Kehl, *Boss Rule in the Gilded Age* (U. of Pittsburgh Press, 1981), pp. 32–33; Frank B. Evans, *Pennsylvania Politics, 1872–1877: A Study in Political Leadership* (Pennsylvania Historical Commission, Harrisburg, PA, 1966), pp. 12–13. The chief bond

between Cameron and Adams seems to have been Adams' attraction to Cameron's much younger wife, Elizabeth, a niece of John and William T. Sherman of Ohio.

29. Kehl, *Boss Rule,* p. 63.
30. *Ibid.,* pp. 29, 64–67.
31. *Ibid.,* pp. 27–28.
32. *Ibid.,* p. 27.
33. *Ibid.,* pp. 105–13.
34. *Ibid.,* p. 117.
35. Richard L. McCormick, *The Party Period and Public Policy* (Oxford U. Press, New York, 1986), p. 293.

Chapter 8.   Third-Party Challenge: Populist Uprising

1. James L. Sundquist, *Dynamics of the Party System: Alignment and Realignment of Political Parties in the United States* (Brookings, Washington, DC, 1983), p. 116.
2. *Ibid.,* pp. 112–14.
3. Wilfred E. Binkley, *American Political Parties: Their Natural History* (Knopf, New York, 1962), p. 259.
4. John D. Hicks, *The Populist Revolt* (U. of Minnesota Press, Minneapolis, 1931), pp. 26, 31, 32.
5. Hamlin Garland, *A Son of the Middle Border* (Macmillan, New York, 1917), pp. 359, 361.
6. Hicks, *Populist Revolt,* p. 160.
7. Garland, *Son,* p. 357.
8. Hicks, *Populist Revolt,* pp. 155–59.
9. *Ibid.,* pp. 301–05.
10. *Ibid.,* pp. 42–43.
11. *Ibid.,* pp. 172–77; C. Vann Woodward, *Tom Watson: Agrarian Rebel* (Macmillan, New York, 1938), p. 220.
12. Hicks, *Populist Revolt,* pp. 205–14; Woodward, *Watson,* pp. 168–69.
13. Hicks, *Populist Revolt,* pp. 215–37.
14. Paul Kleppner, *Continuity and Change in Electoral Politics* (Greenwood Press, Westport, CT, 1987), pp. 97–99.
15. Matthew Josephson, *The Politicos* (Harcourt, Brace, New York, 1963), pp. 617, 620.
16. Margaret Leech, *In the Days of McKinley* (Harper, New York, 1959), pp. 52–62.
17. *Ibid.,* pp. 54, 76–77.
18. Thomas Beer, *Hanna* (Knopf, New York, 1929), pp. 20–21, 55, 69.
19. Leech, *McKinley,* p. 67.
20. Beer, *Hanna,* p. 144.
21. Josephson, *Politicos,* p. 661.
22. *Historical Statistics of the United States* (Bureau of the Census, Washington, DC, 1961), p. 74.
23. Seymour Martin Lipsett and Earl Raab, *The Politics of Unreason* (Harper, New York, 1970), p. 95.
24. *Annals of America,* vol. 12 (Encyclopedia Britannica, Chicago, 1968), pp. 100–06.
25. Josephson, *Politicos,* p. 678.
26. *Ibid.,* p. 668.
27. Woodward, *Watson,* p. 293; Josephson, *Politicos,* p. 684.
28. Beer, *Hanna,* pp. 155, 162.

29. Richard Jensen, *The Winning of the Midwest* (U. of Chicago Press, 1971), pp. 283–85.

30. Sundquist, *Dynamics*, p. 166; Kleppner, *The Cross of Culture*, pp. 358–59.

31. Sundquist, *Dynamics*, p. 162; Jensen, *Winning of the Midwest*, p. 285.

32. Irving Stone, *They Also Ran: The Story of the Men Who Were Defeated for the Presidency* (Doubleday, New York, 1943), p. 74; Jensen, *Winning of the Midwest*, p. 287.

33. Kleppner, *Continuity and Change*, p. 73.

34. Sundquist, *Dynamics*, p. 168.

Chapter 9.   Reaction Against Parties: The Progressive Era

1. Herbert Croly, *Progressive Democracy* (Macmillan, New York, 1914), p. 349.

2. Quoted in Daniel Bell, *The End of Ideology* (Free Press, New York, 1962), p. 32.

3. Walter Rauschenbusch, *A Theology for the Social Gospel* (Macmillan, New York, 1917).

4. George E. Mowry, *The California Progressives* (U. of California Press, Berkeley, 1951), pp. 86–104.

5. John D. Buenker, *Urban Liberalism and Progressive Reform* (Norton, New York, 1973), pp. 28, 186. Some Social Gospellers enthusiastically supported Anglo-Saxon triumphalism. The Anglo-Saxon "race," Josiah Strong predicted in 1885, "is destined to dispossess many weaker races, assimilate others, and mold the remainder, until in a very true and important sense it has Anglo-Saxonized mankind." Winthrop S. Hudson, *Nationalism and Religion in America* (Harper, New York, 1970), pp. 115–16.

6. Samuel F. Hays, *American Political History as Social Analysis* (U. of Tennessee Press, Knoxville, 1980), p. 211.

7. *Ibid.*, p. 210. Among the eventual products of this strand of the progressive movement was the Brookings Institution, founded in 1916.

8. Paul E. Peterson, *City Limits* (U. of Chicago Press, 1981), pp. 114–16.

9. Xandra Kayden and Eddie Mahe, Jr., *The Party Goes On: The Persistence of the Two-Party System in the United States* (Basic Books, New York, 1985), p. 41.

10. Robert M. LaFollette, *Autobiography: A Personal Narrative of Political Experiences* (LaFollette, Madison, WI, 1918), p. 209.

11. Walton Bean, *Boss Rueff's San Francisco* (U. of California Press, Berkeley, 1952), p. 5; David R. Mayhew, *Placing Parties in American Politics: Organization, Electoral Settings, and Government Activity in the Twentieth Century* (Princeton U. Press, Princeton, NJ, 1986), p. 222.

12. Michael Paul Rogin and John L. Shorer, *Political Change in California* (Greenwood Press, Westport, CT, 1970), pp. 35–46.

13. *Annals of America* (Encyclopedia Britannica, Chicago, 1968), vol. 12, p. 343.

14. *Ibid.*, vol. 13, pp. 217, 251.

15. Gabriel Kolko, *The Triumph of Conservatism* (Free Press, New York, 1963), pp. 173–74.

16. *Ibid.*, p. 173.

17. Malcolm Moos, *The Republicans* (Random House, New York, 1956), p. 279.

18. Edmund Morris, *The Rise of Theodore Roosevelt* (Coward, McCann, & Geohegan, New York, 1979), pp. 142–43.

19. Moos, *Republicans*, p. 168; Arthur M. Schlesinger, Jr., *The Cycles of American History* (Houghton Mifflin, Boston, 1986), p. 261; Richard L. McCormick, *From Realignment to Reform: Political Change in New York State, 1893–1910* (Cornell U. Press, Ithaca, NY, 1979), p. 132.

20. Morris, *Roosevelt,* pp. 674–75; McCormick, *Realignment to Reform,* p. 145.

21. Ralph M. Goldman, *The National Party Chairmen and Committees: Functionalism at the Top* (Sharpe, Armonk, NY, 1990), p. 199.

22. James A. Kehl, *Boss Rule in the Gilded Age* (U. of Pittsburgh Press, 1981), p. 243.

23. LaFollette, *Autobiography,* p. 409.

24. Kolko, *Conservatism,* p. 73.

25. Archie Butt, *The Intimate Letters of Archie Butt, Military Aide* (Kennikat, Port Washington, NY, 1930), pp. 201, 303. Archie Butt served as military aide to both Theodore Roosevelt and Taft while each was President. He seems to have been the one individual who in 1912 retained the trust of both men. He went down on the *Titanic* on April 15, 1912, ending the last hope, many of their intimates believed, that they would be reconciled.

26. L. White Busbey, *Uncle Joe Cannon: The Story of a Pioneer American* (Holt, New York, 1927), pp. 247–69.

27. Butt, *Intimate Letters,* p. 256.

28. John H. Fenton, *Midwest Politics* (Holt, New York, 1966), p. 45.

29. LaFollette, *Autobiography,* pp. 15, 17; Albert O. Barton, *LaFollette's Winning of Wisconsin (1894–1904)* (Homestead, Des Moines, 1922), pp. 42–45.

30. LaFollette, *Autobiography,* p. 496.

31. Goldman, *National Party Chairmen,* p. 264.

32. Henry E Pringle, *The Life and Times of William Howard Taft,* vol. 2 (Archon, Hamden, CT, 1939), p. 767.

33. *Ibid.,* p. 768

34. Richard C. Bain and Judith H. Parris, *Convention Decisions and Voting Records* (Brookings, Washington, DC, 1973), pp. 178–84.

35. Kolko, *Conservatism,* pp. 195, 200.

36. *Ibid.,* p. 195.

37. *National Party Platforms, 1840–1968* (U. of Illinois Press, Champaign, 1970), pp. 175–83.

38. Kolko, *Conservatism,* p. 197.

39. David Sarasohn, *The Party of Reform: Democrats in the Progressive Era* (U. of Mississippi Press, Jackson, MS, 1989), argues that the Wilson administration represented the triumph of progressivism. The question turns in part, as I will discuss in chapter 12, on varying meanings of "progressive" and "liberal."

Chapter 10. The Progressive Legacy, City Machines, and the Solid South

1. Paul Kleppner, *Who Voted? The Dynamics of Electoral Turnout, 1870–1980* (Praeger, New York, 1982), p. 58.

2. *Ibid.,* p. 59.

3. Larry J. Sabato, *The Party's Just Begun: Shaping Political Parties for America's Future* (Scott, Foresman, Glenview, IL, 1988), p. 224.

4. Leon D. Epstein, *Political Parties in the American Mold* (U. of Wisconsin Press, Madison, 1986), p. 168.

5. LaFollette, quoted in Malcolm E. Jewell, *Parties and Primaries: Nominating State Governors* (Praeger, New York, 1984), p. 7; V. O. Key, *Politics, Parties, and Pressure Groups* (Crowell, New York, 1958), p. 411.

6. Austin Ranney, *Curing the Mischiefs of Faction: Party Reform in America* (U. California

Press, Berkeley, 1975), p. 130; Truman, quoted in William J. Keefe, *Parties, Politics, and Public Policy in America* (Congressional Quarterly Press, Washington, DC, 1988), p. 7.

7. Joseph A. Schlesinger, "The New American Political Party," *American Political Science Review,* vol. 79, no. 4 (December, 1985), p. 1155.

8. Horace Greeley, *Recollections of a Busy Life,* vol. 1 (Kennikat, Port Washington, NY, 1971), p. 313; Joel H. Silbey, *The Partisan Imperative: The Dynamics of American Politics Before the Civil War* (Oxford U. Press, New York, 1985), p. 142.

9. Paul Kleppner, *Continuity and Change in Electoral Politics, 1893–1928* (Greenwood Press, Westport, CN, 1987), pp. 166–67; Robert Goldberg, "Election Fraud: An American Vice," in A. James Reichley, ed., *Elections American Style* (Brookings, Washington, DC, 1987), pp. 184–87.

10. Kleppner, *Continuity and Change,* pp. 167–68.

11. *Ibid.,* pp. 165–66.

12. Richard L. McCormick, *From Realignment to Reform: Political Change in New York State, 1893–1910* (Cornell U. Press, Ithaca, NY, 1979), pp. 141, 231.

13. Martin Shefter, "The Emergence of the Political Machine: An Alternative View," in Willis D. Hawley *et al.,* eds., *Theoretical Perspectives on Urban Politics* (Prentice-Hall, Englewood Cliffs, NJ, 1976), p. 17; George Washington Plunkitt, *Plunkitt of Tammany Hall,* recorded by William L. Riordan (Cameron House edition, 1982), p. 17.

14. M. Craig Brown and Charles N. Halaby, "Machine Politics in America, 1870–1945" (unpublished paper, 1985), pp. 4, 14, 42.

15. Oscar Handlin, *The Uprooted* (Little, Brown, Boston, 1951), p. 190.

16. Ralph G. Martin, *The Bosses* (Putnam, New York, 1964), p. 33.

17. Shefter, "Political Machine," pp. 36, 41; Peter H. Argersinger, "New Perspectives on Election Fraud in the Golden Age," *Political Science Quarterly,* vol. 100, no. 4 (Winter 1985–86), p. 687.

18. David R. Mayhew, *Placing Parties in American Politics: Organization, Electoral Settings, and Government Activity in the Twentieth Century* (Princeton U. Press, Princeton, NJ, 1986), p. 310.

19. Plunkitt, *Tammany Hall,* pp. 3, 11, 25.

20. *Ibid.*

21. John D. Buenker, *Urban Liberalism and Progressive Reform* (Norton, New York, 1973), pp. 4, 196, 208; A. D. Van Nostrand, "The Lomasney Legend," *New England Quarterly* (December, 1948), p. 435; John D. Buenker, "The Mahatma and Progressive Reform: Martin Lomasney as Lawmaker," *New England Quarterly,* vol. 44 (September, 1971), p. 397.

22. Thomas M. Guterbuck, *Machine Politics in Transition: Party and Community in Chicago* (U. of Chicago Press, 1980), p. 8; Buenker, *Urban Liberalism,* pp. 26, 211.

23. Handlin, *The Uprooted,* p. 192.

24. Buenker, *Urban Liberalism,* p. 47–49.

25. *Ibid.,* pp. 56, 87, 122.

26. Walton Bean, *Boss Rueff's San Francisco* (U. of California Press, Berkeley, 1952); Sam Bass Warner, *The Private City: Philadelphia in Three Periods of Its Growth* (U. of Pennsylvania Press, Philadelphia, 1968), p. 218.

27. Walter Dean Burnham, "The Turnout Problem," in A. James Reichley, ed., *Elections American Style* (Brookings, Washington, DC, 1987), pp. 113–14.

28. V. O. Key, *Southern Politics in State and Nation* (Vintage, New York, 1949), p. 665.

29. *Ibid.*, pp. 118, 208–09, 232–33; C. Vann Woodward, *Tom Watson: Agrarian Rebel* (Macmillan, New York, 1938), p. 371.

30. Key, *Southern Politics*, p. 19.

31. *Ibid.*, p. 118; Woodward, *Watson*, pp. 444–47.

32. Key, *Southern Politics*, pp. 232–39.

33. *Ibid.*, p. 262.

34. *Ibid.*, p. 156; T. Harry Williams, *Huey Long* (Knopf, New York, 1969), pp. 130–31.

35. *Statistical Abstract of the United States, 1925* (GPO, Washington, DC, 1926), pp. 207–228; Key, *Southern Politics*, p. 231.

36. *Ibid.*, p. 157.

Chapter 11.   The President as Party Leader: Woodrow Wilson

1. Woodrow Wilson, "Committee or Cabinet Government," and "Cabinet Government in the United States," in *College and State*, vol. 1 (Harper, New York, 1925), pp. 36–37, 109–10.

2. James W. Ceaser, *Presidenial Selection: Theory and Development* (Princeton U. Press, Princeton, NJ, 1979), pp. 197–207.

3. The papers of Woodrow Wilson, Arthur S. Link, ed., vol. XV (Princeton U. Press, Princeton, NJ, 1966), pp. 547–48, quoted by John Milton Cooper, Jr., *The Warrior and the Priest: Woodrow Wilson and Theodore Roosevelt* (Harvard U. Press, Cambridge, MA, 1983), p. 120; Paul Kleppner, *Continuity and Change in Electoral Politics, 1893–1928* (Greenwood Press, Westport, CT, 1987), p. 204.

4. John D. Buenker, *Urban Liberalism and Progressive Reform* (Norton, New York, 1973), pp. 52–53.

5. Cooper, *Warrior and Priest*, pp. 176–77; Buenker, *Urban Liberalism*, p. 52.

6. Richard C. Bain and Judith H. Parris, *Convention Decisions and Voting Records* (Brookings, Washington, DC, 1973), pp. 184–91.

7. William F. McCombs, *Making Woodrow Wilson President* (Fairview, New York, 1931), pp. 208–09.

8. *Annals of America*, vol. 13 (Encyclopedia Britannica, Chicago, 1968), p. 357.

9. Cooper, *Warrior and Priest*, p. 194.

10. Arthur S. Link, *Woodrow Wilson and the Progressive Era: 1910–1917* (Harper, New York, 1954) pp. 64–66.

11. *Ibid.*, p. 233; Walter Dean Burnham, *Critical Elections and the Mainsprings of American Politics* (Norton, New York, 1970), p. 78.

12. Cooper, *Warrior and Priest*, p. 306.

13. *Ibid.*, p. 326.

14. *Ibid.*, p. 334.

15. *Ibid.*, p. 340.

16. Ralph M. Goldman, *The National Party Chairmen and Committees: Factionalism at the Top* (Sharpe, Armonk, NY, 1990), pp. 319–20.

17. Malcolm Moos, *The Republicans* (Random House, New York, 1956), p. 323.

18. Calvin Coolidge, *Autobiography* (Cosmopolitan, New York, 1929), p. 158.

Chapter 12. A Functioning Majority Party: The New Deal

1. Ralph M. Goldman, *The National Party Chairmen and Committees: Factionalism at the Top* (Sharpe, Armonk, NY, 1990), pp. 319–20.

2. John Kenneth Galbraith, *The Great Crash: 1929* (Houghton Mifflin, Boston, 1955), p. 93.

3. *Historical Statistics of the United States* (Bureau of the Census, 1961), pp. 92, 283; Arthur M. Schlesinger, Jr., *The Crisis of the Old Order: 1919–1933* (Houghton Mifflin, Boston, 1957), p. 175.

4. *Ibid.*, p. 232; Herbert Stein, *The Fiscal Revolution in America* (American Enterprise Institute, Washington, DC, 1990), pp. 16–38.

5. *Historical Statistics*, p. 73; Schlesinger, *Crisis*, pp. 249, 184–85.

6. *Ibid.*, p. 278.

7. Geoffrey C. Ward, *A First-class Temperament: The Emergence of Franklin Roosevelt* (Harper, New York, 1989), pp. 85–86, 600.

8. Schlesinger, *Crisis*, p. 286.

9. *Ibid.*, pp. 289–292.

10. James A. Farley, *Jim Farley's Story: The Roosevelt Years* (McGraw-Hill, New York, 1948), p. 22.

11. *Ibid.*, p. 23; Schlesinger, *Crisis*, p. 308.

12. Richard C. Bain and Judith H. Parris, *Convention Decisions and Voting Records* (Brookings, Washington, DC, 1973), pp. 242–44.

13. Schlesinger, *Crisis*, p. 314.

14. *Ibid.*, pp. 433–34.

15. Kristi Anderson, *The Creation of a Democratic Majority: 1928–1936* (U. of Chicago Press, 1970), p. 100.

16. Nancy J. Weiss, *Farewell to the Party of Lincoln: Black Politics in the Age of FDR* (Princeton U. Press, Princeton, NJ, 1983), p. 30.

17. *Ibid.*, p. 31.

18. John Kenneth Galbraith, *American Capitalism: The Concept of Countervailing Power* (Houghton Mifflin, Boston, 1952).

19. For a discussion of the evolution of New Deal ideology, see Alan Brinkley, "The New Deal and the Idea of the State," in *The Rise and Fall of the New Deal Order, 1930–1980*, Steve Fraser and Gary Gerstle, eds. (Princeton U. Press, Princeton, NJ, 1989), pp. 85–112.

20. Barbara Deckard Sinclair, "Party Realignment and the Transformation of the Political Agenda: The House of Representatives, 1925–38," *American Political Science Review*, vol. 78, no. 3 (September, 1979), pp. 944–48.

21. James T. Patterson, *Congressional Conservatism and the New Deal* (U. Press of Kentucky, Lexington, 1967), p. 11.

22. E. Pendleton Herring, "Second Session of the 73rd Congress," *American Political Science Review*, vol. 28 (October 1934), p. 865.

23. Sinclair, "Party Realignment," p. 949; Patterson, *Congressional Conservatism*, p. 13.

24. Goldman, *National Party Chairmen*, pp. 319–20.

25. *Ibid.*, pp. 287–303.

26. Farley, *Farley's Story*, pp. 39–49; Cornelius P. Cotter and Bernard C. Hennessy, *Politics Without Power: The National Party Committees* (Atherton, New York, 1964), p. 144. In the 1980s only about 2,000 federal jobs could be filled completely outside the merit system. David F. Price, *Bringing Back the Parties* (Congressional Quarterly, Washington, DC, 1984), p. 80.

27. Robert E. Sherwood, *Roosevelt and Hopkins: An Intimate History* (Harper, New York,

1948), p. 68. For a thorough account of Roosevelt's attempt to build a national political machine based on both party regulars and programmatic liberals, see Sidney M. Milkis, *The Modern Presidency and the Transformation of the American Party System* (forthcoming).

28. Bruce M. Stares, *The New Deal and the Last Hurrah: Pittsburgh Machine Politics* (U. of Pittsburgh Press, 1970), p. 165.

29. Sidney M. Milkis, "FDR and the Transcendence of Party Politics," *Political Science Quarterly*, vol. 100, no. 3 (Fall, 1985), p. 495.

30. Leon D. Epstein, *Political Parties in the American Mold* (U. of Wisconsin Press, Madison, 1986), p. 142; Stares, *Pittsburgh*, p. 12.

31. Alfred Steinberg, *The Bosses* (Macmillan, New York, 1972), p. 8.

32. Wallace S. Sayre and Herbert Kaufman, *Governing New York City: Politics in the Metropolis* (Russell Sage, New York, 1960), p. 186.

33. Stares, *Pittsburgh*, pp. 18–19.

34. Steinberg, *The Bosses*, p. 8.

35. Alex Gottfried, *Boss Cermak of Chicago* (U. of Washington Press, Seattle, 1962), p. 226; Harold F. Gosnell, *Machine Politics: Chicago Model* (U. of Chicago Press, 1937), pp. 10–13.

36. *Ibid.*, p. 41.

37. *Ibid.*, p. 68.

38. Thomas M. Guterbuck, *Chicago in Transition: Party and Community in Chicago* (U. of Chicago Press, 1980), pp. 6–7; Edward Banfield and James Q. Wilson, *City Politics* (Harvard U. Press, Cambridge, MA, 1963), pp. 117, 40–42.

39. Gosnell, *Machine Politics*, pp. 71–72.

Chapter 13.   Vehicles of Opposition

1. *New York Times*, March 27, 1933, quoted by Arthur M. Schlesinger, Jr., *The Coming of the New Deal* (Houghton Mifflin, Boston, 1958,) p. 3.

2. Werner Sombart, *Why Is There No Socialism in the United States?* translated by Patricia M. Hocking and C.T. Husbands (International Arts and Sciences Press, White Plains, NY, 1976), remains the classic discussion of the causes of socialism's failure to attract political support in the United States. See also Michael Harrington, *Socialism* (Saturday Review Press, New York, 1972), pp. 266–69; and Selig Perlman, *Theory of the Labor Movement* (Kelley, New York, 1949), pp. 167–68.

3. Arthur M. Schlesinger, Jr., *The Politics of Upheaval* (Houghton Mifflin, Boston, 1960), p. 98–104.

4. *Ibid.*, pp. 106–08.

5. *Ibid.*, pp. 111–23; Stanley Kelley, Jr., *Professional Public Relations and Political Power* (Johns Hopkins U. Press, Baltimore, 1956), pp. 33–44.

6. Schlesinger, *Politics of Upheaval*, pp. 29–41.

7. James Hennesey, *American Catholics* (Oxford U. Press, New York, 1981), pp. 27–75; Schlesinger, *Politics of Upheaval*, pp. 16–28.

8. V. O. Key, *Southern Politics in State and Nation* (Vintage, New York, 1949), p. 157.

9. T. Harry Williams, *Huey Long* (Knopf, New York, 1969), p. 3.

10. *Ibid.*, pp. 69, 130, 146.

11. *Ibid.*, p. 5.

12. *Statistical Abstract of the United States, 1938* (Government Printing Office, Washington, DC, 1939), pp. 211–29; Robert Penn Warren, *All the King's Men* (Harcourt, New York, 1974), p. 393. Long's career inspired three other significant novels: Sinclair Lewis, *It Can't Happen Here* (Signet, New York, 1970); John Dos Passos, *Number One* (Houghton Mifflin, Boston, 1943); and Adria Locke Langley, *A Lion Is in the Streets* (McGraw-Hill, New York, 1945).

13. Williams, *Long,* p. 5.

14. Schlesinger, *Politics of Upheaval,* p. 67.

15. *Ibid.,* p. 65.

16. Williams, *Long,* p. 8.

17. Hennesey, *American Catholics,* p. 114.

18. Walter Dean Burnham, "The Turnout Problem," in A. James Reichley, ed., *Elections American Style* (Brookings, Washington, DC, 1987), p. 114.

19. Schlesinger, *Politics of Upheaval,* p. 230. The aide was the astute Thomas Corcoran, "Tommy the Cork."

20. James T. Patterson, *Congressional Conservatism and the New Deal* (U. of Kentucky Press, Lexington, 1967), p. 101.

21. *Ibid.,* pp. 108, 117–19.

22 *Ibid.,* p. 121.

23. *Ibid.,* p. 119.

24. *Ibid.,* p. 124.

25. John F. Manley, "The Conservative Coalition in Congress," *American Behavioral Scientist,* vol. 17, no. 2 (November/December, 1973), pp. 223–46.

26. Martha H. Swain, *Pat Harrison: The New Deal Years* (U. of Mississippi, Jackson, MS, 1978), pp. 155–60; James F. Byrnes, *All in One Lifetime* (Harper, New York, 1958), pp. 99–100.

27. Patterson, *Congressional Conservatism,* pp. 339–52.

28. Sidney M. Milkis, "FDR and the Transcendence of Party Politics," *Political Science Quarterly,* vol. 100, no. 3 (Fall, 1985), p. 496.

29. Manley, "Conservative Coalition," pp. 235–39.

30. *Ibid.,* pp. 231–32.

31. James L. Sundquist, *Dynamics of the Party System: Alignment and Realignment of Political Parties in the United States* (Brookings, Washington, DC, 1983), p. 227.

32. Barbara Deckard Sinclair, "Party Realignment and the Transformation of the Political Agenda: The House of Representatives, 1925–38," *American Political Science Review,* vol. 78, no. 3 (September 1979), pp. 944–48.

33. *Ibid.,* p. 950; Manley, "Conservative Coalition," p. 232.

34. Patterson, *Congressional Conservatism,* pp. 136–38.

35. *Ibid.,* p. 257.

Chapter 14. Fission of Party Coalitions

1. Ralph M. Goldman, *The National Party Chairmen and Committees: Factionalism at the Top* (Sharpe, Armonk, NY, 1990), pp. 396–409; Leon D. Epstein, *Political Parties in the American Mold* (U. of Wisconsin Press, Madison, 1986), p. 207.

2. Robert E. Sherwood, *Roosevelt and Hopkins: An Intimate History* (Harper, New York, 1948), p. 123.

3. *Ibid.,* p. 128.

4. *Ibid.,* pp. 148,177.

5. Goldman, *National Party Chairmen,* p. 411.

6. James A. Farley, *Jim Farley's Story* (McGraw-Hill, New York, 1948), pp. 248–51.

7. Richard Norton Smith, *Thomas E. Dewey and His Times* (Simon & Schuster, New York, 1982), pp. 303–06; Steve Neal, *Dark Horse: A Biography of Wendell Willkie* (Doubleday, New York, 1984), pp. 45–79.

8. Edward J. Flynn, *You're the Boss* (Viking, New York, 1947), p. 156.

9. Richard C. Bain and Judith H. Parris, *Convention Decisions and Voting Records* (Brookings, Washington, DC, 1973), pp. 259–61.

10. Neal, *Willkie,* pp. 142–80; Sherwood, *Roosevelt and Hopkins,* pp. 186–201.

11. Neal, *Willkie,* pp. 316–19.

12. Harry S Truman, *Memoirs, Vol. 1: Year of Decisions* (Doubleday, New York, 1955), pp. 190–93; Cabell Phillips, *The Truman Presidency: The History of a Triumphant Succession* (Macmillan, New York, 1966), pp. 39–47.

13. Truman, *Year of Decisions,* pp. 555–59; Norman D. Markowitz, *The Rise and Fall of the People's Century: Henry A. Wallace and American Liberalism, 1941–1948* (Free Press, New York, 1973), pp. 41–53.

14. Robert J. Donovan, *Conflict and Crisis: The Presidency of Harry S Truman, 1945–1948* (Norton, New York, 1977), pp. 223–24.

15. *Ibid.,* pp. 225–28; James F. Byrnes, *All in One Lifetime* (Harper, New York, 1958), pp. 375–76.

16. George F. Kennan, *Memoirs: 1925–1950* (Little, Brown, Boston, 1967), pp. 301–04.

17. Ralph Straetz and Frank Munger, *New York Politics* (New York U. Press, 1960), p. 31.

18. *Ibid.,* p. 31; Wallace S. Sayre and Herbert Kaufman, *Governing New York City: Politics in the Metropolis* (Russell Sage, New York, 1960), p. 160.

19. James T. Patterson, *Mr. Republican: A Biography of Robert A. Taft* (Houghton Mifflin, Boston, 1972), p. 385.

20. Byrnes, *Lifetime,* p. 387; Donovan, *Conflict,* pp. 281–87; Patterson, *Taft,* p. 371.

21. *Ibid.,* p. 385.

22. Donovan, *Conflict,* pp. 342, 360–61; Markowitz, *Rise and Fall,* pp. 267–73.

23. Donovan, *Conflict,* pp. 342–43; Markowitz, *Rise and Fall,* pp. 264–68.

24. Nancy J. Weiss, *Farewell to the Party of Lincoln: Black Politics in the Age of FDR* (Princeton U. Press, Princeton, NJ, 1983), pp. 37–40, 241–49.

25. *Ibid.,* p. 295.

26. Donovan, *Conflict,* p. 31.

27. *Ibid.,* pp. 352–56.

28. Patterson, *Taft,* pp. 259, 319.

29. Donovan, *Conflict,* p. 404; Stephen E. Ambrose, *Eisenhower,* vol. 1 (Simon & Schuster, New York, 1983), p. 478.

30. Interview with Ronald Reagan, January 4, 1978.

Chapter 15.   Decline of State and Local Machines

1. For useful accounts of the national committees in the 1950s, see Cornelius P. Cotter and Bernard C. Hennessy, *Politics Without Power in the National Party Committees* (Atherton, New York, 1964); and Hugh A. Bone, *Party Committees and National Politics* (U. of Washington Press, Seattle, 1958).

2. *Ibid.*, pp. 104, 211; Stephen E. Ambrose, *Eisenhower,* vol. 2 (Simon and Schuster, New York, 1985), p. 294; Ralph M. Goldman, *The National Party Chairmen and Committees: Factionalism at the Top* (Sharpe, Armonk, NY, 1990), pp. 511–19.

3. *Ibid.*, pp. 449–66.

4. *Ibid.*, pp. 451–52.

5. *Ibid.*, pp. 460–61; James L. Sundquist, *Politics and Policy: The Eisenhower, Kennedy, and Johnson Years* (Brookings, Washington, DC, 1968), pp. 405–07.

6. *Ibid.*, pp. 407–10.

7. *Ibid.*, pp. 409–14. Galbraith, however, squelched an effort by another member of the economic subcommittee, Leon Keyserling, chairman of the Council of Economic Advisers under Truman, to promote an even more expansionary policy. Philip A. Klinkner, *The Road Back: Response of American Parties to Electoral Detente* (forthcoming).

8. Edwin O'Connor, *The Last Hurrah* (Little, Brown, Boston, 1956), p. 374.

9. A. James Reichley, *The Art of Government: Reform and Organization Politics in Philadelphia* (Fund for the Republic, New York, 1959).

10. Thomas M. Guterbuck, *Machine Politics in Transition: Party and Community in Chicago* (U. of Chicago Press, 1980), pp. 14–15.

11. Mike Royko, *Boss: Richard J. Daley of Chicago* (Dutton, New York, 1971), p. 4.

12. *Ibid.*, p. 61.

13. David R. Mayhew, *Placing Parties in American Politics: Organization, Electoral Settings, and Government Activity in the Twentieth Century* (Princeton U. Press, Princeton, NJ, 1986).

14. Robert J. Huckshorn, *Party Leadership in the States* (U. of Massachusetts Press, Amherst, 1976), pp. 111–12.

15. Roger Lutchin, "Power and Policy: American City Politics Between Two World Wars," in Scott Greer, ed., *Ethics, Machines, and the American Urban Future* (Schenkman, Cambridge, MA, 1980), p. 26.

16. Edward C. Banfield and James Q. Wilson, *City Politics* (Harvard U. Press, Cambridge, MA, 1963), pp. 207–08.

17. *Ibid.*, p. 208.

18. Reichley, *Art of Government,* p. 98.

19. Raymond E. Wolfinger, "Why Political Machines Have Not Withered Away and Other Revisionist Thoughts, "*Journal of Politics,* vol. 34, no. 2 (May, 1972), pp. 367–68.

Chapter 16.   Movement Politics: The Republican Hard Right

1. James L. Sundquist, *Politics and Policy: The Eisenhower, Kennedy, and Johnson Years* (Brookings, Washington, DC, 1968), pp. 134–42, 481–89.

2. Theodore C. Sorensen, *Kennedy* (Harper, New York, 1969), p. 465.

3. Interview with Nelson Rockefeller, March 24, 1978.

4. This analysis is based largely on personal experience with the progressive Republicans while I served during the 1960s on the staffs of Senator Kenneth Keating of New York and Governor William Scranton of Pennsylvania, and in 1976 on the staff of President Gerald Ford. For an extended account and analysis of the progressive Republicans, see Nicol C. Rae, *The Decline and Fall of the Liberal Republicans from 1952 to the Present* (Oxford U. Press, New York, 1989).

5. F. Clifton White with William J. Gill, *Suite 3505: The Story of the Draft Goldwater Movement* (Arlington, New Rochelle, NY, 1967), pp. 263–79; Theodore H. White, *The Making of the President, 1964* (Atheneum, New York, 1965), p. 82.

6. A. James Reichley, *Conservatives in an Age of Change: The Nixon and Ford Administrations* (Brookings, Washington, DC, 1981), pp. 22–28; James T. Patterson, *Mr. Republican: A Biography of Robert A. Taft* (Houghton Mifflin, Boston, 1972), p. 330.
7. Richard John Neuhaus later analyzed the swing against a religious presence in the ceremonial aspects of public life in *The Naked Public Square* (Eerdmans, Grand Rapids, MI, 1984).
8. Daniel A. Mazmanian, *Third Parties in Presidential Elections* (Brookings, Washington, DC, 1974), p. 116.
9. For Goldwater's political philosophy, see particularly Barry Goldwater, *The Conscience of a Conservative* (Victor, Shepherdsville, KY, 1960).
10. White, *Making of the President, 1964,* pp. 126–29.
11. John G. Francis, "The Political Landscape of the Mountain West," in Peter F Galderisi, Michael S. Lyons, Randy T. Simmons, and Francis, eds., *The Politics of Realignment: Party Change in the Mountain West* (Westview, Boulder, CO, 1987), pp. 19–31.
12. John C. Green and James L. Guth use the term "hard right" in "The Price of Power: Republican Party Factionalism in the Reagan Era," paper delivered at the 1987 meeting of the American Political Science Association in Chicago, to designate much the same group I had earlier called "fundamentalists." "Hard right" has the advantage of avoiding the more specifically religious connotation of "fundamentalists."
13. Byrnes, elected governor in 1950, had defected from the Democratic party to support Eisenhower for President in 1952.
14. Sorenson, *Kennedy,* p. 489.
15. John H. Kessel, *The Goldwater Coalition: Republican Strategies in 1964* (Bobbs-Merrill, Indianapolis, IN, 1968), pp. 68–71.
16. Rae, *Liberal Republicans,* p. 64.
17. F. Clifton White, *Suite 3505: The Story of the Draft Goldwater Movement* (Arlington House, New Rochelle, N.Y., 1967), p. 332; Robert D. Novak, *The Agony of the GOP: 1964* (Macmillan, New York, 1965), p. 441.
18. White, *Making of the President, 1964,* p. 303.
19. Phyllis Schlafly, *A Choice Not an Echo* (Pere Marquette, Alton, IL, 1964).
20. *American National Election Survey,* 1964.
21. Norman H. Nie, Sidney Verba, and John R. Petrocik, *The Changing American Voter* (Harvard U. Press, Cambridge, MA, 1976), pp. 301, 336.
22. Sundquist, *Politics and Policy,* pp. 493–96.
23. David W. Reinhard, *The Republican Right Since 1945* (U. of Kentucky Press, Lexington, KY, 1983), pp. 210–11.
24. Lou Cannon, *Reagan* (Putnam, New York, 1982), pp. 86, 93, 103; Ronald Reagan, with Richard G. Hubler, *Where's the Rest of Me?* (Duell, Sloan, and Pearce, New York, 1965), 157–58, 297.
25. Cannon, *Reagan,* pp. 102–3; Adam Clymer, "A Star Is Born," in *Reagan the Man, the President,* Hedrick Smith, et al. (Macmillan, New York, 1980), p. 10.

Chapter 17. Reform Politics: Amateur Democrats

1. *Gallup Poll,* vol. 3 (Random House, New York, 1972), p. 2106.
2. James L. Sundquist, *Politics and Policy: The Eisenhower, Kennedy, and Johnson Years* (Brookings, Washington, DC, 1968), p. 498.

3. *Ibid.*, p. 497; *Gallup Poll,* vol. 3, p. 2038; Frederick G. Dutton, *Changing Sources of Power* (McGraw-Hill, New York, 1971), p. 226.

4. David S. Broder, *The Party's Over: The Failure of Politics in America* (Harper, New York, 1972), pp. 62–63.

5. For the evolving role of the New Hampshire primary, see *Media and Momentum, The New Hampshire Primary and Nomination Politics,* Gary R. Orren and Nelson W. Polsby, eds. (Chatham House, Chatham, NJ, 1987).

6. Theodore H. White, *The Making of The President, 1968* (Atheneum, New York, 1969), p. 166.

7. *Ibid.*, p. 124.

8. *Ibid.*, p. 125; Warren E. Miller and Teresa E. Levitan, *Leadership and Change: The New Politics of the American Electorate* (Winthrop, Cambridge, MA, 1976), p. 48.

9. Nelson W. Polsby, *Consequences of Party Reform* (Oxford U. Press, New York, 1983), pp. 23–26; Lewis Chester, Godfrey Hodgson, Bruce Page, *American Melodrama* (Dell, New York, 1969), p. 344.

10. For a contrary argument, see Nelson W. Polsby, "What If Robert Kennedy Had Not Been Assassinated?" in *What If? Explorations in Social-Science Fiction,* Polsby, ed., (Lewis, Lexington, MA, 1982), pp. 148–50.

11. Richard C. Bain and Judith H. Parris, *Convention Decisions and Voting Records* (Brookings, Washington, DC, 1973), p. 327.

12. Chester, et al., *American Melodrama,* pp. 660–61. The vote against Humphrey was divided between McCarthy and Senator George McGovern, who was backed by some delegates elected for Kennedy and unable to bring themselves to support McCarthy.

13. A. James Reichley, "The Rise of National Parties," in *The New Direction in American Politics,* John E. Chubb and Paul E. Peterson, eds. (Brookings, Washington, DC, 1985), pp. 182–83.

14. *Ibid.*, p. 184. See also Polsby, *Consequences of Party Reform,* p. 27; Austin Ranney, *Curing the Mischiefs of Faction: Party Reform in America* (U. of California Press, Berkeley, 1975); David E. Price, *Bringing Back the Parties* (Congressional Quarterly, Washington, DC, 1984), pp. 145–50; William J. Crotty, *Decision for the Democrats: Reforming the Party Structure* (Johns Hopkins U. Press, Baltimore, 1978); and Byron F. Shafer, *Quiet Revolution: The Struggle for the Democratic Party and the Shaping of Post-Reform Politics* (Russell Sage, New York, 1983).

15. James Q. Wilson, *The Amateur Democrat* (U. of Chicago Press, 1962), pp. 2–5. Some who participated in the clubs argue that Wilson underestimated their social aspect.

16. *Ibid.*, pp. 151, 131, 132.

17. *Ibid.*, p. 195.

18. For thorough accounts of the post-1968 reform process within the Democratic party, see Crotty, *Decision for the Democrats;* Shafer, *Quiet Revolution;* and Polsby, *Party Reform.*

19. Shafer, quoted by Price, *Bringing Back the Parties,* pp. 148–50.

20. *Ibid.*, pp. 150–52. Loophole primaries were eliminated by the Democrats for the 1992 nomination process.

21. *Ibid.*, pp. 152–55; *Democratic Party of the U.S. v. LaFollette,* 450 U.S. 107 (1981).

22. *Cousins* v. *Wigoda,* 419 U.S. 477 (1975).

23. "The Democratic Delegates: Who Are They?" *Washington Post,* August 25, 1996; "The Republican Delegates: Who Are They?" *Washington Post,* August 11, 1996.

Chapter 18.   The New Giants: National Party Organizations

1. See, for example, Joseph A. Schlesinger, "The New American Political Party," *American Political Science Review,* vol. 79 (December 1985), pp. 1152–68.
2. I served as a policy consultant on the Ford White House staff from May through December 1976 and became to some extent involved in President Ford's campaign.
3. Interview with William Brock, January 22, 1985.
4. Xandra Kayden, "Parties and the 1980 Presidential Election," in Campaign Finance Study Group, *Financing Presidential Campaigns* (Harvard U. Press, Cambridge, MA, 1982), p. 11.
5. David Adamany, "Political Parties in the 1980s," in *Money and Politics in the United States: Financing Elections in the 1980s,* Michael J. Malbin, ed. (American Enterprise Institute, Washington, DC, 1984), p. 80; Leon D. Epstein, "Party Confederations and Political Nationalization," *Publius,* vol. 12 (Fall 1982), p. 86.
6. Interview with Rodney Smith, January 9, 1987.
7. A. James Reichley, *Religion in American Public Life* (Brookings, Washington, DC, 1985), pp. 319–24. As John White has pointed out, "the larger portion of the Reagan strategy was a reiteration of traditional values." John Kenneth White, *The New Politics of Old Values* (University Press of New England, Hanover, NH, 1988), pp. 49–50.
8. Henry C. Kenski and William Lockwood, "Catholic Voting: The Shift from New Deal Loyalist to Critical Swing Vote," paper delivered at the annual meeting of the American Political Science Association, San Francisco, 1990; Timothy A. Byrnes, *Catholic Bishops in American Politics* (Princeton, U. Press, Princeton, NJ., 1991), pp. 82–91.
9. For a useful examination of the Republican National Committee during the 1980s, see Tim Hames, *Power Without Politics: The Republican National Committee in American Political Life,* doctoral dissertation, Oxford University, 1990.
10. Based on figures obtained from releases by the Federal Election Commission, Washington, D.C.
11. *Ibid.*
12. Interview with Lynn Cutler, December 9, 1987.
13. Interview with Brian Lunde, January 9, 1986.
14. Interviews with Brian Atwood, December 21, 1984; Martin Franks, January 8, 1985; and Audrey Sheppard, July 12, 1988.
15. Interview with Barney Frank, January 23, 1985; Gary D. Wekkin, "The New Federal Party Organization," paper delivered at the annual meeting of the American Political Science Association in New Orleans, 1985, p. 19; Brooks Jackson, *Honest Graft* (Knopf, New York, 1988), pp. 84–85.
16. Federal Election Commission release, May 5, 1988.
17. For a thorough description and analysis of national party financing, see David B. Magleby and Candice J. Nelson, *The Money Chase* (Brookings, Washington, DC, 1990).
18. Interview with Thomas Hofeller, December 15, 1986.
19. Interview with Lunde.
20. Paul S. Herrnson, *Party Campaigning in the 1980s* (Harvard U. Press, Cambridge, MA, 1988), pp. 78–79.
21. Larry J. Sabato, *The Party's Just Begun: Shaping Political Parties for America's Future* (Scott, Foresman, Glenview, IL, 1988), pp. 81–85; Thomas B. Edsall, "GOP Committees a Bonanza for Ex-Aides and Relatives," *Washington Post,* January 14, 1987.

22. Interviews with Representatives William Clinger (R, Pennsylvania), Robert Edgar (D, Pennsylvania), Mickey Edwards (R, Oklahoma), Walter Fauntroy (D, District of Columbia), Barney Frank (D, Massachusetts), William Frenzel (R, Minnesota), Newt Gingrich (R, Georgia), James Leach (R, Iowa), Joseph McDade (R, Pennsylvania), Jim Moody (D, Wisconsin), David Price (D, North Carolina), Buddy Roemer (D, Louisiana), William Thomas (R, California), and Vin Weber (R, Minnesota).

23. Federal Election Commission release, July 25, 1990; Jackson, *Honest Graft*, p. 89.

24. *Ibid.* House Democrats have become considerably more dependent than Senate Democrats on PAC contributions and vigorously resist abolition or limitation of PACs.

25. Interviews with Brock; and Robert Strauss, September 24, 1986.

26. Interview with Tim Hyde, January 4, 1985.

27. Paul S. Herrnson, "Political Parties and Election Campaigns: The Role of Party Organizations in House Races," paper delivered at the annual meeting of American Political Science Association in New Orleans, 1985, p. 6. In the late 1980s the Republican campaign committees had so little success raising money for challengers from most business PACs that they substantially reduced their efforts.

28. Interviews with Richard Lugar, January 18, 1985; Kirk O'Donnell, January 24, 1986; Vin Weber, February 6, 1986; and Sheppard. For a discussion of reasons for increased party cohesion in Congress, see Samuel C. Patterson and Gregory A. Caldeira, "Party Voting in the United States Congress," *British Journal of Political Science,* vol. 18 (January, 1988), pp. 111–30.

29. Interview with Pamela Adkins, March 4, 1986.

30. Interview with Jennifer Dunn, March 17, 1986.

31. David Wessel, "GOP Lawmakers Limit Role in Deficit Package," *Wall Street Journal,* June 25, 1990. Frenzel retired at the end of 1990.

32. *American National Election Study, 1984.*

33. Interview with James Baker, March 1, 1985.

34. Interviews with Frank Fahrenkopf, January 15, 1985; and William Lacy, January 11, 1985.

35. A. James Reichley, "The Rise of National Parties," in *The New Direction in American Politics,* John E. Chubb and Paul E. Peterson, eds. (Brookings, Washington, DC, 1985), p. 194.

Chapter 19. State Parties: Seeking New Roles

1. See particularly Cornelius P. Cotter, James L. Gibson, John F. Bibby, Robert J. Huckshorn, *Party Organizations in American Politics* (Praeger, New York, 1984), pp. 13–39; and *The Transformation of American Politics: Implications for Federalism* (Advisory Commission on Intergovernmental Relations, Washington, DC, 1986), pp. 95–162.

2. *Elrod v. Burns,* 427 U.S. 347 (1976).

3. *Rutan v. Republican Party,* 88 U.S. 1872 (1990).

4. Interview with Tom Lamm, November 3, 1988.

5. Interviews with Jim Carey, October 11, 1985; and Calvin Sutker, October 8, 1985.

6. Interview with Gordon Durnil, October 10, 1985.

7. Interviews with Carey; Earl Baker, November 3, 1988; and Frank Hollman, June 11, 1986.

8. Interview with Durnil.

9. Interviews with Buie Seawell, October 12, 1987; and Jennifer Dunn, March 17, 1986.

10. Interviews with Royal Masset, October 30, 1986; and Marty Conners, October 1, 1986.

11. Interview with Bobby Kahn, September 30, 1986.

12. Barbara G. Salmore and Stephen A. Salmore, "The Transformation of State Electoral Politics," in *The State of the States,* Carl E. Van Horn, ed. (*Congressional Quarterly,* Washington, DC, 1989), p. 195.

13. *Ibid.,* p. 196; interview with William Cabala, April 25, 1989.

14. Salmore and Salmore, "Transformation," p. 196. See also Malcolm E. Jewell, "A Survey of Campaign Fund-Raising by Legislative Parties," *Comparative State Politics Newsletter* (1986).

15. Salmore and Salmore, "Transformation," p. 194.

16. Tom Loftus, "The New 'Political Parties' in State Legislatures," *State Government,* no. 58 (1985), pp. 109–10; interview with Loftus, October 16, 1987. In 1990 Loftus ran unsuccessfully as Democratic candidate for governor of Wisconsin.

17. Mark Rom and Andrew Aoki, "How Big the PIG? Wisconsin Campaign Contributions, Legislative Vote Scores, and the Party in Government," paper delivered at the annual Northeast Political Science Association in Philadelphia, 1987, found that in Wisconsin from 1978 to 1982 recipients of legislative campaign contributions had "a slightly lower [party unity] vote score than non-recipients." But this is not surprising, since the campaign committees put their money into marginal districts where members are often excused from voting the party line on difficult issues. What is perhaps more significant is the finding by Rom and Aoki that incumbents showed "slightly greater loyalty" after a close election in which campaign committee contributions may have provided crucial assistance. For a discussion of the relationship between governors and their parties, see Alan Rosenthal, *Governors and Legislatures: Contending Powers* (Congressional Quarterly Press, Washington, DC, 1990), pp. 17–20.

Chapter 20.   Local Parties: Getting along Without Patronage

1. Frank J. Sorauf, *Party Politics in America* (Little, Brown, Boston, 1968), p. 63. "All politics is local" has also been attributed to Mayor Richard Daley, Sr., and apparently originated with the turn-of-the-century humorist, Finley Peter Dunne. "Chicago Journal," *New York Times,* November 25, 1990.

2. Willis D. Hawley, *Nonpartisan Elections and the Case for Party Politics* (Wiley, New York, 1973), pp. 16–17.

3. Cornelius P. Cotter, James L. Gibson, John E Bibby, Robert J. Huckshorn, *Party Organizations in American Politics* (Praeger, New York, 1984), p. 57.

4. William Crotty, "Local Parties in Chicago," in *Political Parties in Local Areas,* William Crotty, ed. (U. of Tennessee Press, Knoxville, 1986), p. 160.

5. Interview with George Dunn, October 31, 1984. Dunn, for many years the good right arm of Richard Daley the elder, retired in 1989.

6. Interview with Joseph Vignola, June 12, 1986. Vignola resigned as city controller in 1988 to run, unsuccessfully, as Democratic candidate for the United States Senate.

7. Interview with Roman Pucinski, October 7, 1985.

8. Interview with Lucien Blackwell, June 12, 1986.

9. Interview with William Meehan, June 12, 1986.

10. Larry J. Sabato, *The Party's Just Begun* (Scott, Foresman, Glenview, IL, 1988), p. 95; Tom Watson, "All-Powerful Machine of Yore Endures in New York's Nassau," *Congressional Quarterly* (August 17, 1985), pp. 1623–25.

11. Interview with Joseph Margiotta, April 3, 1986.

12. Watson, "All-Powerful Machine," p. 1624.

13. Interview with Donna Ashby, October 10, 1985.

14. Interview with Jacqueline Bowen, October 10, 1985.

15. Interview with J. R. Mathews, October 1, 1986.

16. Interviews with George Strake, November 2, 1986; and Fred Meyer, October 28, 1986.

17. Interview with Marty Conners, October 1, 1986.

18. Interview with Sandy Kress, October 28, 1986.

19. Rob Gurwitt, "Waxman, Berman and Allies Aim to Shape National Policy," *Congressional Quarterly* (August 17, 1985), pp. 1620–23.

20. *Ibid.*

21. Interview with Michael Berman, March 19, 1986.

22. Interview with John Emerson, March 18, 1986.

Chapter 21.   Rebuilding the Parties

1. David Broder, *The Party's Over* (Harper & Row, New York, 1972), p. xvi; Walter Dean Burnham, *The Current Crisis in American Politics* (Oxford Univ. Press, New York, 1982), p. 232; William J. Keefe, *Parties, Politics and Public Policy in America* (Congressional Quarterly Press, Washington, DC, 1988), p. 283.

2. L. Sandy Maisel, *Parties and Elections in America* (Rowman & Littlefield, Lanham, MD, 1999), p. 499.

3. Daniel M. Shea and John C. Green, "The State of the Parties at Century's End," in *The State of the Parties: The Changing Role of Contemporary Parties,* Third edition, ed. Shea and Green (Rowman & Littlefield, Lanham, MD, 1999), p. 3.

4. For a defense of patronage by a former critic, see "Patronage, Please," *The New Republic,* July 23, 1990.

5. Larry J. Sabato, *The Party's Just Begun: Shaping Political Parties for America's Future* (Scott, Foresman, Glenview, IL, 1988), p. 230.

6. Robert A. Dahl, "The American Oppositions," in *Political Oppositions in Western Democracies,* Dahl, ed. (Yale University Press, New Haven, CT), pp. 64–65. Dahl concedes that a multi-party system "would also have generated costs" but insists that "does not gainsay the costs of the present system." Theodore J. Lowi, "Presidential Power: Restoring the Balance," *Political Science Quarterly,* vol. 100, no. 2 (Summer, 1985), p. 207. Lowi admits that "the potential for fragmentation is very great in the United States" but maintains this danger is offset by the benefits he claims would come from a multi-party system.

7. For a thorough presentation of the case for third parties, see Steven J. Rosenstone, *Third Parties in America* (Princeton U. Press, Princeton, NJ, 1984).

8. *Outside Money,* ed. David Magleby (Rowman & Littlefield, Lanham, MD, 2000); Herbert E. Alexander, ed., *Comparative Political Finance in the 1980s* (Cambridge U. Press, New York, 1989); David Magleby and Candice Nelson, *The Money Chase* (Brookings, Washington, DC, 1990); *Campaign Reform: Insights and Evidence,* ed. Larry M. Bartels (Princeton U. Press, Princeton, NJ, 1998).

9. For an argument for public subsidization of parties, see Sabato, *Party's Just Begun,* pp. 216–18.

10. For a detailed proposal for provision of free television time to parties, see Sabato, pp. 218–21.

11. Leon Epstein, *Political Parties in the American Mold* (U. of Wisconsin Press, Madison, 1986), pp. 156–57; Sabato, *Party's Just Begun,* p. 203.

12. Kay Lawson, "How State Laws Undermine Parties," in *Elections American Style,* A. James Reichley, ed. (Brookings, Washington, DC, 1987), pp. 240–60; Malcolm Jewell, "Political Parties and the Nomination Process," *Comparative State Politics Newsletter,* no. 7 (February, 1986).

13. Some of these regulations may already be unconstitutional under recent court decisions, but states need to get them off their books.

14. *Tashijian* v. *Republican Party of Connecticut,* 479 U.S. 215 (1986); and *Eu* v. *San Francisco County Democratic Central Committee,* 109 U.S. 1013 (1989).

15. Howard A. Scarrow, "Political Parties and the Law," paper delivered at the annual meeting of the American Political Science Association in San Francisco, 1990.

16. A Brookings Survey in 1986 of Democratic neighborhood clubs in Baltimore found that many of these clubs still function as primary centers of community life.

17. Sabato, *Party's Just Begun,* p. 180.

18. Everett Carll Ladd, "A Better Way to Pick Our Presidents," *Fortune* (May, 1980).

19. James W. Ceaser, "Improving the Nomination Process," in *Elections American Style,* Reichley, ed. pp. 29–51.

ACKNOWLEDGMENTS

M ORE EVEN THAN MOST, this book is the product of the author's entire career up to the present time. I am indebted to the many politicians, political activists, scholars, and journalists who over many years have taught me how parties work and act.

I wish particularly to thank colleagues and friends who read all or part of the manuscript and gave much helpful criticism and advice: Walter Beach, John Chubb, John Coolidge, Anthony Downs, William Frenzel, Stephen Hess, Charles O. Jones, Robert Katzmann, Philip Klinkner, David Magleby, Thomas Mann, Candice Nelson, Pietro Nivola, Mancur Olson, Gillian Peel, Paul Peterson, Bert Rockman, Bruce Smith, Herbert Smith, Gilbert Steiner, Donald Stokes, Richard Valelly, and Joseph White. James L. Sundquist read the entire manuscript and provided many useful suggestions—the latest installment in discussions and debates that now go back more than three decades.

I am grateful to the Brookings Institution and its president Bruce MacLaury for generously supporting my research and writing with human and financial resources; and to the Ford Foundation and the Dillon Fund for generous research grants. Robert Faherty gave valuable counsel throughout the project. The Brookings library and its staff, particularly Laura Walker and Susan McGrath, ran down many elusive sources and citations.

Renuka Deonarain effectively administered the entire project. Bliss Austin, Timothy Bladek, Christopher Brandt, Daniel Kolb, Navid Mahmoodzadegan, Sara Pozefsky, David Sandman, Tami Trost, and Gina Young were congenial and efficient researchers. Diane Hodges, Judith Newman, Sandra Riegler, and Eloise Stinger gave administrative support. Robin Donaldson performed computer calculations for tables and figures. Vida Megahed, Renee Peel-Scaife, Toni Williams, and Susan Thompson provided secretarial assistance. Eileen Stubenrauch typed the final manuscript. I thank them all.

At The Free Press, Erwin A. Glikes, president, and Peter Dougherty, senior editor, gave much valuable guidance and encouragement. Everett Sims did a first-rate job of copy editing, and Edith Lewis efficiently directed production.

Finally, I am, as always, grateful to my wife, Mary, and my children, Douglas, Richard, and Susan, for their loyal patience and support.

Washington, DC

INDEX